Enter the Dragon

Enter the Dragon

China in the International Financial System

Edited by Domenico Lombardi and Hongying Wang

ISBN 978-1-928096-15-3 (paper)
ISBN 978-1-928096-16-0 (ebook)

The opinions expressed in this publication are those of the authors and do not necessarily reflect the views of the Centre for International Governance Innovation or its Board of Directors.

Published by the Centre for International Governance Innovation.

Printed and bound in Canada.

Cover design by Sara Moore and Melodie Wakefield.
Page design by Melodie Wakefield.

Centre for International Governance Innovation
67 Erb Street West
Waterloo, ON Canada N2L 6C2

www.cigionline.org

Contents

Preface

Domenico Lombardi and Hongying Wang

The rise of China as an economic powerhouse in recent decades has been nothing short of a miracle, and has been a matter of pride for the Chinese, a magnet of interest for international businesses and a source of anxiety for some of China's economic and strategic competitors. More recently, the world has come to notice the increasing profile of China in the international financial system in particular. The establishment of the New Development Bank and the Contingent Reserve Arrangement with the other BRICS (Brazil, Russia, India, China and South Africa) nations, the Asian Infrastructure Investment Bank and the Silk Road Infrastructure Fund are only a few of the international projects that China has pursued in the last couple of years. The apparent massive show of financial muscle by China, in turn, has attracted a great deal of attention from around the world.

These developments highlight the remarkable evolution of China's role in the international financial system, from an outsider to an insider, from a peripheral actor to a major player and from a rule follower to a rule maker. As China evolves rapidly, it is important for scholars, policy makers and the broader public to understand China's intentions, capabilities and strategies of financial statecraft, and what they mean for China's own future development and for the international financial system. Can China implement and sustain further reforms in its economy, including its financial sector? How will China act or react in the international financial system as it grows in influence? Will China continue to adapt to the current institutions or will it shape them according to its own vision? *Enter the Dragon: China in the International Financial System* aims to shed light on these questions.

This book is the result of cooperation among scholars based in China, North America and Europe, who come from different areas of specialization in economics and political science. We are grateful to a number of anonymous peer reviewers, who have helped improve the quality of the book through their comments and suggestions. Special thanks go to Coby Hu for his valuable research assistance, and to Jennifer Goyder and Carol Bonnett for their careful editing of the entire manuscript. Last but not least, we thank Benjamin J.Cohen, who suggested the title of the book.

Acronyms and Abbreviations

ABMI	Asia Bond Market Initiative
ADB	Asian Development Bank
AIIB	Asian Infrastructure Investment Bank
AMCs	asset management companies
APEC	Asia-Pacific Economic Cooperation
APT	ASEAN Plus Three
ASEAN	Association of Southeast Asian Nations
BCBS	Basel Committee on Banking Supervision
BRIC	Brazil, Russia, India and China
BRICS	Brazil, Russia, India, China and South Africa
CA	current account
CBRC	China Banking Regulatory Commission
CMI	Chiang Mai Initiative
CMIM	Chiang Mai Initiative Multilateralized
CNH	offshore RMB market
CNY	onshore RMB market
CPC	Communist Party of China
CPSS	Committee on Payment and Settlement Systems
CRA	Contingent Reserve Arrangement
CRD	Capital Requirements Directive and Regulation
ECB	European Central Bank

EER	exogenous expansionary rate
ERPT	exchange rate pass-through
Ex-Im	export-import
FDI	foreign direct investment
FSAP	Financial Sector Assessment Program
FSB	Financial Stability Board
FSF	Financial Stability Forum
FTA	free trade agreement
FTA	free trade account
FTN	free trade account for non-resident
FX	foreign exchange
G7	Group of Seven
G8	Group of Eight
G10	Group of Ten
G20	Group of Twenty
GFC	global financial crisis
IASB	International Accounting Standards Board
ICBC	Industrial and Commercial Bank of China
IMF	International Monetary Fund
IMFC	International Monetary and Financial Committee
IOSCO	International Organization of Securities Commissions
IPE	international political economy
JODI	Joint Organisations Data Initiative
MAP	Mutual Assessment Process
MBS	mortgage-backed securities
MMF	money market fund
MNC	multi-national corporation
MoC	Ministry of Commerce
MoF	Ministry of Finance
MoFA	Ministry of Foreign Affairs
NDB	New Development Bank
NDRC	National Development and Reform Commission
NII	net investment income
NIIP	net international investment position
NPC	National People's Congress
NPL	non-performing loan

OCLGFEA	Office of the Central Leading Group for Financial and Economic Affairs
ODI	overseas direct investment
OTC	over-the-counter
PBoC	People's Bank of China
PLA	People's Liberation Army
PPP	purchasing power parity
PRC	People's Republic of China
PTM	price-to-market
QDII	qualified domestic institutional investor
QE	quantitative easing
QFII	qualified foreign institutional investor
RMB	renminbi
ROSC	Report on the Observance of Standards and Codes
RQFII	RMB qualified foreign institutional investor
RRR	reserve requirement ratio
S&P	Standard & Poor's
SAFE	State Administration of Foreign Exchange
SASAC	State Asset Supervision and Administration Commission
SCO	Shanghai Cooperation Organization
SCSRC	Standing Committee for Supervisory and Regulatory Cooperation
SDRs	Special Drawing Rights
SFTZ	Shanghai Free Trade and Financial Zone
SIFMA	Securities Industry and Financial Markets Association
SOE	state-owned enterprise
SSBs	standard-setting bodies
SWIFT	Society for Worldwide Interbank Financial Telecommunication
TFP	total factor productivity
TPP	Trans-Pacific Partnership
TTIP	Transatlantic Trade and Investment Partnership
WMP	wealth management product
WTO	World Trade Organization

Introduction

Domenico Lombardi and Hongying Wang

n the early 1990s, China's economy began to experience a remarkable transformation. Growing at a rate of about 10 percent per year, China's economy has become the second largest in the world, and by some calculations even the largest (see Figure 1). For instance, according to the International Monetary Fund (IMF), China's GDP at US$17.6 trillion when measured in purchasing power parity (PPP) terms surpassed that of the United States in 2014. In terms of trade, China has evolved from a closed economy into the largest goods-trading nation, with trade measuring over 50 percent of its GDP. Additionally, significant strides have been made in its domestic financial market. Since the inception of the Shanghai and Shenzhen stock exchanges in 1990, the total value of stocks traded has surged from zero to over 70 percent of GDP. From 1997 to 2014, the local currency bond market grew from 3.6 percent of GDP to over 50.6 percent. Similarly, the previously non-existent corporate bond sector has flourished into a US$2 trillion market, or 35.8 percent of China's bond market, in 2014 (see Figure 2).

While China has integrated its real economy — in particular manufacturing — into the global trade network, there has been lacklustre progression in the internationalization of its financial market (Subacchi et al. 2012; Dobbs, Leung and Lund 2013; Craig et al. 2013). Indeed, a number of contentious factors — including a managed exchange rate policy coupled with stringent regulation of capital flows — have kept China's financial market relatively isolated from its trading partners (Maziad and Kang 2012). However, following the global

Figure 1: GDP Growth of BRIC and Advanced Economies, 1993–2015

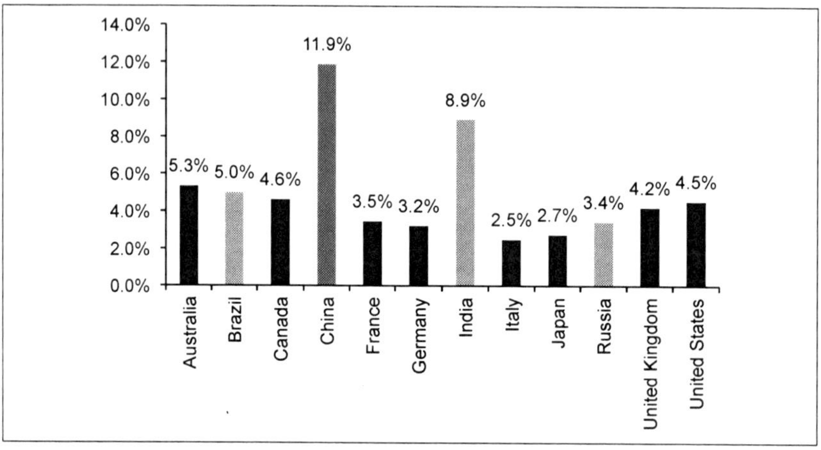

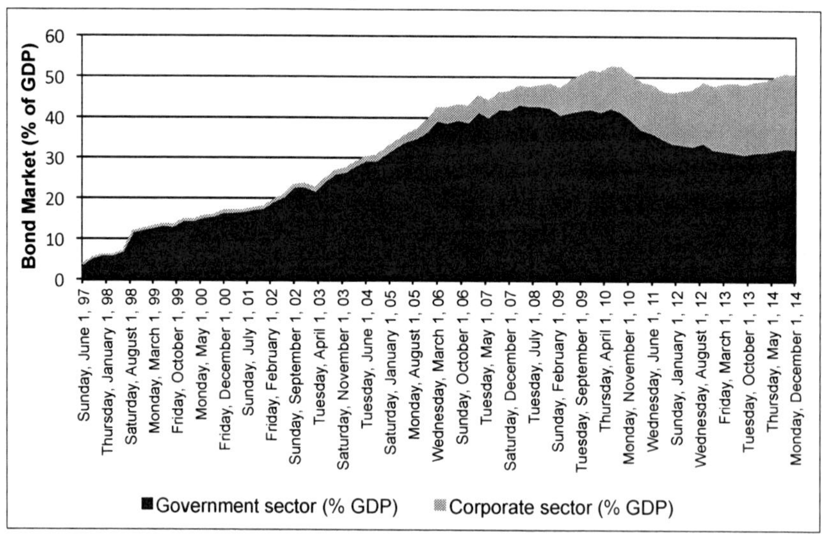

Data source: IMF World Economic Outlook database (2015).
Note: The figures measure the average growth rate of PPP-adjusted GDP in US dollars between 1993 and 2015. Figures for 2014 and 2015 are estimated by the IMF.

Figure 2: China's Local Currency Bond Markets, 1997–2014

Data source: ADB AsianBondsOnline database.

financial crisis (GFC) of 2007–2009, the Chinese government unveiled a series of policy initiatives to foster the international role of its currency, the renminbi (RMB).

Thanks to China's economic size, global trade networks, and gradual capital account liberalization and financial development, the international use of the RMB has significantly expanded. The RMB is now the fifth-most-commonly used world payments currency, a significant jump from its ranking as the thirty-fifth-most-used payments currency in 2010.[1] Similarly, RMB cross-border settlements aggregated to more than US$800 billion by 2014, and now cover all of China's balance-of-payments items, including the capital account, despite its still restricted status in 2014.

To further promote the international use of the RMB, the People's Bank of China (PBoC) has to date promoted a series of RMB offshore hubs and bilateral currency swap arrangements with countries and central banks. As of May 2015, the PBoC has bilateral currency swap arrangements with over 30 countries and territories, 14 of which are designated "offshore RMB centres" with official RMB clearing banks.[2] As may be expected from these recent developments, RMB internationalization and China's broader role in the global financial system have attracted increased attention. Given that its economy continues to grow, the country will inevitably wish to modify some aspects of the international monetary order. At the same time, as China further integrates into the international financial system and increases the RMB's exposure to global ebbs and flows, it will open itself up to a number of new risks associated with global interconnectedness, as demonstrated by the GFC.

To address some of these concerns, *Enter the Dragon: China in the International Financial System* brings together experts from both inside and outside of the People's Republic of China (PRC) to explore issues regarding RMB internationalization and China's integration with the global financial and monetary system.

---

1   This is according to data by the Society for Worldwide Interbank Financial Telecommunication (SWIFT), which provides financial institutions worldwide information about financial transactions.

2   As of May 2015, these include Hong Kong, Macau, Taiwan, Singapore, the United Kingdom, Germany, South Korea, France, Luxembourg, Qatar, Canada, Malaysia, Australia and Thailand.

The book is divided into three parts, each devoted to a specific dimension of the broader topic. The first part tackles questions surrounding RMB internationalization, such as China's motivations to internationalize its currency, noteworthy obstacles and the process being used to attempt to achieve it. The second part focuses on broader issues concerning China's rise, in particular those related to the country's financial integration with the rest of the world and the politics behind them. The third part discusses important issues concerning China's role in global financial governance and dialogue.

RMB Internationalization

The explicit promotion of RMB internationalization by the Chinese government and the rapid pace of its development are somewhat unusual occurrences in the history of international finance. Why has Beijing been so eager to expand the international use of the Chinese currency? Which processes are being used to achieve RMB internationalization? What are the consequences of China pushing for the internationalization of it currency? How much further is RMB internationalization likely to go, given domestic and foreign political and economic constraints?

The first part of the book includes chapters that examine these and related questions. Juan Carlos Martinez Oliva first explores the geopolitical considerations for currency internationalization and their relation to the RMB. His chapter documents the growing international importance of the RMB and the political ambitions of the PRC in the Asia-Pacific region — particularly vis-à-vis the perceived threat of US dominance. In doing so, it examines China's involvement in regional economic and financial initiatives, as well as its "soft" and "hard" power status in the East Asian region, all in the context of RMB internationalization. He argues that RMB internationalization, at least from the perspective of the Chinese government and its elites, is a deliberate political strategy that focuses on East Asia with China at the centre. Martinez Oliva further notes that the Chinese yuan has a high chance of matching the US dollar as a world reserve currency in the long run. However, in the short run, a prerequisite is for the RMB to first become a major regional currency in East Asia for trade and investment.

Complementing this geostrategic perspective, Alex He offers insights into the domestic forces behind China's push for the use of the RMB globally. He argues that the major incentive behind the PBoC's push for RMB internationalization is its desire to propel domestic economic reforms (liberalizing the capital account, exchange rate and interest rate). This political dynamic goes alongside several other considerations, including the need to reduce the exchange rate risk faced by Chinese enterprises in international markets, reducing China's exposure to the US dollar, and to increase the "prestige" of the RMB and bolster Shanghai as a financial centre.

Barry Eichengreen discusses and evaluates the "sequencing problem" in regards to currency internationalization. Eichengreen identifies three main approaches to RMB internationalization. The first is the "gradualist" approach characterized by the need to progressively reform China's domestic financial market prior to setting sights on complete financial liberalization. In contrast, the "big bang" approach favours moving RMB internationalization at a much faster pace, whereby the PRC simultaneously pursues policy reform on several fronts. The last approach, denoted as the "phased" strategy, seeks to promote RMB internationalization while still maintaining capital account restrictions by: relaxing the capital account in a manner that reconciles the need for financial stability; promoting offshore centres where RMB-denominated transactions can be cultivated; and designing an insulated, special trade and financial zone onshore that supports RMB-denominated transactions with the rest of the world. Eichengreen believes the last is the best approach, which he argues has indeed been the choice China has employed so far.

The chapter by Qiyuan Xu evaluates the impact of RMB cross-border settlements on China's domestic interest rates, asset prices and foreign exchange reserves. Xu observes that RMB export settlement schemes at the initial stage do not affect the PRC's interest rates or asset prices, and further, that they slow down the accumulation in the PBoC's foreign exchange reserves. In contrast, he finds a non-trivial impact of RMB import settlement schemes on the Chinese economy through changes in the interest rate. The schemes also increase the cost for the PBoC through additional accumulation of foreign reserves as a result of the interest rate changes. Regarding schemes to promote RMB flows for financial purposes, such as the RMB Qualified Foreign Institutional Investor program, this chapter contends that such schemes will not exert pressures on the PBoC, but will instead affect asset prices through the money market. If the RMB flows are large enough, they can exert significant influence on the Chinese domestic interest rates. As a result, Xu proposes that RMB settlements for financial purposes should be regulated with quotas in the interim, although in the long run these items should be liberalized.

To conclude the part on RMB internationalization, Randall Germain and Herman Mark Schwartz explore the political limits to China's RMB internationalization efforts. They examine a number of political requirements and adjustment costs associated with issuing a global currency. The key insight offered is through a historical comparison between China and traditional international currency issuers: Great Britain and the United States. From this, Germain and Schwartz argue that China does not meet the conditions required to effectively issue a global currency, and that the PRC's political system will not be able to adequately reorganize its economy to support an international currency. This is because China will need to circulate the RMB internationally through net import increases, and by moving away from investment and export production to consumption. They argue that this would subtract power from Chinese elites and the Communist Party, resulting in the current agents in power resisting the required reforms, and thus preclude the RMB from rivalling the US dollar.

China's Financial Internationalization

China's financial sector, as mentioned earlier, has been undergoing a slow but steady transformation toward liberalization, development and "opening up." This raises a number of new questions: What financial policies has the Chinese government adopted to encourage and accommodate the opening up of China's financial sector? How have China's financial policies influenced its economy? What are the political factors behind China's foreign financial policy? How might China's financial internationalization be extended beyond its current scope? Addressing these questions, the second part of this book explores several aspects of the broader internationalization process and implications it has for financial policy and development in China.

Hailong Jin, Domenico Lombardi and Coby Hu probe the constraints of macroeconomic policies in relation to the exchange rate management pursued by the Chinese government. They first document the PBoC's large accumulations of foreign reserves while, at the same time, the yuan-dollar exchange rate remained relatively stable for over a decade from 1994 to 2005. Both of these factors point to a managed exchange rate policy. However, the chapter finds that the cost associated with this policy has been high. In addition to the standard cost of loosing monetary policy independence, the return on the PBoC's foreign reserves — specifically on US dollar assets — was too low to justify the continued purchase of foreign assets by issuing yuan. Moreover, the authors conclude that the PBoC's exchange rate policy imposes other constraints on China's macroeconomic environment, namely, the cost of inflation, which disrupts real economic activities, and the cost of the implicit tax imposed on Chinese banks in the form of high reserve ratio requirements.

Turning to a political analysis, David A. Steinberg focuses on the domestic sources of China's foreign financial and monetary policies, in particular, the policies regarding capital controls, exchange rates and foreign reserves. The central argument is that the overall costs and benefits of a given financial policy are ambiguous for a nation, but each policy creates clear winners and losers among different socio-economic groups. In China, as elsewhere, the government tends to adopt policies that serve the interests of the politically powerful groups. The retention of capital controls and the continued intervention in the foreign exchange market, resulting in the accumulation of large amounts of foreign reserves, are policies that favour some groups in China at the expense of other groups. Under the current political regime, the power balance is extremely tilted in favour of the winners. The prospect for substantial change of China's foreign financial policy is dim for the foreseeable future because of the absence of political reform.

Stuart S. Brown and Hongying Wang analyze the status of China's emergence as a major international creditor. They dissect sources and consequences of the PRC's status as an international creditor, as well as its connection with Beijing's underlying economic development model. The chapter suggests that China's net creditor status has not been as beneficial to China financially or politically as one might expect. Moreover, they contend that China's transition to a domestic demand-oriented economy would actually reduce its net creditor position. This would lead China's economic fundamentals to be more balanced, thus providing a better foundation for global influence. Brown and Wang argue that US dominance will continue, largely thanks to the depth and liquidity of US capital markets as compared to those in China. They conclude that in order to achieve a status similar to the United States, Beijing must introduce fundamental changes in its economy, which is difficult given its political system.

In the final chapter of the second part, Liu Dongmin examines the prospect of developing China's local government bonds to fill a gap of global safe assets. He contends that a key indicator for the potential for the RMB's internationalization is its role as a reserve currency held by central banks. He argues that this requirement is directly related to the size of the bond market. Bonds, especially those issued by the government, denominated in its currency, must be considered a global safe asset with high credit ratings — as is the case for both US and UK government debt. He recommends that the PRC government increase the supply of treasury bonds in onshore and offshore markets and concurrently impose the needed reforms on bonds, especially local government bonds, sales and regulation, focusing on market transparency and liberalization.

China in International Financial Governance

Accompanying China's integration into the international financial system has been its increased involvement in global financial governance. What kind of an actor has China been in international financial institutions? How will it act in the future? What forces have shaped China's preferences and capacities in global financial governance? The chapters in the third part will address some of these questions.

Bessma Momani examines how Beijing's increasing power and influence have shaped debates at the IMF, including those on IMF governance, economic surveillance and IMF Special Drawing Rights (SDRs). On the first issue, Momani cites China's concerns regarding the dominance of IMF governance by the United States and its allies. Driven by to these concerns, China has argued in favour of a shift in IMF voting rights to developing countries, but this reform has repeatedly been stalled by US Congress. On the second issue, Momani argues that the PRC's focus has been to urge the IMF to put more emphasis on surveying developed economies, most notably the United States due to its position as issuer of the global reserve currency. Finally, the chapter documents China's push for a larger role of the IMF's SDR, which China sees as necessary, in part due to the upward trend in multipolarity of trade, finance and even political power. The conclusion indicates that the future of China's approach to the IMF is hard to predict given the tension between China's identity as a developing country and an emerging great power.

Evaluating a similar trend, Alex He provides a detailed analysis of China's engagement with the Group of Twenty (G20) economies. The chapter explores Beijing's policies, agenda and goals, and how they relate to the country's participation in the G20. He argues that China views such a forum as an ideal platform for contributing to global economic governance. He highlights the changing approaches taken by the Chinese, specifically the departure from the defensive and isolated stance, in response to repeated criticisms of China's exchange rate policy, to an active and open stance where China plays a part in dealing with global issues such as the European debt crisis and the GFC. He contends that the PRC's desire to participate in the G20 does not stem from an interest in becoming an agenda-setter, but instead from gaining prestige by promoting an important mechanism for global cooperation.

Next, David Kempthorne probes China's relations with international financial standard-setting bodies, such as the Basel Committee on Banking Supervision and the Financial Stability Board (FSB). He points out that despite the growth of its financial market, China still plays a meagre role in international finance when compared with the United States and Europe. He sees China as lagging far behind developed nations in regulatory expertise, which makes it difficult for China to influence international financial regulations. In terms of international compliance, Kempthorne contends that China has been largely compliant with Basel III capital adequacy standards as well as the FSB's standards for shadow banking reforms. Nonetheless, he acknowledges some divergence in China from international standards, in particular, from its lack of transparency when dealing with financial transactions within the industrial sectors. He concludes that the PRC is unlikely to influence the work of these financial standard-setting bodies in the near future.

In the last chapter of the final part, Hongying Wang explores China's accelerated engagement in minilateral financial arrangements — agreements and institutions involving cooperation with regional neighbours and fellow developing countries, such as the Chiang Mai Initiative, the Asian Infrastructure Investment Bank (AIIB), the New Development Bank (NDB) and the Contingent Reserve Arrangement (CRA). In particular, the chapter considers China's underlying motivations for participating in such plurilateral financial cooperation, as well as the effect of such bodies on existing global financial governance. Wang describes the establishment of the AIIB, CRA and NDB as part of a more active foreign economic policy, but does not see these China-backed arrangements as a threat to the existing international financial order in the near term. She argues that the international community should accommodate these changes and encourage the PRC to maintain an open form of minilateralism, just as the West should keep its own minilateralism open to China.

Conclusion

The questions concerning the internationalization of the RMB, the global integration and development of China's financial sector, and the country's role in international financial institutions and governance are important for scholars and policy makers as they contemplate how best to cope with the transformation of the international financial system resulting from the rise of China, and its associated challenges and risks. The significance of these topics will no doubt increase as the PRC continues to expand — in terms of both economic might and political clout. As this book argues, the PRC will continue to pursue and push for a greater role in international economic cooperation, financial dialogue and politics.

Against this backdrop, the goal of this volume is to further the debate regarding many of the questions that accompany China's ascendance as an international financial power. Rather than simply focusing on economic analysis, much of this book is devoted to a broader conceptual approach that draws on a number of fields covering the spectrum between economics and political science. Indeed, the aim of this volume is to demonstrate that China's economic rise is a highly political process. The origins of the country's ascendance in the international financial system and the consequences of this development can only be understood by incorporating political as well as economic analysis. We hope *Enter the Dragon* contributes to the ongoing discourse over China's political interests, its agenda for economic and financial cooperation, as well as the domestic and international implications of China's economic rise.

Works Cited

Craig, Sean R., Changchun Hua, Philip Ng and Raymond Yuen. 2013. "Development of the Renminbi Market in Hong Kong SAR: Assessing Onshore-Offshore Market Integration." IMF Working Paper. www.imf.org/external/pubs/ft/wp/2013/wp13268.pdf.

Dobbs, Richard, Nick Leung and Susan Lund. 2013. "China's Rising Stature in Global Finance." *McKinsey Quarterly*. July. www.mckinsey.com/insights/winning_in_emerging_markets/chinas_rising_stature_in_global_finance.

Maziad, Samar and Joong Shik Kang. 2012. "RMB Internationalization: Onshore/Offshore Links." IMF Working Paper.

Subacchi, Paola, Helena Huang, Alberta Molajoni and Richard Varghese. 2012. *Shifting Capital: The Rise of Financial Centres in Greater China.* A Chatham House Report. www.chathamhouse.org/sites/files/chathamhouse/public/Research/International%20Economics/r0512shiftingcapital.pdf.

Part One

RMB Internationalization

1

China's Power and the International Use of the RMB

Juan Carlos Martinez Oliva

The Chinese will want to share this century as co-equals with the United States.
— Lee Kuan Yew (2013)

The rapid rise of the renminbi (RMB) in the international arena is the result of a deliberate series of well-engineered actions intended to spread the Chinese currency all over the world. Chinese authorities initially proceeded with caution, but soon accelerated the pace toward a growing use of RMB in foreign trade and in financial transactions; they have also encouraged its use in central banks' foreign exchange reserves. These steps demonstrate a strong resolve by China to turn the RMB into a broadly accepted currency at the international level. In the face of such unusual developments, the motivation of China's authorities has been called into question.

When trying to quantify the net financial benefits of currency internationalization, economic literature, in most cases, restricts the analysis to a limited number of measurable factors, such as the reduction of transaction costs and uncertainty deriving from a third country's currency fluctuations, and the benefits accruing from seigniorage, viewed as an interest-free loan from foreigners holding the national currency. Recent studies investigating the above effects conclude that a currency hegemon such as the United States derives little benefit from the international role of its currency, or even that a reduced role would be beneficial, and therefore advisable.[1]

Based on the above conclusion, one would be inclined to dismiss currency internationalization as a desirable option. The question of why China has placed RMB internationalization on its wish list would, nonetheless, remain unanswered.

In an insightful paper on the benefits and costs of currency internationalization, Benjamin J. Cohen remarked that in a discussion largely dominated by economists, it is hard for a political scientist not to note the glaring omission of geopolitics.[2] Taking stock of Cohen's enlightening remark, the present chapter will set out to enrich the conventional analysis of currency internationalization by embedding in it geopolitical consideration and power analysis. This will be done by putting together apparently heterogeneous elements, such as the process of RMB internationalization, China's involvement in regional economic and financial initiatives, and China's exercise of soft and hard power, particularly, but not exclusively, in the East Asian region.

An appealing feature of an international currency, it is worth remembering, is that its universal recognition as a means of exchange, store of value and unit of account involves a special status and represents a source of power for the issuer, and hence an "exorbitant privilege."[3] The connection between power and money is a very close one, as Robert Mundell reminds us.[4] From the early stages of the rise of the Roman Empire, at the end of the second Punic war, until the end of the third century AD, the *denarius argenteus* marked the territory of the empire, and represented the most tangible sign of Rome's power.[5] Thirteen centuries later, the silver Spanish dollar, or *real de a ocho*, similarly spread along the Spanish empire until nineteenth century — it was the most stable and least debased currency in the Western world throughout its entire existence, and a

---

1   An overview of such studies is found in Cohen (2012). More recently Williamson (2013) confirmed that the benefits for the United States from being the dollar's issuer are outweighed by the constraints that being a monetary hegemon pose to exchange rate management.

2   "Yet in the literature on currency internationalization, geopolitics rarely enters. The eight-hundred pound gorilla is sitting there, but hardly anyone, it seems, wants to talk about it" (Cohen 2012, 27).

3   The expression was first coined by Valéry Giscard d'Estaing, then the finance minister of France, to define the international hegemony of the dollar.

4   "Great powers have great currencies" (Mundell 1993). Among the international political scientists who have investigated the issue are Charles Kindleberger, Susan Strange and Benjamin J. Cohen. See Cohen (2010).

5   Yet Roman coins also circulated outside the empire, reaching the farthest parts of the known world. See Martinez Oliva (2007).

benchmark for the currencies to come.[6] At the end of World War II, the United States picked up the reins of global leadership that were slipping from Britain's hands,[7] and the US dollar replaced the pound sterling, which was the main world money in the age of the gold standard.[8]

Geopolitical considerations add a welcome touch of sophistication to the interpretation of the interaction between dominant currencies and the power of the issuer, and to the motives lying behind the desire to internationalize a currency. Such considerations may provide a convincing explanation of why countries find it helpful and convenient to settle their foreign payments in a dominant currency that is universally accepted and keeps a stable value, according to a behavioural pattern that seems to have remained broadly unchanged throughout centuries.

The interaction between an international currency and the power of its issuer is of special interest to the present work, as it is particularly relevant in the analysis of China's motivations to internationalize the RMB. In this view, it is argued, if the international use of a currency is pushed far enough, it can trigger a virtuous circle based on cross-feeding effects. A powerful country can create incentives for a more intense use of its currency by its clients and partners; conversely, being the issuer of a powerful currency allows extracting benefits, both economic and strategic, from other countries, thus increasing a country's power. In sum, a monetary hegemon may internalize benefits from a widespread use of its currency while network externalities create compelling reasons to perpetuate its monetary dominance across its area of influence.[9]

That currency internationalization may mutually interact with power and security considerations is a concept rarely found in economic literature. According to Cohen (2012), while security considerations are, in few instances, taken into account among possible determinants of the choice of a currency for international transactions, the reverse possibility that currency

---

6   The Spanish dollar became the trade standard even in the Far East. Later, local currencies such as Western powers' "trade dollars," the Hong Kong dollar and the first Chinese yuan coins were minted with the same specification (weight, size, purity) as a Spanish dollar.

7   The paraphrase is intentional from Will Clayton's historical memo of May 1947: "The reins of world leadership are fast slipping from Britain's competent but now very weak hands. These reins will be picked up either by the United States or by Russia."

8   An extensive description of those events is found in Gardner (1969).

9   For a thorough discussion on the self-feeding mechanism of international monetary power, see Henning (2012).

internationalization may bring about sizeable positive security effects has been generally overlooked. This means assuming that the benefits in terms of power from issuing an international currency are not necessarily limited to the economic field. As Cohen himself puts it, monetary autonomy "can also make it easier to defend against political or military pressures from the outside" (ibid., 16).[10]

In line with the above considerations, the present chapter views the process of RMB internationalization as an element of a deliberate strategy aimed at creating an East Asian economic community with China at its centre. In this mould, the rise of the RMB would represent a relevant tool in the diplomatic and strategic effort to achieve the goal of President Xi Jinping's Asian dream of an "Asia for the Asians."[11] Consistent with its regional grand strategy, China is looking to win neighbouring countries' support and friendship while keeping a leader's attitude on strategic issues such as territorial sovereignty, and maritime rights and interests. By introducing security implications, China's stated intention to "properly handle territorial and island disputes" adds relevance to the geopolitical aspects of the analysis.[12] Rather than as an autonomous process, RMB internationalization can, therefore, be viewed as a functional element of China's power strategy to enhance its geopolitical role in the East Asian region.

Establishing RMB offshore centres around the world, creating a network of swap agreements with a large number of central banks, projecting new RMB-based regional financial institutions, and reinforcing its charm offensive and soft power while strengthening its strategic and military capabilities, can thus be viewed as mutually sustaining elements of China's blueprint.

---

10   In this view, by receiving active support by client states, a monetary hegemon is able to increase its geopolitical capabilities.

11   The concept was clearly expressed in President Xi's remarks at the Fourth Summit of the Conference on Interaction and Confidence Building Measures in Asia: "it is for the people of Asia to run the affairs of Asia, solve the problems of Asia and uphold the security of Asia" (Xi 2014). President Xi explicitly used the term "Asia for Asians" in South Korea sometime later (Harold 2015).

12   See, for example, President Xi's address at the central foreign affairs meeting held on November 28 to 29, 2014, in Beijing (http://news.xinhuanet.com/english/china/2014-11/30/c_133822694.htm).

The Irresistible March of the RMB

Money is a good soldier, sir, and will on.
— William Shakespeare, *The Merry Wives of Windsor*

China is fast acquiring the status of a major international currency for the RMB. According to SWIFT data, as of January 2015, the Chinese currency ranks fifth among currencies used in global payments, up from thirteenth at the beginning of 2013. The RMB overtook the Canadian and Australian dollar as a global payments currency in November 2014, and now stands just one step behind the Japanese yen, the British pound, the euro and the US dollar.[13] Further achievements are likely to materialize soon.

That the RMB might be close to getting full international status was less clearly apparent few years ago than today, when at the November 2008 Group of Twenty (G20) summit meeting — during the height of the international financial crisis — Chinese President Hu Jintao urged a new international financial order that would be "fair, just, inclusive, and orderly." On further occasions, China reiterated its concern about the stability of a dollar-based international monetary system.[14] A few months later, on March 2009, People's Bank of China Governor Zhou Xiaochuan, moving from President Hu's call for a better global financial system, suggested, in an extensively quoted essay "Reform of the International Monetary System," that the outbreak of the crisis and its spillovers to the entire world reflected "inherent vulnerabilities and systemic risks in the existing international monetary system" (Zhou 2009). While openly challenging the role of the US dollar, he advocated the need to create an international reserve currency that would be "disconnected from economic conditions and sovereign interests of any single country" and might remain stable in the long run, thus removing the inherent deficiencies caused by using credit-based national currencies (ibid.).[15] The financial crisis exposed China's vulnerability due to its huge stock of dollar-denominated reserves.

---

13   See SWIFT RMB Monthly Tracker 2015 (www.swift.com/products_services/renminbi_reports).

14   Such as, for example, the Economic Leaders' Meeting of the Asia-Pacific Economic Cooperation forum in Lima, Peru, on November 7–26, 2009.

15   There is a striking resemblance in Governor Zhou's words of the famous attack by General Charles de Gaulle, in a press conference on February 4, 1965, on the dollar's unique status under Bretton Woods rules: "Cette sorte de facilité unilatérale qui est attribuée à l'Amérique, contribue à faire s'estomper l'idée que le dollar est un signe impartial et international des échanges alors qu'il est un moyen de crédit approprié à un Etat." (This sort of unilateral benefit assigned to America, contributes to blur the idea that the dollar is an impartial and international means of exchange rather than a credit instrument in favour of a single country [author's own translation] (http://fresques.ina.fr/de-gaulle/fiche-media/Gaulle00105/conference-de- presse-du-4-fevrier-1965.html).

China's dilemma was similar to that of Europe in the early 1970s. Europe proved unable to offset the adverse spillover effects of US inflationary policies under Nixon's administration, descending from the huge military cost of the Vietnam War, a situation that created serious friction between the two sides of the Atlantic.[16]

In July 2009, China announced a pilot program aimed at settling its foreign trade in RMB rather than in US dollars. It was the start of the Hong Kong offshore market (CNH), which provided Chinese authorities a fully controllable testing environment that might help evaluate the impact of new policy choices in international banking and finance.[17] Chinese authorities employed Qualified Foreign Institutional Investor (QFII) and Qualified Domestic Institutional Investor standards for foreign and domestic investors respectively, to soften the limits placed on cross-border capital flows.[18]

Things have moved fast since then. According to estimates by the Hong Kong Monetary Authority, between April 2013 and February 2015, the average daily turnover of real-time gross settlements in offshore RMB increased from 60 to 112 (Lee 2015). The very high degree of financial specialization of Hong Kong is confirmed by the ratio between its share in international currency settlements and its share of world GDP (2.68 percent), slightly higher than the corresponding ratio for Britain (2.55 percent), but well above the corresponding ratio in the euro area (1.71 percent), in the United States (1.90 percent) and in Japan (0.40 percent). The equivalent ratio for mainland China lags behind at 0.14 percent.[19]

A fast-growing network of swap lines is contributing to intensifying the use of the RMB as a trade settlement currency across the world. According to some observers, China's swap lines may be viewed as "a cross-section of its geopolitical aims"; indeed, they include a sample of China's national interests ranging from

---

16   James and Martinez Oliva (2007) report that "by July 1971 the state of diplomatic relations between the United States and Europe was so deteriorated that Secretary Connally felt… that the strengthening of European economy and the Europeans' aim at a stronger monetary integration could be a threat for the United States, given 'the degree of resentment against the U.S. and the dollar' that he could sense in his discussions with the Europeans."

17   The creation in Hong Kong of an offshore centre as an experimental environment for financial testing can be viewed as fully consistent with the model of "adaptive authoritarianism," which has been described as characterizing China's policy generation pattern in past years. In this context, Heillman (2008) highlights Chinese authorities' ability to "encourage and protect broad-based local initiatives and filter out generalizable lessons"; such a model has in many instances proven successful in generating fruitful links between central and local initiatives. Rodrik (2006) notes "China carved out special economic zones where foreign investors had access to a free trade regime."

18   See Martinez Oliva (2012).

19   Author's calculations based on BIS data (www.bis.org/publ/rpfx13fx.pdf).

key Asian partners (Hong Kong, Singapore, Malaysia, Indonesia, Thailand) to oil-exporting countries (United Arab Emirates, Qatar), and including strategically relevant neighbours such as Mongolia and Kazakhstan (Lanman and Kennedy).[20]

Extending credit lines across the world can also be viewed as a sign of China's effort to reinforce the role and credibility of its currency by playing the monetary leader. In the worst moments of the 2008 international financial crisis, consistent with its role as the world's banker, the United States acted as a lender of last resort. To that end, the Federal Reserve Bank of New York arranged emergency dollar credit lines through swap arrangements with the European Central Bank, the Bank of Japan, the Bank of England and the Swiss National Bank to provide the needed amount of liquidity to the market. Meanwhile, the United States for the first time established swap lines with four major emerging market economies (Brazil, Mexico, South Korea and Singapore). The political economy of that decision seems to be that, following divergences between the United States and Europe on how the international monetary and financial system should be reformed, the United States aimed at strengthening its relationship with strategically important emerging market economies, thus reinforcing its leverage in the new global system.[21]

China has learned fast to use currency and finance to pursue its foreign policy goals. On October 13, 2014, China and Russia signed a three-year currency-swap line of US$24 billion (Xie 2014). While it is uncertain if the initiative can effectively help Russia to cope with its worst economic crisis since the default year 1998, it is an example of a political attitude aimed at reinforcing useful strategic alliances while displaying its ability to bypass the sphere of action and influence of the International Monetary Fund (IMF). Arguably, the challenge is more apparent than real as the sanctions on Russia might induce the Fund to reject any formal request of assistance from Russia, in the unlikely case that such a request comes. Similar considerations may hold for China's assistance to Argentina and Venezuela, as these countries would hardly meet the conditions for an IMF program. In March 2015, the Chinese government signed trade and investment agreements to loan Argentina US$7.5 billion to develop energy and transportation infrastructure projects. China and Argentina also agreed to a loan for US$4.7 billion from a group of Chinese banks led by the China Development Bank for the construction of two hydroelectric dams in

---

20   Recent deals signed last November with Kazakhstan, in particular, amount to US$14 billion. It is worth recalling that Kazakhstan is the world's leading producer of uranium and its uranium exports to China, which has 22 nuclear reactors, and 26 under construction, was part of previous deals.

21   For an extended analysis of that unprecedented decision by the Fed, see Chey (2012).

Patagonia (Raszewski 2014). Since 2007, China has extended over US$50 billion in loans to Venezuela in return for guarantees of future oil deliveries. In the face of Venezuela's difficult situation, China agreed on the extension to Venezuela of a further US$4 billion cash-for-oil in July 2014. Venezuela is currently exporting over 600,000 barrels of oil per day to China, more than half of which is already going toward repayment of previous loans (Kaiman 2015). In such circumstances, one might therefore argue that China is exercising its ability to frustrate US foreign policy while at the same time collecting potential allies and clients across the world.

In order to facilitate settlements and clearing in RMB, a growing number of offshore centres have been established by China. Following Hong Kong's rise as the first and still most relevant RMB offshore financial centre, clearing banks have been created in Macau, Taipei and Singapore. The status and reputation of the RMB, as well as its operational capabilities, have been further enhanced by the birth of new RMB financial hubs in London, Frankfurt, Paris, Seoul, Luxemburg and Sydney. Arguably, while the creation of offshore centres in Asia can partially be explained by the convenient geographical proximity with China, geopolitical considerations — largely associated with the aim of establishing a well-rooted area of influence in East Asia — have the largest share in Beijing's choice. Clearing RMB transactions across the world with ease represents a powerful incentive to adopt the RMB as the East Asian trading and financial currency by countries whose major trading partner is, in most cases, China itself, and which, in some cases, have sizeable surpluses of RMB to be spent across the world.

In the case of Europe, other considerations might be playing a role, including a long history of mutual trade relations; the benefit of operating in a well-established and highly developed financial space; the convenience of having RMB financial centres that can settle their operations at different time zones, as a midpoint connector between Asia and North America. Since Europe represents China's largest trading partner, creating a structure that encourages and facilitates settlement in RMB involves further advantages in terms of reinforcing the RMB's role as a settlement currency.[22]

Finally, QFII quotas have been granted to Singapore (RMB 50 billion), London (RMB 80 billion) and Taiwan (RMB 100 billion). More recently, QFII quotas amounting to RMB 80 billion have been assigned to Frankfurt, Paris and Seoul.

---

22   Interestingly, in a recent survey of 24 firms active in the Chinese market, more than half of the interview respondents expressed the belief that Europe as a whole will play a key role in the RMB internationalization process. See Aite Group (2014).

Hong Kong's quota of RMB270 billion still makes it the largest of all the RMB financial centres. The total QFII quota globally is therefore at RMB740 billion as of end-December 2014.[23]

In conclusion, Chinese authorities have successfully triggered a high-intensity process that will probably achieve a full global status for its currency soon. The RMB becoming a competitive reserve currency does not, however, imply that China is able, or willing, to displace the dollar from its status of global dominant currency.[24] A broad set of empirical studies all found a strong tendency toward the creation of an East Asian bloc of regional currencies led by the RMB.[25] As a matter of fact, China's moves seem more consistent with a far more attainable multi-step strategy to create financial networks that can enable it to be easily traded internationally, enhance its use in East Asia for trade and investment, and eventually turn it into the dominant East Asian currency and a pivotal element of China's economic power strategy in the region.

While China's policy choices on the RMB seem consistent with a successful achievement of regional monetary dominance in East Asia, it is highly unlikely that China will be able to eclipse the dollar at the global level, and almost certainly not a goal of Chinese authorities at the present stage.[26] The following section will argue that the rise of the RMB may be seen as part of a visible strategy to support the creation of regional finance and development institutions, thus creating China's area of influence. Unlike the conventional claim that China might be aiming at challenging the role of the United States as a global hegemon, and eventually replacing it, it seems more convincing that China is pursuing a peer-to-peer status with the United States, and an even distribution of roles in the new global monetary order.

---

23   See www.ife.com.cn/content-32-305-1.html.

24   See, for example, Prasad and Ye (2013).

25   A comprehensive survey of such empirical studies is found in Subramanian and Kessler (2013). Among them, Henning (2012) finds evidence of the forming of a loose but effective "RMB bloc" with China by countries such as Malaysia, Thailand, Singapore and the Philippines; South Korea has also participated tentatively since the global financial crisis.

26   The sequence from the (certain) regional affirmation to the (uncertain) global affirmation of RMB is noted in Eichengreen (2011): "China on the other hand has indicated that it aspires to make the renminbi a leading reserve currency in its own right, starting presumably in Asia." Four years later, while noting that the RMB is already a dominant currency in East Asia, Subramanian and Kessler (2013) suggested "if trade were the sole driver, a more global RMB bloc *could* emerge by the mid-2030s, but complementary reforms of the financial and external sectors *could* considerably expedite the process" (emphasis added).

An Asian Bretton Woods from the Ashes of Global Governance Reform

Especially powerful states usually pursue regional hegemony.
— J. J. Mearsheimer (2001)[27]

In December 2010, the IMF board of governors approved proposals leading to a major renovation of the Fund's quotas and governance, which would take into account the change in size and relevance of emerging economies. IMF leaders nonetheless failed to implement the governance and quota reforms agreed to in advance of the October 2012 annual meeting in Tokyo — the set deadline for a final decision — causing disappointment and resentment within emerging markets and developing countries. New deadlines have all been regularly missed.[28]

Among emerging economies, China was the most damaged, in light of the broad discrepancy between the size of its economy — the largest worldwide according to recent IMF calculations — and its quota. Quite amazingly, China is the fastest-growing country in historical experience from 1870 on. When China's leader Deng Xiaoping started a set of full-fledged reforms in 1982, China represented 2.2 percent of the world's GDP. That figure recorded a sevenfold increase in 30 years, to 14.6 percent in 2012. Among other powers that were at the start of their economic descent, such as Germany, Japan, the Soviet Union and the United States, only the latter was able to nearly double its share of world GDP in 30 years since the beginning of its rise.[29] At the end of 2014, China's share of the world's GDP had reached 16.5 percent in real purchasing power parity terms, as against 16.3 percent of the United States, while China's quota is 3.8 percent, close to much smaller countries' quotas, and far lower than the US quota of 16.8 percent.[30] China's reformed quota would amount to 6.1 percent, thus becoming the third country of the IMF, after the United States

---

27   Elsewhere, the author explains that "although a state would maximize its security if it dominated the entire world, global hegemony is not feasible, except in the unlikely event that that a state achieves nuclear superiority over its rivals."

28   While President Obama's administration had endorsed the reform since the very beginning, US Congress has repeatedly refused to ratify the agreement. The G20 finance ministers and central bank governors communiqué in September 2014 continued to urge the United States to ratify the reforms agreed to in 2010 by year-end, with no success.

29   According to a recent analysis conducted by Daniel Kliman, a senior adviser for Asia at the German Marshall Fund. Kliman (2014) compares China's rise over a 30-year period (1982–2012) with that of the United States (1870–1900), Germany (1870–1900), the Soviet Union (1945–1975) and Japan (1960–1990).

30   By owning an overwhelmingly large quota, the United States has the power to block major IMF decisions requiring a 85 percent majority.

and Japan.[31] The lack of governance reform has also created frustration and resentment in other countries, such as Brazil, India and Turkey, whose larger quota following the reform would give them a greater say in the IMF business.

Not surprisingly, in July 2014, at their sixth summit held in Fortaleza and Brasília, the heads of state and of government of the BRICS (Brazil, Russia, India, China and South Africa) adopted the Fortaleza Declaration and Action Plan, the Agreement on the New Development Bank (NDB), the Treaty for the Establishment of a BRICS Contingent Reserve Arrangement (CRA) and agreements among BRICS Development Banks and Export Credit Insurance Agencies. The NDB is meant to mobilize resources for infrastructure and sustainable development projects; the CRA will provide a framework for the provision of liquidity through currency swaps in response to actual or potential short-term balance-of-payments crises.

While the new institutions are unlikely to replace the IMF and World Bank in the near future, still the question has been raised of whether, in the longer run, competition between the old and the new institutions might bring about fragmentation and regionalization, and if the future shape of the international financial system will reflect the balance of power between the developing and the developed world rather than the intent to pursue cooperative strategies.[32]

Such considerations become particularly relevant if one looks at the recent developments in the field of multilateral trade arrangements in East Asia as part of the largely incompatible strategies of China and the United States to play a leading role in the region.

The progress of Trans-Pacific Partnership (TPP), a multilateral free trade agreement (FTA) whose negotiations started in 2010 with the aim of bringing together countries along the Pacific Rim, was a serious concern in China since the beginning. The TPP represents a very sensitive area in diplomatic relations, for it is viewed as the economic centrepiece of the broader American "pivot" or "rebalancing" strategy in East Asia.[33] The main preoccupation of Chinese policy makers and academic analysts is that the TPP agenda, which now counts

---

31   See www.imf.org/external/np/sec/pr/2011/pdfs/quota_tbl.pdf.

32   On the basis of historical experience, this might not necessarily be true; for example, Henning (2002) stated that the European Payments Union, while perceived as a direct assault to the IMF territory, skillfully handled intra-European payments during the 1950s and paved the way for current account convertibility in the region. For a comprehensive analysis of regional arrangements today see Lombardi (2010); Kawai and Lombardi (2012).

33   The US pivot strategy was started by Hillary Clinton's article "America's Pacific Century," which appeared on *Foreign Policy* on October 11, 2011. Clinton's basic idea is that the development of the Asia-Pacific, where nearly half of the world's population resides, is of vital importance to American economic and strategic interests.

12 countries participating in the negotiations,[34] may represent "a centrifugal force arising to rip asunder the regional economic integration of East Asia" (Yuan 2012). In this light, the US motivation behind the TPP is seen in China as mostly geopolitical rather than economic.

According to Chinese analysts, the "TPP reflects the fact that the United States is taking a substantive step on its strategy of returning to the Asia-Pacific region" (Fu quoted in Song and Yuan 2012). As a strategy to contain China's rise in East Asia by reducing Asian Pacific countries' economic dependence on their powerful neighbour, the TPP is viewed as potentially destabilizing. Chinese authorities might perceive a policy aimed at inducing Association of Southeast Asian Nations (ASEAN) countries to adopt policies in favour of the United States as an unacceptable threat to its status in the East Asian region. Moreover, some Chinese scholars regard the TPP as potentially creating "trade diversion" in favour of TPP members, and therefore damaging China's economic interest.

For different reasons, the debate on the TPP is also very lively in the United States. While the Chinese accusation that the United States is using the TPP as a strategic and political-military tool is rejected by US political scientists,[35] American liberal economists such as Robert Reich, Paul Krugman, Jeffrey Sachs and Joseph Stiglitz criticize the TPP for its emphasis on protecting investors; for ignoring relevant issues such as environmental protection and income inequality; for its potential negative impact on jobs, trade and GDP growth and income distribution; and for the lack of transparency of the process.[36]

A further source of debate in the United States is whether the TPP should address the issue of exchange rate manipulation, the practice through which some countries, by keeping their currencies artificially weak, achieve an unfairly competitive advantage on international trade markets. Fred Bergsten, a senior fellow and director emeritus at the Peterson Institute for International Economics, and Jared Bernstein, former chief economist to US Vice President Joe Biden, both highlight the harmful consequences of currency manipulation on the US current account balance and jobs, and insist that the TPP needs to include rules to restrict such behaviour and sanctions to severely enforce those rules.[37]

---

34   Namely Australia, Brunei, Canada, Chile, Japan, Malaysia, Mexico, New Zealand, Peru, Singapore, the United States and Vietnam.

35   See, for example, Frost (2013).

36   Stiglitz (2014) has pictured the TPP as one aspect of the larger problem represented by the US "gross mismanagement of globalization." Krugman (2014) has claimed "the push for T.P.P. seems almost weirdly out of touch with both economic and political reality." Robert Reich, an academic scholar at Berkeley, and a former Secretary of Labor in the Clinton administration, has defined TPP as "the worst trade deal you never heard of" (see http://robertreich.org/).

37   See Bergsten (2015); Bernstein (2015).

With the clear purpose of countering the perspective of a growing US presence in East Asia, China started in past years to sign bilateral and multilateral FTAs with a number of countries from East Asia and elsewhere.[38] Extending economic benefits to neighbours via FTAs allowed China to deepen its soft power in the area, and gain trust and friendship among countries that had a past history of political and military confrontation with China.

More recently China's strategy has become more coordinated and ambitious. In opposition to the TPP, China has conceived and promoted its own concept of a free trade area of the Asia-Pacific, along with the Asian Infrastructure Investment Bank (AIIB). Washington's fear is that the Chinese initiative might undercut the TPP, as well as the World Bank, the IMF and the Asian Development Bank (ADB), and reinforce Chinese commercial power in the area, while, in parallel, Chinese military presence would progressively grow, stretching from the East China Sea to the entire South China Sea.

China's official position on the AIIB is that Asia has a massive need to fund infrastructure, with a financial gap that, according to a joint study of ADB and Asian Development Bank Institute (2009), amounts to US$8 trillion from 2009 to 2020. Financing such a huge gap is well beyond the funding capabilities of the ADB and the World Bank. Indonesia alone, for example, is said to need US$230 billion to enhance its poor infrastructure, which constrains growth.[39] The Greater Mekong sub-region, connecting less developed parts of Vietnam, Laos, Cambodia and Thailand, is estimated to need about US$50 billion.

Although the AIIB will start with authorized capital of US$100 billion and funds of US$50 billion, its resources will be fully concentrated on infrastructure, differently from the ADB and World Bank, whose firepower has to deal with a lot more development areas, such as education, gender inequality, environmental sustainability and health. Moreover, China's presence in the infrastructural projects of its neighbours is already relevant, in spite of political disagreement with the United States and Japan, who accuse China of buying political influence in the area, and of disregarding social and environmental issues.[40]

---

38   According to Jiamin Jin, a senior fellow at the Fujitsu Research Institute, China's FTA partners can be divided in the following four categories: greater China economic region; neighbouring countries and regions; resource producers; and developed countries. See Yuan (2012).

39   According to the World Bank (2014), in the absence of higher growth rates, Indonesia will not be able to accommodate the 15 million new workers who will join the country's labour force by 2020.

40   For example, following dissident pressure, Myanmar's government in September 2011 ordered the suspension of a controversial hydroelectric project financed and led by a state-owned Chinese company.

In spite of official declarations of cooperative intentions and goodwill by all parties, the AIIB's relationship with the ADB and World Bank does not look simple, even at this very early stage.[41] US officials have reportedly lobbied against the development bank with unexpected determination and engaged in a vigorous campaign to persuade important allies to stay away from the project.[42] South Korea, Indonesia and Australia were persuaded to abstain from signing up as founding members, in spite of the interest they initially expressed. In January 2015, nonetheless, 26 countries met in Mumbai as prospective founding members of the AIIB.[43] Furthermore, in March 2015 Britain shockingly announced its intention to join the new bank as a founding member, thus opening a decisive breach in the anti-AIIB front. While Britain's initiative lifted a US-resented reaction, Germany, France and Italy followed suit; Denmark and Australia did the same shortly after, thus marking a neat Chinese win in terms of international credibility and influence.

According to Simon Tay (2014), a Singaporean academic scholar and social scientist, the reality has changed since the years when Washington could keep Japan and others from supporting calls for an Asian monetary fund during the Asian financial crisis of 1997-1998. According to Tay, a better strategy might be that not only US allies but also the United States join a truly Asian bank that may help enhance infrastructure, and reinforce an effective cooperative process across the region.[44]

Both the Asian and European response can be viewed as shaped by the same aim to participate in the benefits accruing from cooperating with a country whose international power is growing quickly, and whose currency is rapidly acquiring the status of an international currency. Indeed, one might argue, the attitude of countries participating in the AIIB was affected by the rapid rise of the RMB, which has enhanced the reputation of China and gathered a very broad consensus and interest, as shown in the previous section. Consistent with a model where economic and geopolitical considerations are mutually reinforcing,

---

41   For a thorough assessment of the "battle of the banks" see Momani (2014).

42   See Perlez (2014).

43   The countries are Bangladesh, Brunei, Cambodia, China, India, Indonesia, Kazakhstan, Kuwait, Laos, Malaysia, Maldives, Mongolia, Myanmar, Nepal, New Zealand, Oman, Pakistan, the Philippines, Qatar, Saudi Arabia, Singapore, Sri Lanka, Tajikistan, Thailand, Uzbekistan and Vietnam.

44   It is perhaps worth recalling that, likewise for the case of China, which joined the Inter-American Development Bank in 2008 as a funding member, the United States might request to join the AIIB with a similar status.

one can also argue that, aside from the disagreement on how the issue of global economic governance reform has been managed so far, the main raison d'être for China's choice to establish the AIIB appears to be that of reinforcing China's hegemony in East Asia.

Once operational, the AIIB will almost certainly have strong ties with the process of RMB internationalization. The AIIB's expanding activity will soon require it to access private funding; this means that, in the near future, the AIIB will tap private resources via financial market instruments to collect infrastructure funding. Such a move would allow the mobilization of private savings across Asia and impose market discipline, thus improving the quality of the project financed.

While the initial endowment is largely based on China's huge stock of US dollar reserves, one may easily foresee that the financing activity of the AIIB will increasingly rely on RMB operations. The mobilization of private resources via the private market, while being promoted and scrutinized from headquarters in Beijing, will obviously be handled in the main Asian financial centres of Hong Kong and Singapore, with relevant implications for the prestige of the RMB. In the same fashion as the International Finance Corporation, the private sector arm of the World Bank Group, which helps developing domestic capital markets by issuing local currency debt, the AIIB might prove a powerful tool in developing the use of the Chinese currency in international markets in the future. Conversely, a growing presence of RMB on the international financial market would enhance and facilitate AIIB activity and presence across the world. Regional trade and investment arrangements will therefore interact with and mutually reinforce the RMB's role as East Asia's main currency, thus contributing to a stronger affirmation of China's power in the region.

Hard Power and Soft Power in China's Regional Policy in East Asia

> *Friendship is something in the soul. It is a thing one feels.*
> *It is not a return for something.*
> — Graham Greene, *The Heart of the Matter*

At the height of disagreement between the United States and Europe, in mid-1971, on the then so-called "dollar imperialism," US Treasury Secretary John Connally regretfully noted that monetary discussions and questions on settlements of US external deficits should have been "linked together with discussions of trade, economic, and defense matters. The monetary questions cannot be considered in a vacuum" (Connally quoted in James and Martinez Oliva 2007). That economic processes and political decisions cannot be easily disentangled into single parts to be subjected to a piecemeal approach, at the cost of oversimplification and misjudgment, also applies to the process of RMB internationalization.

The previous section has highlighted how RMB internationalization goes hand in hand with China's attempt to create an all-Asian infrastructure bank under its control, in a process that resembles the creation of the International Bank for Reconstruction and Development by the United States. This section will argue that for a regional strategy of broad proportions and large ambitions, such as China's, to succeed, it must also take into account the need to gather consensus and political support from its prospective partners, allies and clients. This means establishing close and enduring friendship ties in the region.

A July 8, 2014, *Washington Post* article claimed that "China has no friends" (Wyne 2014). According to the article, China's historical aversion to creating alliances, its authoritarianism, its assertiveness in territorial disputes with neighbours and its inward-looking policies are among the factors contributing to its isolation.

Recent trends nonetheless show that things might be less straightforward than *The Washington Post*'s analysis suggested. China seems to have learned in recent years that building a leader's role in East Asia necessarily requires overcoming the fears and reservations of neighbouring countries, who are worried about suffering from excessive interference or control by their mighty neighbour. It also entails the need to pledge economic support, and reassure other countries that, under the common denominator of mutual economic interest, China will still respect their political independence. At the same time, according to some analysts, China is downgrading the strategic priority of its relations with the Western world. It seems, therefore, less inclined to accept criticism and interference on sensitive policy topics.[45]

Chinese policy analysts have described how China's foreign policy stance has changed and evolved in past years with the intent to pursue a stricter connection with its East Asian neighbours. Following a turbulent period that began in 1949, the year the People's Republic of China was founded, the Chinese government sought to re-establish relations with the United States in 1972, under the Nixon administration, with the common interest of cooperating against the Soviet Union. A turn in China's attitude came in 1982, when the 12th Congress of the Chinese Communist Party started a new course, based on an independent and self-reliant foreign policy of peace. Under the guidance of the principle of non-alignment, China distanced itself from both the United States and the Soviet Union, and undertook independent initiatives in both the diplomatic and the economic playing fields. Bolder economic reform followed, which paved the way to China's economic takeoff. The change in China's views on foreign relations brought about a consistent refusal to resort to alliance, discarded as an old-fashioned diplomatic tool from the Cold War period.

In the past few years, Beijing has nonetheless started to reconsider the potential benefits of alliance. A few years ago, Feng Zhang, a distinguished social scientist of moderate views, warned Washington that the threat of a strengthening of America's strategic dominance in the Asia-Pacific might be the major factor behind Beijing's diplomatic rethinking. If adopted as a policy, this "could produce a Cold War-style confrontation that no one really wants" (Zhang 2012).[46] The paradigm of alliance gets alarming hawkish tones in the analysis of Dai Xu, a People's Liberation Army (PLA) Air Force colonel in charge of the Chinese Institute for Maritime Security and Cooperation Studies. According to Dai (2014), the United States would be "leading a coalition of oceanic countries to encircle the Eurasian continent from the east to west." In this light, Dai views cooperation between China and Russia as means to rebalance international politics. The alliance would, in the future, include other countries in the area, such as Iran, thus helping counterweight the US influence; it would even "force countries like Japan…to develop friendly ties with China" (ibid).[47]

---

45   The process, which has been described as China's big diplomacy shift, is viewed as a potential source of tension with the developed world. See Heath (2014).

46   After reviewing the state of the intellectual and policy debate on establishing alliances, the author concluded that America's consolidation of its strategic position in the Asia-Pacific may seem a merely defensive posture to Washington and its regional allies, but it is highly offensive to many Chinese strategists.

47   According to some commentators, the emergence of hawks in public debates might be part of a good cop-bad cop strategy implemented by Beijing to affect diplomatic negotiations on controversial issues; for others, it would simply reflect enlarged freedom of speech in China. See Lague (2013).

The rise of the RMB would take centre stage in this strategy, according to Di Dongsheng, from Renmin University of China, who suggests that foreign-policy experts closely connected to the PLA see an accelerated pace of RMB internationalization favourably, on the grounds of their belief in the "great-currency great-power nexus" (Di 2013). In the past, some countries have been preoccupied with the strategic implications of the RMB rise. For example, Yuriko Koike (2013), a member of the House of Representatives of Japan and former minister of defence stated: "It is unclear how exactly China hopes to use the renminbi's rise as a geopolitical tool. The country's opacity calls for caution." Quite clearly, the implications of this relevant statement may conversely apply to China's other neighbours, who may feel the appeal of the RMB rise, as a sign of the growing power and influence of a country that seems ready to extend unconditional financial support to its friends.

M. Taylor Fravel (2012), a political scientist from MIT, has provided a thorough description of the process that has led China to gradually soften its foreign policy stance after maritime tensions in the South China Sea peaked in 2011. The bottom line is that China has realized that threatening states in Southeast Asia and therefore increasing US involvement in the region risked undermining its broader foreign policy goals. In Fravel's view, Chinese authorities have adopted a more moderate approach to prevent alliances of Southeast Asian countries against China, to reduce their incentive to create stronger ties with the United States and to diminish the latter's role in intervening to maintain security in the area and to settle disputes among states in the region.

Concluding that China is unilaterally and assertively trying to create a pan-Asian economic and institutional order as a response to its hegemonic ambitions would be, nonetheless, misleading. Looking at how Asian regionalism has developed in the last two decades, one would find that in the aftermath of the Asian financial crisis of 1997-1998, countries in the region have acted under the common driver of achieving cohesion and finding collective solutions to common problems.[48]

Evan Feigenbaum, an experienced analyst of Asian geopolitics, suggests that the 1997-1998 financial crisis contributed to fuelling the impression that the United States was giving little attention to Southeast Asia's economic problems, thus reinforcing regional connections among Asian countries. The severe economic troubles the region experienced may be seen as a main cause for East Asia's

---

48   "Collective action was deemed necessary to address the root causes of the crisis and help solving structural weaknesses related to market development and regulatory frameworks which were — and to a large extent still are — generalized throughout the region" (Capannelli 2011). A thorough analysis of how regionalism is developing in today's Asia is found in Frost (2008).

quest for a local solution, and for the development of pan-Asian views in the region.[49] Even Japan, a close US ally, he adds, with a strong trans-Pacific identity has "long incubated a variety of pan-Asian ideas and ideologies," particularly on the issue of monetary integration (Feigenbaum 2015). As a matter of fact, the aborted Japanese initiative to create an Asian monetary fund gave origin to the Chiang Mai Initiative, which established bilateral swaps among Southeast and Northeast Asian countries.[50]

In a recent book, Lee Kwan Yew, one of Asia's greatest statesmen, suggested that Americans will eventually have to share their prominent world position with China.[51] Treating China as an enemy will induce a counter-strategy to demolish the United States in the Asia-Pacific. Such a strategy might be already at work. In a talk with a group of officials from India and Myanmar in July 2014, Chinese President Xi Jinping stated that a new architecture of Asia-Pacific security cooperation that is open, transparent and equality-based should be worked out, because "the notion of dominating international affairs belongs to a different age" (Xinhua 2014.) At the same time, China has not ceased to demonstrate its maritime strength in the South China Sea to show "strong willingness to counter U.S influence in the region" (Ekman quoted in Associated Press 2014). To reinforce its influence, China is using its growing global economic dominance and its neighbours' dependence on Chinese trade exchanges while pledging generous economic incentives as a means to shift the power balance in favour of China. For example, in 2014 Beijing tried to downplay the strong confrontation with Vietnam on maritime claims by removing an oil rig that had triggered violent anti-Chinese reactions the Vietnamese public, and by stating the intention to improve relations between the two countries.[52]

That China is building up "plenty of soft power" is forcefully advocated by Trevor Moss (2013), an independent observer of Asian politics, defence and security, who describes how the Chinese model exerts a profound interest and appeal in Africa, where China has committed US\$74 billion to local projects

---

49   "Across the region, elites came to view the United States as arrogant and aloof, dictating clichéd solutions to skeptical Asians….The United States continue to pay a price for those perceptions to this day" (Feigenbaum and Manning 2009).

50   While addressing concerns in the United States, and elsewhere, about the implications of such regional financial initiatives, Randall Henning (2002) suggested that: "accepting regional initiatives would have useful diplomatic benefits for the United States. Blocking East Asian initiatives in the past has eroded US standing in the region; accepting some of these proposals shields the United States from criticism for taking a blocking position."

51   See Yew (2013). The founding father of modern Singapore, Lee Kwan Yew is acclaimed as one of the most influential politicians of the twentieth century.

52   While China has shown interest in making amends with Vietnam, also by sending senior officials to Hanoi, the maritime dispute is continuing, after Vietnam submitted its position to an international arbitration tribunal, following the initiative taken by the Philippines and later endorsed by several other countries.

since 2000, and has already delivered around US\$50 billion, benefitting 50 out of 54 African states. But this is also true for other areas such as Latin America, Eastern Europe and, obviously, for some parts of Asia, where China might be perceived differently than in the Western world. The feeling, in those areas, that China can be viewed as a reliable long-term ally is in net contrast with the perception by Western commentators who only look at how China is viewed in North America, in Western Europe and in those Asian countries that are afraid of China.

Chinese Premier Li Keqiang's proposals at the Naypyitaw regional summit in November 2014 are a further example of how the Chinese "stick-and-carrot" strategy is played, by reinforcing its strategic presence in the South China Sea while pledging stronger trade and development involvement with smaller countries. China is continuing its soft-power offensive by pouring money into the AIIB and the NDB, as mentioned before, and in pushing ahead the initiative for a Maritime Silk Road Bank. All these moves suggest that China is getting ready to fill the global power vacuum that a reduced regional role of the United States in Asia might eventually create.

Lee Kwan Yew maintains that it is up to the United States to choose between engaging and isolating China. When China has enough power, it will be faced with the decision on whether to be a hegemon and create its sphere of influence in East Asia, or be a good international citizen. It is in everybody's interest to give China incentives to choose cooperation rather than confrontation. If China is not offered a peaceful way to get access to markets and resources, the world will need to live with a pushy China. In Lee Kwan Yew's words, "the United States can through dialogue and cooperation with China chart a course to manage China's transition in the next 20 or 30 years into a big power" (quoted in Allison and Blackwill 2013).

Conclusions

RMB internationalization is among the most dynamic processes in the most dynamic economy of the last 140 years. As in natural evolutionary processes, the expense of energy in economics must be warranted by rational motives. This chapter has tried to analyze the motivation behind the huge effort undertaken by Chinese authorities in terms of political economy considerations, particularly in the realm of power and geopolitics.

The interaction between the growing international importance of the Chinese currency and the aim of China to create its own area of influence in Southeast Asia suggest the presence of a deliberate strategy where the two objectives are mutually consistent and cross reinforcing. The apparent reluctance of the United States to surrender its own influence in the area, which is viewed as a big economic opportunity as well as a central element of US strategic agenda, suggests a number of considerations on the shape that the future relationship between China and the United States might take.

The latest report of the US National Intelligence Council,[53] "Global Trends 2030: Alternative Worlds," notes that the United States has tended to systematically underestimate the growth of China's power in past years, and highlights that the most plausible best-case outcome would be that China and the United States collaborate on a range of issues, leading to broader global cooperation.[54] Former Treasury Secretary Paulson recently expressed similar conclusions: "The US-China relationship is the most important relationship in the world.... You can't solve the world's greatest challenges unless the two countries work together" (Paulson quoted in Paulson Institute 2015).

The scenario might actually be less rosy, though. It is sometimes claimed that China is trying to replicate what the United States did when it pushed the European powers out of the Western Hemisphere — that is, push the United States out of Asia. This would be broadly consistent with President Xi Jinping's stated "Chinese dream" of a new geopolitical order in Asia built by the governments of that region — with Beijing playing an outsized role. While the United States still dominates the South China Sea, its naval presence has decreased since the Reagan years, and might go even lower by the 2020s as the result of its massive fiscal debt. At the same time, the Chinese navy, the second-most powerful in the world, is growing very quickly.[55]

There are, nonetheless, clear reasons to be in favour of the optimistic view, the materialization of which might largely depend on the United States, and on its willingness to invite China to share the global stage. In this scenario, both the United States and China should find the most appropriate ways to collaborate in a relationship between equals. When such an optimistic scenario could materialize is hard to predict. President Xi's statement that the Pacific Ocean is big enough for the United States and China seems to be a step in the right direction, even if he seems far less accommodating on issues related to the South China Sea. On the US side, in spite of the growing pressures by national security and diplomatic experts, current and future US administrations

---

53   The National Intelligence Council is the centre for mid-term and long-term strategic thinking within the United States intelligence community. Eminent scholars such as Joseph Nye and Richard Cooper are among its past directors.

54   "China's power has consistently increased faster than expected…A comprehensive reading of the four [past] reports leaves a strong impression that [we] tend toward underestimation of the rates of change" (National Intelligence Council 2012).

55   See Kaplan (2014).

might find it hard to surrender parts of world leadership to China. Still, the US diplomatic failure in the AIIB controversy has demonstrated that times have changed, and that many countries, including historical allies of the United States, seem today less prone than in the past to adhere to a model strictly based on American hegemony, and rather inclined to a multilateral approach to the bigger economic issues. A first step forward might be reinforcing collaboration between the two big powers on less contentious fields, such as global terrorism or climate change, as a helpful strategy to enhance mutual trust and knowledge, and to pave the way to more engaging forms of cooperation in the future.

The rapid rise of the RMB as an international currency shows how fast global economic relations may change in the global economy. If that trend is to continue, the Chinese currency might someday score very high among international currencies. It is quite likely that sometime in the future, in a matter of years or decades, the RMB will be on equal footing with the US dollar as a world reserve currency. But what matters most in the shorter run is that there is a very good chance the RMB will become the major regional currency in East Asia, and a powerful vehicle for trade and investment across the area. Such an outcome should be viewed not as a threat, but as helpful and desirable at the regional level, and as a source of stability for the overall international monetary system.

Author's Note

I wish to thank without implication Lorenzo Bencivelli, Terence Chong, Stefano Fenoaltea, Randall Henning, Yifan Hu, Massimo Roccas, Lucio Scandizzo, Liping Zhang and an anonymous referee for helpful comments. The opinions expressed are my own and do not necessarily represent those of the Bank of Italy or the Eurosystem.

Works Cited

Aite Group. 2014. "Internationalizing the Renminbi: Weaving a Web for the Next World Currency." Research commissioned by Clearstream, May.

Allison, G. and R. Blackwill. "Interview: Lee Kwan Yew on the Future of U.S.-China Relations." *The Atlantic*, March 5.

Asian Development Bank and the Asian Development Bank Institute. 2009. *Infrastructure for a Seamless Asia.* http://adb.org/sites/default/files/pub/2009/2009.08.31.book.infrastructure.seamless.asia.pdf.

Associated Press. 2014. "China's Prospects for New Thinking on Asian Alliances Weaken as It Pursues Territorial Claims." Fox News, July 10. www.foxnews.com/world/2014/07/10/china-prospects-for-new-thinking-on-asian-alliances-weaken-as-it-pursues/.

Bergsten, C. F. 2015. "The Truth About Currency Manipulation — Congress and the Trans-Pacific Partnership." *Foreign Affairs*, January 18.

Bernstein, J. 2015. "How to Stop Currency Manipulation." *The New York Times*, January 9.

Capannelli, G. 2011. "Institutions for Economic and Financial Integration in Asia: Trends and Prospects." ADBI Working Paper Series No. 308, September.

Chey, H. 2012. "Why Did the US Federal Reserve Unprecedentedly Offer Swap Lines to Emerging Market Economies during the Global Financial Crisis? Can We Expect Them Again in the Future?" GRIPS Discussion Paper 11-18, National Graduate Institute for Policy Studies, Tokyo, Japan, January.

Cohen, B. J. 2010. "Currency and State Power." Paper presented at the conference Back to Basics: Power in the Contemporary World, Princeton University, October.

————. 2012. "The Benefits and Costs of an International Currency: Getting the Calculus Right." *Open Economies Review* 23: 13–31.

Di, D. 2013. "The Renminbi Rise and Chinese Politics." In *The Power of Currencies and Currencies of Power*, edited by A. Wheatley. London and New York, NY: The International Institute for Strategic Studies, Routledge.

Dai, Xu. 2014. "Vigorous Eurasian Community Needed to Counter US Hegemonic Ambition." *Global Times*, June 15.

Eichengreen, B. 2011. "What Kind of Economic and Financial Leadership Does the World Expect of China? Lessons from Two Historical Episodes." In *Medium- and Long-term Development and Transformation of the Chinese Economy*, Cairncross Economic Research Foundation.

Feigenbaum, E. A. 2015. "The New Asian Order." *Foreign Affairs*, February.

Feigenbaum, E. A. and R. A. Manning. 2009. *The United States in the New Asia*. Council on Foreign Relations, Council Special Report N. 50, November.

Fravel, M. T. (2012), "South China Sea: What Issues and Whose Core Interests?" Paper presented at the 6th Berlin Conference on Asian Security: The US and China in Regional Security, Berlin, June 18-19.

Frost, E. L. 2008. *Asia's New Regionalism*. Boulder, CO: Lynne Rienner.

———. 2013. "Strategic Implications of TPP: Answering the Critics." *Asia Pacific Bulletin*, No. 220, July.

Gardner R. N. 1969. *Sterling-dollar Diplomacy: The Origins and the Prospects of our International Economic Order*. New York, NY: McGraw-Hill.

Harold, S. 2015. "Asia for the Asians." www.afpc.org/publication_listings/viewPolicyPaper/2696.

Heath, T. 2014. "China's Big Diplomacy Shift." *The Diplomat*, December.

Heillman, S. 2008. "From Local Experiments to National Policy: The Origins of China's Distinctive Policy Process." *The China Journal* 59: 1–30.

Henning, C. R. 2002. *East Asian Financial Cooperation*. Institute for International Economics, Policy Analyses in International Economics 68.

———. 2012. "Choice and Coercion in East Asian Exchange Rate Regimes." Peterson Institute for International Economics, Working Paper series, WP 12-15, September.

James, H. and J. C. Martinez Oliva. 2007. "Too Much for One Country: The United States and the Bretton Woods System, 1958–1971." In *International Monetary Cooperation Across the Atlantic*, edited by H. James and J. C. Martinez Oliva. Frankfurt am Main: C. Adelmann.

Kaiman, J. 2015. "China Agrees to Invest $20bn in Venezuela to Help Offset Effects of Oil Price Slump." *The Guardian*, January 8. www.theguardian.com/world/2015/jan/08/china-venezuela-20bn-loans-financing-nicolas-maduro-beijing.

Kaplan, R. D. 2014. *Asia's Cauldron: The South China Sea and the End of a Stable Pacific."* New York, NY: Random House Publishing Group.

Kawai, M. and D. Lombardi. 2012, "Financial Regionalism." *Finance & Development* 49 (3), September.

Kliman, D. 2014. "Is China the Fastest-Rising Power in History?" *Foreign Policy*, May.

Koike, Y. 2013. "The New Shape of Asia." In *The Power of Currencies and Currencies of Power*, edited by A. Wheatley. London and New York: The International Institute for Strategic Studies, Routledge.

Krugman, P. 2014. "No Big Deal." *The New York Times*, February 27.

Lague, David. 2013. "Special Report: China's Military Hawks Take the Offensive." Reuters, January 17.

Lanman, S. and S. Kennedy. 2014. "Fed Crisis Program Becomes China's $500 Billion Influence Tool." Bloomberg. December 24.

Lee, E. 2015. "RMB: More Than Just Another Currency!" Presentation at the 5th Global Securities Financing Conference, Hong Kong, April 28. https://clearstream-events.com/userfiles/file/Esmond_Lee_-_RMB_-_more_than_just_another_currency.pdf.

Lombardi, D. 2010. "Financial Regionalism: A Review of the Issues." Brookings Institution Issues Paper, November.

Martinez Oliva, J. C. 2007. "Monetary Integration in the Roman Empire." In *From the Athenian Tetradrachm to the Euro: Studies in European Monetary Integration*, edited by P. Cottrell, G. Notaras and G. Tortella. Aldershot, UK: Ashgate.

———. 2012. "The Challenges of Renminbi Internationalization." Peterson Institute for International Economic, *China Economic Watch* (blog), March 23. http://blogs.piie.com/china/?p=1180.

Mearsheimer, J. J. 2001. *The Tragedy of Great Power Politics*. New York, NY: W. W. Norton and Company Inc.

Momani, B. 2014. "The Battle of the Banks." CIGI Commentary, November. www.cigionline.org/sites/default/files/momani_1.pdf.

Moss, T. 2013. "Soft Power? China Has Plenty." *The Diplomat*, June.

Mundell, R. A. 1993. "EMU and the International Monetary System: A Transatlantic Perspective." Austrian National Bank Working Paper 13.

National Intelligence Council. 2012. "Global Trends 2030: Alternative Worlds." December. www.dni.gov/nic/globaltrends.

Paulson Institute. 2015. "Paulson Institute Co-hosts High-Level Panel at Council on Foreign Relations." January 29. www.paulsoninstitute.org/events/2015/01/29/paulson-institute-co-hosts-high-level-panel-at-council-on-foreign-relations/.

Perlez, J. 2014. "U.S. Opposing China's Answer to World Bank." *The New York Times*, October 9.

Prasad, E. and L. Ye. 2013. "The Renminbi's Prospects as a Global Reserve Currency." *Cato Journal* 33 (3): 563–70.

Raszewski, E. 2014. "UPDATE 1—China Lends Argentina $7.5 billion for Power, Rail Projects." Reuters, July 19. http://uk.reuters.com/article/2014/07/19/argentina-china-idUKL2N0PT2N220140719.

Rodrik, D. 2006. "Goodbye Washington Consensus, Hello Washington Confusion? A Review of the World Bank's Economic Growth in the 1990s: Learning from a Decade of Reform." *Journal of Economic Literature* 44 (4): 973–87.

Song, G. and W. J. Yuan. 2012. "China's Free Trade Agreement Strategies." *The Washington Quarterly* 35 (4): 107–119.

Stiglitz, J. E. 2014. "On the Wrong Side of Globalization." *The New York Times*, March 15.

Subramanian, A. and M. Kessler. 2013. "The Renminbi Bloc Is Here: Asia Down, Rest of the World to Go?" Peterson Institute for International Economics, Working Paper Series, WP 12-19, August.

Tay, S. 2014. "Asian Bank Will Not Just Be China's Domain." *China Daily Europe*, October 31.

Williamson, J. 2013. "The Dollar and U.S. Power." In *The Power of Currencies and Currencies of Power*, edited by A. Wheatley. The International Institute for Strategic Studies. London and New York: Routledge.

World Bank. 2014. "Indonesia: More Infrastructure, Skills, Better Market Regulation Needed for Higher Growth." Press release, June 24.

Wyne, Ali. 2014. "5 Reasons China Has no Friends." *The Washington Post*, July 8.

Xi, Jingping. 2014. "Remarks by Chinese President Xi at the Fourth Summit of the Conference on Interaction and Confidence Building Measures in Asia." May 30. www.cfr.org/regional-security/remarks-chinese-president-xi-fourth-summit-conference-interaction-confidence-building-measures-asia/p33637.

Xie, Ye. 2014. "Ruble Swap Shows China Challenging IMF as Emergency Lender." Bloomberg, December 22. www.bloomberg.com/news/articles/2014-12-22/yuan-ruble-swap-shows-china-challenging-imf-as-emergency-lender.

Xinhua. 2014. "Chinese President Calls for Greater Democracy in Int'l Relations." Xinhua, June 28. http://news.xinhuanet.com/english/china/2014-06/28/c_133445551.htm.

Yew, L. K. 2013. *Lee Kuan Yew: The Grand Master's Insights on China, the United States and the World*. Interviews and selections by G. Allison and R. D. Blackwill, with A. Wyne. Cambridge, MA: MIT Press.

Yuan, W. J. 2012. "The Trans-Pacific Partnership and China's Corresponding Strategies — A Freeman Briefing Report." Center for Strategic and International Studies, Washington DC, September.

Zhang, F. 2012. "China's New Thinking on Alliances." *Survival: Global Politics and Strategy* 54 (5): 129–148.

Zhou, X. 2009. "Reform the International Monetary System: Essay by Dr Zhou Xiaochuan, Governor of the People's Bank of China." March 23. Bank for International Settlements. www.bis.org/review/r090402c.pdf.

2

The Political Logic of RMB Internationalization: A Unique Journey to a Major Global Currency

Alex He

RMB internationalization, while a goal in and of itself, is, in practice, developing into a propeller for the People's Bank of China (PBoC) to achieve the ultimate goal of domestic financial reform — liberalizing the capital account, exchange rate and interest rate. The unique route of renminbi (RMB) internationalization taken under the concurrently controlled capital account and exchange rate is why this process has evolved into a booster for domestic financial reform. Since launching the cross-border RMB trade settlement scheme in July 2009, many RMB offshore markets and currency swap arrangements have been created, a process that is likely to continue. Accompanying theoretical and empirical studies, Chinese and otherwise, have highlighted the concurrent economic and political forces propelling the internationalization process. These combined forces raise several questions: How can we assess the separate roles played by economic factors and political considerations? How do the two determinants interact in shaping policy outcomes? Is the leading role played by the market or a government strategy? If it is a government strategy, what sequencing or reform road map has been, or is being, pursued? Is it one based on economic theory[1] or a path influenced profoundly by political considerations?[2]

This chapter answers these questions by performing a political analysis of the motivation behind the internationalization process, and the road map being used to achieve it. It discusses how RMB internationalization originated from the idea of China's rise within the international monetary system. Further, Chinese leaders were worried following the 2008 global financial crisis (GFC) about China's excessive dependence on the US dollar. In practice, this worry evolved into a process to push domestic financial reform aimed at liberalizing the capital account, market-based interest rate and exchange rates.

This chapter first reviews the literature on the concept of an international currency and its economic and political determinants, and then examines motivations for RMB internationalization. Second, it explores the connection between RMB internationalization and China's rise in international financial markets. Third, it focuses on the political considerations embodied in the actual internationalization process, including the role of domestic financial reform in transforming China's economic development model from export and investment driven to consumption driven, as well as the opponents and supporters for the reforms.

International Currencies: Determinants of Internationalization

Concepts of International Currencies

An international currency is one that is commonly used outside of a domestic country's currency. All or part of its function — the classic three functions of money (unit of account, medium of exchange and store of value) — can be transferred to the international level. This concept based on monetary function was defined by Benjamin J. Cohen (1971) and refined by Peter Kenen (1983)

---

1   Normally, the economy theory concerning RMB internationalization is the initial liberalization of interest rate and market-based exchange rates, allowing for the openness of the capital account and RMB internationalization to take its course naturally.

2   For instance, there is a so-called "reversed coercing path" of RMB internationalization prevailing in Chinese academia. It begins with RMB internationalization in the form of cross-border trade settlements and the establishment of offshore RMB markets and swap agreements before the resulting internationalization-related pressures push for the liberation of exchange rates, interest rates and the capital account.

Table 1: Roles of an International Currency

Function of Currency	Governments	Private Actors
Unit of account	Anchor for pegging local currency	Denominating trade and financial transactions
Medium of exchange	Vehicle currency for foreign exchange intervention	Invoicing trade and financial transactions
Store of value	Foreign exchange reserves	Investment on financial assets

Data sources: Kenen (1983) and Frankel (2011).

into six combinations of the three functions of international currency in private and public transactions (see Table 1). Among these three, the function as a store of value represents the highest level of internationalization of a currency (the reserve currency).

Susan Strange (1971) studies the political considerations in the evolution of international currencies, classifying them into four categories in her study of sterling: master, top, negotiated and neutral. This political economy typology of international currencies was updated by Eric Helleiner (2008) to include the influence political economy has on currencies. His research focuses more on the top currency and negotiated currency concepts.

Master currencies — of a hegemonic or imperial state that coerce their use by other states, such as the pound in the sterling area and the French franc in the previous franc zone — and neutral currencies — no desire for international use, such as the Swiss franc and the German deutschmark — both have their limitations and do not possess universal significance, as they apply only within a certain historical context (Strange 1971). By contrast, the top currency — one most favoured by the world market for various monetary purposes due to its economic superiority, such as the US dollar in the 1950s — as well as negotiated currencies — occur when the issuing state bargains or negotiates politically with other states for their use of its currency, offering inducements such as military and diplomatic support or economic benefits, such as the pound in the postwar period and the US dollar in the 1960s — both have examples in the modern world. To some degree, today's dollar can still be considered a top currency, and today's RMB, as judged by the path and ways by which the Chinese government promotes it, can be a proper example of a negotiated currency. Helleiner (2008) points out that a negotiated currency can also be a currency on the rise, and is not necessarily one that has lost or is losing political dominance as a master currency or economic dominance as a top currency. Such is the case of the RMB.

Economic and Political Determinants of Currency Internationalization

Economic and political determinants together define the concept of an international currency. Accordingly, studies on international currency issues should focus on both indispensable aspects. The political factors have attracted less recognition than the vast attention economists have awarded this topic, but are equally deserving. Scholarly research in the political economy arena has provided some analytical frameworks for further study on the subject, but more is warranted. Scholars conclude that the fundamental determinants of international currency status are economic size, confidence in the currency and depth of financial markets (see Frankel 1992; 2011; Eichengreen and Frankel 1996; Chinn and Frankel 2008). Helleiner (2008) categorizes various economic factors of major determinants of currency internationalization into three broader attributes — confidence, liquidity and transactional networks.

Recent studies argue that the effects of economic size and transactional networks (network externalities) on international currency choice are in fact not very strong. Paul Krugman (1984) and Menzie Chinn and Jeffrey Frankel (2007) point out that the international use of a currency is non-linearly related to the issuing country's economic size. Barry Eichengreen (2005; 2011) and Eichengreen and Marc Flandreau (2010) argue that network externalities have a weak connection with currency use as a store of value, although a potentially strong connection may exist with its use as a medium of exchange. They also point out that advances in information technology have substantially lowered the transaction costs of using multiple international currencies.

Two other determinants, liquidity (also referred to as depth of financial markets) and confidence, receive less doubt as to the influence of their attributes on currency internationalization. Economically, confidence in a currency can be affected by diverse factors, including monetary and fiscal policies, as well as the issuing country's current account and net-debtor position (Tavlas and Ozeki 1992). Or as Helleiner (2008) puts it, foreigners' confidence in a currency — in particular as a store of value and unit of account — is inspired through consistent stability, an attribute that is usually linked to sound macroeconomic fundamentals in the issuing country. Confidence in a currency, however, can be derived not only from economic fundamentals but also from the broader international security power of the issuing country (Strange 1971). It can also be influenced profoundly by domestic politics and institutions. Andrew Walter (2006) notes that the stable value of pound, which inspired such confidence abroad, was linked to Britain's limited government, narrow electoral franchise and a conservative financial sector control exhibited by the Bank of England.

Following the same logic, a contrary example is that the broader uncertainties surrounding the strength of European political cooperation and the inability of Europe to project its power in a unified manner at the international level — not just in monetary affairs, but also in political and security affairs — undermines confidence in the euro (Cohen 2004; 2007; Henning 1997; 2000; McNamara 2008).

Economists believe that the existence of well-developed and open financial markets in the issuing country, which lower the currency's transaction costs, is another salient economic attribute of an international currency (Lim 2006). Frankel (2011) generalizes the economic factor as the development of its financial markets, in particular their depth, liquidity, dependability and openness. For example, full development of the US financial markets after the creation of the Federal Reserve in 1913, as well as London's financial markets in the nineteenth century, laid the foundation for the rise of the dollar and pound, respectively, as international currencies. In contrast, the tightly regulated financial markets in Japan and Germany were frequently referred to as the principal obstacles of the internationalization of the yen and the Deutschmark (Aliber 1964; Tavlas 1991). Political scientists explain two structural factors that promote the international standing of a currency: the political context characterized by limited, constitutional government and pro-creditor legal frameworks (Stasavage 2003; Walter 2006); and the political legitimacy of a domestic financial order in the eyes of low-income groups (Seabrooke 2006). Helleiner (2008) reiterates that political agencies can play a role in the construction of financial systems that support international currency leadership. He highlights the creation of the Federal Reserve System in the cultivation of the dollar's international role. The creation of this system by US policy makers helped boost liquidity in dollar-based New York financial markets through activities such as rediscounting and open market purchases.

Why China Pushes for RMB Internationalization: A Literature Review

Based on the conditions discussed above, one can argue that the RMB certainly has the potential to evolve into a major international reserve currency. Its capacity to do so is underscored by the size of China's economy — second largest in the world — current account surplus and accompanying expectations for RMB appreciation. However, the full development of financial markets (characterized in particular by depth, liquidity, dependability and openness), which China lacks, constitutes an indispensable precursor for an international currency. Furthermore, by the criteria of liquidity, breadth and openness, Chinese financial markets still have a long way to go before they catch up to those of other major currencies (Frankel 2011). Internationalization of the RMB was started and pushed on the perception of China not yet needing to liberalize its capital account, as well as China not having finished its market-based exchange rate formation regime reform and not having finalized its market-oriented reform of interest rates. This is an unusual pattern, as it defies the logic of classic economics, which states that a currency's internationalization comes with the requirements of a liberalized capital account, a fully market-based exchange rate formation regime and an unregulated interest rate being met.

A unique path based on both political and economic considerations has been taken to push RMB internationalization, a path that cannot be fully explained by economic or monetary determinants alone. Frankel (2011) raises three hypotheses regarding China's consideration in pushing RMB internationalization. The first is that China seeks the advantages of international currency status: seigniorage, convenience for its firms and international prestige. The second hypothesis claims that China does not fully realize the tensions between its simultaneously pursued goals of internationalization and maintaining a competitively valued currency. The third is that an elite few in China (both government officials and academic scholars) push to promote shifting the economy from being export driven to domestic sector driven, and they believe that financial opening, the easing of financial repression and RMB appreciation would contribute to that strategy. Ulrich Volz (2013) argues that RMB internationalization has been triggered mostly by China's domestic need for financial reform, along with the country's defensive reaction to its excessive dependence on the US dollar. Studies from a political economy approach by Chinese scholars have produced significant results. Based on their research, reasons for China's surging interest in promoting the RMB internationalization since 2009 could be summarized as follows.

First, one reason is to avoid the exchange rate risk facing Chinese firms and to promote trade by reducing transaction costs (He 2009; Zhang Ming 2013; Gao and Yu 2011; Huang and Lynch 2013; Yu 2014). RMB internationalization would lead to more foreign trade and financial transactions being invoiced and settled in RMB, resulting in enterprises not needing to hedge the exchange rate risk. Specifically, the considerable exchange rate fluctuation of the dollar — the main international trade settlement currency — in the GFC underscored the massive risks facing China and most of its neighbouring countries and regions. It is the GFC that initially pushed the Chinese government to promote cross-border RMB trade settlements (to reduce transaction costs for China and its regional trading partners), thus insulating China from the exchange rate risks of multiple cross-border capital flows denominated principally in US dollars. In this way, smooth development of trade relations between China and its regional partners could also be secured and maintained.

A second motivation may be to ease the negative effects on China's economy brought about by developed economies' quantitative easing (QE) policies since the GFC. While the Fed's QE plus the US Treasury's intervention succeeded in stabilizing US financial markets, they brought rapid expansion of the Fed's balance sheet (Yu 2014). The potential for a devaluation of the US dollar, resulting in significant capital losses on China's foreign exchange reserves, became the biggest concern for Chinese leaders in the years following the GFC. The QE policy and consequent devaluation of the US dollar exerted great pressure on the RMB and other emerging economies' currencies. Affected currencies appreciated, causing global excess liquidity, which resulted in short-term capital inflow, inflation and asset price increases in emerging countries, including China. Currency appreciation to a certain level would negatively affect the export and economic growth in China and other emerging countries. Some analysts thus conclude that RMB internationalization reflects China's strategy to deal with international currency competition during the negative environment caused by loose monetary policies carried out by developed economies since the GFC (see, for example, Mao and Qin 2013). In the long run, more widely used RMB in trade settlements, and perhaps as a reserve currency, should help prevent the negative spillovers caused by the Fed's "irresponsible" policies, such as the three-round QE policy seen over recent years.

Third, RMB internationalization would increase China's international economic and political prestige. Additionally, RMB internationalization would allow the Chinese monetary authority to collect seigniorage from the rest of world. As international standing of RMB expands, international loans and investments would be executed increasingly more often through Chinese financial institutions, effectively boosting Shanghai as a financial centre (Gao and Yu 2011). In short, a successful RMB internationalization would be seen by China's leaders and elites as a symbol of China's rise in the international financial sphere.

Fourth, RMB internationalization is a new booster for China's financial reform (Huang 2009; Wang 2011; He and Ma 2011). Under international currency status, reform of the RMB's market-based exchange rate and interest rate will be required. This unavoidable prerequisite implies that liberalization of the exchange and interest rates could generate as profound a change to China's financial market openness as China's entry into the World Trade Organization (WTO) did (Zhang Ming 2013). Development of offshore RMB markets would build up more pressure on exchange rate and interest rate reforms (He and Ma 2011; Wang 2011; Wu 2011). The powerful vested interest groups that obstructed the advancement of liberalization of exchange and interest rates constitute the most difficult part of China's financial system reform. That difficulty forced the PBoC to first promote RMB internationalization in the form of trade settlements, in order for channels to be created that would allow these RMB to flow back, which would build up great pressure on the need to realize RMB convertibility under the capital account. This is called the "reversed coercing mechanism" in China's financial reform.

Some scholars have different perspectives on whether using RMB internationalization as a force to push domestic financial reform will work. Zhang Bin (2011) argues that until 2011, development of Hong Kong's offshore markets only forced the Chinese monetary authority to buy more foreign reserves and suffer the financial loss caused by the RMB appreciation against the dollar. Future development of Hong Kong's offshore market is expected to make a greater impact on China's regulated exchange and interest rates (deposit rate). Policy for maintaining current exchange rates within the fixed band and regulated deposit rate would be under further pressure. However, it is not yet clear whether the pressure could produce more regulation or market-oriented reform. Yu Yongding (2011; 2012) also observes that the growth of RMB offshore markets brought opportunities for arbitrage, which exerted new pressures on China's macroeconomic management. Whether these pressures could translate into impetus to push domestic financial reform is uncertain.

The studies above provide some insight into RMB internationalization from a political economy perspective. Among them, two motivations are agreed upon by both Chinese and foreign scholars: to increase China's international prestige economically and politically, and to use it to push China's domestic financial reform. Chinese scholars specifically emphasize two additional direct incentives: RMB in cross-border trade settlement to promote trade by eschewing exchange rate risk and lowering transaction costs, and to deal with the pressure on RMB appreciation and actual losses on China's foreign exchange reserves brought by the QE policies and consequent dollar devaluation since the GFC.[3]

These perspectives show a variety of motives for RMB internationalization, both political and economic. However, current research fails to use a broader political and economic background to explore the connection between RMB internationalization and China's views on the US dollar dominance, as well as Chinese top leaders' vision on financial power. It also fails to provide an

---

3   In practice, however, it did not work. On the contrary, more use of the RMB in cross-border trade settlement only increased the accumulation of China's foreign exchange rate reserves. This is explained more fully in the following sections.

integrated analysis on political incentives influencing the road map of RMB internationalization, as well as why interest groups and other domestic factors matter in the policy-making process. This chapter explores the answers to these two questions and, by doing so, a clearer and more comprehensive understanding of the political logic for RMB internationalization emerges.

China's Views on the US Dollar Dominance

China's Concerns over Its Excessive Dependence on the US Dollar

In stark contrast to the popular image of China as the United States' biggest creditor ("America's banker," among the American public), Chinese elites are highly concerned with their excessive dependence on the US dollar (in the form of dollar-denominated assets, including bonds and bills) and the possible severe consequences it could have on China's economic and political stability. China has fallen into a dollar trap.[4] The GFC showcased the real danger facing its extensive foreign reserves of US Treasury bonds and bills. During the GFC, China was put on the brink of massive capital losses on its foreign exchange reserves, especially on its US government-sponsored enterprise bonds (Yu 2014). After the GFC, the perils of holding enormous amounts of dollars became evident: facing a serious deterioration of the US economy, the Fed's QE, while aiming to stabilize the US financial market, led to a sharp decline in the value of the dollar that would severely reduce the value of China's foreign exchange reserves.

A solution to this was to diversify its foreign reserves; however, China's options were limited. China accumulates foreign reserves at a rate of about US$400 billion a year — there is simply no combination of markets in the world capable of absorbing such large amounts as the US Treasury market (Kroeber 2011). Furthermore, China prioritizes safety and liquidity above return (the three objectives for foreign reserve management). In China's eyes, US Treasury securities remain the best choice in terms of safety and return among all investment products in the international financial market (Yu and Liu 2011). Further, China would expose itself to more risk should it stop buying US Treasury securities (Yi 2010). As Lawrence Summers (2004) said, "it is true and can be argued forcefully that the incentive for Japan or China to dump treasury bills at a rapid rate is not very strong, given the consequences that it would have for their own economies." This is what Summers calls a "balance of financial

---

4   In April 2009, Paul Krugman, *New York Times* columnist and Nobel Prize laureate, called this "China's dollar trap." See www.nytimes.com/2009/04/03/opinion/03krugman.html.

terror," wherein China simply cannot stop financing the United States. Or as Krugman (2009) points out, "China now owns so many dollars that it can't sell them off without driving the dollar down and triggering the very capital loss its leaders fear."

The reality is that China never strategically reduced its US Treasury reserves, but instead continues to increase holdings, reaching a record high US$1.3 trillion by May 2013, and as of September 2014 still remains the number one foreign holder of US Treasury securities (Department of the Treasury 2014). Even in the two years following the GFC, when newspapers were filled with stories about China "dumping dollars," China actually increased its holdings of US Treasury securities: from US$618 billion in September 2008 (when China became the foreign country holding the most US Treasury securities for the first time) to US$1.15 trillion in September 2010 (ibid.). According to Nouriel Roubini, an economist at New York University, if the dollar fell by a third against the RMB, China could suffer a capital loss equivalent to 10 percent of its GDP (cited in Ferguson 2005). For that reason alone, the PBoC has every incentive to continue printing RMB in order to buy dollars. Niall Ferguson (2005) believes that China will continue financing America's twin deficits for a longer period than the dollar pessimists expect. Due to lack of adequate domestic support, the solution of liberalizing the exchange rate to avoid the dollar trap has not been an option for China's policy makers. In short, it can be argued that China is at the mercy of the United States, and not the other way around.

One feasible way to eliminate the dependence and the dollar trap is to promote the RMB to an international status. Some economists in China argue that as a long-term strategy, RMB internationalization should be the correct way to eliminate its dollar dependency (He 2009; Xiang 2011; 2013; Cao Yuanzheng 2014). Although the process will take years or even decades, and will bring large economic costs, such as reducing export competitiveness and compromising monetary policy independence, it is still the right solution for stepping out of the dollar trap. In the long run, it can bring vast political and economic advantages.

Other economists in China, however, demonstrate that the current path of RMB internationalization has not reduced China's dependence on the dollar, but instead has led China to accumulate more dollar-denominated assets and increase its exposure to exchange rate risk. On one hand, under the one-way expectation of RMB appreciation in the market, foreign and Chinese exporters are inclined to use RMB as an invoice currency. On the other hand, importers in foreign countries and China are reluctant to use the RMB as an invoice currency, as they may lose possible gains from appreciation. In reality, due to different bargaining powers possessed by foreign and Chinese enterprises, the amount of RMB being used to pay for imports is much higher than the amount received by China's exporters. Overseas investors have incentives to continuously increase holdings of RMB assets under the RMB's unilateral passage for appreciation. Further, to maintain the current fixed exchange rate floating band, China's monetary authorities must continue buying into the increased foreign reserves (Zhang Ming 2011; Zhang and Xu 2012; Yu 2014). Assuming that the latter opinion is correct, what then explains the PBoC continuing to push RMB internationalization along the current route? Are there incentives beyond simply eliminating dollar dependence? To answer this, more considerations need to be explored. The pursuit of RMB internationalization must have greater goals than simply eliminating excessive dollar dependence.

China's Envy Toward, and Doubt Surrounding, US Dollar Hegemony

China's apprehension of its excessive dependence on the US dollar is based on a broader political economic background, involving how China perceives US dollar hegemony. A popular interpretation of the dollar hegemony among China's public and elite can be summarized as follows: it is an international order in which the United States easily gains and even "plunders" (as some scholars term it) the material and financial wealth from the rest of the world.

Following the conclusion of the gold standard in 1971, the dollar standard system formed, and endowed the United States with the financial monopoly that is supported by its national strength. The dollar's unique status as the international currency in this system enables the United States to plunder wealth from the rest of the world, most notably developing countries, in two related ways. First, the United States maintains a twin deficit — current account and fiscal — implying that it seizes material wealth from other countries through US dollar exports in exchange for foreign-made goods. Second, through the issuing of Treasury bonds and the development of financial derivatives, the outflow of the dollar through the current account deficit flows back to the United States. In this way, the United States effectively imports production value and further supports its financial system. This circulation mechanism causes an inner impulse for the United States to print money. Should the mechanism be in danger of breaking, the United States can pay the debts or dilute its debts by printing money. In doing so, it avoids the obligation to pay debts or reduce the amount of debt through devaluating the dollar. The QE policy, in essence, is debt monetization, and the depreciation of the dollar accompanying the QE policy leads to foreign reserves denominated in dollars held by foreign countries to fall substantially.

This, thus, leads foreign countries to suffer while the United States plunders wealth (Li and Li 2014; Wang and Cheng 2011; Zhang 2010).

Chinese scholars' opinions on dollar hegemony echo the idea expressed by some Western economists, such as Niall Ferguson. Instead of calling it "wealth plundering," Ferguson (2005) terms it "tribute." He believes today's Sino-American economic relationship has an imperial attribute: empires traditionally collect tributes from their people. Rather than the "blood and treasure" paid to a traditional empire, today's tribute is effectively paid to the American empire by China and other East Asian economies in the form of underpriced exports and low-interest, high-risk loans. Just as the US Treasury Secretary in the Richard Nixon administration, John Connally, told his European counterparts that "the dollar is our currency, but your problem," Ferguson believes today's United States can say the same to China and other Asian countries. As such, the well-known saying is quoted frequently by Chinese scholars to describe the dollar hegemony and to illustrate their analysis on how the United States plunders wealth from China and other countries.

Some Chinese scholars who hold more radical opinions go further on the dollar hegemony (see Ding and Niu 2014; Qiao 2007; 2014). In their conspiracy-based views, the United States had used the dollar to hammer the Japanese economy into a decade-long recession, effectively destroying the possibility of Japan catching up with the United States economically in the 1980s.[5] These scholars argue that China must remain highly vigilant to the American conspiracy, which is embodied in the measures the United States took to exert pressure on China, including further opening of the financial market, liberalization of the exchange rate and opening of the capital account. Similarly, economists and even officials who advocate for market-based reforms in the fields above are usually criticized as being agents for US multinationals. They further explain a cyclical process in which the dollar hegemony provides the United States with cheap capital from the rest of the world, which is used to finance its military power, and which, in turn, allows it to maintain the dollar's hegemony.

Some of China's more highly regarded economists, however, interpret the dollar hegemony in a neutral way (He 2004; Zhang 2009; Yi 2011; Xiang and Wang 2014). Zhang Yuyan's explanation provides an example: US monetary hegemony allows it to collect seigniorage from the rest of the world because most countries use and reserve the dollar. The dollar circulates beyond the United States and the dollar reserves held by all other economies are only sustainable through a continuous and large US current account deficit, from which the United States

---

5   The Plaza Accord in 1985 was widely used in China as "proof" of the US conspiracy and the trigger of Japan's subsequent recession.

enjoys global resources and services provided by exporting the dollar and dollar-denominated assets. To maintain the stable dollar circulation, the United States must continue to export the dollar and provide enough financial products to meet the demand for trade and overseas reserves.

In these Chinese scholars' opinions, the fundamental problem of the international monetary system lies in the fact that the US monetary authorities only make monetary policies and macroeconomic policies based on their judgments on the US domestic economic situation. In other words, the United States fails to consider negative spillover effects of its monetary policy on other economies. This explains why China proposes to establish a super-sovereign reserve currency and reform the current international monetary system. However, the reform of the international monetary system and the promotion of the International Monetary Fund's (IMF's) Special Drawing Rights are difficult without the support of the United States. Another option left to China then is to push RMB internationalization to fulfill the functions of an international currency (unit of account, means of exchange and store of value), while insisting on pursuing the goals of reforming the international monetary system.

This neutral opinion on the US monetary hegemony is also echoed by some mainstream US economists. Eichengreen (2011) states in his book *Exorbitant Privilege* that one of the big benefits of the dollar's international currency status is that other countries need to provide real resources in order to obtain it. About US$500 billion circulates outside the United States, for which foreigners have had to provide the United States with US$500 billion of actual goods and services. Because of the convenience of dollar securities, foreign banks hold large amounts of US bonds and bills, and are willing to pay more to obtain them. This allows the United States to run an external deficit in the amount of the interest rate differences between what it pays on foreign investment liabilities and the return on its foreign investment, thus allowing it to import more than it exports and consume more than it produces year after year without becoming more indebted to the rest of the world.

Either based on conspiracy or neutral economic analysis, China believes that the secret of the United States as a superpower lies in the dollar hegemony. The dollar's status as the world's currency allows for the use of foreign assistance to support American living standards and subsidize American multinationals. Further, there is no evidence showing that the left-wing, conspiracy-based opinion — epitomized in the bestselling book series, *Currency Wars*[6] — has influenced Chinese leaders' views on the monetary hegemony. It is fair to say, however, that this viewpoint, in addition to neutral opinions from economists, illustrates the importance of monetary power for a sovereign country's economic and political prestige in the modern world. RMB internationalization is China's first necessary step in pursuing its goal of becoming a financial power in the global monetary system.

Chinese Leaders' Vision of Building up China's Financial Power

Chinese leaders have been developing their own understanding of the importance of finance in the modern economy since the beginning of China's new round of economic reform after the 1989 Tiananmen event. Deng Xiaoping's unexpected foresight in 1991 that "finance is the core of modern economy" (Deng 1994) indicated that China's leaders realized the importance of finance in modernizing China's economy. Following in the spirit of the highest direction from Deng, China launched the market-based financial reform in the mid-1990s, and started to "[be] in line with international norms" (or *yu guoji Jiegui*, as translated in Mandarin). The RMB was devalued and a managed floating system was introduced in 1994. China opened its current account by accepting the IMF's Article VIII in 1996 and a road map for capital account liberalization was set (Yu 2014). The initially smooth financial reform, however, took a sudden turn at the outbreak of Asian financial crisis in 1997. During the crisis, the RMB was repegged to the US dollar, capital account liberalization was stopped and capital control was tightened.

Although financial sector reform has been pushed since the 1990s, China's confidence in its strictly regulated financial system increased after it successfully withstood, to a great extent, the Asian financial crisis, which in turn impeded further financial reform. However, integration with the global financial market remained the ultimate goal for Chinese policy makers. The GFC triggered a new round of reform out of China's concern that the dollar trap would lead to large capital losses. The report released at the 18th National Congress of the Communist Party of China (CPC) in 2012 set the goal of financial reform: to "deepen reform of the financial system and improve the modern financial system so that it will better contribute to macroeconomic stability and support

---

6   *Currency Wars* (*Houbi Zhanzheng*), compiled by Song Hongbing in 2007 and a bestseller in China, is a conspiracy theory-based book series that claims Western countries are ultimately controlled by a group of private banks. It has drawn criticism and praise, and is seen as a prominent exponent of economic nationalism. Its sequel and third installment were published in 2009 and 2011, respectively. The sequel, *Currency Wars 2: World of Gold Privilege* was reported as being one of the most popular books in China by late 2009.

development of the real economy."[7] In other words, the modernization of China's financial sector and the building of strong institutions to manage the financial system were priorities. The report also called for reforms to "accelerate development of a multilevel capital market, take steady steps to make interest rates and the RMB exchange rate more market-based, and promote the RMB's convertibility under capital accounts in due course."[8]

The reform platform released from the 3rd Plenary Session of 18th CPC Central Committee in 2013 highlights three points of financial reform: lowering the entry threshold to boost financial market competition; promoting the marketization of interest rates and exchange rate formation, and the opening of capital markets; and managing potential financial risks by administrations and institutions, as well as improving financial infrastructures. Generally speaking, the key point of the reform was to let the market play a decisive role. In August 2013, before the plenum, Premier of the State Council of the People's Republic of China Li Keqiang stated the same financial agenda to the international community at the Summer Davos Forum in Dalian, China.[9] Premier Li said China's financial reform was "a key move of a chess piece to revitalize the whole game of the Chinese economy."[10]

Scholars began to recognize the importance of a fully developed financial market in China's economic growth in the coming years. Compared to the leaders, scholars have become more focused on the integration of China's financial sector into the global financial market and use more direct words to advocate the importance of finance in the global economy. They emphasize finance's function of leverage in the global economic division of labour and believe the competitiveness of a country's financial sector determines, to a great extent, its status in the global economy (Zhang Yugui 2013). Domestically, they believe that market-oriented financial reform is regarded as the core of the next transformation of economic structure. The market-based financial reform would support the rebalancing of growth toward greater domestic demand.

The success of the financial reform will determine the future of China's economic transformation (Huang 2014; Zhang Yugui 2013; World Bank and Development Research Center of the State Council 2013). RMB internationalization — because of China's concerns regarding market-oriented reform on exchange rate formation and the interest rate, liberalization of the capital account and modernization of the financial system — has become the crucial point that will

---

7   To access the full text of Hu Jintao's report, see http://news.xinhuanet.com/english/special/18cpcnc/2012-11/17/c_131981259.htm.
8   Ibid.
9   See http://topic.chinadaily.com.cn/index/special/sid/505.
10   See http://usa.chinadaily.com.cn/epaper/2013-11/12/content_17097692.htm.

play the pivotal role in China's comprehensive market-based financial reform. Or, as some scholars put it, economic and financial transformations in China constitute the precondition for RMB internationalization. When the structural transformations are finished, the conditions for RMB internationalization should be ripe. The success of the internationalization could be expected, implying that China will have finally fulfilled its strategy in becoming a financial power (Xia 2011; Pan and Wu 2012).

It can be argued that China, as the second-largest economy in the world, deserves its own international currency. The miraculous economic growth in China since the "reform and opening-up" policy (the Chinese economic reform) at the end of the 1970s is built on desired integration into the global economy and the adoption of market-oriented policy. China's entry into the WTO pushed its manufacturers into the international division of labour and contributed greatly to economic growth. Full participation and integration into the global financial market, which would irreversibly connect China's domestic financial market to the global market, is regarded as another key dimension for China's economic progress in the even more intertwined world economy since the dawning of the twenty-first century. Following this logic, in the current credit-based global monetary system, an international currency implies power. RMB internationalization itself is the core of the "Chinese dream"[11] in the financial field and can provide the financial support needed to realize the dream in its entirety.

Eliminating dollar dependence, trying to achieve an equal status to the dollar in the global monetary system and establishing a modern financial system constitute the long-term goals of the broader political background of RMB internationalization. The current internationalization road map is indirect and gradual and intends to achieve these long-term objectives of RMB internationalization through domestic financial reform, despite having increased China's dollar dependence in the initial years — a necessary cost in China's eyes.

---

11   "Chinese dream" is a new term originally used by Chinese President Xi Jinping to describe the nation's rejuvenation, improvement of people's livelihoods, prosperity, construction of a better society and military strengthening. Accordingly, each government department and every walk of life in Chinese society have their roles to play in contributing to the realization of the dream.

Political Logic of the Road Map of RMB Internationalization

An Indirect and Manageable Approach

Despite the academic chorus of appeal for RMB internationalization and the consensus on market-based exchange and interest rate reform (and liberalizing the capital account), the Chinese government has yet to claim a strategy or even publicly address the internationalization process. However, an indirect and manageable approach for RMB internationalization is underway.

Following the GFC, RMB internationalization was promoted as a necessary measure to avoid the risk of China's excessive dependence on the dollar. The Chinese government was not prepared for the increased demand from academic circles to accelerate RMB internationalization, which became more strident in the aftermath of the GFC. China's market-oriented financial reform was far from finished, as the exchange rate and interest rate reform and opening of the capital account were slowly progressing.

The central government recognizes the virtues of China's managed financial system and has confidence in a gradual and manageable approach to financial reform. Chinese scholars and leaders realize the risks of transitioning to a more financially integrated economy, especially the possible impact that capital account liberalization could have on China's economy. The indirect, controllable approach to financial reform is seen as the right choice for China. Facing the great appeal for RMB internationalization, economists and PBoC officials have been studying the gradual manner or middle way to promote RMB internationalization on the condition of a regulated capital account and limited convertibility. The consensus was reached that it could be started from promotion of cross-border trade settlement.

The RMB has been widely used in China's neighbouring countries and regions to settle border trade years before the GFC, and a series of studies have since been done by Chinese scholars (Xu 2014). In July 2009, the State Council's Administrative Measures on Pilot Projects for RMB Cross-Border Trade Settlement (PBoC 2009) was issued,[12] officially initiating the cross-border trade settlement and symbolizing an acceleration of RMB internationalization.

---

12   This was jointly issued by the PBoC, the Ministry of Finance, the Ministry of Commerce, the General Administration of Customs, the State Administration Taxation and the China Bank Regulatory Commission — six ministries of the State Council (China's cabinet).

Despite the rapid progress of RMB internationalization in trade settlement in recent years, deposits of overseas residences, RMB bonds, RMB cross-border loans, RMB overseas direct investment, the introduction of RMB qualified foreign institutional investors and RMB swap agreements with other central banks, Chinese authorities continue to keep a low public profile regarding the RMB internationalization process.[13] It was not until the beginning of 2011, one and half years after the acceleration of RMB internationalization, that the Chinese authority first officially mentioned the wording, albeit in a consistently overlooked document (Xu 2014). Chinese officials describe the process of RMB internationalization as a "let market-take-its-course" situation, and internationalization will be realized when conditions are ripe.[14] In reality, however, Chinese authorities actively push RMB internationalization by the means mentioned above. It appears the Chinese government took a subtle "do-without-saying" approach to RMB internationalization.

This gradual and manageable approach to RMB internationalization follows the same model as the reform of exchange rate formation since 2005 — the first serious step in China's market-based financial reform. China did not fully liberalize at once, but instead followed a gradual means of regulation through a managed floating exchange rate regime based on market supply and demand in reference to a basket of currencies. In the following years, it proved to be a way of avoiding risk, as the government thought the negative impact on the whole economic situation was being controlled. Similarly, the current Chinese government believes that it is still not in a position to fully push market-based exchange rate and interest rate reform, two prerequisites for the internationalizing of its currency (according to the classical theory on sequencing a currency's internationalization). The path chosen for RMB internationalization was thus still gradual and even circuitous. The best option left to reformers is to promote the cross-border trade settlement and establishment of offshore RMB markets. In doing so, the two prerequesites for RMB internationalization can be achieved.

China's concern about the control of foreign capital over its financial market, and consequent encroachment on its financial sovereignty caused by market-based reform, also contributes to its gradual and manageable means of achieving RMB internationalization. Combined with Chinese leaders' emphasis on the importance of finance, China's tight grip on financial power and worry over foreign control of its financial markets is understandable. China will likely

---

13   For detailed progress on RMB internationalization, please refer to the paper by Yu (2014).

14   Yi Gang, deputy governor of the PBoC, expressed this opinion when interviewed by journalists from the official Xinhua news agency on March 1, 2013. See http://rmb.xinhua08. com/a/20130301/1130481.shtml. Jia Kan, director of the Research Institute for Fiscal Science at the Ministry of Finance, published an article to explain this perspective in 2012. See http://paper.people.com.cn/rmlt/html/2012-02/22/content_1006917.htm?div=-1.

never relinquish control of its financial market and would be very reluctant to let foreigners play a significant role in its domestic financial markets, which, according to Kroeber (2011), is crucial if China wants to let the RMB become a substantial reserve currency.

All things considered, the current approach taken in internationalizing the RMB is quite unique. What is seen as a more "normal" approach would be to push market-based reform on exchange and interest rates and liberalize the capital account, as this will naturally lead to internationalization of the RMB. The reality, however, is that in spite of unfinished market-oriented reform on exchange and interest rates and a still strictly regulated capital account, the Chinese government, albeit in a low-profile way, pushes RMB internationalization by ways of cross-border trade settlement, establishment of offshore RMB markets and swap agreements with other central banks.[15]

Behind the indirect and manageable approach taken for RMB internationalization, there are deeper reasons that need to be explored, such as the so-called reverse coercing mechanism — the most plausible explanation.

Capital Account Liberalization in the Name of RMB Internationalization

The fundamental problem with the current road map for RMB internationalization, according to Yu (2014), is that China cannot provide liquidity to the rest of the world without increasing its foreign liabilities correspondingly, due to China running a current account surplus. Ultimately, China's current means of RMB internationalization — i.e., relying on RMB trade settlement to provide offshore markets RMB liquidity — will lead China to hold increasingly more dollar-denominated assets, which is exactly what it is trying to avoid by promoting RMB internationalization. As a result, the goal of RMB internationalization would never be realized. To make it worse, one of the most serious consequences of the current approach is the rampant exchange and interest rate arbitrage. Profits from arbitrage are the major driving force of current RMB internationalization, causing China to suffer great welfare loss.

The regulated exchange rate mechanism is to blame for the failure. Based on the expectation of RMB appreciation, certain progress has been made on the current path of internationalization under dual control of the exchange rate and capital account; however, this progress is unsustainable. Since September

---

15   The amount of RMB that has been activated only accounted for a tiny part of the total size of RMB in the swap agreements. For example, only RMB 4.169 billion had been activated out of RMB 296 billion in the third quarter of 2013 (1.4 percent) (PBoC 2013).

2011, the reversal of expected RMB appreciation has set back the process. Additionally, turmoil in global financial markets would also lead to a huge amount of capital denominated in RMB assets being converted to US dollars. Regardless, the consequences of reduced holdings of RMB assets and of trading volume of RMB cross-border trade settlements prove that the government-led initiatives of currency internationalization under controlled exchange rate and capital account are unstable.

The performance of the RMB internationalization process in 2014 further proved this instability. That year marked the first net depreciation (over the course of a year) of the yuan relative to the US dollar in five years. As the strong dollar emerges and the Chinese economy slows down, market expectations for RMB appreciation have declined substantially. Consequently, the process of RMB internationalization has slowed down, even though the Chinese government has bolstered it by establishing offshore RMB centres in Canada and Australia, two developed economies, as well as introduced other measures for further opening of its capital account, such as the enlargement of RMB Qualified Foreign Institutional Investors quotas and the kick-off of the Shanghai-Hong Kong Stock Connect. The increase of offshore RMB deposits in Hong Kong in 2014 was the smallest in 21 months, and once even declined mid-year. The share of China's goods trade settled in RMB dipped to 13.2 percent in July 2014, the lowest since October 2013 (Global Research of Standard Chartered 2014).

Given all these constraints and setbacks to RMB internationalization, two important questions still remain: What is the reasoning behind opting for the current road map? And why does the PBoC continue using the current means of RMB internationalization despite the apparent lack of stability and sustainability?

The answers lie in the liberalization of the capital account. Following the current approach, the PBoC is actually pushing capital account liberalization under the guise of RMB internationalization. First, opening RMB trade settlements and developing offshore RMB markets are ways of relaxing capital account control (Yu 2011). Currency swap agreements signed between the PBoC and other central banks are another way to break through capital account control, ostensibly in the name of RMB internationalization, by providing anticipation of adequate liquidity to encourage more use of RMB in overseas markets (Zhang and Xu 2012). This explains why RMB trade settlements, development of offshore RMB markets and currency swap agreements were still pushed forcefully after 2011, although scholars had pointed out the inherent defects of RMB internationalization under the current path and had called for a halt (Yu 2011; Zhang and Xu 2012). In November 2014, the beginning of the

Hong Kong-Shanghai Stock Connect "through train" — which allows Chinese mainland investors to buy Hong Kong shares and international investors to gain access to one of China's two stock markets via Hong Kong-based brokerages — provided another nudge to further open the door of the capital account without having to directly lift China's capital control. As Charles Li, chief executive of Hong Kong Exchanges and Clearing said, the scheme marked a breakthrough point for the two-way opening of mainland China's capital account (Li 2014).

The liberalization of the capital account is a policy goal supported by authoritative official documents, which justifies the current approach the PBoC is using to promote RMB internationalization. It is worth noting that while neither the PBoC nor any other departments ever mention RMB internationalization or the relationship between RMB internationalization and capital account liberalization in their official documents and statements, liberalization of the capital account — a desired, if not the primary, consequence of RMB internationalization — is specified as a priority in such authoritative documents as the "12th Five-Year Plan," the report of the 3rd Plenary Session of the 18th CPC Central Committee.

Therefore, the PBoC insisted on its policy and proposed a period of "strategic opportunity" for capital account liberalization in 2012 (Research Team of Statistics and Analysis Department of PBoC 2012b) and has continued to push to liberalize the capital account since, despite many economists warning of the great danger it could bring to China's economy. In practice, the PBoC did not intend to push capital account liberalization in one swing. The proposed strategic opportunity was more of an announcement on the importance and urgency for the capital account to be liberalized. The current approaches of RMB internationalization have actually indirectly broken through the capital account control. In this way, capital account liberalization does not have to directly confront the powerful interest groups, but instead provides a logical and feasible path for domestic financial reform under the current political and economic background in China.

Coordinated and Controllable Way for China's Financial Reform

An important supplementary explanation for the PBoC's efforts for the liberalization of the capital account is that the PBoC does not seek to promote the policy in a rigid way. According to what Deputy Governor Yi Gang said in a recent debate with Yu Yongding, the PBoC is concurrently promoting the liberalization of the interest rate, the exchange rate and the capital account "in a coordinated way" (Sina Finance 2014). This is also what the PBoC February 2012 policy research report indicates (Research Team of Statistics and Analysis

Department of PBoC 2012b). It claims that classic economic theory, "the impossible trinity" (or "trilemma"), has its limitations and does not apply to China's current situation. One of the key limitations of the theory is that it does not take the "intermediate states" of each component of the triangle into account. For example, between the fixed and fully liberated exchange rate system, there is an intermediate state of being neither fully regulated nor fully liberated. This constitutes the theoretical foundation for the coordinated means of promoting China's financial reform.

Some other influential economists in China, such as Xia Bin,[16] endorse the PBoC's opinion on the gradual model of China's coordinated reforms of the three important policy goals (Xia 2014). Xia believes the sequencing is no longer the key for China's financial market reform, as both exchange rate reform and liberalization of the capital account have already made some progress. Further complicating the situation is the ongoing effort to internationalize the RMB, effectively adding a new heavyweight variable to China's financial market reform. RMB internationalization, in its current state, is pushed under a regulated exchange rate and unfinished capital account liberalization, and should not follow an abstract theory. This is not a case that has ever occurred in Western classical economic textbooks, and there is no experience China can learn from.

The PBoC is emphasizing that at present, the conditions for accelerating the capital account liberalization are ripe, and are promoting the market-oriented exchange and interest rate reform, as well as liberalization of the capital account in a coordinated way. China's choice is to promote the exchange rate, interest rate and capital account liberalizations simultaneously in an alternative way, launching whichever reform once the conditions for it are ripe. In this way, some combination of measures would be taken and the risks reduced.

Based on its own calculation and confidence in the current gradual approach, the PBoC did not follow the ideal sequencing. Judging from some comments of PBoC officials, such as Deputy Governor Yi Gang and former Deputy Governor Wu Xiaoling, the PBoC is promoting the use of the RMB as a settlement and investment currency, which will bring great external pressure to liberalize the capital account. Only after the liberalization of the capital account is achieved can interest and exchange rate reform be realized. This is what Yu (2014) calls the PBoC's "functional approach" to RMB internationalization, or as other scholars refer to it, the "reversed coercing approach." Meanwhile, at

---

16   Xia Bin is the director-general of the Financial Research Institute at the Development Research Center of the State Council and a former member of the monetary policy committee of the PBoC.

the request of other countries,[17] signing currency swap agreements with foreign central banks is a supplement to the basic PBoC approach to promoting RMB internationalization.[18]

At present, the PBoC is under much more criticism regarding the slow pace of interest and exchange rate reforms. Some analysts believe the current policy combination of slow exchange rate reform and promotion of capital account and RMB internationalization is not ideal, based on the rampant exchange rate and interest rate arbitrage caused by the policy (Yu, Zhang and Zhang 2013). The PBoC should recognize that a more flexible exchange rate could offset negative impacts of further liberalizing the capital account. The PBoC's slow-moving exchange rate reform in recent years lies in the greatest difficulties facing them. Some progress was made when certain favourable conditions were prepared, such as the devaluation of the RMB in 2014. In March 2014, the PBoC widened the RMB exchange rate trading band to two percent and began to gradually reduce its regular intervention on the foreign exchange markets. Yi Gang believes that by the end of 2014, RMB exchange rate flexibility had increased and a two-way fluctuation for the RMB exchange rate was forged (Yi 2014).

RMB Internationalization as a Propeller and Important Collateral Goal for Further Financial Reform in China

It is evident that PBoC officials understand the sequencing for RMB internationalization is important and should adhere to the following order: reform of market-based interest rate and exchange rate formation mechanism, convertibility of RMB under capital account and then complete the RMB internationalization. However, exchange and interest rate reforms are facing too many difficulties and it is very hard to break the powerful vested interest groups in state-owned enterprises (SOEs), the "big four" — four state-owned commercial banks — and local governments, which are supported and protected by the current financial repression-based economic development model. As

---

17   The PBoC's swap agreements with South Korea in December 2008 and other countries' central banks in the first months of 2009 were all signed at these countries' requests (Ba 2009). In recent years, many swap agreements were also at the request of other countries' central banks for different reasons — for example, Argentina, Malaysia and Indonesia for trade settlement currency, and Russia, the Philippines, Cambodia and Belarus for reserve currency (Yang 2014).

18   The PBoC did not zealously promote the swap agreements with other countries. Personal interview with Xu Qiyuan.

Wu Xiaoling (2011), vice chairperson of the Financial and Economic Affairs Committee of the National People's Congress, said in 2001, "it is too difficult to reach consensus among all the parties concerned with how to reform the exchange rate regime." The PBoC has to shift to another means of exchange rate reform — first by promoting RMB internationalization, then taking advantage of the pressures brought by RMB internationalization to promote the convertibility of the RMB under capital accounts and, lastly, fulfilling the exchange rate reform.

It works in this way: under the current approach for RMB internationalization, cross-border trade settlement and establishment of offshore RMB markets would lead to large amounts of offshore RMB. The offshore RMB trading hubs themselves also function as the mechanisms to provide channels for overseas RMB to flow back to China, which ensure that RMB internationalization could proceed. The amount of capital flow, in turn, will exert great pressure on the still-controlled capital account and exchange rate.

In reality, the mechanism may not necessarily bring success, but may bring China losses in the form of exchange rate and interest rate arbitrage, as argued by some scholars (see Zhang Bin 2011; Yu 2011; 2012). This, however, is viewed as a necessary cost of RMB internationalization and realization of the greater goal of China's financial reform. RMB internationalization under current routes is the second-best choice for China. The best choice — the liberalization of exchange and interest rates first — however, is not feasible under present circumstances. Furthermore, with the market expectation for the RMB turned into depreciation from appreciation, and the PBoC further relaxing control of the exchange rate in 2014, the arbitrage activities became less profitable and the cost was reduced. The dilemma is that with the reduction of the cost, the process of RMB internationalization also slowed down accordingly.

Therefore, it would be fair to say that RMB internationalization is being used as a booster for domestic financial reform, and it is a collateral goal of the latter. For China's difficult financial reform, it seems the reversed coercing mechanism is in fact a practical option for the PBoC and its supporters.

RMB internationalization is a crucial tool that would achieve two key goals of China's economic development: globally, it will enhance the competitiveness of China's international finance, and progressively shake off the constraints brought about by current global monetary system regulations dominated by developed countries; and domestically, it will boost the financial reform, efficiently advancing China's economic development. In China's view, the US dollar's hegemony and policy consequences arising therefrom, such as its actual veto power at the IMF, the negative externalities of the US monetary policy, and constant and huge current account and fiscal deficits, could bring an unfavourable impact on China's economic development. China will be more competitive financially and more capable of seizing the initiative in international monetary policy coordination and its international status would be promoted upon the RMB becoming a major reserve currency. Domestically, it will push a series of market-oriented financial reforms involving the exchange rate, interest rate, bank sector and capital market.

China's top leaders have a clear understanding of RMB internationalization's position in China's financial reform (Cheng 2014).[19] It is clear that the ultimate goal of China's financial reform is in fact not RMB internationalization itself, but is instead the building of a moderately prosperous society by 2020. Wu Xiaoling emphasizes that the PBoC is paying more attention to how to promote market-based domestic financial reform, rather than how to push the RMB toward becoming an internationalized currency, and, thus, the era of the RMB is yet to come (Wu 2014). Governor Zhou Xiaochuan also stresses that for RMB internationalization, the PBoC primarily focus on finishing its "homework," including lifting unnecessary restrictions for the use of the RMB, such as legal and business regulations, gradually pushing to realize RMB capital account convertibility. The PBoC is creating conditions for more wide use of the RMB, and will not set a prearranged speed, rhythm and point for it (Zhou 2014).

At the same time, RMB internationalization itself as a collateral goal is also important in view of the political and economic benefits it could bring to China. It would be ready to be realized if the set goals of financial reform are achieved. This provides another explanation why the PBoC is still promoting RMB internationalization in its unique way, even though no country has ever taken initiative to push internationalization of its currency — primarily because of the potentially extreme cost and responsibilities.

Logic behind Gradual RMB Internationalization: The Key to China's Economic Structure Transformation

The fundamental reason for the reversed coercing method of financial reform lies in the difficulties of the market-oriented exchange rate and interest rate reform — normally, the prerequisites for the full internationalization of a currency. Among them, the market-based interest rate system takes up the core of China's current financial reform and is a fundamental constraint for real market-oriented exchange rate reform and liberalization of the capital account.

---

19   Cheng Siwei is a famous economist and vice chair of the 9th and 10th Standing Committee of the National People's Congress.

According to interest rate parity theory, while the domestic interest rate is regulated, liberalization of the exchange rate will lead to large exchange rate fluctuations, widened interest rate spread and great amount of cross-border capital flows, all of which impact domestic monetary policy. In China today, regulated interest rates will lead to a distorted exchange rate and an impossible-to-set reasonable fluctuation interval under the current, regulated exchange rate system. Additionally, the long-term ceiling on the deposit interest rate and maintenance of low nominal interest rates will put an upward pressure on China's exchange rate. In short, a market-based interest rate constitutes the precondition of the liberalization of exchange rate.

Eighteen years after the market-based interest rate reform began in 1996, the most important deposit rate still remains untouched, and is now the only regulated interest rate.[20] Scholars, both domestic and foreign, agree that the financial repression, with its centrepiece in regulated interest rates, comprises the core of the financial system in China (Huang 2014; Cao Tong 2014; Sender 2012; Lardy 2012; Ito and Volz 2013). The financial repression, which had been implemented since the reform and opening-up policy began more than 30 years ago, guaranteed that household wealth was transferred to governments and SOEs. It constitutes the most important foundation of China's current economic growth model, characterized by investment and exports. It also constitutes a key element to the CPC's influence over the Chinese economy.

Market-oriented interest rate reform is thought to be the most difficult part of financial reform in China. It intends to change the financial repression policy, and is essential for moving China from the current economic growth model — investment- and export-driven — to a consumption-driven growth path. This constitutes a departure from the most successful economic growth model over the past 30 years, and cannot be realized without grand determination from the top policy makers in China.

The greatest difficulty comes from the opposition of the powerful vested interest groups that benefit from the current financial repression and growth model. They tend to oppose policy changes such as exchange and interest rate liberalization, which are logically linked to RMB internationalization, without being directly against RMB internationalization per se. Premier Li Keqiang expressed his opinion on these powerful interests and the difficulty to push the reform at his inaugural press conference in March 2013 by saying "sometimes stirring vested interests may be more difficult than to stir the soul" (Zhang 2013).

---

20   On August 25, 2015, the PBoC declared it would liberalize deposit rates with a term over one-year deposit, a further important step in the market-oriented reform on the interest rate, but it would still maintain its control on the one-year benchmark deposit rates.

Main Restrictive and Supportive Forces of RMB Internationalization

Main Restrictive Forces

Large State-owned Commercial Banks

Although competing and benefitting from a role in offshore RMB clearing banks, large commercial banks constitute a significant de facto restrictive force for RMB internationalization by vigorously maintaining the regulated deposit rate.

Large commercial banks in China enjoy substantial subsidies brought by negative real deposit rates. In 2011, average interest income accounted for 80 percent of total bank income (China Banking Regulatory Committee 2012, 8). Former Deputy Governor of the PBoC Wu Xiaoling called the banks' profits "unreasonable." Current Mayor of Chongqing Huang Qifan said that banks' net interest spread in China is two percent higher than those in other countries (Su and Lou 2012). Zhang Weiying (2011), a well-known economist from Peking University, describes the state-owned banks' method of profiting "easy money" through its monopoly status as being based on the logic of a gangster — a deposit rate of 1.2 percent and a lending rate of 5.6 percent provide a spread that even a fool could make money from. A study by US scholar Nicholas Borst echoes Zhang's criticism. He describes how since the PBoC mandated the ceiling on deposit rates and a floor on lending rates, banks in China have lived with a comfortable margin of around three percent (Borst 2012).

At present, deposit rate control is the only one remaining in China's interest rate reform, which, according to official sources, has been viewed as the most crucial and risky step, and therefore remains untouched. As an important prerequisite to RMB internationalization, interest rate reform was opposed fiercely by large commercial banks because it would result in the deposit-loan spread narrowing significantly, which would have serious repercussions on bank profitability. The four biggest state-owned banks, which dominate the banking system, had an average return on equity of about 25 percent in 2011 (Orlik and Reilly 2012). Facing questions from the public on their excessive profits in 2012, some leaders of China's biggest banks were quick to deny the profits (Su and Lou 2012). This is a sign of the potential difficulties deposit rate reform may face, as the leaders will not succumb easily.

State-owned Industrial Enterprises

Some state-owned industrial enterprises might benefit from RMB settlements of trade and outward direct investment — two channels of RMB internationalization — however, as the major borrowers of China's current financial system and receivers of cheap funding from the state-owned banking system, state-owned industrial enterprises strongly opposed financial market reform, most notably the untouched deposit rates. This puts them on the list of de facto restrictive forces of RMB internationalization. Even the lending rates have been marketized since 2013, unregulated deposit rates will accordingly lead to the rise of lending rates, and will erode the relatively high profitability of SOEs. After an investigation trip to Zhejiang Province in 2012, Chair of All-China Federation of Industry and Commerce Huang Mengfu noted that a percentage of SOEs' profitability comes from transfer payments of interest rates, as they can get a loan from the bank at a fairly low rate. The interest rate on petty loans averages at 20 percent, much higher than the 10 percent rate that large-size private enterprises would be happy with. The SOEs, however, can get loans from a bank with a 5.3 percent lending rate (Liu 2013). A competition with the private sector on lending from banks would benefit overall welfare at the expense of SOEs. According to *The Nature, Performance and Reform of the State-owned Enterprises*, a book published by the Unirule Institute of Economics (2012), the absolute majority of a RMB 10 trillion loan went to SOEs in 2010.

Export Industries

Exchange rate liberalization would result in significant appreciation against the US dollar.[21] China's export industries, with support from the powerful National Development and Reform Commission (NDRC) and the Ministry of Commerce — as well as the coastal provinces in which export industries account for a large percentage of GDP and job opportunities — formed a powerful interest group that opposed the fully market-based exchange rate reform. Since the beginning of the exchange rate reform in 2005, reformers have consistently witnessed the influence of the loose coalition of interest groups. Although some export enterprises have benefitted from RMB trade settlement since it was officially initiated in 2009, limiting factors such as current foreign

---

21   Under the current regulated capital account, more capital will still find ways to flow in China and push RMB to appreciate. The RMB has appreciated for eight years since the beginning of exchange rate reform in 2005. Recently, the expectation for one-way RMB appreciation has gone down with the decline of China's current account surplus and unstable fluctuation of cross-border capital flow. Furthermore, with the Fed formally ending the QE policy in 2014, the RMB could enter into the passage for depreciation against the US dollar. It would reduce the pressure from China's export sector and thus lead to a window of opportunity for exchange rate reform.

trade structure[22] and Chinese exporting enterprises' lack of bargaining power determine that 90 percent of Chinese foreign trade enterprises still choose to settle in US dollars (Wang 2014), and still greatly oppose the risk of a fully liberalized exchange rate.

The NDRC

With its nickname "miniature State Council," the NDRC — the macroeconomic management agency under State Council — is the major policy maker and implementer of China's financial repression policy that guarantees the low-cost huge investment to sustain China's economic development in the past decade. The policy, centred on low interest rates, depresses household income and contributes to the buildup of the country's property bubble by causing a much larger allocation of investment into real estate. The prevailing interest rate system also contributes to serious distortions in capital allocation and exacerbates macroeconomic imbalance in the Chinese economy (Lardy 2012).

Local Governments

According to Chinese Academy of Social Sciences researcher Justina Lee (2013), the massive debt held by local governments in China amounting to RMB 20 trillion — or, according to data released by the China Bank Regulatory Commission in 2013, RMB 9.7 trillion — has become one of the major obstacles faced in the liberalization of interest rates. Interest rate liberalization, which would drive up deposit and lending rates, will significantly increase the government's borrowing costs and debt levels (Zhang Bin 2011). The massive amounts of debt held by local governments would be a source of systemic risk to China's financial market if it seeks to liberate its deposit rate before solving the problem. This concern turns local governments into major forces of opposition to the interest rate reform, specifically to the loss of control over the deposit rate (ibid.).

Real Estate and Construction Industries

China's real estate and related construction industries have developed into a large pillar of economic growth since the country's market-oriented housing system reform in 1998. The thriving of industries can be attributed to the great amount of cheap loans from state-owned banks (as they profit from the negative real deposit rates). With the introduction of a RMB 4 trillion stimulus package after the GFC in 2008, the real estate industry re-boomed and became closely bound to the highly invested banks. The negative real deposit rates and lack

---

22   For example, companies from China's main trade partners (i.e., developed economies such as the United States and European countries) favour not using the RMB in trade settlements; commodities are settled with the US dollar.

of alternative investment opportunity pushed a large amount of money into the real estate market, which boosted the development of the property market en route to a property bubble. The sustainable development of the real estate market, with its huge size and supporting role in economic growth (plus its being bound together for better or worse with financing from banks and local governments), makes it a powerful interest group that prefers to keep the current regulated interest rate system.

These groups have not openly opposed RMB internationalization because it is widely interpreted and accepted as part of the goal of full economic nationalism. This goal symbolizes the elevation — perhaps to the same level as the United States — of China in the global economy upon the intended rise of the RMB as an international currency. The groups are not in a convenient position to oppose a policy for promoting China's rise as a financial power. However, the desired internationalization of the RMB will necessitate market-oriented exchange rate and interest rate reform, which endangers these groups' fundamental interests. Their opposition is the primary reason for the uniqueness of the internationalization process and its irregularity compared to the classic means of currency internationalization.

Main Supporting Forces

The current route of RMB internationalization under the dual control of the capital account and the exchange rate highlights the PBoC's dominance in governing the process. It nails down the support from top leaders, which guarantees the cooperation of other relevant government agencies such as the Ministry of Finance and the China Banking Regulatory Committee, which are essentially in an auxiliary position and are capable of offering technological support to the process. The economic nationalism implications of RMB internationalization, from another point of view, create a favourable public opinion regarding the process.

The PBoC

One of the few agencies countering the many interest groups for RMB internationalization is the PBoC. The capacity the PBoC has for advancing the internationalization of the RMB and related financial market reform largely depends either on its independence relative to central banks in Western countries or — given the lack of central bank independence in China — on the amount of support it can get from the top leaders.

The PBoC is granted power over monetary policy; however, it is not as independent as central banks such as the Fed or Bank of England in Western countries. Significant policies, such as the market-based reform of exchange and interest rates, as well as RMB internationalization, must be decided by the top leaders after consulting relevant agencies and experts. This means that the PBoC has to compete with other government departments (and the powerful interest groups behind them) for influential power.

The biggest advantage the PBoC has lies in its financial sector expertise. It seems as though the initiative of RMB internationalization was shrouded as an economic nationalism policy that is supposed to raise China's status in the international financial market. In this way, it is put in a favourable position to be realized. In practice, it is fair to say that RMB internationalization in part depends on the relative advantage the PBoC has through its expertise of the financial sector, whereas other departments and interest groups lack sufficient knowledge and experience.

The PBoC has, at minimum, two strong points for bidding for support from top leaders. First, the cross-border trade settlement with neighbouring countries and regions turned into a "two birds with one stone" policy. It is the centrepiece of current RMB internationalization, and will help enhance economic and political relations with these countries. As such, the fact that Hong Kong's economic development benefitted from the establishment of an offshore RMB market would result in an increasingly stable political situation, which is a big concern for Chinese leaders. It is also an important step for RMB internationalization because of Hong Kong's status as an international financial centre. The Chinese government's continued effort in the fall of 2014 to initiate the Hong Kong-Shanghai Stock Connect through-train as arranged amid the months-long street protests in Hong Kong — albeit a number of days delayed — demonstrated this point.

Second, the PBoC's policy priority is to liberalize the capital account. This policy goal conforms to the financial reform goal made in the reform agenda at the 3rd Plenary Session of 18th CPC Central Committee. Wu Xiaolin (2011) said that within five years, China should be able to realize the convertibility of the RMB under the capital account. The report released by the PBoC in February 2012 claimed that China was in a period of "strategic opportunity" for capital account liberalization, and it should be accelerated (Research Team of Statistics and Analysis Department of PBoC 2012a). It also reassured the skeptical academics that there would be no large risks resulting from China opening its capital account. As Yu Yongding (2014) observes, the PBoC's intention to use RMB internationalization to promote capital account liberalization has become increasingly clear over time.

Top Leaders and Their Aides

There are more important dynamics involved in the liberalization of the capital account: it was endorsed by President Xi's top economic adviser and the prime architect of China's new economic reform, Liu He. Liu was elevated to the director of the Office of the Central Leading Group for Financial and Economic Affairs (OCLGFEA), a White House National Economic Council-like agency, which advises President Xi and the other six members of the Politburo Standing Committee, China's final arbiters of power. Reform-minded Liu, with long experience as an adviser for top leaders and close connection with President Xi, is believed to have significant power over China's economic and financial policy making (Wang 2013; Lian 2013).

Historically, external forces were frequently used to realize the reform agenda in China's modern and contemporary era. The risk is that reformers who seek foreign pressures were always criticized as "looking to enhance their status by relying on foreign powers" (in Chinese, *xie yang zi zhong*), or in some cases were even called traitors by conservatives. The power and influence commanded by reformers could effectively protect them from attacks by conservatives and promote the reforms, just as former Premier Zhu Rongji promoted China's economic reform with China's entry into the WTO in 2001. The current market-oriented financial reforms seemingly gained support from top leaders, although the opposing forces still remain powerful. Liu He's connection with President Xi, Governor Zhou's unusual remaining in office and Premier Li Keqiang's pro-reform financial measures all demonstrate the support from the top leaders.

Liu's philosophy of taking advantage of external forces to push domestic reforms matches the current means of RMB internationalization promoted by the PBoC. In 2010, Liu said that "from the perspective of China's long history, a unified domestic drive and external pressures have been keys to success" and that "domestic drive often needs to be activated by external pressure" (Yu 2013; Davis and Wei 2013). Similarly, RMB internationalization was used to press domestic financial reform, in particular the liberalization of the capital account. In the financial sector, Zhou is an important ally that Liu worked with for years. The PBoC's financial liberalization reform has support from Liu in addition to two important personnel changes. First, Vice Governor of the PBoC, Yi Gang was quietly named the deputy director of the OCLGFEA in April 2014. For years, Yi and Zhou have been pushing to make it easier for money to flow in and out of the country and to give the market a greater role in setting both exchange rates and interest rates (Davis and Wei 2013). Second, Fang Xinhai, who was invited back to work at China's financial sector by Zhou, joined the OCLGFEA in 2013 and is responsible for crafting a financial liberalization plan.

Favourable Public Opinion

Historically, the PBoC has frequently lost battles for exchange and interest rate reform-related policy influence with the more powerful NDRC and the Ministry of Commerce. Now, in the case of RMB internationalization, there is certainly a role reversal in the PBoC's favour. The sentiment of economic nationalism and the accompanying idea of a much larger international role for the RMB gaining momentum are very much helping the internationalization process by forging a consensus that would see, should the RMB become a major international reserve currency, China approach the status the United States has in the global monetary system and proclaim its successful rise in global financial field. As Bob Davis from *The Wall Street Journal* believes, the PBoC indeed could take advantage of its financial expertise to push market-based financial reform under the favourable atmosphere (Wei and Davis 2014). With these advantages, the PBoC began its plan for the internationalization in the aftermath of the GFC. As some foreign observers argue, China's financial reform would help give the PBoC unconditional control of the monetary base (Goodfriend and Prasad 2006). It now sets the tone for the macroeconomic policy and reform agendas (Wei and Davis 2014).

Conclusion

The process of RMB internationalization will proceed with China trying to push it through setting up more RMB offshore markets in European cities such as London, Frankfurt, Paris and Luxembourg, as well as North American cities such as Toronto. China continues to sign currency swap agreements with developing and emerging economies. The basic logic behind the moves above are the same as previously mentioned: to promote a gradual enlarging of the international use of the RMB — geographically it follows the specific road map of first targeting the neighbouring regions before spreading use in BRICS countries (Brazil, Russia, India, China and South Africa) and other emerging countries via currency swap agreements — and the final goal of full internationalization. Functionally, the goal is to become a settlement currency first, then an investment currency and lastly a reserve currency.[23]

---

23   Of course, in practice, this is not a rigid process that RMB internationalization followed. Some countries already chose RMB as one of their options for foreign exchange reserve with China's efforts (Chatterjee and Armstrong 2014).

Behind these measures and trends for the goal of RMB internationalization lies the PBoC's real goal of pushing for domestic financial reform in the coming years: liberalization of the capital account and market-oriented exchange and interest rate reforms. Ultimately, intensifying the reform should be the true goal of China's full modernization by 2020. By then, China may hold greater chances to realize the long-term objectives of RMB internationalization — eliminating dollar dependence and trying to achieve an equal status with the dollar in the global monetary system, as well as establishing a modern financial system.

In general, the prospect of RMB internationalization and the underlying goal of promoting domestic financial reform depend on the following: determination of top leaders to deepen reforms of China's growth model; the PBoC's expertise and ability to use it wisely; the political wisdom of supporting leaders and scholars; and how much strength and efforts the reformers exert against the powerful and extremely adamant opposition. Specifically, the current means of internationalization relies highly on the expectation for RMB appreciation, which implies unsustainability. The process of RMB internationalization beginning to lose its momentum with the devaluation of the RMB against the dollar in 2014 proved this risk.

2014 witnessed the decrease of expectations for RMB appreciation, as well as the strengthening of the dollar. This worries Chinese policy makers with the great possibility of large-scale capital flight. Consequently, it would trigger a more prudent policy toward the liberalization of capital account, and the development of offshore RMB markets would be shadowed, thus resulting in a downward progress of the RMB internationalization.

On the other hand, the two-way exchange rate fluctuation that occurred during 2014, in addition to implying a more flexible exchange rate formation mechanism, effectively eliminated the almost exclusive expectation for the RMB to continuously appreciate. Furthermore, the Chinese economy is expected to continue to develop in a sustainable way in coming years and the sheer size of its economy and trade volume indicate the great demand for yuan. The RMB should continue to appreciate in the long run, although it is expected to experience a two-way fluctuation in the coming years with the expected continued strengthening of the dollar. For the PBoC, a natural two-way floating exchange rate is an important policy goal, and achieving it would further benefit the RMB internationalization process by improving confidence in the RMB, rather than potential arbitrage opportunities, as well as further benefit financial market reform in China.

Both officials and scholars are well aware of the possible negative impact that may arise as a result of liberalizing the capital account. Although it appeared the

PBoC had already made its decision and declared China as being in a period of "strategic opportunity" for capital account liberalization in 2012, the process is still very complicated and at some point may stop or even reverse. These potential occurrences can be observed from the PBoC's recently changing tone regarding capital account liberalization, as it has reverted to a more cautious attitude and adjusted its policy accordingly in 2014.

As far as time is concerned, both PBoC officials and economists in China agree that RMB internationalization is a long-term process that will take years, or perhaps even decades. The PBoC's gradual manner and cautious attitude toward promoting the interest and exchange rates in combination with top policy makers' hesitance regarding capital account liberalization increase the potential for the reform to turn into a decades-long process. Reformers in China will be required to use any means necessary to wear down the opposition. Such is the nature of gradual reforms of this magnitude.

Acknowledgements

The author would like to thank Domenico Lombardi, Samuel Howorth, Xu Qiyuan and Zhang Bin, as well as several anonymous referees, for helpful comments and suggestions.

Works Cited

Aliber, Robert Z. 1964. "The Costs and Benefits of the US Role as a Reserve Currency." *Quarterly Journal of Economics* 78: 442–56.

Ba, Shusong. 2009. "2009, Renminbi Guojihua de Qibu zi Nian" [2009, the Beginning Year of the RMB Internationalization]. eeo.com.cn, May 19. www.eeo.com.cn/zt/50forum/bzgcj/2009/05/19/138003.shtml.

Borst, Nicholas. 2012. "Are Chinese Banks Too Profitable?" Peterson Institute of International Economics. *China Economic Watch* (blog), March 29. www.piie.com/blogs/china/?p=1191.

Cao, Tong. 2014. "Cunkuan Lilv Fangkai Mianlin Liangnan Xuanze" [Liberalization of Deposit Rate Facing Dilemma]. Finance.sina. com.cn, July 7. http://finance.sina.com.cn/money/bank/bank_hydt/20140707/081619625197.shtml.

Cao, Yuanzheng. 2014. "Huigai he Kuoda Shiyong Renminbi Jianshao dui Meiyuan Yilai" [Exchange Rate Reform and Reducing the RMB Reliance on the US Dollar]. *Zhongguo Jinrong Xinxi Wang.* http://rmb.xinhua08.com/a/20140331/1308879.shtml.

Chatterjee, Saikat and Rachel Armstrong. 2014. "REUTERS SUMMIT-China Currency Claims a Bigger Share of Reserve Manager Portfolios." Reuters, October 29. www.reuters.com/article/2014/10/29/china-summit-reserves-reuters-summit-idUSL4N0SO3VK20141029.

Cheng, Siwei. 2014. "Shinian Zuoyou Jiben Shixian Renminbi Guojihua" [Basically Achieving the RMB Internationalization in About a Decade]. *Shanghai Shang Bao* [*Shanghai Business Daily*], February 28.

China Banking Regulatory Committee. 2012. *2011 Annual Report.* Chinese Version.

Chinn, Menzie and Jeffrey Frankel. 2007. "Will the Euro Eventually Surpass the Dollar as Leading International Reserve Currency?" In *G7 Current Account Imbalances: Sustainability and Adjustment*, edited by Richard Clarida. 283–338. Chicago, IL: University of Chicago Press.

———. 2008. "Why the Euro Will Rival the Dollar." *International Finance* 11 (1): 49–73.

Cohen, Benjamin J. 1971. *The Future of Sterling as an International Currency.* London: Macmillan.

———. 2004. *The Future of Money.* Princeton, NJ: Princeton University Press.

———. 2007. "Toward a Leaderless Currency System." Paper presented at Wither the Key Currency? workshop, Cornell University, Ithaca, New York, October 12–14.

Davis, Bob and Lingling Wei. 2013. "Meet Liu He, Xi Jinping's Choice to Fix a Faltering Chinese Economy." *The Wall Street Journal*, October 6.

Deng, Xiaoping. 1994. *Selected Works of Deng Xiaoping, 1982–1992.* Beijing: Foreign Languages Press.

Department of the Treasury. 2014. "Major Foreign Holders of Treasury Securities." September 16. www.treasury.gov/ticdata/Publish/mfhhis01.txt.

Ding, Yifan and Niu Wenxin. 2014. *Meiyuan Baquan* [*The Dollar Hegemony*]. Chengdu: Sichuan People's Publishing House.

Eichengreen, Barry. 2005. "Sterling's Past, Dollar's Future: Historical Perspectives on Reserve Currency Competition." NBER Working Paper No. 11336. May.

———. 2011. *Exorbitant Privilege: The Rise and Fall of the Dollar and the Future of the International Monetary System*. London: Oxford University Press.

Eichengreen, Barry and Marc Flandreau. 2010. "The Federal Reserve, the Bank of England and the Rise of the Dollar as an International Currency, 1914-39." Prepared for the BIS Annual Research Conference, Lucerne, June 24-25.

Eichengreen, Barry and Jeffrey Frankel. 1996. "The SDR, Reserve Currencies, and the Future of the International Monetary System." In *The Future of the SDR in Light of Changes in the International Financial System*, edited by Michael Mussa, James Boughton and Peter Isard. Washington, DC: IMF.

Ferguson, Niall. 2005. "Our Currency, Your Problem." *The New York Times*, March 13. www.nytimes.com/2005/03/13/magazine/13WWLN.html?_r=0.

Frankel, Jeffrey. 1992. "On the Dollar." In *The New Palgrave Dictionary of Money and Finance*. London: MacMillan Press Reference Books.

———. 2011. "Historical Precedents for the Internationalization of the RMB." Paper for the workshop organized by the Council on Foreign Relations and the China Development Research Foundation, Beijing, November 1.

Gao, Haihong and Yu Yongding. 2011. "Internationalization of the Renminbi." In *Currency Internationalization: Lessons from the Global Financial Crisis and Prospects for the Future in Asia and the Pacific*. 105–24. Bank for International Settlements.

Goodfriend, Marvin and Eswar Prasad. 2006 "Monetary Policy Implementation in China." BIS Papers No. 31. December.

Global Research of Standard Chartered. 2014. "Offshore Renminbi — Slow but Steady." September 8.

He, Dong and Ma Jun. 2011. "Ping Dui Renminbi Guojihua de Jige Wujie" [Several Misunderstandings on Renminbi Internationalization]. *Zhongguo Jingji Guancha* [*China Economic Review*] 7.

He, Fan. 2004. "Meiyuan Baoquan dui Shijie de Yingxiang" [The Dollar Hegemony's Influence on the World Economy]. *Xuexi Shibao* [*Studies Times*], November 19.

———. 2009. "Renminbi Guojihua de Xianshi Xuanze [The Pragmatic Choices of the RMB Internationalizaiton]." *Guoji Jingji Pinglun* [*International Economic Review*] 7-8: 8–14.

Helleiner, Eric. 2008. "Political Determinations of International Currencies: What Future for the US Dollar?" *Review of International Political Economy* 15 (3): 354–78. August.

Henning, C. Randall. 1997. "Cooperating with Europe's Monetary Union." *Policy Analyses in International Economics* 49. Washington, DC: Institute for International Economics.

———. 2000. "US–EU Relations after the Inception of the Monetary Union: Cooperation or Rivalry?" In *Transatlantic Perspectives on the Euro*, edited by C. Randall Henning and Pier Carlo Padoan. Washington, DC: Brookings Institution Press.

Huang, Haizhou. 2009. "The RMB Internationalization: A New Propeller for Reform and Opening Up." *Guoji Jingji Pinglun* [*International Economic Review*] 7-8: 5–7.

Huang, Yiping. 2014. "Jinrong Gaige Hexin shi Lilue Shichanghua he Renminbi Guojihua" [The Core of Financial Reform Is Interest Rate Marketization and RMB Internationalization]. *Jingji Cankao Bao* [*Economic Information Daily*], June 9.

Huang, Yukon and Clare Lynch. 2013. "Does Internationalizing the RMB Make Sense for China?" *Cato Journal* 3.

Ito, Hiro and Ulrich Volz. 2013. "China and Global Imbalances from a View of Sectorial Reforms." *Review of International Economics* 21 (1): 57–71.

Kenen, Peter. 1983. "The Role of the Dollar as an International Currency." Group of Thirty Occasional Papers No. 13.

Kroeber, Arthur. 2011. "The Renminbi: The Political Economy of a Currency." Shaping the Emerging Global Order Paper Series. Brookings Institution. www.brookings.edu/research/papers/2011/09/07-renminbi-kroeber.

Krugman, Paul. 1984. "The International Role of the Dollar: Theory and Prospect." In *Exchange Rate Theory and Practice*, edited by John Bilson and Richard Marston. 261–78. Chicago: University of Chicago Press.

———. 2009. "China's Dollar Trap." *The New York Times*, April 3. www.nytimes.com/2009/04/03/opinion/03krugman.html?_r=0.

Lardy, Nicholas. 2012. "Sustaining Economic Growth in China." East Asia Forum, February 5. www.eastasiaforum.org/2012/02/05/sustaining-economic-growth-in-china/.

Lee, Justina. 2013. "Local $1.6 Trillion Debt Pile Impedes Rate Freedom: China Credit." *Bloomberg*, November 14. www.bloomberg.com/news/2013-11-14/local-1-6-trillion-debt-pile-impedes-rate-freedom-china-credit.html.

Li, Charles. 2014. "Shen Gang Tong Reng Zai Taolun Jieduan" [Shenzhen-Hong Kong Stock Connect Is Still in Discussion]. *Zhongguo Zhenquan Wang* [Cnstock.com], December 2. http://news.cnstock.com/news/sns_yw/201412/3262534.htm.

Li, Xiao and Li Junjiu. 2014. "Meiguo Baquan Diwei Pinggu Yu Xinxing Daguo Yingdui" [Assessing Current US Hegemonic Position and Strategic Measures of Newly Emerging Great Powers]. *Shijie Jingji Yu Zhengzhi* [*World Economics and Politics*] 1: 114–41.

Lian, Zhong. 2013. "Liu He: Ni Dui Zhongguo you Duo Zhongyao?" [Liu He: How Much Important to China?]. *Lianzheng Liaowang* [*Honesty Outlook*] 11. http://news.sina.com.cn/m/rectitude/.

Lim, Ewe-Ghee. 2006. "The Euro's Challenge to the Dollar." IMF Working Paper 06/153.

Liu, Wei. 2013. "Guoqi Wei Wang' [SOE Is the King]. *Nanfang Zhoumo* [*Southern Weekly*], January 3.

Mao, Changqing and Qin Peijing. 2013. "Renminbi Guojihua: Buzhuo Yu Shiji" [RMB Internationalization: Steps and Opportunities]. Project Entrusted by Sino-US Financial Seminar at Harvard University. Research Department of CITIC Securities.

McNamara, K. 2008. "A Rivalry in the Making? The Euro and International Monetary Power." *Review of International Political Economy* 15 (3): 439–59.

Orlik, Tom and David Reilly. 2012. "China's Dinosaur Banks Must Evolve." *The Wall Street Journal*, April 5. http://online.wsj.com/news/articles/SB1000142405270230407200457732364240536 7110.

Pan, Liying and Wu Jun. 2012. "Tixian Guojia Hexin Liyi De Renminbi Guojihua Tuijin Lujing" [The Roadmap for RMB Internationalization That Embodies China's Core Interests]. *Guoji Jingji Pinglun* [*International Economic Review*] 3: 99–109.

PBoC. 2009. "Administration Rules on Pilot Program of Renminbi Settlement of Cross-border Trade Transactions." www.pbc.gov.cn/publish/english /964/2009/20091229135722061684633/20091229135722061684633} _.html.

———. 2013. *China Monetary Policy Report, Quarter Three, 2013.* November 5.

Qiao, Liang. 2007. "Meiyuan Baquan Yu Lingwai Yizhong Zhanzheng" [The Dollar Hegemony and Another Type of War]. Zhongshan Ribao [*Zhongshan Daily*], October 10.

———. 2014. "Qiaokai Jinrong Baquan De Neihe" [Crack the Kernel of Financial Hegemony]. Preface for *Pricing Power* by Zhang Jie. http://blog.sina.com.cn/s/blog_5d98f6740102uz9e.html.

Research Team of Statistics and Analysis Department of PBoC. 2012a. "Woguo Jiakuai Ziben Zhanghu Kaifang De Tiaojian Jiben Chengshu" [Conditions for Accelerating the Liberalization of Capital Account in China are Basically Ripe]. PBoC. February 23.

———. 2012b. "Xietiao Tuijin Lilv Huilv Gaige he Ziben Zhanghu Kaifang" [Promote the Interest Rate and Exchange Rate Reform, as well as the Liberalization of Capital Account in a Coordinated Way]. PBoC. April 17.

Seabrooke, Leonard. 2006. *The Social Sources of International Financial Power.* Ithaca, NY: Cornell University Press.

Sender, Henny. 2012. "China Should Give Its People Greater Freedom on Investment." *Financial Times*, March 30.

Sina Finance. 2014. "Yu Yongding Yi Gang Jibian Renminbi Lilv Shichanghua: Yanghang Tai Xiaoxin Le" [Yu Yongding and Yi Gang Debate on the Marketization of RMB Exchange Rate: The PBoC Is Overcautious]. finance.sina.com.cn, http://finance.sina.com.cn/ hy/20140419/131918853420.shtml.

Stasavage, David. 2003. *Political Economy of a Common Currency — The CFA Franc Zone since 1945.* Aldershot: Ashgate Publishers.

Strange, Susan. 1971. *Sterling and British Policy: A Political Study of an International Currency in Decline.* Oxford: Oxford University Press.

Su, Manli and Lou Sailing. 2012. "Yinhang Hangzhang Fouren Baoli Shuo" [Governors of Banks Denied Extravagant Profits]. *Xin Jing Bao* [*The Beijing News*], March 12.

Summers, Lawrence. 2004. "The United States and the Global Adjustment Process." Speech at the third annual Stavros S. Niarchos Lecture Institute for International Economics, Washington, DC, March 23.

Tavlas, George S. 1991. "On the International Use of Currencies: The Case of the Deutsche Mark." *Essays in International Finance* 181. Princeton, NJ: Princeton University. March.

Tavlas, George S. and Yuzuru Ozeki. 1992. "The Internationalization of Currencies: An Appraisal of the Japanese Yen." IMF Occasional Paper No. 90.

Unirule Institute of Economics. 2012. *The Nature, Performance and Reform of the State-owned Enterprises.* World Scientific Publishing Company.

Volz, Ulrich. 2013. "All Politics Is Local: The Renminbi's Prospects as a Future Global Currency." In *Financial Statecraft of Emerging Market Economies: "The New Kids on the Block" and Global Rebalancing,* edited by Leslie Armijo and Saori Katada. London: Palgrave Macmillan.

Walter, Andrew. 2006. "Domestic Sources of International Monetary Leadership." In *International Monetary Power,* edited by David M. Andrews. Ithaca, NY: Cornell University Press.

Wang, Xi and Cheng Zongfei. 2011. "Meiyuan Weiji Daolai Hai You Duoyuan" [How Far Is It from the Dollar Crisis?]. *Renmin Luntan* [*People's Tribune*] 21.

Wang, Xin. 2011. "Ruhe Kan Renminbi Guojihua Guocheng Zhong de Wenti yu Shouyi" [How to Evaluate the Problems and Benefits in the Process of the RMB Internationalization]. China Finance 40 Forum. July 26.

Wang, Ying. 2014. "Jiucheng Waimao Qiye Reng Wuyuan Renminbi Jiesuan. Zhuanjia Cheng Peitao Zhengce Youdai Wanshan" [90 Percent of Foreign Trade Enterprises Still Miss RMB Settlement. Experts Say Supporting Policies Needed to Be Prompted]. *China Enterprise News,* July 28.

Wang, Zhiyue. 2013. "Zhinang Liu He" [The Brain Truster Liu He]. *Diyi Caijing Ribao* [*China Business News*], October 11.

Wei, Lingling and Bob Davis. 2014. "China's Central Bank Prevails in Policy Battles over Economic Future." *The Wall Street Journal,* June 8.

World Bank and Development Research Center of the State Council. 2013. *China 2030: Building a Modern, Harmonious and Creative Society.* Washington, DC: World Bank. doi: 10.1596/978-0-8213-9545-5.

Wu, Xiaoling. 2011. "Dingceng Sheji he Jinrong Tizhi Gaige" [Top Layer Design and the Reform of Financial System]. *Shanghai Security*, August 27.

———. 2014. "'Renminbi De Shidai' Hai Meiyou Daolai" [The Era of RMB Is Yet to Come]. Chinanews.com, March 22. www.chinanews.com/gn/2014/03-22/5982181.shtml.

Xia, Bin. 2011. "Reminbi Guojihua Shi Zhongguo Jinrong Zhanlue Buju De Zhongyao Yi Zhao Qi" [RMB Internationalization Is an Important Stunt in the Layout of China's Financial Strategy]. Jingji Cankao Bao [*Economic Information Daily*], October 24.

———. 2014. "Zhongguo Jinrong Gaige De Luoji" [The Logic of China's Financial Reform]. Shanghai Zhengquan Bao [*Shanghai Securities News*], May 23.

Xiang, Songzuo. 2011. "Tuijin Renminbi Guojihua Zouchu Meizhai Xianjing" [Promote RMB Internationalization to Get Rid of the Trap of Dollar Debts]. *Zhengquan Ribao* [*Securities Daily*], August 22. http://zqrb.ccstock.cn/html/2011-08/22/content_257435.htm.

———. 2013. "Tuijin Renminbi Guojihua Jianshao dui Meiyuan Yilai" [Promote RMB Internationalization to Lessen China's Dollar Exposure]. Zhongguo Zhenquan Wang [Cnstock.com], October 10. www.cnstock.com/v_news/sns_jrgc/201310/2777903.htm.

Xiang, Weixing and Wang Guannan. 2014. "'Jinrong Kongbu Pingheng' Shijiao Xia de Zhongmei Jinrong Xianghu Yilai Guanxi Fenxi" [China-US Financial Interdependence Relationship: An Analysis Based on the Perspective of 'Balance of Financial Terror']. *Guoji Jinrong Yanjiu* [*Studies of International Finance*] 1.

Xu, Qiyuan. 2014. "Renminbi Guojihua: Gainian, Zhenglun yu Zhanwang" [RMB Internationalalization: Concept, Discussion and Outlook]. Research Center of International Finance Working Paper No. 2014-09. Institute of World Economics and Politics, Chinese Academy of Social Sciences.

Yang, Tao. 2014. "Huobi Huhuan Xin Jucuo de Duochong Yiyi" [Multiple Significances of the New Measures of Currency Swap]. *China Finance* 12.

Yi, Gang. 2014. "Yanghang Zhubu Tuichu Changtai Shi Waihuishichang Ganyu" [PBoC Is Gradually Withdrawing Its Regular Intervention on the Foreign Exchange Markets]. Xinhuanet.com, December 22. http://news.xinhuanet.com/fortune/2014-12/22/c_127323232.htm.

Yi, Xianrong. 2010. "Waihui Chubei Buchi Meiguo Guozhai Chi Shenme" [Foreign Reserves: No US Treasuries?, Then What?]. Zhongguo Ribao Wang [Chinadaily.com.cn], February 22. www.chinadaily.com.cn/zgrbjx/2010-02/22/content_9481244.htm.

———. 2011. "Zhongguo Weihe Hai Buduan Zhengchi Meizai" [Why China Still Increase Its Holding of US Treasuries]. *Jinghua Shibao* [*Beijing Times*], August 18. http://news.xinhuanet.com/fortune/2011-08/18/c_121876597.htm.

Yu, Ying and Liu Dong. 2011. "Guo Shuqing Tan Jiegou Jiangju" [Guo Shuqing on Problems of China's Economic Structure]. *Zhengquan Shichang Zhoukan* [*Securities Markets Weekly*] 30.

Yu, Yongding. 2011. "Ying Zanting Chutai Renminbi Guojihua Xin Zhengce" [Suspend Introducing New Policy on the RMB Internationalization]. *Diyi Caijing Ribao* [*China Business News*], December 15.

———. 2012. "Cong Dangqian De Huilv Bodong Kan Renminbi Guojihua" [The Current RMB Exchange Rate Volatility and RMB Internationalization]. *Guoji Jingji Pinglun* [*International Economic Review*] 1: 18–26.

———. 2014. "How Far Can Renminbi Internationalization Go?" ADBI Working Paper Series No. 461. February.

Yu, Yongding, Zhang Bin and Zhang Ming. 2013. "Zhongguo Ying Shen dui Ziben Zhanghu Kaifang" [China Must Act with Caution on Liberalization of Capital Account]. *Financial Times* [Chinese Version, ftchinese.com], June 4.

Zhang, Bin. 2011. "Hong Kong Li'an Renminbi Shichang Fazhan de Kunhuo" [Problems on the Development of Hong Kong's Offshore Renminbi Market]. Research Center for International Finance Policy Review No. 2011-069. Institute of World Economics and Politics, Chinese Academy of Social Sciences.

Zhang, Bin and Xu Qiyuan. 2012. "Huilv yu Ziben Guangzhi Xia de Renminbi Guojihua [RMB Internationalization in the Context of Exchange Rate and Capital Account Control]." *Guoji Jingji Pinglun* [*International Economic Review*] 4: 63–73.

Zhang, Ming. 2011. "Renminbi Guojihua: Jiyu Zai'an He Li'an de Liangzhong Shijiao" [The RMB Internationalization: Two Perspectives Based on Onshore and Offshore]. *Jinrong yu Jingji* [*Journal of Finance and Economics*] 8: 4–10.

———. 2013. "Renminbi Guojihua: Zhengce, Jinzhan, Wenti Yu Qianjing [The RMB Internationalization: Policy, Progress, Problem and Prospect]." *Jinrong Pinglun* [*Chinese Review of Financial Studies*] 2.

Zhang, Monan. 2010. "Meiyuan Lanfa Dengyu Caifu Lueduo" [Overissue of US Dollar Equal to Wealth Plundering]. *Renmin Ribao* [*People's Daily*], November 11.

Zhang, Weiying. 2011. "Shichang Zhidu Zui Daode" [Market System is the Most Moral]. *Nanfang Zhoumo* [*Southern Weekly*], July 16.

Zhang, Xudong. 2013. "Li Keqiang Tan Gaige Tiaozhan: Chudong Liyi Bi Chuji Linghun Hai Nan" [Li Keqiang on the Challenges Facing Reform: Stirring Vested Interests More Difficult Than to Stir the Soul]. *China Business News*, March 18. http://finance.sina.com.cn/china/20130318/012514859895.shtml.

Zhang, Yugui. 2013. "Jinrong Gaige Jueding Jingji Zhuanxing Chengbai" [Financial Reform Determines Whether the Economic Transformation Can Succeed]. *Jingji Cankao Bao* [*Economic Information Daily*], September 24.

Zhang, Yuyan. 2009. "Quanqiuhua Shidai De Shijie Geju Xianzhuang Yu Zhanwang" [The World Order in the Era of Globalization: Status Quo and Prospect]. *Wen Hui Bao*, August 29.

Zhou, Xiaochuan. 2014. "Renminbi Guojihua Yao Zuohao 'Jiatingzuoye' Huilv Bianhua Guanzhu Zhongqi Qushi" [RMB Internationalization Requires Finishing Its 'Homework' and Pay Attention to Mid-term Trend in Exchange Rate Changes]. Xinhuanet.com, March 11. http://news.xinhuanet.com/politics/2014-03/11/c_119712241.htm.

3

Sequencing RMB Internationalization

Barry Eichengreen

enminbi (RMB) internationalization is a process as well as a state and a goal of Chinese policy. Whether the RMB is widely used as a unit of account, means of payment and store of value in international transactions by private and public sector entities — these being the core functions of an international currency — is not a question that admits a yes-or-no answer. There are different degrees of RMB internationalization, and the degree to which the currency has been internationalized is something that has changed and will continue to develop over time. Internationalizing the RMB will entail a series of steps by Chinese policy makers that similarly have to be implemented over time. Those steps will not all be taken at once. Rather, they will be sequenced — sensibly, it is hoped.

This chapter focuses on this sequencing problem — on the process of RMB internationalization. It does not revisit the question of whether RMB internationalization is an appropriate goal of Chinese policy. Nor does it assess its implications for the rest of the world.[1] Instead, this chapter asks how the process of RMB internationalization will unfold, seeking to identify key steps. It then analyzes in what order those steps should be taken and how they should be related to one another.

There are parallels between this question and the questions in related literature in economics. Most obviously, there is the literature on sequencing capital

---

1   I have covered these issues elsewhere. See, for example, Eichengreen (2013a, 2013b) and Eichengreen and Kawai (2014).

account liberalization, where questions include what components of the capital account should be liberalized first and what components should be liberalized later, and how the removal of restrictions on transactions on capital account should be related to other economic and financial reforms. Since capital account liberalization is a necessary condition for currency internationalization by a country starting from China's position, the literature on the former is directly relevant to the latter.

More generally, there is the literature on the order of economic liberalization in the transition from a controlled or planned economy to a market system.[2] Here questions include how the liberalization of international transactions should be sequenced with the privatization of state-owned enterprises (including banks) and the removal of controls on prices (not least the prices of bank loans and deposits). China may no longer be a planned economy in the classic sense, but significant elements of central control remain. Neither is it a fully marketized economy, in other words. Its banks are still majority state owned, which affects their lending and how they are viewed by international investors. Although Chinese policy makers have taken steps to liberalize interest rates, significant controls on rates remain, which is something that has implications for RMB internationalization.

Then there is the literature on financial development, which asks: what steps should be taken to promote the development of deep and liquid financial markets, and in what order should they be taken? In part, the connections between this literature and the literature on RMB internationalization run through work on capital account liberalization, since it is sometimes argued that capital account liberalization stimulates financial development by subjecting domestic financial institutions to the chill winds of international competition and by helping to create a more diverse investor base that makes for a more liquid market. But the literature on the sequencing of measures to foster financial development is relevant more generally, since the development of deep and liquid financial markets is another necessary but not sufficient condition for currency internationalization.

Finally, there is the literature on the connections between economic liberalization and political liberalization.[3] Issues here include whether the prevailing economic and political regimes are compatible with one another. Or do economic reforms, in order to be fully credible and irreversible, have to be accompanied by political reforms? Conversely, do political reforms in the direction of greater openness

---

2   See, for example, McKinnon (1991) and Lavigne (1995).
3   See, for example, Haggard and Webb (1994), Giuliano, Mishra and Spilimbergo (2010) and Mo and Weingast (2013).

and contestability increase the likelihood of economic reforms in the same direction? In the context of RMB internationalization, there are two implied questions: Must China transform its political system in the direction of greater openness and contestability in order for the RMB to be seen as an attractive international currency by residents and non-resident investors?[4] And will the economic and financial liberalization that is integral to the process weaken the regime's political control, with implications for the openness, contestability and perhaps even the stability of the Chinese political system?

The second section of this chapter seeks to clarify what is meant by an international currency. The third section then considers these related literatures on sequencing in more detail in an effort to draw out their implications for RMB internationalization. Several possible sequencing strategies are then described, and the final section concludes in favour of one.

What Do We Mean by an International Currency?

An attractive international currency has three essential attributes: size, stability and liquidity.[5] Size refers to the fact that the issuing country must have a scale that allows it to engage in a large volume of international transactions. This will render the currency a natural habitat for residents engaged in international transactions and foreigners doing business with them, since the currency employed in that context can be used for a variety of other transactions at minimal cost. To the extent that network increasing returns are important in money and finance, a large volume of cross-border transactions by agents predisposed to using that currency, other things being equal, will make it attractive for still others to follow, broadening and accelerating the process of currency internationalization still further.[6] The association between issuing-country GDP and the volume of its overseas trade and financial transactions on the one hand and the use of assets denominated in its currency as reserves and in private foreign investments on the other is one of the more robust regularities in the literature on the demand for international currencies, consistent with this view.[7]

---

4   Residents, as well as non-residents, will presumably have a choice of what currency to hold when the RMB is fully internationalized.

5   As argued at more length in Eichengreen (2014).

6   The so-called "new view" of international currency status questions the strength of those network increasing returns, suggesting that there is room for more than one consequential international currency, but it does not dismiss their existence entirely. See Chitu, Eichengreen and Mehl (2013) and Eichengreen, Chitu and Mehl (2014).

7   Chinn and Frankel (2005) provide a review of the relevant literature and a model in which the demand for a currency as international reserves depends heavily, in non-linear fashion, on country size.

Second, the currency in question and the financial markets of the country issuing it must possess a suitably high level of stability in order to be attractive to international users. The currency must be stable in the sense of maintaining its value, while the financial markets of the issuer must be stable in order to reassure holders that this value will similarly be maintained in the future. Instability of the real economy — deep recession or a sharp slowdown in growth — may similarly erode confidence among residents and foreigners insofar as it augurs financial problems and creates uncertainty about the policy response.

History supports this emphasis on stability. Although a variety of factors admittedly help to account for why the dollar played no international role prior to 1913, despite the fact that the United States had already been the world's largest economy in the 1870s, one factor surely was the instability of US financial markets.[8] Both sterling and the dollar then saw their international currency status damaged by the economic, financial and currency crises of the 1930s. The recurrent currency and balance-of-payments crises experienced by Britain after World War II similarly go a long way to explaining the erosion of sterling's international currency role. Stability is clearly important for the international store-of-value function — for the willingness of central banks to hold their foreign reserves in a particular unit and of private investors to include it in their internationally diversified portfolios. But it is also important more broadly, that is, for other international currency functions.

Finally, liquidity is a key attribute of an international currency. Both private and official investors want to know not just that the currency will hold its value but also that they will be able to adjust their portfolios — to buy and sell securities denominated in that unit — at low cost (with low bid-ask spreads) without moving prices against themselves. History supports this emphasis as well. The market in US government bills — the dominant reserve and international asset — is far and away the most liquid market in the world, so measured. Prior to 1914, the London market in sterling-denominated assets was unsurpassed for its liquidity, and the illiquidity of US financial markets was a major factor limiting international use of the dollar.

Conversely, the relatively limited liquidity of markets in treasury bills goes a long way toward explaining why the Japanese yen failed to gain market share more rapidly as an international and reserve currency in the 1980s and 1990s (Fukuda and Cong 1994). Marc Flandreau and Clemens Jobst (2009) show more generally that differences in market liquidity, as measured by various proxies for bid-ask spreads, help to explain the number of international markets in which different national currencies have historically been used and traded.

---

8   That "variety of factors" is treated at length in Eichengreen (2011).

Literature on Sequencing

The literature on the sequencing of reforms during the transition from a planned to a market economy focuses on issues such as whether it is preferable to liberalize goods or financial markets, and the current or capital account of the balance of payments, first. While there are dissents — such as Ronald McKinnon (1991) — most analyses conclude in favour of liberalizing goods markets and the current account first. Intuitively, if goods markets are heavily distorted, financial liberalization may cause resources to flow into the wrong sectors, where the undistorted productivity of investment is low (Brecher and Diaz-Alejandro 1977). In the Chinese context, this literature is largely academic in any case, since China has long since opted to proceed with trade liberalization first.

Another focus of this literature is the sequencing of interest rate decontrol. There is little disagreement about the need to move to market-determined interest rates once the economy has been fully opened and the commercialization and privatization of state-owned enterprises are largely complete. But whereas some authors argue that it is important to remove interest rate ceilings and floors early in the liberalization and opening process, others argue that higher borrowing costs may impose undue hardships on firms still subject to controls on the prices of their products, leading to unnecessary bankruptcies. Relevant to the Chinese case, they argue that the removal of ceilings on deposit rates may so squeeze bank margins as to lead banks to gamble for survival by making higher-risk, higher-interest-rate loans.[9] These warnings point to the need to strengthen prudential supervision and regulation, internal controls, and the balance sheets of the banks themselves before decontrolling interest rates.[10]

The literature on the sequencing of capital account liberalization is closely related to the sequencing of RMB internationalization, as noted, because an open capital account is a prerequisite for full currency internationalization. A closed capital account is an obvious barrier to all but the most basic trade-related international transactions, since in this case the currency will be accepted in payment for exports only if it can be used for purchases of imports from suppliers in the same country. This was the case in the early stages of RMB internationalization, circa 2009, when only select Chinese companies in select regions were permitted to settle their trade-related transactions in RMB and the majority of cross-border financial transactions in the currency were still prohibited. Circa 2009-2010, the ratio of daily Chinese RMB foreign exchange turnover to daily Chinese exports and imports of goods and services was

---

9   See Calvo and Coricelli (1995) for an introduction to the debate.
10   As argued, for example, by Feyzioglu, Porter and Takas (2009).

approximately one. For other more financially developed and open economies, the ratio was considerably higher (McCauley and Scatigna 2011, 69).

If the capital account is partially open, as in China at the time of writing, then the currency will be usable for a specified range of international financial transactions as well. But it will be able to compete on a level playing field with the dominant international currency or currencies only if it can be used freely for financial transactions — that is, only if the capital account of the issuing country has been considerably, or fully, liberalized. From this flows the argument that capital account liberalization is necessary, but not sufficient, for currency internationalization.

So, for China to elevate the RMB to the first rank of international currencies, it must liberalize the capital account. What do we know about the optimal and desirable sequencing of the latter? For several decades after World War II, theorists and practitioners saw capital account liberalization as appropriate only for countries with impeccably strong economic and financial credentials, which in practice meant the United States. For other countries, the view was that they should wait until their domestic financial markets and international balance of payments were significantly stronger. The fact that there was a reluctance to adjust exchange rates, making for the persistence of competitive imbalances, and that countries like the United Kingdom had large external debt overhangs informed this reluctance to move faster.

But, because a liberalized capital account was a distant prospect, not much attention was paid to the sequencing of policies needed to achieve it. This changed in the next period, which saw its apex in the mid-1990s. This period was marked by a sharp swing toward the view that the capital account should be liberalized early in the reform process. The 1990s saw the growth of international capital flows following the Brady deals that drew a line under the Latin American debt crisis, encouraging the notion that there were now benefits to be had by countries capable of attracting the ample foreign funds on offer. The growing volume of capital flows also encouraged the belief that controls were ineffectual and that it was futile for countries to attempt to regulate the capital account. It was better, the conclusion followed, for governments to subject themselves to the discipline of the market by throwing open the capital account. Support for this view was nurtured as much by skepticism that policy makers could be trusted to do the right thing if left to their own devices as by confidence that market discipline was vigorous and effective.[11]

---

11   A telling example is Dornbusch (1998).

Recall that this was also a period of domestic financial liberalization and deregulation, notably in the United States. The same ideology that supported domestic financial deregulation and liberalization similarly encouraged external financial deregulation and liberalization, of which the United States was a leading exponent. The 1990s were when European countries removed their residual restrictions on transactions on capital account. Japan removed its remaining restrictions on currency transactions and foreign bank entry into the country. Emerging market countries that acceded to the Organisation for Economic Co-operation and Development, such as South Korea and Mexico, moved in the same direction, as mandated by that organization's Code of Liberalisation. Discussions within the International Monetary Fund (IMF) of whether capital account convertibility should be an obligation of members encouraged the presumption that countries should move toward an open capital account sooner rather than later. Thus, the same belief set that encouraged "light touch regulation" at the national and international levels encouraged the presumption in favour of early capital account liberalization.

This experiment did not end happily. The Mexican "tequila crisis" of 1994-1995, the Asian crisis of 1997-1998 and the global credit crisis of 2008-2009 were fuelled by volatile capital flows made possible by capital account liberalization pursued in isolation from the requisite supporting policies. This experience led emerging markets, then the international policy community and finally the IMF to adopt a more nuanced position on capital account liberalization.

The new conventional wisdom is summarized by IMF (2012). The Fund describes two tracks — capital flow liberalization and supporting reforms — as going hand in hand. Supporting reforms include revising the domestic legal framework to strengthen creditor rights and to support the development and operation of domestic capital markets; improving accounting and statistical standards so that investors are able to make informed decisions; creating a lender of last resort to ensure the provision of emergency liquidity to the market through the establishment of an independent central bank and international agreements on swap lines and credits; and strengthening prudential supervision, financial regulation and private risk management. As these processes get underway, it becomes prudent to begin liberalizing foreign direct investment (FDI) inflows. When the supporting reforms are more advanced, it is then appropriate to begin liberalizing FDI outflows, other long-term capital flows and select short-term flows (starting with trade finance and inward investment in the equity market by qualified foreign investors). As significant capital market development occurs in response to these measures and the supporting reforms themselves become deeper and broader, it then becomes timely to relax remaining restrictions on capital flows, in particular short-term flows.

Thus, this new conventional wisdom does not recommend that countries first complete the process of financial development and reform before opening the capital account, which was, to a first approximation, the view in the 1950s and 1960s. Nor does it suggest that they should throw open the capital account early in the reform and development process, which is a crude characterization of the Washington Consensus of the 1990s. Rather, it is an "integrated approach [that] envisions proceeding through successive, and often overlapping, phases" (IMF 2012, 24).

While there is a vast literature on financial development, its determinants and its relationship to economic growth, studies focusing on the sequencing of policies to foster financial deepening and development are relatively few. One strand of literature focuses on the sequential development of markets and institutions. There, it is argued that banks tend to develop first, since they are best able to cope with imperfections in the information and contracting environment that otherwise hinder the flow of finance to small- and medium-sized enterprises by developing long-term relationships with their clients. Bond markets develop next, since debt is senior to equity and therefore will be attractive to investors in an uncertain environment. Equity markets, which allow investors to share in extraordinary profits and place bets on competing technologies, develop later. In this view, policy makers seeking to foster deep and liquid financial markets should start by promoting the growth of the banking system, followed by bond markets and finally equity markets, while recognizing that there is a role in a relatively mature financial system for all three. China's experience is consonant with this view, insofar as the country started with a bank-centred financial system before developing significantly sized bond and equity markets.[12]

Another strand of literature focuses on whether financial development should start with legal reform or political reform.[13] The literature on law and finance has a considerable history, but was given new life by Rafael LaPorta et al. (1998), who provided cross-country evidence that countries with legal rules that effectively protect corporate shareholders and creditors (in particular countries with a common-law tradition) tend to have the most active and best-developed financial markets. In contrast, in countries with less investor-friendly legal systems, companies go public less frequently, banks play a larger role relative to

---

12   The same pattern is evident in a variety of other historical instances. But there are exceptions, as noted by Rajan and Zingales (2003). They cite the case of Japan, which relied fairly heavily on securities markets in the late nineteenth and early twentieth centuries before moving to a bank-based financial system.

13   In fact, there has been a lively debate over this question in the context of China. See Zhao (2006).

security markets, corporate ownership is concentrated and the voting premium (the price of shares with high voting rights relative to that of shares with low voting rights) is larger. In other words, financial markets are less liquid in such countries. This suggests that China should start with legal reforms that strengthen creditor rights as it seeks to deepen and develop its financial markets in a manner consistent with the goal of RMB internationalization.

A competing interpretation of the sequencing of measures to foster financial development questions the exogeneity of legal rules and points to political reform as a precondition for financial development. Douglass North (1990), Mancur Olson (1993), and Raghuram Rajan and Luigi Zingales (2003) emphasize reforms of political institutions that give creditors voice in the choice of policies. North and Barry Weingast (1989), generalizing from the case of England's Glorious Revolution, emphasize the importance of political checks and balances that limit the arbitrary exercise of power, including the power to expropriate, by the executive. Charles Calomiris and Stephen Haber (2014) point to the role of political institutions that encourage competition among political entities. This view suggests that in order to develop its financial markets to the point where RMB internationalization becomes viable, China will first have to reform its political system.

Finally, there are the connections between financial development and capital account liberalization. It has been argued that capital account liberalization, by exposing domestic financial institutions to foreign competition and increasing the diversity of the investor base, can play a positive role in financial development. Or at least this was argued until a series of crises associated with premature capital account liberalization threw financial development off track. The empirical literature on these connections is large and inconclusive.[14] The modern synthesis, insofar as there is one, is that capital account liberalization has a positive impact on financial development only when institutions for contract enforcement, information dissemination and prudential supervision and regulation have reached a certain minimum threshold.[15] Again, this suggests that a considerable period of time may have to pass, during which the institutions in question are strengthened, before it will be productive for China to fully open its capital account with the goal of fostering financial development.

---

14   My own review and summary is Eichengreen (2003).
15   See, for example, Ito (2005) and Eichengreen, Gullipalli and Panizza (2011).

The Gradualist Approach

The literature on sequencing reviewed in the preceding section is consistent with the Chinese preference for "crossing the river by feeling the stones beneath one's feet." It points to the need for very considerable progress in reforming domestic financial markets and institutions before removing the residual restrictions on international financial transactions that limit international use of the RMB. Moreover, a brief review of what China needs to do to successfully strengthen, reform and develop its financial sector underscores that considerable time will be needed to implement the financial reform measures needed for successful RMB internationalization.

Since the Chinese financial system remains heavily bank based (consistent with the experience of other countries), reform necessarily starts with the banking system. Although the big five Chinese banks have been commercialized — they have been instructed to make lending and investment decisions on a commercial, profit-maximizing basis — they remain majority state owned, and their senior executives, including their chairpersons and presidents, are still appointed by the Chinese Communist Party. Consequential business decisions are still made by party committees rather than boards of directors. Bank lending still favours the state sector broadly defined. More generally, this state of affairs raises questions about whether the decisions of senior bank executives and managers are informed by non-commercial motives.[16]

The record of policy lending in other middle-income countries is not entirely positive. That record suggests that insofar as banks perceive themselves as doing the government's bidding, their management may be inclined to take excessive risks and otherwise take steps that jeopardize the profitability and even continued existence of their institutions. It follows that foreigners, in particular, will be reluctant to maintain significant deposits in Chinese banks until the banks in question are privatized or otherwise distanced from the policy-making process.[17]

Sound banks are well-capitalized banks. Headline numbers suggest that Chinese banks are adequately capitalized and have healthy loan-to-deposit ratios.[18] But many of the banks have off-balance-sheet assets acquired through the sale of wealth-management products that are not captured by those headline numbers. Many wealth-management purveyors offer purchasers a guarantee of high interest rates. If at some point the loans and investments made by the banks'

---

16   See the discussion in Huang, Li and Wang (2013).

17   An analysis of the World Bank report in question is Davis (2013).

18   The latest figures available from the World Bank at the time of writing (for 2012) put bank capital (tiers one through three) as a share of assets at 6.3 percent.

wealth-management arms are insufficient to cover the guaranteed interest payment, the banks will then be required to bring those obligations back onto their balance sheets, depleting their capital.[19] This in turn raises the question of whether the banks need to be better (or pre-emptively re-) capitalized early in the financial reform process.

Putting the banks on a firm commercial footing further presupposes the existence of a resolution mechanism so that bad banks can be allowed to fail without destabilizing the system. In late 2014, the People's Bank of China (PBoC) released the consultative draft of a retail deposit insurance scheme, which is one precondition for a bankruptcy plan for financial institutions. But a full resolution scheme remains to be developed.

Another priority is to widen the regulatory perimeter, bringing wealth-management products and other parts of the shadow banking system under formal regulation and strengthening supervision and regulation more generally. The China Banking Regulatory Commission (CBRC) took a step in this direction in 2013 by requiring commercial banks to register their wealth-management products prior to selling them to the public. But registration is still a far cry from requiring the banks to carry these assets on their balance sheets and hold capital against them. Wealth-management products might be regarded as attractive by foreign investors lured by the prospect of a guaranteed high interest rate and the expectation of RMB appreciation. Thus, liberalizing the capital account further and allowing wealth management companies to compete for foreign customers could be a fatal mistake were it to proceed prior to extension of effective oversight.

Adequate supervision and regulation will require upgrading the quality of such oversight, notably by the CBRC, which shares responsibility for financial regulation with the PBoC. The CBRC has been criticized for moving too slowly to rein in the off-balance-sheet activities of state-controlled banks and address the weaknesses of the country's small banks in particular. It is criticized for moving too slowly on deposit-rate liberalization because it is close to the state banks, which oppose liberalization that will require them to compete for deposits. Finally, the CBRC has been taken to task for failing to coordinate more closely with the PBoC. These are indications of the need to upgrade the quality of regulation, all the more urgently as domestic and international financial transactions are further liberalized.

---

19   The problem is not unlike that created by the special-purpose investment vehicles operated by banks in the United States and Europe before the financial crisis. As in the United States, weakness in the construction sector, in which Chinese wealth-management vehicles have invested, could be the precipitating event.

China's remaining limits on bank lending rates were removed in July 2013; however, controls on bank deposit rates remain an issue because the state banks resist decontrol and because binding controls feed the growth of the wealth-management industry. Governor Zhou Xiaochuan of the PBoC has expressed his "personal preference" for fully liberalizing deposits and interbank lending rates by 2016, although, as noted, other branches of government may be reluctant to move in this direction. Those other observers emphasize that full interest rate liberalization is prudent only when supervision and regulation have been strengthened sufficiently to ensure that banks do not take on excessive risk simply to offset narrower net interest margins and only once the banks' management and internal controls have been strengthened so as to cope with increased volatility of both rates and margins. These challenges tend to be an issue especially for small city and rural commercial banks. That many observers expect an interval of another five to 10 years before interest rate decontrol is complete, may be an indication that they anticipate it will take that long for regulators and management to prepare adequately.[20]

Financial reform and development efforts have long since extended to developing a deep and liquid market in RMB-denominated securities as well. Bond market development, in particular, is important for currency internationalization, since many investors prefer to hold their foreign currency assets in this form. Chinese bond market capitalization is significant, in excess of US$5 trillion. That said, the country has a long way to go before the depth and liquidity of its bond market rival those of the United States. US bond market capitalization is roughly 10 times China's. The Chinese market is dominated by government issuance; although the corporate bond market is growing, it remains relatively small. Turnover, adjusted for market size, is again only a tenth of that of the US market. Many Chinese bonds are held to maturity by banks and other institutional investors, and 95 percent of transactions are on the interbank over-the-counter (OTC) market, where bonds are purchased and sold by banks and other institutions. The lack of exchange-based trading limits price transparency and discovery, since third parties are not privy to transactions, while creating additional counterparty risk.

The Chinese authorities have been taking a number of steps to accelerate bond market development. In 2012, they expanded the Qualified Foreign Institutional Investor (QFII) and RMB Qualified Foreign Institutional Investor (RQFII) programs through which foreign investors can gain access to the interbank bond market as a way of increasing investor diversity. Still, access of foreign

---

20   More than half of senior executives of Chinese financial institutions surveyed by Deloitte in 2012 anticipated that it would take another five to 10 years to complete the process of interest rate liberalization (see Federal Reserve Bank of San Francisco [2014]).

investors to the interbank bond market remains limited, since the authorities are concerned to control the total volume of borrowing on the interbank market while reform of the banking system is still underway. In 2013, the State Council then required all transactions on the interbank market to be booked through the National Interbank Funding Center and required additional documentation of transfers of ownership. The council authorized trading of government debt futures as a risk management tool with the goal of encouraging participation and market liquidity. In 2014, the government authorized 10 provinces and cities to issue bonds in their own names and to assume responsibility for interest and principal payments for the first time, important steps in the development of a local government bond market.[21]

Finally, the National Development and Reform Commission, which regulates the issuance of bonds by non-listed corporations, has attempted to promote the growth of the corporate bond market by giving more issuers the status where they only need to register to issue bonds, instead of undergoing a lengthy approval procedure. But then the first bond defaults (by Chaori Solar in early 2014) caused the commission to backtrack. This reversal reflects the existence of trade-offs between the size of the bond market on the one hand and its stability and liquidity on the other, at least in the short run.

The Chaori event is viewed as positive insofar as it signals that corporate bonds do not enjoy an implicit government guarantee, and highlights the need for investors and issuers to engage in due diligence. But it points also to the dangers of liberalizing and opening corporate debt markets prior to putting in place sound management practices and strengthening the incentives for responsible corporate borrowing. It highlights the importance of upgrading corporate governance as part of the financial development push. China continues to rank low relative to other middle-income countries on standard corporate governance ratings like that of KPMG.

While China has adopted corporate governance regulations resembling those of the United States, implementation lags.[22] Financial reporting standards are lax. Accountability of directors to private shareholders is limited. In 2013, China ranked eightieth in the world in terms of the strength of its auditing and reporting practices, according to the Global Competitiveness Report of the World Economic Forum. Here, China is significantly behind the economies whose currencies the RMB aspires to compete with, such as the United States, the United Kingdom, the euro zone and Japan. These corporate governance

---

21   Previously, local governments were able to issue debt only indirectly through local government financing vehicles, if at all.

22   See Morck and Yeung (2014) and Piotroski (2014).

and control problems result in concentrated corporate ownership and limited private external financing, characteristics of the corporate sector that are not obviously compatible with the development of deep and liquid bond and equity markets.

The common implication of these observations is that China will require time to develop larger, more stable and more liquid financial markets capable of appealing to international investors. It will need time to develop those markets to the point where the balance of risks and rewards from opening them fully to international investors tips decisively in the direction of rewards.

The Big Bang Approach

The problem with gradualism is that it is, well, gradual. Progress may be so slow that the destination is never reached. Entrenched interests resisting specific reforms, such as state banks opposed to deposit-rate liberalization and exporters skeptical of the merits of the more flexible exchange rate that will have to accompany larger international financial flows, have more time to mobilize in opposition. The complementarities among reforms that can exist if policy makers move simultaneously on several fronts will go unexploited.

These are arguments for moving faster. In the extreme, currency internationalization might be used as a lever to force domestic reforms. Yiping Huang, Ran Li and Bijun Wang (2013) assert that "many officials" view RMB internationalization this way. By rapidly removing remaining restrictions on the use of RMB for transactions on capital account, Chinese policy makers will have no choice but to move to a more flexible exchange rate now, rather than later, in order to accommodate the larger volume of financial flows. Deposit rates will have to be decontrolled now, rather than later, regardless of the preferences of the banks, since depositors dissatisfied by the rates of interest on offer will be free to shift their funds abroad.

Similarly, the authorities will have to redouble their efforts at strengthening supervision and regulation of the banking and financial system, since banks will have more scope for increasing their leverage by borrowing abroad in order to fund risky investments. Regulators will have to move quickly to strengthen corporate governance and financial transparency requirements, and Chinese firms will be compelled to comply, since investors dissatisfied by governance and transparency standards will be free to invest abroad. China will reform faster in such circumstances, the argument goes, because it has no choice.

The obvious objection to a strategy designed to force other entities, whether banks, firms or regulators, to do the right thing is that those other entities may not cooperate. If they do not respond as expected, the results could be unfortunate, or worse. History is littered with the corpses of countries that have liberalized financial markets and opened the capital account of the balance of payments prematurely, resulting in financial crises rather than reform and financial development.

Having seen a number of such crises in the neighbourhood, Chinese policy makers are aware of the risks. Radical big-bang-style reform, moreover, is not the Chinese way. The post-1979 history of policy reform is dominated by limited experimentation and then gradual generalization of experiments that succeed.[23] The Chinese approach of dual-track reform, where only certain sectors or activities are liberalized while others remain controlled in the interest of social, economic and financial stability, epitomizes the point. Their successful experience with dual-track reform presumably renders Chinese officialdom skeptical of the practical importance of arguments prioritizing policy complementarities.

Still, there is the possibility that the government, in its enthusiasm for RMB internationalization, is proceeding with capital account liberalization faster than warranted, given the state of domestic financial reform and development. Cautious critics of Chinese policy warn of putting the cart before the horse. A related danger is that capital account liberalization may be approaching the point where the authorities lose control — where there are so many channels through which capital can flow in and out of the country that residual controls are no longer effective. At this point the capital account will open spontaneously whether the authorities like it or not.

Phased Strategies

The alternative is a phased strategy where the authorities seek to actively promote RMB internationalization while maintaining significant restrictions on the capital account. This can be done by relaxing capital account restrictions in a manner designed to reconcile the need for continued restrictions in the interest of financial stability with the desire to promote RMB-based international financial business, fostering the development of offshore financial centres where RMB-denominated transactions can be cultivated, and creating a special trade

---

23   Pre-1979 policy changes, from the Great Leap Forward to the Cultural Revolution, is a different story, but their legacies only reinforce the point.

and financial zone onshore insulated from the rest of the economy but free of barriers to RMB-denominated transactions with the rest of the world.[24]

Selective Capital Account Liberalization

China's phased approach to capital account liberalization dates from 2002, when qualified foreign institutional investors (initially offshore subsidiaries of mainland asset managers with a base in Hong Kong) were permitted to buy and sell a limited range of RMB-denominated exchange-traded securities in China. 2004 then saw authorization for residents of Hong Kong and Macau to open RMB-denominated deposit accounts in the two offshore financial centres. 2006 saw creation of the Qualified Domestic Institutional Investor Program, which licensed Chinese asset managers to sell mutual funds of overseas stocks and bonds to local investors. The first RMB-denominated bonds issued in Hong Kong by international companies seeking to fund investments on the mainland ("dim sum bonds") were then floated in 2007.

In 2009, designated Chinese companies were authorized to settle trade-related transactions with Hong Kong, Macau and the Association of Southeast Asian Nations in RMB, and in 2010, this authorization was expanded to the rest of the world. Overseas banks involved in RMB cross-border trade settlement were permitted to invest the RMB funds they thereby accumulated in the Chinese interbank bond market. And in 2011, authorization to settle commercial transactions in RMB was extended from designated firms to the rest of the Chinese economy.

The authorities have focused on enhancing the access to the Chinese market of "qualified" foreign institutional investors expected to adopt "a long-term, buy-and-hold strategy" (Zhao and Liu n.d.). Licensing appears to be a function of location (initially, only institutional investors based in Hong Kong were regarded as trustworthy and licensed), accumulated business experience, the size of assets under management, and general business reputation, where "long-term investors" such as mutual funds, pension funds, insurance companies and sovereign wealth funds have been given preference. RQFII quotas have been increased repeatedly, and the range of assets that can be purchased by qualified foreign investors has been widened steadily. This focus on buy-and-hold investors can be seen as a strategy for liberalizing the capital account without exposing Chinese financial markets to capital flow reversals and news-induced capital flight. As for whether so-called buy-and-hold investors in fact buy and hold, time will tell.

---

24   I explore these options in Eichengreen (2014). The present section is an update to that material.

In November 2014, China opened a link between the Hong Kong and Shanghai equity market, giving Chinese savers a channel through which to invest a portion of their savings in overseas stocks and Hong Kong residents greater scope for investing in the Shanghai market. In its early phases, the Shanghai-Hong Kong "Stock Connect," as this program is known, is only open to eligible investors in Hong Kong and China, who are permitted to trade only eligible shares. Amounts are limited to an aggregate quota of US$48 billion in purchases for Hong Kong residents, while the quota for mainland investors starts at US$40 billion.[25] If the pilot phase runs smoothly, then these quotas will presumably be increased. Again, limiting the scheme to eligible investors and designated shares can be seen as a strategy for avoiding the risk of equity price bubbles and crashes due to capital flow surges and reversals.

The combined result of these measures has been to promote select types of capital flows, in practice inflows more than outflows. On the outflow side, the Qualified Domestic Institutional Investor scheme has not met its quotas; take-up is reportedly less than 40 percent (ANZ Research 2014, 3). Southbound flows via the Shanghai-Hong Kong Stock Market Connect have averaged less than four percent of its daily quota as of late 2014. All this suggests that continued progress on a phased approach to RMB internationalization will require, in addition, other measures.

Offshore Financial Centre

Promoting offshore RMB financial centres is another phased strategy for currency internationalization. Encouraging transactions in RMB-denominated assets and the extension of RMB-denominated loans and trade credits offshore allows foreign banks to familiarize themselves with the business and widens international use of the currency. To the extent that Chinese entities are active offshore, they too gain experience in doing business with foreign counterparties and in managing the associated exposures and risks. Expertise acquired offshore can then be transferred to China, once mainland-based banks are permitted to engage in a broader range of RMB-based transactions with foreign counterparties and foreign banks are permitted to enter the Chinese market.

Hong Kong emerged first as a major offshore RMB centre because of its proximity, financial sophistication, the relatively large share of Chinese exports routed through it, and because of Beijing's political control of the territory (from 1997). Hong Kong remains far and away the single largest repository of offshore RMB deposits, the most important market for issuance of dim sum bonds, and

---

25   These quotas constrain only buy orders; sell orders, in contrast, are permitted at any time
      without limit.

the leading offshore source of RMB trade credit. But China has done a good job at ginning up competition among foreign financial markets, many of which now want to develop into offshore RMB centres in order to capture what is presumed to be a growing volume of RMB-related business.

Three constraints on banks in offshore financial centres are the existence of only a limited pool of RMB-denominated financial instruments offshore, possession of a relationship with a Chinese bank through which RMB-based transactions can be settled and securing RMB-denominated liquidity to cover an open position. The first constraint is more binding for some offshore centres than others. Thus, Taipei was recently able to become the most important centre for offshore RMB deposits, surpassing even Hong Kong, because of its very large current account surplus with China, in settlement of which its exporters can take RMB claims. But without RMB inflows through either the current or capital account, financial institutions in other offshore centres have limited resources with which to make RMB-denominated loans and investments.[26]

Table 1: Offshore RMB-clearing Banks

Country	City	Bank	Date	Source
China SAR	Hong Kong	BoC	2003.12	PBoC
China SAR	Macau	BoC	2004.08	PBoC
Taiwan	Taipei	BoC	2012.12	BoC
Singapore	Singapore	ICBC	2013.04	MAS
United Kingdom	London	China Construction Bank	2014.06	UK Gov
Germany	Frankfurt	BoC	2014.06	Bloomberg
South Korea	Seoul	Bank of Communications	2014.07	Bloomberg
France	Paris	BoC	2014.09	WSJ
Luxembourg	Luxembourg	ICBC	2014.09	ICBC
Qatar	Doha	ICBC	2014.11	Reuters
Canada	Toronto	ICBC	2014.11	WSJ
Malaysia	Kuala Lumpur	BoC	2014.11	Reuters
Australia	Sydney	BoC	2014.11	Bloomberg

Source: Author.

Note: Acronyms used in this table: BoC — Bank of China; ICBC — Industrial and Commercial Bank of China; MAS — Monetary Authority of Singapore; SAR — Special Administrative Region; WSJ — *Wall Street Journal*

---

26   It is sometimes said that China has to shift from current account surplus to deficit so that other countries can run surpluses against it and accumulate RMB-denominated claims offshore. This is not quite right, given that capital accounts are also being progressively liberalized (see above) and such claims can also be accumulated through capital flows. But given the gradual pace of capital account liberalization, which I argue elsewhere is apt to continue, the prevailing pattern of current account balances clearly favours some offshore centres relative to others.

To address the second problem, clearing and settlement, the Chinese authorities have designated one of their big domestic banks as the official clearing bank for each authorized offshore RMB centre. The designated clearing banks for different offshore financial centres are listed in Table 1.

To address the third problem, liquidity, the PBoC has negotiated RMB swap lines with the central banks of foreign financial centres, enabling those central banks to obtain the RMB needed by their respective domestic financial institutions and pass this on to the latter as needed. The assured provision of RMB liquidity should in turn allow foreign monetary authorities to authorize the banks they regulate to incur RMB exposures, or at least allow those foreign central banks to feel more comfortable about doing so. Those RMB swap arrangements, their amounts and their dates of negotiation are shown in Table 2.

As a result of these initiatives, competition for offshore-RMB-centre status is intense. London has emerged as a centre for the issuance of dim sum bonds, and the UK government was the first non-Chinese issuer of RMB-denominated sovereign debt.[27] Frankfurt hopes to capitalize on the presence of the big German banks and on the fact that it is home to the European Central Bank, which maintains a swap line with the PBoC. Taipei, Seoul and Singapore are all seeking to compete with Hong Kong for the status of principal Asian offshore financial centre. The peculiar absence of the United States from this competition may reflect the dominance of the dollar in both US and international markets for trade credit and international bond issuance or perhaps the political delicacy of negotiating an RMB swap line with China. In particular, were the Fed to negotiate a swap line with China, it is likely that elements in Congress would be highly critical and accuse the central bank of, in effect, making foreign policy, given China's traditional status as a geopolitical rival to the United States and now as the second global superpower. That said, there are those in San Francisco who would seek to capitalize on the absence of other offshore RMB centres from their and adjoining time zones.

This strategy of relying on offshore financial centres is working in the sense that the volume of offshore RMB deposits, issuance of dim sum bonds and other measures of international activity involving the currency have been rising steadily. Chinese and foreign banks are growing accustomed to dealing with one another and in the currency, although the pace and extent of their learning is difficult to gauge. Chinese banks are bringing their new knowledge back home, and foreign banks are more willing to engage in RMB-based business

---

27   It plans to use the receipts to augment and diversify the currency composition of its international reserves.

Table 2: RMB Swap Arrangements

Country	Date	Amount in RMB	Other Amount	Source
South Korea	2008.12	180 billion	38 trillion won	Garcia-Herrero and Xia (2014)
Hong Kong	2009.01	200 billion	227 billion HKD	Garcia-Herrero and Xia (2014)
Malaysia	2009.02	80 billion	40 billion MYR	Garcia-Herrero and Xia (2014)
Belarus	2009.03	20 billion	8 trillion BYB	Garcia-Herrero and Xia (2014)
Indonesia	2009.03	100 billion	175 trillion IDR	Garcia-Herrero and Xia (2014)
Argentina	2009.03	70 billion	70 billion peso	Garcia-Herrero and Xia (2014)
Iceland	2010.06	3.5 billion	66 billion ISK	Garcia-Herrero and Xia (2014)
Singapore	2010.07	150 billion	30 billion SGD	Garcia-Herrero and Xia (2014)
New Zealand	2011.04	25 billion	N/A	Garcia-Herrero and Xia (2014)
Uzbekistan	2011.04	0.7 billion	N/A	Garcia-Herrero and Xia (2014)
Mongolia	2011.05	5 billion	N/A	Garcia-Herrero and Xia (2014)
Kazakhstan	2011.06	7 billion	N/A	PBoC
Russia	2011.06	N/A	N/A	PBoC
South Korea	2011.10	360 billion	64 trillion won	PBoC
Hong Kong	2011.11	400 billion	490 billion HKD	Garcia-Herrero and Xia (2014)
Thailand	2011.12	70 billion	320 Thai baht	PBoC
Pakistan	2011.12	10 billion	140 billion Pakistan rupee	PBoC
United Arab Emirates	2012.01	35 billion	20 billion dirham	PBoC
Malaysia	2012.02	180 billion	90 billion MYR	PBoC
Turkey	2012.02	10 billion	3 billion Turkish lira	PBoC
Mongolia	2012.03	10 billion	2 trillion tug	PBoC
Australia	2012.03	200 billion	30 billion Australian dollar	PBoC
Ukraine	2012.06	15 billion	19 billion hryvnia	PBoC
Singapore	2013.03	300 billion	60 billion SGD	Bloomberg
Brazil	2013.03	190 billion	60 billion real	PBoC
United Kingdom	2013.06	200 billion	20 billion pound	PBoC
Iceland	2013.09	3.5 billion	66 billion ISK	PBoC
Hungary	2013.09	10 billion	375 billion Hungarian forint	PBoC
Albania	2013.09	2 billion	35.8 billion lek	PBoC
Indonesia	2013.10	100 billion	175 trillion IDR	PBoC
European Union	2013.10	350 billion	45 billion euro	PBoC
Switzerland	2014.07	150 billion	21 billion Swiss francs	PBoC
Argentina	2014.07	70 billion	90 billion peso	PBoC
Mongolia	2014.08	15 billion	4.5 trillion tug	PBoC
Sri Lanka	2014.09	10 billion	225 billion LKR	PBoC
Russia	2014.10	150 billion	815 billion rubles	PBoC
South Korea	2014.10	360 billion	64 trillion won	PBoC
Qatar	2014.11	35 billion	N/A	Reuters
Hong Kong	2014.11	400 billion	505 billion HKD	PBoC
Canada	2014.11	200 billion	30 billion CND	PBoC

Source: Author.

Note: Currency codes used in table: HKD — Hong Kong dollar; MYR — Malaysian ringgit; BYB — Belarussian ruble; ISK — Icelandic króna; SGD — Singapore dollar; IDR — Indonesian rupiah; LKR — Sri Lankan rupee; CDN — Canadian dollar.

in China. The principal source of dissatisfaction concerns the speed of progress. That dissatisfaction in turn spurs the quest for alternatives, including the one to which this chapter now turns.

Onshore Free Trade and Financial Zones

An alternative to relying on offshore centres as a testing ground for liberalized financial markets and capital flows is creating a similar zone onshore, free of barriers to the rest of the world but insulated from the remainder of the Chinese economy. This is what the Chinese authorities sought to do in 2013 when announcing their intention to create a Shanghai Free Trade and Financial Zone (SFTZ).[28]

In December 2013, the PBoC issued a blueprint as to how the SFTZ would work.[29] It described those plans as:

- Trade in merchandise between the SFTZ and the rest of the world would be largely free of customs and licensing formalities.

- Entities doing business in the SFTZ would be permitted to open free trade accounts (FTAs) for use in local and foreign currency transactions. Non-residents would be permitted to open free trade accounts for non-residents (FTNs) as soon as national treatment principles with their countries of residence were established. Holders of FTAs and FTNs would then be permitted to freely transfer funds between offshore accounts and onshore non-resident accounts; funds could similarly be transferred freely between FTAs and FTNs.

- Authorized commercial banks would set up an FTA clearing unit separate from their onshore clearing systems — that separation being what would presumably prevent capital controls still applying in the rest of China from being evaded. Capital account transactions such as loan repayments and FDI could then be funded with these accounts.

- Corporates with accounts in the SFTZ could invest overseas without pre-approval. Residents with FTAs could invest in foreign securities markets and freely transfer income generated in the free trade zone to offshore accounts.

- Non-residents would be allowed to use funds in their FTNs to invest in onshore securities markets without restriction, as would resident

---

28   An earlier attempt to create a free financial zone that has attracted less attention and activity was in Qianhai, a commercial district of Shenzhen.

29   The remainder of this description of intentions draws on that opinion as distilled in Eichengreen (2014).

corporations with FTAs, while corporates in the free trade zone would be allowed to issue RMB-denominated bonds on the onshore market.

- Corporations, non-bank financial institutions and other institutional entities registered in the zone could borrow on offshore markets and bring that funding back onshore. They would be permitted to access offshore derivatives markets to hedge the risks of foreign currency borrowing.[30]

The goal, then, was to remove all substantial restrictions on financial transactions between the Shanghai zone and the rest of the world, and thus to use the zone as an onshore testing ground for capital account convertibility and a magnet for attracting foreign financial intermediaries. The corresponding dangers were that something could go wrong with the Chinese banks and enterprises operating inside the zone. In addition, there could be leakages between the SFTZ and the rest of the economy, undermining the effectiveness of China's capital-control regime and creating financial vulnerabilities elsewhere. Previous experience suggests that the longer these "Chinese walls" remain in place, the better financial markets become at finding ways of evading them. It is not clear why the SFTZ should be different.

Officials are clearly aware of these risks. They have been moving deliberately in implementing their blueprint, disappointing the over-optimistic expectations of naïve observers, some of whom were led to believe by the initial announcement that the free trade and financial zone would be completed within a year.[31] In fact, progress in the first year through September 2014 was widely characterized as modest. In the first nine months of 2014, cross-border fund flows in the Shanghai zone totalled US$25 billion, only 15 percent of total cross-border flows in and out of Shanghai-based entities.[32] The zone has done more to facilitate the inward and outward movement of goods than financial services, at least to date.[33]

To be sure, there have been accomplishments.[34] Banks in the SFTZ have been permitted to open some of those special free trade zone accounts designed to allow easier transfer with overseas accounts, although use of those accounts for foreign transfers remains tightly controlled for the moment. Multinational corporations have been permitted to more freely transfer capital from and to

---

30   In this way foreign exchange positions would be squared or covered within the free trade zone and offshore markets (positions elsewhere in China will not be able to be used to square positions in the free trade zone, again reflecting the assumption of binding capital controls between the free trade zone and the rest of China).

31   See, *inter alia*, Palmioli and Heal (2014).

32   See Du (2014).

33   Shen (2014) describes the most visible change within the zone as the availability of cheap directly imported shellfish from Vietnam and Mozambique.

34   Described at more length by Palmioli and Heal (2014).

their overseas accounts via their special RMB cash pools in the SFTZ. In March 2014, the central bank removed the upper limit on foreign-currency deposit rates offered by lenders in the zone (in contrast to the rest of the economy where such ceilings remained — see above).

Finally, to facilitate foreign trade and investment, a simplified reporting procedure was introduced, also in March 2014, whereby companies in the zone only need to issue an annual report as a public announcement instead of going through an annual inspection. There has been an effort to encourage FDI in the SFTZ, by banks and others, by streamlining approval procedures and eliminating red tape. In particular, the authorities have moved to a "negative list" system where forms of FDI in the zone that are not expressly prohibited are now presumed to be permissible.[35]

Permitting authorized Chinese banks and firms along with foreign-headquartered banks and firms doing RMB business in Shanghai to engage in cross-border financial transactions without restriction is a faster and more powerful way of encouraging them to acquire expertise in such business, compared to their relying on limited contacts with banks and firms in offshore financial centres. It is also riskier. Leakages between the SFTZ and the rest of the economy could undermine the effectiveness of the prevailing capital-control regime, with unintended financial consequences. It should not be a surprise in this light that the authorities, given their penchant for caution, have moved slowly in developing their free trade and financial zone. More likely than not, they will continue doing so.

Conclusions and Recommendations

China will soon be the largest economy in the world, if it is not already.[36] Since it will be not only the largest economy but also the single most important trading nation, it makes sense that its currency should play a consequential international role. But size and the volume of a country's trade alone do not international currency status make, as the experience of the United States in the late nineteenth and early twentieth centuries similarly underscores.[37]

In order to successfully internationalize the RMB, in the sense of enhancing its attractiveness as an international unit of account, means of payment and

---

35   As Jane Jiang (2014) puts it, "the negative list constitutes an affirmative statement that a business may conduct any activity unless specifically restricted or prohibited. This approach is fundamentally different from the regime in the rest of China, where businesses are told what they can do."

36   Different metrics and conversion factors produce somewhat different results.

37   Again, this is a central point of Eichengreen (2011).

store of value, China will have to build deep and liquid financial markets open to the rest of the world. In practice, such markets, like Rome, are not built in a day. Nor is building them without risk. Financial liberalization and opening are fraught with difficulty. The experience of the euro area illustrates the problems that can flow from removing capital controls before prudential supervision and regulation have been adequately rationalized and strengthened. This is not an experience that China should seek to emulate.

Consequently, the country is likely to adopt a cautious and gradual approach to financial development, capital account liberalization and RMB internationalization. But the problem with a gradual approach is that the train may never reach the station. This, in turn, points to the desirability of strategies capable of accelerating the process of currency internationalization without also exposing the financial system and the economy to unnecessary risks. Selective capital account liberalization that focuses on buy-and-hold investors and capital inflows rather than outflows, the negotiation of swap arrangements with foreign central banks and the promotion of offshore financial centres are three obvious means to these ends. They are the options on which the Chinese authorities have focused so far. They are the options that they should continue to pursue.

Works Cited

ANZ Research. 2014. "CNY: Breaking Down the Depreciation Talk." FX Insight, *ANZ Research*. December 11.

Brecher, Richard and Carlos Diaz-Alejandro. 1977. "Tariffs, Foreign Capital and Immiserizing Growth." *Journal of International Economics* 7 (4): 317–22.

Calomiris, Charles and Stephen Haber. 2014. *Fragile by Design: The Political Origins of Banking Crises and Scarce Credit*. Princeton, NJ: Princeton University Press.

Calvo, Guillermo and Fabrizio Coricelli. 1995. "Output Collapse in Eastern Europe: The Role of Credit." In *Eastern Europe in Transition: From Recession to Growth?* edited by Mario Blejer, Guillermo Calvo, Fabrizio Coricelli and Alan Gelb, 92–105. Washington, DC: The World Bank.

Chinn, Menzie and Jeffrey Frankel. 2005. "Will the Euro Eventually Surpass the Dollar as Leading International Reserve Currency?" In *G7 Current Account Imbalances: Sustainability and Adjustment*, edited by Richard Clarida, 283–335. Chicago, IL: University of Chicago Press.

Chitu, Livia, Barry Eichengreen and Arnaud Mehl. 2013. "When Did the Dollar Overtake Sterling as the Leading International Currency: Evidence from the Bond Markets." *Journal of Development Economics* 111: 225–45.

Davis, Bob. 2013. "World Bank Mulling Sweeping Proposals for China Reform." *The Wall Street Journal*, August 1.

Dornbusch, Rudiger. 1998. "Capital Controls: An Idea Whose Time is Past." In *Should the IMF Pursue Capital-Account Convertibility?* edited by Stanley Fischer, Richard Cooper, Rudiger Dornbusch, Peter Garber, Carlos Massad, Jacques Polak, Dani Rodrik and Savak Tarapore, 20–27. Essays in International Finance No. 207, International Finance Section, Department of Economics, Princeton University.

Du, Roger Yu. 2014. "Shanghai Free Trade Zone Takes It Slow." *Global Risk Insights*, November 9.

Eichengreen, Barry. 2003. "Capital Account Liberalization: What Do the Cross-Country Studies Tell Us?" *World Bank Economic Review* 15: 341–65.

———. 2011. *Exorbitant Privilege: The Rise and Fall of the Dollar and the Future of the International Monetary System.* New York, NY: Oxford University Press.

———. 2013a. "Renminbi Internationalization: Tempest in a Teapot?" *Asian Development Review* 30: 148–64.

———. 2013b. "Number One Country, Number One Currency?" *World Economy* 36: 363–74.

———. 2014. "Pathways to Renminbi Internationalization." In *Internationalisation of the Renminbi: Pathways, Implications and Opportunities*, edited by Barry Eichengreen, Kathleen Walsh and Geoff Weir, 5–50. Sydney: Centre for International Finance and Regulation.

Eichengreen, Barry, Livia Chitu and Arnaud Mehl. 2014. "Network Effects, Homogenous Goods and International Currency Choice: New Evidence from an Older Era." ECB Working Paper No. 1651. March.

Eichengreen, Barry, Rachita Gullipalli and Ugo Panizza. 2011. "Capital Account Liberalization, Financial Development and Industry Growth: A Synthetic View." *Journal of International Money and Finance* 60: 1090–106.

Eichengreen, Barry and Masahiro Kawai. 2014. "Issues for Renminbi Internationalization: An Overview." ADBI Working Paper No. 454. January.

Federal Reserve Bank of San Francisco. 2014. "China's Interest Rate Liberalization Reform" *Asia Focus*. May.

Feyzioglu, Tarhan, Nathan Porter and Elod Takas. 2009. "Interest Rate Liberalization in China." IMF Working Paper WP09/171. August.

Flandreau, Marc and Clemens Jobst. 2009. "The Empirics of International Currencies: Network Externalities, History and Persistence." *Economic Journal* 119: 643–64.

Fukuda, Shin-Ichi and Ji Cong. 1994. "On the Choice of Invoice Currency by Japanese Exporters: The PTM Approach." *Journal of the Japanese and International Economies* 8: 511–29.

Garcia-Herrero, Alicia and Le Xia. 2014. "China's Financial Liberalization: New Challenges and Opportunities." BBVA Banking Watch, May 27.

Giuliano, Paola, Prachi Mishra and Antonio Spilimbergo. 2010. "Democracy and Reforms: Evidence from a New Dataset." IMF Working Paper WP/10/173. July.

Haggard, Stephan and Steven Webb. 1994. *Voting for Reform: Democracy, Political Liberalization and Economic Adjustment*. New York: Oxford University Press for the World Bank.

Huang, Yiping, Ran Li and Bijun Wang. 2013. "The Last Battles of China's Financial Reform." Unpublished manuscript, Crawford School of Management, Australian National University.

IMF. 2012. "The Liberalization and Management of Capital Flows: An Institutional View." November 14. Washington, DC: IMF.

Ito, Hiro. 2005. "Financial Development in Asia: Thresholds, Institutions and the Sequence of Liberalization." Unpublished manuscript, Portland State University. April.

Jiang, Jane. 2014. "Reconsidering Shanghai's Free Trade Zone." *Nikkei Asian Review*, November 26.

La Porta, Rafael, Florencio Lopez-de-Silanes, Andrei Shleifer and Robert Vishny. 1998. "Law and Finance." *Journal of Political Economy* 106: 1113–55.

Lavigne, Marie. 1995. *The Economics of Transition from Socialist Economy to Market Economy*. New York, NY: St. Martin's Press.

McCauley, Robert and Michela Scatigna. 2011. "Foreign Exchange Trading in Emerging Currencies: More Financial, More Offshore." *BIS Quarterly Review* (March): 67–75.

McKinnon, Ronald. 1991. *The Order of Economic Liberalization: Financial Control in the Transition to a Market Economy.* Baltimore, MD: Johns Hopkins University Press.

Mo, Jongryn and Barry Weingast. 2013. *Korean Political and Economic Development: Crisis, Security and Institutional Rebalancing.* Cambridge, MA: Harvard University Press for the Harvard University Asia Center.

Morck, Randall and Bernard Yeung. 2014. "Corporate Governance in China." *Journal of Applied Corporate Finance* 26 (3): 20–41.

North, Douglass. 1990. *Institutions, Institutional Change and Economic Performance.* Cambridge: Cambridge University Press.

North, Douglass and Barry Weingast. 1989. "Constitutions and Commitment: The Evolution of Institutions Governing Public Choice in Seventeenth-Century England." *Journal of Economic History* 49 (4): 803–32.

Olson, Mancur. 1993. "Dictatorship, Democracy and Development." *American Political Science Review* 87 (3): 567–76.

Palmioli, Giovanni and Adam Heal. 2014. "Structural Economic Reform in China: The Role of the Shanghai Free Trade Zone." *ESCAP Trade Insights* 3, November. UN Economic and Social Commission for Asia and the Pacific.

Piotroski, Joseph. 2014. "Financial Reporting Practices of China's Listed Firms." *Journal of Applied Corporate Finance* 26 (3): 53–60.

Rajan, Raghuram and Luigi Zingales. 2003. "The Great Reversals: The Politics of Financial Development in the Twentieth Century." *Journal of Financial Economics* 69: 5–50.

Shen, Hong. 2014. "One Year On, Shanghai Free Trade Zone Disappoints." *The Wall Street Journal.* September 28. http://online.wsj.com/articles/one-year-on-shanghai-free-trade-zone-disappoints-1411928668.

World Economic Forum (various years). *Global Competitiveness Report.* Zurich: World Economic Forum.

Zhao, Samuel and Sheldon Liu. n.d. "A Guide to the Qualified Foreign Institutional Investors Scheme for Navigating Investment into China." New York and Hong Kong: Brown Brothers Harriman.

Zhao, Suiseng. 2006. *Debating Political Reform in China: Rule of Law vs. Democratization.* London: Routledge.

4

Assessing the Potential of RMB Trade Settlement

Qiyuan Xu

n July 2009, China launched a renminbi (RMB) trade settlement pilot scheme. Since then, the acceleration of RMB internationalization has made remarkable progress.

First, there is the development of RMB cross-border settlement. In addition to the pilot program of RMB settlement in trade and direct investment, a series of supporting measures under the financial account have also been implemented, such as RMB Qualified Domestic Institutional Investors, RMB Qualified Foreign Institutional Investors (RQFII) and RMB cross-border loans. From the second quarter of 2009 to the fourth quarter of 2014, the amount of RMB cross-border trade settlement accumulated to RMB 16.6 trillion. At the same time, RMB settlements of foreign direct investment (FDI) and overseas direct investment (ODI) exceeded RMB 1 trillion. By the end of April 2014, RQFII amounted to RMB 215.6 billion. The pilot program of RMB cross-border loans has already launched within the Qianhai area in Shenzhen, the free trade zone in Shanghai and Tianjin Eco-city.

Second, there is the construction of the RMB offshore market in Hong Kong (CNH) and other international financial centres. The current layout of RMB offshore markets in the Asia-Pacific region (including Macau, Taiwan, Australia, Korea, Japan and Association of Southeast Asian Nations [ASEAN] countries) is widely established and extends to the European market. In order to develop the RMB offshore market, more and more economies have assigned currency swaps with the People's Bank of China (PBoC) at the same time, to construct the RMB-clearing platform. So far, there is a preliminary worldwide RMB network composed of three types: the RMB onshore market; the RMB offshore centre; and the RMB offshore hubs (Subacchi and Huang 2012) that correspond to Shanghai, Hong Kong and other offshore markets, such as London, Singapore, Taiwan China, Frankfurt, Paris and Luxembourg.

RMB internationalization has made great progress both in cross-border settlement and offshore market development. These contributed to advancing the RMB's international function as a medium of exchange. According to statistics reported by SWIFT, the RMB surpassed the Australian dollar and became the fifth-largest payment currency in December 2014. Meanwhile, the RMB keeps rising for the commitment of bilateral currency swap lines between China and other economies, which reached RMB 3.1 trillion by January 2015. In addition, the network for the RMB directly trading against other major currencies, such as the Japanese yen, Australian dollar, New Zealand dollar and the British pound, has been established. Some countries have begun to consider, or already hold, RMB assets as their official reserves.

The authorities have, so far, made great achievements on RMB internationalization in last five years. But there is some skepticism and worry about the smooth progress continuing. If RMB appreciation is no longer sustainable, the "hot money"-dominated RMB cross-border settlements could suddenly stop, which might also cause instability in the CNH (offshore RMB) market. The investigation by Fan He et al. (2011) identified CNH deposits as hot money, which carries some potential risks. Eichengreen also pointed out that if the public believes the RMB will continuously appreciate, then only the agents who receive payments in RMB have the motivation to participate in RMB internationalization (quoted in Wei and Davis 2011). In this case, the settlement will inevitably be imbalanced.

The analysis by Garber (2011) argued that with the expectation of RMB appreciation, even RMB settlements based on real businesses have the appearance of speculation and, therefore, can exert influence on China's economy. Similarly, Li et al. (2013) analyzed to what extent the role of expectation of RMB appreciation plays in RMB cross-border settlements. The conclusion is that although the impact from the expectation of RMB appreciation to RMB settlements is statistically significant, the effect of appreciation expectation is not dominant.[1]

In the beginning of 2013, taking advantage of RMB trade settlements, there were large-scale flows of hot money into China through fake trade invoices, aiming to earn profits from the interest rate spreads and exchange rate gap between onshore and offshore markets (Wu and Xu 2014). This indicates that speculation was an important driver for RMB cross-border settlement, at least in early 2013.

Now that the US Federal Reserve System has started to exit the quantitative easing policy, the RMB exchange rate has a depreciation expectation. This is troublesome. Xiao Lisheng (2015) points out that there has been a bottleneck for RMB internationalization since 2014, because the RMB exchange rate has become more volatile and the absolute appreciation expectation has disappeared.

As we can see, RMB internationalization has made great progress while facing deep skepticism. So far, RMB internationalization has benefitted from the RMB exchange rate gap and interest rate spread between the onshore and offshore market. What are the prospects for RMB internationalization in the future, if the appreciation expectation reverses? This chapter will assess the potential for RMB trade settlement.

The Framework for the Assessment

Assessment Based on the Currency Functions

Based on Benjamin J. Cohen (1971), Peter B. Kenen (1983) refined the three most important functions for international currency: unit of account, medium of exchange and store of value. As shown in Table 1, there are six combinations for the three functions in official and private cases. It has become a popular

---

1   In the onshore market, CNY reflects the RMB exchange rate with limited regulations, while in the offshore market, CNH reflects the RMB exchange rate based on market mechanisms. Therefore, the gap between CNH and CNY reflects RMB exchange rate expectation. If the RMB exchange rate against the US dollar in the CNH market is more expensive than the CNY market, it means RMB appreciation expectation exists. With this background, in order to make arbitrage, importers will transfer RMB payments to the CNH market through connected party transactions, and then exchange more US dollars with the same amount of RMB and lastly pay the foreign exporters with US dollars. In this way, RMB appreciation expectation leads to more RMB cross-border settlement, especially in imports. Since 2009, the payment of RMB accounted for more than 60 percent of the total RMB settlements. See Zhang and Xu (2012) and Xu and He (2015). Without the gap between CNH and CNY, this type of RMB settlement driven by arbitrage will disappear.

Table 1: Official and Private Use of Currency Functions

Currency Functions	Official Use	Private Use
Unit of account	Anchor for pegging currency	Denominating trade and financial products
Medium of exchange	Vehicle currency for intervention in the foreign exchange market	Invoicing trade and financial transactions
Store of value	Foreign exchange reserve	Financial investment

Source: Kenen (1988).

framework to measure and forecast the potential for an international currency (Chinn and Frankel 2007; Gao and Yu 2011; Frankel 2012).

The literature on what determines reserve currency status is fairly well established. As summarized by Jeffrey Frankel (2012), three points are important: The first is the fundamental determinants, in particular the size of the country or region. The second is how open and developed a country's financial markets are. The third factor is the confidence in the value of the currency.

These three factors also correspond to the three functions. A large economy has the advantage of transaction network externality, so that the currency can play the role of a unit of account or a medium of exchange. An open and developed financial market will meet the demand of financial liquidity, and confidence in the currency value provides the expectation of safety and a stable yield, both of which will contribute to a currency as a function for store of value.

Although these three factors sound reasonable, they could be challenged. Regarding the first factor, economic size, in itself, does not necessarily make sense with regard to global value chains. China is the world's factory, and also the world's assembly line, which is a low value-added position in the global value chain. Processing trade accounted for 36 percent of China's foreign trade in 2014. For example, China's exports of iPhones to the United States earned billions of surpluses in US dollars. In relatively crude value-added terms, however, China adds only a small share, say 3.95 percent, of domestic value added to the iPhone, corresponding to the value of the assembly work (Organisation for Economic Co-operation and Development-World Trade Organization 2012). In this case, due to the low value-added position in the global value chain, processing enterprises will be forced to make the trade settlement in the currency that favours the foreign counterparty. On the contrary, if a processing trade such as the iPhone is settled in RMB, then the majority of the iPhone's added value will be exposed to the exchange rate risk. Therefore, considering the feature of processing trade and its share in China's foreign trade, the expectation of the RMB's potential as an invoicing currency should be brought down. It is not as optimistic as China's economic size shows. In addition, more factors will be presented to explain the inconsistencies between China's economic size and its position in the global production network. Therefore, the data on China's economic size probably overestimates the RMB's potential for trade settlement.

For the second factor, an open and developed financial market results from a well-behaved free market and an effective institution. For the third factor, a currency gains confidence in the global market in the short and mid term through a stable exchange rate and a relatively low inflation rate, which is supported by prudent monetary policies operated by an independent central bank. But from the long-term view, the Balassa-Samuelson effect will dominate the exchange rate and lead the anticipation.[2]

Assessment Based on Transaction Network and Specialization Network

The Young theorem states that not only is the level of division of labour dependent on the extent of the market, but also the extent of the market is determined by the level of division of labour, so that they are two like sides of the same coin. (Young 1928). Yang Xiaokai (1990) further demonstrates the point by means of inframarginal analysis.[3] From a view beyond the domestic market, the expansion of the extent of the market from a domestic to an international market originates at the level of the domestic division of labour. At the same time, the development of the domestic division of labour is driven by a larger domestic market extent and a higher efficiency of the domestic transaction network (Yang 1999).

Cohen (1998) defines a money's domain, which combines the influence of state-imposed territoriality (visible hand) with that of market-generated transactional networks (invisible hand). On the one hand, the government imposes influence through money issuance and monopoly of currency management. On the other hand, there is an invisible (market) hand, which plays a role through the transaction network. Generally, the visible hand of the government is effective within political jurisdictions, while the invisible hand of the market plays a more important role in currency deterritorialization.

---

2   Countries with high productivity growth also experience high wage growth, which leads to higher real exchange rates. The effect was proposed by economists Bela Balassa (1964) and Paul Samuelson (1964).

3   Inframarginal economics is applying inframarginal analysis to studies of network effects of division of labour and various economic problems associated with different features of the network pattern of division of labour. Inframarginal economics make it possible to make the network of division of labour endogenous. See Yang (1990).

As a result, behind an international currency there is a mutual promotion between the efficiency of the transaction network and the degree of specialization. The mutual promotion makes an economy more important in the global value chain and keeps economic growth stable. The internationalization of an economy's currency is just the expansion of its specialization network (Xu and Li 2008).

International trade captures the features of a cross-border transaction network and a specialization network. Studying the fundamentals in international trade is critical for assessing a currency's internationalization.

A historical account of the yen's internationalization is insightful. In the 1980s and 1990s, discussions focused mainly on financial market liberalization. Japanese Prime Minister Ryutaro Hashimoto announced plans in November 1996 to accelerate and broaden financial reforms by creating "free, fair, and global" markets (Osaki 2005). He called these reforms the "Japanese big bang," based on their similarity to Britain's 1986 big bang. Japan's big bang encompassed all the financial sectors. But the yen's internationalization did not behave well because of Japan's big bang. For example, as an index of the yen's internationalization, in 1995 before the big bang, the yen occupied seven percent of the currency compositions of official foreign exchange reserves, while after the big bang it declined to three percent within 10 years (IMF 2009). With a liberalized financial market, studies of yen's internationalization focus more on trade sector. In 2007, the former adviser to Japan's prime minister, Takatoshi Ito, investigated the international trade settlement of Japanese multinational enterprises (Ito et al. 2011). The traditional assessment method, based on the real economy, is at the forefront of the yen's internationalization.

This chapter first provided an overview of the existing literature and illustrated a framework to make an assessment. In the second part, China's international trade will be analyzed, in particular structural information reflecting China's position in the global transaction network and specialization network. The third part will focus on the pricing power of China's export enterprises, and then assess the potential of the RMB as an invoicing currency in export settlement. The final section will make concluding remarks and provide some policy advice.

The Structure of China's International Trade

The most prominent features of China's foreign trade structure are huge volumes and a large trade surplus. There are also four other characteristics that cannot be overlooked: foreign-owned enterprise, which contributed 46 percent for both exports and imports in 2014 (these data have fluctuated around 50 percent in the last decade); processing trade, which accounts for 36 percent of total imports and exports; primary commodities, which accounted for 33 percent of total imports in 2014, although most of the primary commodities prices declined at the same time; and China still relies heavily on demand from EU countries, and the United States, which account for 35 percent of China's total export (National Bureau of Statistics of China 2015).

The first of the six features mentioned above is a favourable condition for RMB internationalization, while the others are restraining factors.

First, with a total trade volume of nearly US$3 trillion, China has, since 2010, become the largest exporter and second-largest importer, second only to the United States (IMF 2015). This is obviously a beneficial factor driving the RMB to become an international currency.

On the other hand, the trade surplus was US$182 billion in 2010 and US$383 billion in 2014, respectively (ibid). There are no indications that the huge surplus in foreign trade will fade away. As a result, it will be difficult for China to export RMB through the trade account, which is necessary for an international currency to make provisions for its liquidity in the offshore market.

So far, the proportion of RMB settlement for imports is much higher than for exports. This enables a net outflow of RMB through the trade account. However, Chinese importers do not benefit from the RMB settlement with the background of RMB appreciation expectation, unless they can make arbitrage between onshore and offshore markets profitable. Of course, the arbitrage works well through an expectation of RMB appreciation. Nevertheless, it can clearly be seen that exporting RMB liquidity through arbitrage is unsustainable in the long run.

Yin Jianfeng (2011) describes two models from the history of currency internationalization. One is "trade settlement plus offshore market" and the other is "capital account plus multinational enterprises." The latter is more sustainable from a long-term perspective, while the former is more fragile, or even dangerous, as seen with the Japanese yen during the 1980s and 1990s. As discussed above, RMB internationalization has, thus far, developed typically in the model of trade settlement plus offshore market. The huge trade surplus acts as a constraint on RMB internationalization.

As mentioned above, foreign-owned enterprises accounted for about half of China's foreign trade for decades. In the global production network, the business decisions of foreign enterprises are generally made by parent companies. Therefore, the subsidiary corporations in China are not fully independent. For Chinese companies, RMB settlement is favourable in order to eliminate the exchange rate risks. But for the subsidiaries of the multinational enterprises in China, RMB settlement is not necessarily helpful. For a foreign-owned enterprise based in China, the balance sheet of its parent company is denominated in yen, euro or US dollars, thus, RMB settlement is not necessarily attractive for it. Therefore, it is always difficult for foreign companies in China to accept the RMB settlement. Of course, when RMB appreciation is predictable, foreign enterprises will be interested in RMB settlement. However, it should be noted that their interests exist only under the conditions of RMB appreciation expectation. Therefore, the sustainability of the speculative RMB settlements is doubtful.

Processing trade accounted for 36 percent of China's foreign trade in 2014. Processing trade includes mainly two types of trade: processing with imported materials and process materials supplied by clients. As an example of the latter case, Chinese company A imports accessories from Japanese company B, which cost A RMB 9,500. Company A assembles the accessories and then exports them back to B, receiving RMB 10,500 in return. In this case, the total trade volume is RMB 20,000. But in order to save the costs for remittances, B just pays the difference of RMB 1,000 to A. It means that even if all the cross-border transactions, RMB 1,000, are settled in RMB, it accounted for only five percent of the total trade volume.

For the case of processing with imported materials, enterprise A will import from foreign company C and then export to another foreign company, D. But Chinese processing trade companies are in a low value-added position in the global value chain. As in the case of iPhones mentioned above, due to the low value-added position in the global value chain, processing enterprises are always forced to choose the settlement currency in favour of the foreign counterparty. Considering the share of processing trade in China's foreign trade, the expectation of the RMB's potential as an invoicing currency should be brought down.

Furthermore, the proportion of primary commodities is rather high in China's imports — 33 percent in 2014, despite the fact that their prices declined. This means two things: First, the RMB will be excluded in import settlement to the extent that primary commodities are always denominated and settled in US dollars. Second, for some Chinese exporters, imports are the main cost. But at least a substantial part of the import cost, such as the primary commodities, are denominated and settled in US dollars. Under the condition, if the exports are settled in RMB, the Chinese exporters will face greater exchange rate risk or higher risk management costs. The above two aspects restrict the use of RMB in cross-border settlement. Since Japan has also been quite dependent on resource imports, the Japanese yen's internationalization has been restrained for the same reason (Ito et al. 2011).

Finally, China still relies heavily on demand from developed economies, and even more so in recent years. In 1997, nearly 60 percent of China's exports were to Asian economies, while in 2014, it declined to 51 percent. Thirty-five percent of China's exports were to Europe and North America, and in 2014 it increased to 40 percent. In international trade between a developed and a developing economy, the currency of the developed economy is usually selected as the invoicing currency (Grassman 1973). Therefore, the potential of RMB internationalization will be restricted with such trade directions.

It is worth noting that even the yen failed to play a leading role in Japanese exports within Asia. In this area, most Japanese exports are denominated and settled not in yen, but in US dollars. Ito et al.'s (2011) investigation revealed that subsidiaries of Japanese multinational enterprises in other Asia economies, say Malaysia, process intermediate goods that are imported from Japan, and then export the final product to the United States. In this case, Japan, Malaysia and the United States constitute a triangular trade. Because Malaysia subsidiaries ultimately exported to the US market, the US dollar dominated the trade settlement between Malaysia and the United States.

Furthermore, it is difficult or more expensive for Malaysia subsidiaries to manage the exchange rate risks. Consequently, the parent company based in Tokyo will make settlements with subsidiaries in Malaysia in US dollars so as to transfer the risks to the parent company, which is much better at dealing with such risks. As a result, the parent company based in Japan exports to Malaysian subsidiaries and settles in US dollar. The outcome is that the proportion of dollar-denominated trade still remains high in east Asia.

The proportion of internal trade within Asia appears to be high, but a substantial ratio is intermediate trade. Asia remains highly reliant on the final demand from European and American markets. A report by the Asian Development Bank (2008) pointed out that in terms of traditional trade data, the Asian economies export 51.8 percent inside the area, and 48.2 percent outside the area. However, if intermediate goods are excluded, the trade of final products shows a different outcome. The above two ratios would be revised to 32.5 percent and 67.5 percent, respectively.

Chinese companies have invested more in emerging and developing economies in recent years. Correspondingly, international trade grew rapidly between China and these economies. Before rising overseas investments, China exported directly to developed economies such as the United States. It could be expected that China will export more via a third country to the United States. However, such changes will not fundamentally change the pattern of the global production network. Continuing in this path, the yuan will encounter the same problem as the yen experienced with triangular trade.

As mentioned above, the huge trade volume has a positive effect on RMB internationalization, but China's large trade surplus and high reliance on the final demand from European and American markets have restricted the optional path of RMB internationalization. Foreign-owned enterprises occupied 46 percent of China's foreign trade in 2014. Foreign trade enterprises overall lack pricing power. Processing trades accounted for 36 percent of the foreign trade in 2014, and there is as high dependence on imported primary commodities. All these factors will restrain the long-term potential of RMB internationalization (see Table 2).

Finally, all the negative factors are closely related to the enterprises' international competitiveness. From the point of view of the micro economy, invoicing currency in international trade is definitely selected by the multinational enterprises that enjoy global market power. All major international currencies are supported by a large number of multinational companies that are highly competitive. In contrast, most Chinese multinational enterprises listed in the Fortune 500 rely heavily on the domestic monopolistic advantages and protection policies. Such enterprises could hardly be expected to be competitive in the global market. From this perspective, the potential for RMB internationalization is rather limited and there is a long way to go.

Table 2: The Impacts from Trade Structure to the Potential of RMB Settlement

China's Trade Structure	Impact on RMB Trade Settlement
Huge trade volume	Positive
Large surplus, dependence on the developed markets	Path constraint
Foreign-owned enterprises (46%)	Negative
Processing trade (36%)	
Reliance on imported bulk commodities (33%)	

Source: Author.

An Assessment of Pricing Power of Chinese Enterprises

When bargaining in the international market, a company's pricing power is a critical factor, and which currency is selected to be dominant and the invoicing currency is inevitably included in the international trade contract. Generally speaking, enterprises always prefer to select domestic currency for settlement, so as to reduce exchange costs and avoid exchange rate risks. Therefore, the selection of invoicing currency is ultimately a pricing power competition between both sides of the deal. The final decision certainly can be favoured by stronger pricing ability, while the counterparty with weaker pricing power will bear more costs or exchange rate risk.

If a company has no pricing power or weak power, it could hardly have a voice in selecting the invoicing currency in the international bargaining. In cases where domestic companies lack pricing power, the use of domestic currency as invoicing currency is confined to the following two conditions: First, foreign enterprises demand changes for the contracts, such as changing the price, in order to shift the cost of exchange rate risk hedging. Second, with the expectation of RMB appreciation, foreign exporters to China will probably prefer to accept the RMB as invoicing currency. But the condition is unfavourable for domestic importers. Eichengreen (2011) also points out that if the public believes the yuan will continuously appreciate, then only the agents who receive payments in RMB have the motivation to participate in RMB internationalization. In this case, the settlement will inevitably be imbalanced. Moreover, this type of imbalance is based on the expectation of RMB appreciation.

In accordance with the lower value-added position in the global production network, Chinese enterprises have relatively weak pricing power in international trade. In 2008, the People's Bank of China (PBoC) carried out an investigation that involved the largest 18 provinces in terms of international trade volume. It showed that among 1,121 foreign trade enterprises, 10 percent have no pricing power at all, 47.4 percent of them have weak pricing power, while only 42.6 percent of the total are endowed with strong pricing power (Xu 2010). Even for those with strong power, a considerable number of them are foreign-owned enterprises. As mentioned earlier, the foreign-owned enterprises could not be the micro foundation for RMB internationalization.

In a general model, Engel (2006) shows that firms would set prices in their own currencies, i.e., producer currency priced if the prices would exhibit high exchange rate pass-through (ERPT), while they would choose to set prices in the destination market currencies, i.e., local currency priced, if the prices exhibit low ERPT.[4] Based on Engel (2006), Li Cui, Chang Shu and Jian Chang (2009) draw the conclusion that if a producer has sufficient market power, it can decide to have its exports invoiced in its own currency and keep its profit margin unchanged, which is the case of zero price-to-market (PTM), but full ERPT to export prices in the buyer's currency.[5] While the theoretical analysis is constructed considering the individual exporters, it can also be expected that a similar result exists at an aggregate level. That is to say, the higher ERPT to the destination markets, the more the exporters' currency would be used as the invoicing and settlement currency.

As Cui, Shu and Chang (2009) have shown, even considering Chinese enterprises' weak pricing power, the potential of RMB settlement in China's export will increase to 20–30 percent if the RMB is fully convertible. It would be inferior to the yen's past performance, which was about 40 percent. But considering China's foreign trade volumes, it would still be high.

However, processing trade occupies a big ratio in China's foreign trade, and it is processing trade that destroys the theoretical link between pricing power and the ERPT effect.

Mordechai Kreinin (2004) considered the global production networks and pointed out that production sharing changes the role of pass-through, to the extent that a country's exports enter into its imports and its imports become part of its exports.

For example, suppose that the appreciation of the RMB is passed through completely in the import channel. It will result in a decrease in the RMB price of component imports into China. And suppose it is, in turn, fully passed through to the RMB price of the assembled vehicle. Therefore, the dollar price will rise only to the extent that the vehicle contains China's value added. That is, the ERPT effect on exports denominated in one currency is offset by the exchange rate effect on the import expressed in the other currency.

The real world is more complicated. Production sharing is popular in East Asia. Korea, Japan, China and the ASEAN countries are heavily involved in the production network, in which China mainly plays a role as an international assembly line. For example, Japan exports intermediate goods to China, then

---

4   ERPT is a measure of how responsive international prices are to changes in the exchange rate. When ERPT is higher, the producer will transfer more exchange rate changes to the prices in destination market. When it is lower, the producer will absorb more exchange rate changes and transfer fewer changes to the prices in destination market.

5   When the exchange rate changes, some exporters will stabilize foreign currency prices in destination market in order to maintain their market share. This is a behaviour called price-to-market (PTM). A zero PTM behaviour shows that there is no ERPT effect, while a one PTM behaviour shows a complete ERPT effect.

China assembles the components and finally exports the finished goods to the United States. At the same time, the RMB is supposed to peg against the dollar, and the yen is relatively flexible.

Suppose yen appreciation is fully passed through to the RMB's price of component imports into China. Then the RMB cost for Japanese vehicle companies in China will increase accordingly. However, owing to their market power, Japanese vehicle enterprises have strong pricing power in global market. Yen appreciation will be finally passed through to dollar price in the US market. At the same time, the RMB is still pegged to dollar.

In the case above, it appears that companies in China enjoy an extremely high pass-through effect. They could raise the dollar price for exports even as the RMB exchange rate stays constant. But this kind of high pass-through effect will not necessarily result in RMB settlements for two reasons. First, the export companies in China are Japanese multinational enterprises, not Chinese. Second, to avoid the exchange rate risk, the Japanese companies will prefer to settle the international trade with yen or dollars, but not RMB. The yen is the home currency — it is consistent with the asset, which is either denominated in yen in the Tokyo stock market or in dollars in the New York stock market.

Thus, it can be seen that Japanese companies could export to the United States via China's assembly line. This type of three-country model results in two characteristics in China's exports. First, 38 percent of China's total exports, a much higher level than general cases, are indirectly contributed by foreign companies, such as Korean and Japanese companies. Secondly, 46 percent of China's total exports are classified as section 16 and 17 of the Harmonized Commodity Description and Coding System.[6] Generally, these two sections are capital- and technical-intensive industries, and the exporters in the sections have a relatively strong pricing power. But in the case of China, these two sections are typically in the processing trade section in exports (Chen, Li and Lu 2007; Yang 2012), which means they will not be favourable to sustainable development for RMB trade settlement, although such kinds of exports appear to enjoy pricing power.

---

6   The Harmonized Commodity Description and Coding System, generally referred to as "Harmonized System" or simply "HS," is a multi-purpose international product nomenclature developed by the World Customs Organization. It comprises about 5,000 commodity groups, each identified by a six-digit code, arranged in a legal and logical structure, and is supported by well-defined rules to achieve uniform classification. Section 16 — Machinery and mechanical appliances; electrical equipment; parts thereof; sound recorders and reproducers, television image and sound recorders and reproducers, and parts and accessories of such articles. Section 17 — Vehicles, aircraft, vessels and associated transport equipment.

Cui, Shu and Chang (2009) studied the pass-through effect of China's exports without considering the global production network and processing trade, hence they overestimate the potential of the RMB as an invoicing currency in cross-border trade, and consequently overestimate the potential of RMB internationalization.

Since processing trade accounted for 38 percent of exports, the estimation of Cui, Shu and Chang (2009) could be applied to only 62 percent of export settlements in 2014. Cui, Shu and Chang (2009) concluded that the potential of RMB settled in exports was 20–30 percent according to the panel regression on the price-to-market (PTM) coefficients. As explained above, we know that processing export trade, which accounted for 38 percent of the total, could hardly make the RMB an invoicing currency; the conclusion of Cui, Shu and Chang (2009) about the proportion 20–30 percent should be converted to 12.4–18.6 percent.

As shown in Figure 1, the share of RMB as a denominating currency in exports reached 20.3 percent by December 2014. Meanwhile, the potential ratio estimated by the authors ranges from 12.4 to 18.6 percent, which appears to tell us that the share of RMB as an invoicing currency exceeded the upper limit of the potential level in 2014.

Figure 1: The Proportion of RMB Settlement in Cross-border Trade

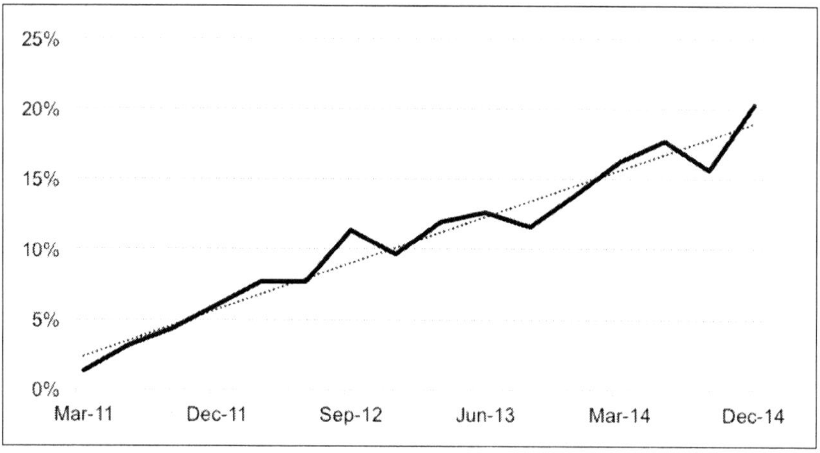

Data source: PBoC, CEIC data (www.ceicdata.com/en/countries/china).

But what should be underlined is the difference between the two currency functions: the RMB as a denominating currency and an invoicing currency. The PTM coefficient drawing from the regression analysis of Cui, Shu and Chang (2009) captures the pricing power of China's exports. A company with strong pricing power would like the deal to be denominated in domestic currency so as to avoid the exchange rate risk. At the same time, if a deal is only settled in RMB, but denominated in US dollars, it would be meaningless for China's exporter to reduce the exchange rate risk. As a result, the function of the RMB as a denominating currency is more important to China's exporters than the RMB as an invoicing currency. Furthermore, the links among pricing power, the PTM coefficient and the possibility of the RMB as a denominating currency have been discussed. Unfortunately, data about the RMB playing the role of denominating currency is not available. The data on RMB settlement must be used as a substitution.

However, due to their difference, the RMB settlement could be misleading for understanding the RMB's position as a denominating currency. As a matter of fact, compared with the role of an invoicing currency, the RMB has fallen behind in its role as a denominating currency to some extent. In some trade settlements, the RMB is the invoicing currency while it is still dominated in US dollars in contracts. According to the PBoC's data in 2012 and 2013, the RMB was the denominating currency for 50 percent of RMB trade settlements (Li 2013). If the ratio of 50 percent is kept the same in 2014, the share of RMB settlement in export should be cut by 50 percent. According to the estimation, the share of RMB as denominating currency occupied 10.15 percent of the total export. It means 10.15 percent of China's export was both settled and denominated by RMB. However, there is also another 10.15 percent of the export, which was just settled but not denominated by RMB.

It is clear that there is more potential to explore the RMB's role as a denominating currency. The estimation taking into account processing trade shows the potential level is 12.4 percent to 18.6 percent, while the ratio in 2014 just recorded 10.15 percent. However, there is another 10.15 percent RMB settlement in the total trade, which is settled in RMB but not denominated by RMB. For the second 10.15 percent RMB settlement, it is not supported by exporters' pricing power. On the contrary, it could be a settlement arbitrage or carry trade, which takes advantage of the RMB exchange rate difference and the interest rate gap between onshore and offshore market. As a result, for the achievement of RMB settlement in export, the sustainability of the second 10.15 percent RMB settlement is questionable.

Concluding Remarks

There has been both big progress and deep skepticism in RMB internationalization. In order to understand the RMB's prospects, we try to assess the potential of RMB settlement based on the transaction network and specialization network. As mentioned in the first part of this chapter, an international currency results from a virtuous circle between the efficiency of the transaction network and the degree of specialization.[7]

Because international trade captures the features of a cross-border transaction network and specialization network, the fundamentals of China's performance in international trade are studied to assess the potential of RMB internationalization.

The result is complicated by both positive and negative factors. The huge volume of trade is positive through the network effect for RMB internationalization, but the large trade surplus and high reliance on the final demand from developed markets had restricting effects. Foreign-owned enterprises occupied 46 percent in China's foreign trade in 2014, and processing trades accounted for 36 percent of the foreign trade in 2014. As well, there is a high dependence on imported primary commodities (CEIC 2015). All these factors will restrain the long-term potential of RMB internationalization.

All the negative factors are all closely related to the enterprises' international competitiveness. In the third part of this chapter, the links among pricing power, PTM coefficient and the possibility of RMB as a denominating currency were discussed. It was estimated that the potential share for RMB as a denominating currency in exports ranges from 12.4 percent to 18.6 percent. But the real performance of RMB had reached 20.3 percent by December 2014. Then the difference was explained based on the different meaning between denominating currency and invoicing currency. Finally, it was pointed out that in 2014, half of the achievement of RMB settlement in export was not supported by the exporters' pricing power, and the sustainability of the half is questionable. The half of the achievement of RMB settlement in export was fundamentally supported by the exporter's pricing power, which can be regarded as a solid part of RMB settlement progress. At the same time, the other half was mainly driven by carry trade and arbitrage between the onshore and offshore RMB market, which can be regarded as a fragile part of RMB settlement. There is further

---

7   See section Assessment Based on Transaction Network and Specialization Network.

space for the solid part to expand; at the same time, the fragile part could be at least partly collapsed with the conditions changing in the global market. The evolution of the RMB's position as an international currency depends on the trade-off between the above two.

So far, the pricing power of Chinese companies is rather weak, and the international trade structure has posed barriers to RMB cross-border settlement in many areas. Nevertheless, profit-driven companies, with increasing competitiveness in the international market, can serve as a supportive micro-foundation for RMB internationalization. Based on the current conditions, two major policies could be adopted from the national level to promote the RMB function as the unit of account (denominating currency) and invoicing currency (settlement currency) in cross-border trade.

First, the RMB's role in cross-border trade settlement should be promoted from the government level. Specifically, RMB internationalization should be promoted through the international economic assistance and loans; trading platforms of primary commodity futures should be set up in Shanghai, so as to leverage China's position as a major buyer in the international market and raise the international influence of the RMB pricing futures. In this way, it might be possible to turn negative factors, such as China's heavy dependence on primary commodities, into positive ones. The possibilities of using bilateral domestic currencies in the primary commodities trade with other resource-exporting countries should be explored.

Second, other structural reforms could be adopted at the national level to improve the potential for RMB internationalization: to reduce the policy distortion, improve domestic market competition conditions, and foster the competitiveness of Chinese companies to become competitive multinational companies in international market; to improve China's trade structure, reduce dependence on processing trade and promote trade structure upgrading; to develop new energy and new technology to reduce the dependence on importing primary products; and to promote productive services and improve companies' capability of autonomous innovation.

Works Cited

Balassa, Bela. 1964. "The Purchasing Power Parity Doctrine: A Reappraisal." *Journal of Political Economy* 72 (6): 584–96.

CEIC. 2015. www.ceicdata.com.

Chen, Xuebin, Li Shigang and Lu Dong. 2007. "Exchange Rate Pass-through to Chinese Export Prices and Exporters' Capability of Pricing to Market." [In Chinese.] *Economic Research Journal* 12: 106–17.

Chinn, Menzie and Frankel Jeffrey A. 2007. "Will the Euro Eventually Surpass the Dollar as Leading International Reserve Currency?" In *G7 Current Account Imbalances: Sustainability and Adjustment*, edited by Richard H. Clarida, 283–38. Chicago, IL: University of Chicago Press.

Cohen, Benjamin J. 1988. *The Geography of Money*. Ithaca, NY: Cornell University Press.

Cui, Li, Shu Chang and Chang Jian. 2009. "Exchange Rate Pass-through and Currency Invoicing in China's Exports." *China Economic Issues*, Number 2/09. Hong Kong Monetary Authority. July.

Engel, Charles. 2006. "Equivalence Results for Optimal Pass-through, Optimal Indexing to Exchange Rates, and Optimal Choice of Currency for Export Pricing." *Journal of the European Economic Association* 4 (6): 1249–60.

Frankel, Jeffrey A. 2012. "Internationalization of the RMB and Historical Precedents." *Journal of Economic Integration* 27 (3): 329–65.

Gao, Haihong and Yongding Yu. 2011. "Internationalisation of the Renminbi." In *Currency Internationalisation: Lessons from the Global Financial Crisis and Prospects for the Future in Asia and the Pacific*, 105–24. Bank for International Settlements.

Garber, Peter. "What Currently Drives CNH Market Equilibrium?" For the Council on Foreign Relations/China Development Research Foundation Workshop on the Internationalization of the Renminbi, October 31–November 1, Beijing.

Grassman, Sven. 1973. "A Fundamental Symmetry in International Payment Patterns." *Journal of International Economics* 3: 105–16.

He, Fan, Zhang Bin, Zhang Ming, Xu Qiyuan and Zheng Liansheng. 2011. "Hong Kong RMB Offshore Market: Current Situations, Perspectives, Problems and Risks." [In Chinese.] *International Economic Review* 3.

IMF. 2009. "Currency Composition of Official Foreign Exchange Reserves." June 30.

———. 2015. International Financial Statistics (CD-ROM).

Ito, Takatoshi, Koibuchi Satoshi, Sato Kiyotaka and Shimizu Junko. 2011. "Currency Invoicing Decision: New Evidence from a Questionnaire Survey of Japanese Export Firms." Center on Japanese Economy and Business, Working Paper Series, No. 293, March.

Kenen, Peter B. 1988. "International Money and Macroeconomics." In *World Economics Problems*, edited by K. A. Elliott and J. Williamson. Washington, DC: Institute for International Economics.

Kreinin, Mordechai. 2004. "Global Production Networks and Regional Integration." In *Empirical Methods in International Trade: Essays in Honor of Mordechai Kreinin*, edited by Michael G. Plummer. Northampton, MA: Edward Elgar Publishing, Inc. 136–38.

Li, Bo. 2013. "The Perspective for RMB Cross-border Settlement." [In Chinese.] China Finance.

National Bureau of Statistics of China. 2015. www.stats.gov.cn/english/.

Organisation for Economic Co-operation and Development-World Trade Organization. 2013. "Trade in Value-Added: Concepts, Methodologies and Challenges." Joint Organisation for Economic Co-operation and Development-World Trade Organization Note.

Osaki, Sadakazu. 2005. "Reforming Japan's Capital Markets." *Public Policy Review* 1 (1): 3–18.

Samuelson, Paul A. 1964. "Theoretical Notes on Trade Problems." *Review of Economics and Statistics* 46 (2): 145–54.

Subacchi, Paola and Helena Huang. 2012. "The Connecting Dots of China's Renminbi Strategy: London and Hong Kong." International Economics Briefing Paper No. 2012/02, Chatham House.

Wei, Lingling and Bob Davis. 2011. "China Stumbles in Yuan Grand Plan." *The Wall Street Journal*, July 15.

Wu Haiying and Xu Qiyuan. 2014. "An Estimation of China's Real Export Amount." [In Chinese.] *China's External Economic Environment Monitor*. Chinese Academy of Social Sciences Working Paper No. 1, April 25. www.iwep.org.cn/news/730753.htm.

Xiao Lisheng. 2015. "RMB Internationalization in Hong Kong: Current Situations, Problems and Perspectives." [In Chinese.] RCIF Policy Brief No. 0072015, Chinese Academy of Social Sciences.

Xu, Qiyuan and Li Jing. 2008. "Currency Internationalization from the Perspective of International Specialization." [In Chinese.] *Journal of World Economy* 2: 30-39.

Xu, Qiyuan. 2010. "Yen's Internationalization: Lessons for China Yuan." [In Chinese.] *Chinese Review of Financial Studies* 2: 114–21.

Xu, Qiyuan, and He Fan. 2015. *The Influence of RMB Internationalization on the Chinese Economy: Theory and Policy.* CIGI Paper No. 58.

Yang, Biyun. 2012. "Estimation and Comparative Analysis on the Exchange Rate Pass-through into Price of Processing Trade and General Trade." [In Chinese.] *World Economy Study* 10: 35–47.

Yang, Xiaokai. 1990. "Development, Structural Changes, and Urbanization." *Journal of Development Economics* 34 (1-2): 199–222.

———. 1999. "Division of Labor and Specialization: A Literature Review." [In Chinese.] In *The Frontier of Contemporary Economics*, edited by Min Tang and Yushi Mao, vol. 3. Beijing: The Commercial Press.

Yin, Jianfeng. 2011. "RMB Internationalization Trade Settlement Plus Offshore Market or Capital Account Opening-up Plus Multinationals? — Lessons from Japan's Yen Internationalization." [In Chinese.] *International Economic Review* 4.

Young, Allyn. 1928. "Increasing Returns and Economic Progress." *The Economic Journal* 152: 527–42.

Zhang, Bin and Xu Qiyuan. 2012. "RMB Internationalization with the Limited Control of Exchange Rate System and Capital Account." [In Chinese.] *International Economic Review* 4: 63–73.

5

The Political Limits to RMB Internationalization

Randall Germain and Herman Mark Schwartz

What are the domestic political requirements that are needed for the renminbi (RMB) to become a genuine "international" currency?[1] Debate about the outlook for successful internationalization of the RMB, or the extent to which it might become a rival to the dollar, largely concentrates on China's international economic policies and/or on the global economic environment. This chapter focuses instead on the domestic requirements for RMB internationalization, not because they are more important, but rather because the domestic and international bases for an international currency are interlocked and cannot be considered separately. We develop a framework that highlights the domestic adjustment costs that a state must accommodate before its currency can carry the weight of internationalization. A critical part of an international currency's political economy is constituted through the institutions and policies a state uses

---

1   We are here distinguishing between an international currency and an international reserve currency. International reserve currencies are those included by governments in their official foreign currency holdings. At present, for example, the principal international reserve currencies are the US dollar and euro (which, according to International Monetary Fund [IMF] Currency Composition of Official Foreign Exchange Reserves data, comprise approximately 62 percent and 23 percent of reported official holdings respectively), followed by the pound sterling, yen, Swiss franc, and Canadian and Australian dollars. For our purposes, an international currency is more than a reserve currency; it also serves as the main vehicle through which international exchange is denominated, and more importantly, as the means by which demand at the global level is transmitted. Thus conceived, an international currency is an integral political foundation for the organization and operation of the global political economy. We expand on this in Germain and Schwartz (2014).

to negotiate sustainable social trade-offs around those costs. Historically, democracies have been the only political regime type capable of meeting the domestic adjustment costs associated with running an international currency. These costs stem from the employment and capital losses that an international currency generates in the course of augmenting global demand. The normal operation of capitalist markets produces deflationary tendencies (Veblen 1978; Schumpeter 1939). A country emitting an international currency can offset this deflation via trade deficits, but these necessarily harm some domestic groups. Democracies seem more adept at managing the social conflict generated among political and economic classes and, in particular, elites as they contend for the finite resources states use to ameliorate the costs of an enduring trade deficit. This is possibly why the very small universe of historical examples of countries supplying a genuine international currency has, to date, been populated by democracies, although we are cautious about generalizing from this small sample.

This chapter has four sections. First, we develop our framework for considering the domestic political requirements for running an international currency through a selective engagement with the literature. This framework highlights how an international currency emitter must generate new global demand through an interlocking set of political, financial and economic arrangements that are simultaneously acceptable at home and abroad. We next explore how the two historical cases of international currencies in the global economy — sterling and the dollar — reflect the successful domestic political institutional compromises emphasized by our framework. In the British gold standard case, new demand arose from rising real consumption by the working class. In the US fiat currency case, new demand came from a political economy that generated new internationally saleable assets, most importantly in the form of housing-debt-related securities. The third section then examines China and the RMB with respect to this framework, outlining how much of the literature on RMB internationalization overlooks the critical domestic elements for successful currency internationalization. Finally, we assess the extent to which the Chinese state is able to negotiate the domestic adjustment costs that internationalization will generate, and how it might evolve in order to meet these costs.

We argue that China presently is ill equipped to meet the trade-related costs of an international currency, and that it would have to reorganize its economy in ways that facilitate democratization in order to do so. An international currency emitter adds to global demand by putting its currency into global circulation. The resulting balance-of-payments deficits necessarily impose costs on some domestic groups. As we demonstrate below, during the pound sterling era agricultural interests in Britain suffered, but landowners and rural labour alike were compensated by the possibility of emigration (Offer 1991a; Schwartz 2010). In the US dollar era, unskilled manufacturing labour and other low-income groups lost ground, but were compensated through the possibility of rising home equity and cheaper consumer non-durables (Schwartz 2009). As in the British and US cases, export-oriented firms today dominate China's political economy, but to a much greater extent. Chinese state-owned enterprises are privileged within the financial system, penalizing domestic savers and suppressing domestic consumption growth. This helps to generate very large trade surpluses, which act as a drag on global demand. We concur with Pettis (2014), who points out that China currently subtracts from, rather than augments, global demand by running significant trade surpluses. Allowing a large volume of RMB to circulate internationally thus requires shifting demand from investment for export production to domestic consumption. This would add to global demand by substantially increasing China's net imports of consumer products and services. Such a shift, however, implies a reduction in the power of state elites and their associated state-owned enterprises (SOEs) and local government investment bodies (Hung 2013). This development would threaten the political status quo in China, and will thus be resisted by the Communist Party and indeed the Chinese state more generally. For this reason, we do not expect the internationalization of the RMB to proceed to the point where it genuinely rivals the US dollar as the world's pre-eminent international currency.

Internationalizing Currencies: International versus Domestic Considerations

Recent debate on international currencies has focused on potential challenges to US dollar hegemony and on the effects on the dollar stemming from the 2008-2009 financial crisis (see, for example, Helleiner and Kirshner 2009; Cohen and Benney 2014; Drezner 2014; Kirshner 2014). With a few exceptions (see, for example, Wang, Huang and Fan 2015), the terms of the debate focus almost entirely on the international conditions and foundations of currency internationalization even though they contemplate scenarios ranging from continued dollar dominance to a multipolar or leaderless international monetary system. The international conditions range from, among other things, the depth of financial markets (Drezner 2014) to multidimensional sources of power (Kirshner 2014; Norloff 2014; Stokes 2014) to the fundamental ability to print money and have it accepted by other official authorities through central bank networks (Helleiner 2014). These international foundations matter. But this focus ignores the role of domestic considerations in currency internationalization. To highlight these domestic foundations for establishing and then sustaining an international currency, we return to three early theorists who considered international currencies using a more integrated political economy framework: Robert Triffin, Charles Kindleberger and Susan Strange. We extrapolate from their thinking to outline the domestic negotiations and institutions required to successfully internationalize a currency.

Robert Triffin (1960) was among the first to note the growing contradiction between the role the US dollar played in the global economy of the early Bretton Woods period and its fixed link to gold. The critical point in Triffin's analysis is his recognition that regardless of who supplied an international currency, global monetary stocks had to expand to stave off global deflation. The need for growth in aggregate demand has been an enduring feature of the global political economy throughout the post-1945 period, even though the way an international currency facilitates this demand has changed over time. While such increases are necessary for global economic expansion to occur, the form of expansion is also necessarily political in inception and operation. Triffin thus elaborated what became known as the Triffin dilemma, whereby the expansion of the global money supply via the accumulation of dollar balances abroad facilitated the growth of other countries' reserves (and thus their ability to support economic growth), but at the cost of undermining future confidence in the dollar's value in relation to gold. For Triffin (1960, 63), in a fixed exchange rate regime, "further increases in dollar balances cannot be relied upon to contribute substantially and indefinitely to the solution of the world illiquidity problem." Triffin thought it illogical and problematic to have world liquidity, and by extension the entire international system of convertible currencies, rely on the outflow of a single dominant national currency. He preferred to internationalize the provision of world liquidity.[2]

Charles Kindleberger (1981) adds to this key insight by outlining the international role of New York as a global financial centre. During the Bretton Woods period, New York financial institutions provided intermediation by borrowing short domestically and lending long globally. Global demand, in other words, was not simply a function of the amount of imports a leading economy consumed, but could be mediated through the creation and distribution of financial assets (cf. Schwartz 2009). At the time Kindleberger wrote (the late 1960s), the balance of payments of the American economy consisted of trade and current account surpluses but very large capital account deficits; outflows of American foreign direct investment (FDI) and portfolio capital (along with military spending

---

2   Here Triffin agreed with John Maynard Keynes about the need for a banking union, but not
    with his solution (Triffin 1960, 90–93).

abroad) drove increases in global monetary stocks. This required intermediation via a globally oriented US network of financial institutions (Germain 1997). Where Triffin stressed the question of how to meet the demand for additional world liquidity, Kindleberger emphasized the channels through which that demand flowed.

Finally, Susan Strange (1971) connects the external demand for dollars to fund increases in global monetary stocks, or liquidity, to domestic politics. Shortly before the demise of the fixed link between gold and the dollar, she noted that the American economy was particularly vulnerable to the effects of international monetary shocks because of the way in which the central position of American capital markets in the global economy amplified those disturbances. Paradoxically, a top currency country (in our terms, the country that emits the world's main international currency) was more, not less, vulnerable to fluctuations in global demand (Strange 1971, 226-27).[3] Strange recognized that the central monetary problem of the 1920s and 1930s was the reduction in global demand generated by French and US trade surpluses (cf. Falkus 1971). This mirrored the persistent downward pressure on both agricultural and manufactured goods prices in the nineteenth century. The only way to boost liquidity and demand in the global economy, therefore, was for a dominant economy to run trade deficits. However, Strange also recognized that a country issuing the world's top currency needed to offset the domestic costs generated by the pressures associated with running such a currency.[4] She associated those costs primarily with welfare provision to low- and medium-skilled labour, whose jobs were displaced by rising imports (Strange 1971, 227). She also noted that these groups fared worse in the United States than in other Organisation for Economic Co-operation and Development (OECD) countries. As was the case with Britain and sterling, she argued that the United States could only run the world's top currency successfully if it cushioned marginal domestic groups from the dislocations they would face. This was the key political cost of running an international currency.

Triffin, Kindleberger and Strange lead us to recognize the link between an international currency and global demand, extend the means of providing demand to include financial intermediation and connect the provision of global demand (and its fluctuation) to domestic costs in the international currency emitter and the need somehow to ameliorate these costs. We consider these

---

3   Strange provided a typology of international currencies that included what she called top, master, negotiated and neutral currencies, depending on the degree of political control involved in their creation and use (Strange 1971, 217).

4   Strange (1971) ran against prevailing intellectual currents in identifying the sensitivity of US financial markets to international disturbances. Because these markets channelled such large investments abroad, they were acutely responsive to changes in the distribution of the costs and benefits associated with them, whether at home or abroad.

costs in terms of preserving or increasing purchasing power. By preserving or increasing its population's purchasing power, a state running an international currency helps to lift global aggregate demand while simultaneously producing domestic quiescence. We highlight the historical importance of two of the many policies that can affect a population's purchasing power while also adding to global demand: food policies and land- or home-ownership policies.[5] In this we go beyond these early theorists to isolate and explore some of the domestic political arrangements that we believe are central to enabling a state to run an international currency. In the nineteenth century, British free trade policies for cheap food were an historic instantiation of more general policies that lowered the cost of consumer non-durables for low-income groups, thus increasing their purchasing power. Similarly, in the twentieth century, US housing finance policy increased access to credit, and thus to purchasing power, for low- and middle-income groups in America.

Our framework recognizes the international foundations for the international use of a currency, namely convertibility, financial markets capable of performing complex financial transactions, a sufficient volume of the currency in global circulation and, finally, a state capable of negotiating the complex monetary and political arrangements that historically have constituted the international infrastructure of an international currency (cf. Cohen 1971). Our framework, however, further recognizes that a state that issues a genuine international currency must also be able to negotiate the domestic adjustment costs associated with having such a currency. The primary cost arises from the problem of maintaining or expanding purchasing power among the population of the country issuing that international currency. It is thus intimately connected to running either trade or current account deficits, which reduce employment via lost production opportunities or through intense pressure on firms to realize production efficiencies. Although the food and land- and home-ownership policies we single out worked in different ways, they both sought to counter the domestic economic problems generated by the deficits required to run an international currency.

During the nineteenth century, the expansion of free trade occurred simultaneously with the expansion of the franchise to the urban middle class in Britain. Later, defence of free trade (and thus sterling's international role)

---

5   There is a range of such policies that could be examined, including education policy (which impacts skills and social mobility), pensions (which maintains demand among the elderly, one of the poorest demographic sections of any population), income support policies (which reduce the drop in demand when people lose their jobs) and labour market policies (which support demand by matching people and skills with jobs and growth industries). For space purposes, however, we will restrict our remarks to the historically important food and home-ownership policies.

relied, in part, on the growing vote share of the urban working class, for whom imports provided roughly half of food consumption. Similarly, US housing policies sought, among other things, to construct and involve in the political process a mobilized middle class in the context of the Cold War. Later, housing policy became more responsive to the economic demands of newly enfranchised minority groups (Prasad 2012). We think that this suggests, but does not confirm, a relationship between the increased purchasing power needed to expand global demand on the one hand, and mass political support for policies supporting increased purchasing power on the other.

The Historical Record: Sterling, the Dollar and Their Lessons

This section examines the historical record of the British pound and the US dollar to identify how their roles intersect with the domestic foundations for an international currency. Externally, a highly competitive economy must eventually run a trade or balance-of-payments deficit sufficiently large to expand global liquidity if it wants its currency to help global demand expand rather than contract (Triffin 1960). Internally, this means that the state will have to mediate or remediate the distributional conflicts those deficits create among economic sectors and actors. Externally, a market deep and liquid enough to lubricate global trade and investment transactions implies considerable faith on the part of foreign actors in the financial assets that these transactions generate. In our terms, this "faith" validates the future value of these assets. There is also an internal element to this validation, which is the strength or security of property rights in domestic legislation. Thus, an international currency rests on two specific domestic infrastructural foundations that simultaneously address domestic and foreign concerns. The first foundation encompasses state institutions that can ameliorate the losses that trade deficits impose on vulnerable domestic groups. These deficits arise from the way that the international use of the top currency recycles purchasing power abroad. The second foundation encompasses secure property rights that can minimize risks for offshore holders of this recycled purchasing power. How did Britain and the United States construct these two institutional foundations?

During the nineteenth century, the simultaneous consolidation of the world's largest empire and the pre-eminence of British exports of goods, services and capital made the pound sterling the world's primary international currency (Hobsbawm 1975; Schwartz 1989; Langley 2002). Falling prices for British manufactured goods drove a near century of continual deflation under a nominal gold standard system. How did Britain maintain a stable global monetary order and underwrite a growing global economy? Global liquidity and therefore demand increased through the issuance of foreign public and private sterling securities in London, rather than via growth of the gold stocks notionally backing many currencies (de Cecco 1974; Schwartz 2010). Britain recycled its earlier trade surpluses as vendor finance for exports of capital goods to countries capable of supplying its raw material needs. For example, Britain loaned Argentina the cash needed to build a rail system that could then generate interest payments via shipping Argentine food to Britain. Britain's massive trade deficits thus paid for its equally massive current account surpluses, validating its eternal assets.

Food imports, which mushroomed after the repeal of the Corn Laws in 1846, were both the physical manifestation of asset validation and the hinge linking the domestic and international political compromises sustaining sterling. The rising and powerful class of industrial magnates obviously benefited from access to foreign markets. As early as Ricardo (1817), this class was conscious of the benefits that might flow from cheaper food for the growing proletarian population, and also of the connection between real wages, demand and deflation (Gambles 1999). But what about everyone else? British elites faced social unrest as nineteenth century economic expansion created an ever more militant working class (Carr 1946; Cox 1987; Eichengreen 2008). Yet this nascent labour movement did not contest free trade and the centrality of sterling, because falling prices for imported food — the "cheap loaf" — doubled real wages in the nineteenth century. Britain imported 60 percent of its calories by the end of the nineteenth century, and food constituted half of British imports (Offer 1991a, 82, 219). Under relentless import pressure, the price of wheat in Britain fell from 8.26 shillings per bushel in 1820 to 3.84 shillings in 1913 (Clark 2004). By contrast, agricultural imports and falling food prices did hurt rural owners and workers; land prices fell continuously throughout the nineteenth century (Offer 1991b). But a gradually enfeebled landed aristocracy exported their bodies to the colonies as an administrative elite (alongside their workers, who came as settlers), and their capital into urban real estate made increasingly more valuable by the export economy. Sterling's global position facilitated all of this.

The growing food imports that bought domestic social peace also bought external compliance. Rising volumes of raw materials exported to Britain and Europe generated capital gains for those politically influential landholders in the global periphery who could tap into global flows of capital and labour. These peripheral landholders and their bankers in turn parked their earnings in short-term deposits in London, making them short-term creditors on Britain, and thus doubly beholden to sterling. These interlocking domestic and international compromises were a critical political counterpart to the macroeconomic flows that sustained the international role of sterling during the nineteenth century (cf. Ingham 1984).

British property law also helped to secure sterling's position. Weber (1978, 890–92) dismissed British common law for its lack of systematization and calculability, but as he himself noted, the vitality of British capitalism implied some redeeming features for English common law. One of those surely was the spread of common law to Britain's formal colonies and, critically, to the United States. Roughly 70 percent of British investment — and thus sterling circulation — occurred inside the formal British Empire or the United States, and investors in the empire had a right of appeal to the Privy Council. Outside formal empires, the nineteenth century monetary and legal order had a lower degree of institutionalization. The operative international monetary networks were, for the most part, restricted to European financiers and central banks (see, for example, Flandreau 1997; van der Pijl 1998). Yet both British and local investors outside the formal empire showed a strong preference for chartering their firms and listing their debt in London, where it was subject to British law (Guy 1984). Relatively secure property rights assured that sterling remained a currency of choice, rather than necessity, or a top, rather than a master, currency if we adopt Strange's formulation (Strange 1971).

A similar although differently constituted set of interlocking political, economic and social arrangements provided the foundations for the role of the US dollar in the post-1945 global political economy. The American state undertook domestic interventions supporting the dollar's global role that dwarfed what the British state could undertake during the nineteenth century (Cox 1987). The US version of the cheap loaf was the New Deal and Great Society welfare state programs. These both responded to and reinforced significant shifts in electoral political coalitions by extending first welfare benefits and then also civil rights to marginalized and disenfranchised citizens. As with Britain, a few key programs sustaining domestic growth linked the internal and external arenas. Chief among these were deficit-funded military spending and the restructuring of the financial system to support broad home ownership. Both of these generated a tendency toward American balance-of-payments deficits (Houthakker and Magee 1969; Block 1977; Helleiner 1994).

Housing policy played the same role as free trade in agricultural products did for the British in the previous century. Global inflation up to the 1980s devalorized housing debt in the United States. Global disinflation after the 1980s flowed through the US housing finance system as debt refinancing (Seabrooke 2006; Schwartz 2009). Both processes freed up purchasing power for the middle class.

This cash flow supported US imports, which were paid for by generating and exporting dollar-denominated assets, including and perhaps especially mortgage-backed securities (MBS). US MBS constituted nine percent of the global public and private bond market in 2008, which is why an ostensibly domestic market-oriented, non-traded sector could influence the global financial system, and also why the "export" of those MBS could pay for ever-larger US trade deficits (IMF 2009). Those assets were the counterpart to the exports powering growth in key US allies, such as Japan and Germany, and "frenemies," such as China and the Organization for Petroleum Exporting Countries. During the 2000s, the United States accounted for between 50 percent and 80 percent of global trade deficits in any given year (ibid.).

The United States institutionalized the geopolitical compromises forged at Bretton Woods in two formal international organizations, and an array of official networks dominated by the American state. The networks running through the OECD, the Bank for International Settlements and the various "Gs" allowed the United States to assemble a range of contingent political coalitions to manage global economic problems. These organizations, and in particular the World Trade Organization, helped externalize US law to the rest of the world. But even without formal treaties, the power of domestically based institutions, for example, credit rating agencies (Sinclair 2005), gave the United States the same kind of influence over foreign firms that chartering in London conveyed for Britain in the previous century. While the United States has had its share of accounting scandals, minority shareholder rights remain better protected than elsewhere (Gourevitch and Shinn 2005), including China (see chapter 3 of this volume).

This schematic examination of the British and American cases of running an international currency illustrates the critical interlocking connections between their international and domestic foundations. In the nineteenth century, the British decision to open its market to agricultural imports harmed agricultural interests, but it had a larger positive impact on the purchasing power of the growing working classes being forced into factory jobs in the burgeoning textile and manufacturing sectors. This single policy stimulated aggregate demand in the global periphery, as countries such as Canada and Argentina expanded agricultural production for British and European markets, while at the same time placing more purchasing power in the hands of British working classes by dramatically reducing their food bills. Similarly, after World War II, the way in which the US balance of payments worked to stimulate aggregate global demand shifted from public aid and military expenditures (i.e., the Marshall Plan and spending on the Korean and Vietnam wars) to capital outflows and then, after 1980, to the creation and take-up abroad of a wide array of domestically generated financial assets. In the 1990s, a large part of these assets consisted of mortgage-related products linked to the operations of Fannie Mae and Freddie Mac, the government-sponsored entities mandated to make home ownership as widely available as possible to Americans. These policies decreased housing costs, and thus had the effect of increasing the purchasing power of lower- and middle-class Americans. US housing costs largely tracked general price inflation, unlike many other societies. While stagnant real wages after 1970 stemmed in part from the erosion of manufacturing capacity in the face of growing imports from Asia — in other words, from the cost of supplying an international currency — those imports also lowered the cost of consumer non-durables. US prices for consumer non-durables net of food and beverages rose 12 percent more slowly than all prices, from 1990 to 2014, and prices for apparel — virtually all of which is imported, and which constitutes a large portion of low-income groups' consumption — barely rose at all over those 25 years (US Bureau of Labor Statistics 2015).

In both the US and British cases, therefore, the weight of running an international currency was offset by domestic bargains that compensated vulnerable parts of the population. In the British case, food policy and sterling were intimately intertwined; in the US case, housing policy obviously had only domestic origins, but it is hard to believe that the Fed was oblivious to growing foreign acquisition of mortgage backed securities in the 2000s. As we shall see in the following section, this concern with domestic political bargains has yet to make itself felt in the growing literature on the internationalization of the RMB.

China and the RMB: The Intersection of Domestic and International Considerations

The small but growing literature on RMB internationalization runs parallel to the treatment of currency internationalization more generally. The primary focus is on the external economic constraints and functions binding a state wishing to internationalize its currency, rather than the domestic considerations we highlight. Jenkins and Zelenbaba (2012) are exemplary here. Their inquiry into the economic policies that China has adopted to further the international use of the RMB follows Cohen's (1971) early and functionalist taxonomy of roles played by any international currency.[6] Bowles and Wang (2013) provide a thorough but similarly categorized assessment of these policies, which they see originating in China's response to the vulnerability of its exports to fluctuations in the value of the dollar. For them, RMB internationalization is a protective policy that will be successful to the extent that a sustainable, long-term path toward liberalization of the capital account is achieved. Domestic considerations only surface in their analysis in connection to domestic capital markets, which are not yet deep or liquid enough to sustain full liberalization (Bowles and Wang 2013, 1375; Hung 2013).

Analyses of RMB internationalization that do address domestic political considerations do so in one of two ways. On one hand, questions connected to economic growth can foreshadow the kinds of distributional questions we highlight because the size of China's economy is directly related to the prospect of the RMB becoming an international currency. For example, Ito (2010) considers demographic determinants of China's future economic growth, which in turn centrally affects RMB internationalization. However, there is no hint in Ito's analysis of how demographic trends may affect the ability of China to contribute to (or continue subtracting from) global aggregate demand. On the other hand, the question of regime stability often enters the discussion, as when Cohen (2012) concludes his analysis of the future of the RMB by noting that political rigidity in China places important barriers in the way of successful internationalization. However, Cohen does not specify how this rigidity may operate. In effect, most of the literature on RMB internationalization is similar to that on the euro (see, for example, Thimann 2008) in that its primary focus concerns the international arrangements that characterize currency internationalization.

In contrast, as our discussion above suggests, the ability to project a domestic currency into the global economy as a genuine international currency rests on stable domestic political institutions that can generate new demand in global markets via trade deficits, ameliorate the costs that arise from those chronic trade deficits, and provide relatively more secure property rights for domestic and foreign investors than those investors can access elsewhere. China currently faces significant institutional weakness on all accounts. Three facts are central to understanding China's structural problems as well as the weaknesses of official efforts to respond to China's reliance on the US market for growth. First, China

---

6   This taxonomy (Cohen 1971) is a two by three matrix that illustrates the traditional functions of "international" money (to act as a medium of exchange, store of value and unit of account) as they are performed by private and official agents undertaking international monetary and financial transactions. This taxonomy is widely employed in the literature (see, for example, Bowles and Wang 2013; Cohen 2012; Helleiner 2008) and underlies Eichengreen's analysis in this volume (see chapter 3).

averaged trade surpluses of 4.7 percent of GDP from 1999 to 2008; these surpluses are now shrinking, but still averaged three percent from 2009 to 2013 (IMF World Economic Outlook database). Second, although the wage share of GDP is difficult to calculate precisely, the World Bank (2014) estimates that Chinese household final consumption fell from 46 percent of GDP in 2000 to 35 percent in 2008 — a level well below that of every other Asian developing economy (except Singapore, which also has systematic forced saving through its Central Provident Fund). The share of household consumption continued to decline through 2013 to 34.1 percent. Granted, in absolute terms, real household consumption nearly tripled from 1999 to 2013, and real GDP per capita nearly doubled from 1999 to 2008. But much of that gain went into infrastructure investment, real estate and the creation of export capacity. Third, exports jumped from roughly 20 percent to 39 percent of China's GDP from 1998 to 2008, far ahead of the rise in imports, and net exports accounted directly for one-third of growth before the 2008 crisis. In our terms, the Chinese economy has not been adding to aggregate global demand in line with the growth in its economy.

These three facts reflect the core institutional features of the Chinese political economy. China has a largely repressed financial system that captures and channels household savings toward large state-owned or quasi state-owned firms (Bowles and Wang 2013; Gruin 2013). Until recently, savers had almost no choice but to simply deposit money into the state-controlled banking system at essentially negative interest rates. Slightly better off savers could speculate in real estate, although this also tended to reinforce the economy's overreliance on investment for growth. State-owned firms and localities borrowed these savings at low or negative real interest rates. This allowed them to fund the productive and infrastructure investment that has powered Chinese economic growth.

These state-owned firms possess varying degrees of monopoly power, allowing them to systematically capture profits. The spectacular increase in Chinese savings (and thus current account surplus) from 37 percent of GDP in 2000 to over 50 percent in 2007 is largely explained by an increase in the state share of savings from 2.6 percent of GDP in 1999 to 21 percent in 2008 (Yu 2015, 46-47). Most of this is a function of retained earnings by SOEs. Rather than contributing to expanded domestic consumption, SOEs channelled those profits away from mass consumption (Hung 2013, 1355). They serviced their loans and plowed back profits not as increased wages or dividends, but rather as expanded productive capacity or real estate speculation, and most recently as a carry trade against the dollar. Close ties with the Chinese Communist Party assured that these firms were not punished for this mal-investment, perhaps because party elites and their families were skimming SOE profits (Barboza and LaFraniere 2012; Guevara et al. 2014). Some estimates suggest that insiders skimmed as much as US$1 trillion since 2009 (Anderlini 2014). Moreover, families in the top income decile accounted for a disproportionate share — almost 40 percent — of unoccupied housing held for speculative purposes (Chen and Wen 2014, 6). In any case, SOEs' privileged access to bank credit comes at the expense of the rest of the economy. Thus, while SOEs only provided 13 percent of employment in the late 2000s, they accounted for over half of non-agricultural fixed investment (Deer and Song 2011, 22).

China's repressed financial system reduces households' ability to consume, and thus to import. Roughly speaking, savers faced a three percent per year negative interest rate through the 2000s (Pettis 2014). At the same time, the dismantling of the "iron rice bowl" — the old system of employment-based social welfare — and the enforcement of *hukuo* regulations that link eligibility for the new local welfare state to one's registered domicile, put pressure on Chinese households to save large proportions of their income in an effort at self-insurance. The *hukuo* system means that the hundreds of millions of internal migrants in China lack access to the welfare state in the place where they currently work. Chinese households are thus "target savers," who increase their savings in response to low returns, rather than dissaving when interest rates fall. On the one hand, target saving means that China's banking system is flush with funds to lend to the SOEs mentioned above. This is one reason China has been able to mobilize so much savings for investment, and thus attain historically unprecedented rates of growth. On the other hand, target saving drastically reduces Chinese households' ability to consume, and by implication their ability to import.

Local government behaviour reinforces these tendencies toward over-saving and under-consumption. Local government does about 80 percent of state spending in China, but independently raises only about 30 percent of tax revenue. It thus relies on centrally raised and redistributed revenues. More than half of local government revenues come from taxes on local businesses, with another quarter coming from local governments' 25 percent share of the national value-added tax (Wong 2000; Wang and Herd 2013). Alone, this reliance on local businesses for revenue would incline local government to be solicitous of local firms' profitability. But three other factors magnify this orientation. First, perhaps most important, is the orientation to "GDP-ism" and "FDI-ism" — high rates of local growth were a major metric for promotion in the Communist Party until quite recently and, similarly, FDI represented essentially cost-free resources for local officials. Second, land sale and lease revenue contributes another 10 percent of locally controlled funds. Third, local government is relatively corrupt, encouraging collusion among local developers and local governments seeking revenues. Fourth, while land sale taxes represent only 10 percent of local government revenues, they represent discretionary funds for these same governments. These four factors motivate local government to over-borrow and over-develop local real estate, with local firms using access to local government-controlled banks to fund this development. This dovetails with the more general tendency toward over-investment and under-consumption, as we note below.

Finally, unlike either twentieth-century America or nineteenth-century Britain, China also lacks a relatively robust system for guaranteeing property rights (Cohen 2014). Indeed, the entire "Bretton Woods II" argument is premised on the idea that China holds US Treasury bonds as a form of collateral to guarantee that rich country investment in China will not be expropriated (Dooley, Folkerts-Landau and Garber 2004). Chinese corporate accounts are also hardly transparent. Numerous Chinese firms have been delisted from Western exchanges, and the US Securities and Exchange Commission has punished the China-based arms of the big accounting firms for lax auditing standards (Scannell and Bond 2012). Local justice systems in China are susceptible to political and extra-political interference. These conditions of course pertain to many emerging market economies, but these countries are not trying to internationalize their currency. We are not suggesting here that US jurisprudence and accounting standards are without blemish, as the Enron, WorldCom and Madoff scandals show. But as with the debate about English common law in the nineteenth century, the issue is not whether a given system of law and property rights is perfect. The issue is whether it is relatively better than existing alternatives.

China's political economy is thus structurally biased toward the creation of overcapacity and excess exports. This makes it difficult for China to transform the RMB into an international currency, because China cannot supply the world with enough RMB to grow global demand. Furthermore, China limits foreign capital inflows that might accumulate RMB-denominated assets. All other things being equal, China's trade surpluses do exactly the opposite of what the pound and dollar systems did in their respective eras, subtracting from global demand rather than expanding it (Pettis 2014). China's growth certainly has increased the demand for raw material and component parts imports to China. On the other side though, the flood of cheap Chinese exports depresses production in both rich and emerging markets. Trade surpluses reflect a lack of domestic demand that would otherwise absorb local production.[7] If Chinese consumers' purchasing power were higher, China's export surplus would fall as those consumers imported more tourism, health care, education, environmental

---

7   The obvious and perhaps only exceptions to this rule are surpluses by raw materials exporters, who, in essence, are transforming an illiquid asset into liquid assets and, thus, need a surplus in order to accomplish that transformation.

protection, and so on. Externally, Chinese competition displaces manufacturing employment that almost always pays higher wages than do service sector jobs (Autor, Dorn and Hanson 2013). This decreases purchasing power and thus global demand. As with US trade surpluses in the 1920s (Falkus 1971), China's efforts to recycle that demand — to recycle its trade surpluses — took the form of lending to the United States via the purchase of Treasury and agency debt. Rather than internationalizing the RMB, this lending merely reinforces the US dollar's pre-eminent position. Even H. F. Hung (2013), who argues that the US dollar is in decline, acknowledges that China is in something of a dollar trap on account of its large dollar-denominated asset holdings.[8]

China's political economy and its relatively weak property rights intersect in ways that will make durable domestic compromises to support an international currency difficult to attain. If we stylize the situation somewhat, the current normal functioning of the Chinese political economy looks something like this: highly productive small and medium enterprises run by non-party affiliated families and large foreign transnational firms utilize labour-intensive production processes to generate consumer non-durables for export. Export revenues are parked in the central bank, which issues RMB bonds to soak up the RMB it issues to buy dollars. Thrifty families flood the financial system with savings, and the state-owned banking system relends those funds to SOEs at interest rates that encourage those SOEs and, indirectly, local government financing vehicles to overinvest in infrastructure that cannot recover its cost of capital, and to speculate in real estate that similarly cannot generate enough cash flow to service the debt incurred in its construction. Overcapacity in heavy industry and empty apartments are the physical manifestation of reduced household consumption. As of 2014, Chinese researchers estimated that one-fifth of urban housing units were vacant, while real estate construction might account for one-sixth of GDP (Fung 2014). Much like the United States in the 1920s and early 2000s, actors in the Chinese economy are building housing for people whose incomes will not allow them buy that housing at a price sufficient to pay back the cost of construction.

In that context, the trade deficits that would accompany an effort to internationalize the RMB even as a reserve currency would cause considerable domestic financial distress and thus encounter considerable political opposition. On one hand, shifting resources to consumption would reduce both the credit available to overleveraged firms and the demand for heavy industrial and construction inputs. Shifting resources to households also implies a reduction in

---

8   China's US dollar recycling has also put China in the position of lending money at very low
     interest rates to America, which returned the favour by investing globally at high rates of
     return (Schwartz 2009).

retained earnings for state-owned firms. Reduced demand and earnings would put even more pressure on firms that need to roll over large existing loans. At the same time, state-owned firms were engaging in a large cross-border carry trade, indicating a lack of profitable investment opportunities and a search for greater yield (Yu 2013; Schwartz 2015). On the other hand, as Michael Pettis (2014) has long argued, shifting income toward lower income strata in China necessarily involves shifting income away from elites and the enterprises they control. Even reforms that merely raise the cost of capital to privileged firms reduce their income, given the degree of subsidy built into current lending and deposit rates. In the United States, elites operating through a democratic system only conceded the redistributive effects built into the public pension, health and housing policies that supported the dollar's international role when they were faced with depression and then a hot and a cold war. China does not yet face quite this scale of crisis. While redistribution in the United States after 1945 did not "cause" internationalization of the dollar, it made internationalization politically acceptable to domestic groups that experienced losses from the dollar's new global role.

Conclusion

A critical part of an international currency's political economy is constituted via the domestic institutions and policies a state uses to negotiate sustainable social trade-offs around the costs of supplying international demand. An international currency emitter adds to global demand by putting its currency into global circulation. The resulting balance-of-payments deficits necessarily impose costs on some domestic groups. Those costs are the domestic jobs and income lost from running the current account deficits needed to supply the global economy with demand and an expanding money supply. In the only two historical cases of an international currency, a strong degree of democratic politics is associated with the elaboration and institutionalization of these trade-offs. We recognize that linking currency internationalization with democratization is a contested claim, and we cannot say at this point whether democracy is a necessary condition for internationalization. However, this relationship must surely be a fit subject for future research given the striking connection between the costs we have identified with running an international currency and the political trade-offs required to meet those costs. Of course, neither Britain in the nineteenth century nor the United States in the twentieth century had full suffrage. But a large part of the population could vote and was mobilized by elites contending (at least in part) over trade and monetary policy. Elites in both countries offered concessions to lower income groups and to some losing business sectors. These concessions were dual use — they both bought mass compliance and secured an essential foundation for running an international currency. In the British case, free trade around food imports brought rising real wages to the employed part of the working class while allowing Britain's debtors to service their loans with sterling. In the US case, suburbanization helped expand the domestic economy while generating financial assets (MBS) that could be sold offshore. This gave the US middle class rising living standards, plugged the gap in the US balance of payments and helped the global economy grow (Seabrooke 2006; Schwartz 2015).

The challenge today for China and its elites is how to meet these costs. Reorganizing the Chinese economy in ways that facilitate internationalization also opens the door to democratization. Party elites, state-owned enterprises and local government elites dominate China's political economy. All stand to lose from deregulation and de-statization of a financial system that currently subsidizes investments whose profits they harvest. Indeed, the cynical and bottom-up phrase *guo jin min tui* — roughly "state advances, private sector retreats" — has replaced the older top-down policy slogan of "grasp the large, let go of the small." The shortfall in domestic demand that arises from Party and SOE control over profits produces large trade surpluses and thus helps China become internationally competitive, but this narrow interest also means that China's relatively poor citizens subsidize not only their own domestic elites, but relatively rich Americans as well. While a political base for reversing these perverse subsidies exists, it requires activating and mobilizing a mass public. Quite how entrenched elites will voluntarily give up their rents in the absence of countervailing political forces, and substantially expand political participation that will challenge their own privileged position, is for us the critical question to ask about RMB internationalization.

We should note, however, that there are historical parallels in the rest of developing Asia. Both Korea and Taiwan had state-owned banking sectors that loaned to industrial firms at essentially negative interest rates while paying savers even lower rates on deposits. Like China, these countries had demand shortfalls, although Korea periodically had trade deficits in high-growth periods. For both, the shift away from a wholly export-oriented economy occurred in parallel with the end of martial law or authoritarian government and a shift toward higher consumption. The subsequent democratic political regimes of the 1990s reinforced these trends, with Korea experiencing a credit-driven consumer economy rather than an investment economy in the 2000s. As in China, democratization threatened significant entrenched interests. A combination of external pressure and internal pressure — unionized assembly line workers in Korea, the multitude of ethnic Taiwanese small business owners in Taiwan — overcame the residual interest of big firms for subsidized credit. Nevertheless, we believe that the pressure on elite interests in China that would accompany RMB internationalization would be significantly greater, as the consumption deficit in China is larger than was the case in Korea or Taiwan.

Thus, in the absence of something like the depression and war that induced change in America, or the unprecedented conditions that permitted British imperial expansion, we do not expect the internationalization of the RMB to proceed to the point where it genuinely rivals the US dollar as the world's pre-eminent international currency. This degree of internationalization would threaten the political status quo in China. Unless Party elites can find a way to discipline their own membership and shift them toward domestically oriented production and a smaller share of what will still be a growing economy, the Communist Party and indeed the Chinese state more generally will place a clear limit on these changes. Democratization and expanded domestic consumption are ultimately intertwined.

In the nineteenth century, British elites used a steady expansion of the franchise to buy off opposition to the equally steady internationalization of the British economy. Current Chinese policy aims at precisely this process. Can China's Communist Party do the same thing in the face of even greater domestic elite opposition than that which British reformist elites confronted, and without even the limited experience of democracy present in mid-nineteenth century Britain? The fact that the Xi administration must carry out its reform agenda via a selective anti-corruption campaign suggests considerable difficulty, as compared with Britain.[9] Similarly, the reorientation of US international monetary policy (and domestic housing policy) occurred with the enormous tailwind of the 1930s and its expanded social and political mobilization. Given this, the optimistic scenario for RMB internationalization is that it becomes something like the euro: an invoicing currency that also circulates in China's backyard. Yet, despite China's enormous economic heft — on a purchasing power parity basis it is almost as large as the US economy — the RMB has barely attained the status of a regional currency. Although the RMB is now the second-largest currency for denominating letters of credit in transactions through the global Society for Worldwide Interbank Financial Telecommunication (SWIFT) network, its share is roughly nine percent versus 90 percent for the US dollar. Moreover, fully 80 percent of those transactions occur among Chinese and Hong Kong entities. The RMB thus barely functions as a regional currency for China's periphery (Cohen and Benney 2014; SWIFT 2015). This is consistent with the findings in Wang, Huang and Fan (2015), who model the effects of domestic

---

9   Some analysts, notably David Shambaugh (2015), suggest that this process of reform might well lead to a Soviet-style crack-up of the Party.

institutional strength on international use of a given currency. By contrast, the pessimistic scenario involves a credit crash in China as SOEs pour ever-larger sums of borrowed money into unremunerative projects. It is hard to see how China and Chinese consumers could politically accept the costs of current account deficits in that situation, given the consequences of slower growth of incomes and employment. The optimistic scenario may describe what China's elites desire. But it is far from a scenario in which the RMB displaces the dollar.

Authors' Note

We would like to thank Domenico Lombardi and Hongying Wang for extending an invitation to contribute to this volume. We would also like to acknowledge the valuable research assistance of Courtney Lockhart, and the useful comments provided by three reviewers. All errors and omissions remain ours.

Works Cited

Anderlini, J. 2014. "China Has 'Wasted' $6.8tn in Investment, Warn Beijing Researchers." *Financial Times*, November 27. www.ft.com/intl/cms/s/0/002a1978-7629-11e4-9761-00144feabdc0.html.

Autor, D. H., D. Dorn and G. H. Hanson. 2013. "The China Syndrome: Local Labor Market Effects of Import Competition in the United States." *The American Economic Review* 103 (6): 2121–68.

Barboza, D. and S. LaFraniere. 2012. "'Princelings' in China Use Family Ties to Gain Riches." *New York Times*, May 17. www.nytimes.com/2012/05/18/world/asia/china-princelings-using-family-ties-to-gain-riches.html.

Block, F. 1977. *The Origins of International Economic Disorder*. Berkeley, CA: University of California Press.

Bowles, P. and B. Wang. 2013. "Renminbi Internationalization: A Journey to Where?" *Development and Change* 44 (6): 1365–85.

Carr, E. H. 1946. *The Twenty Years Crisis*. London: Macmillan.

Chen, K. and Y. Wen. 2014. "The Great Housing Boom of China." Federal Reserve Bank of St. Louis Working Paper 2014-022A, August. http://research.stlouisfed.org/wp/2014/2014-022.pdf.

Clark, G. 2004. "The Price History of English Agriculture, 1209–1914." *Research in Economic History* 22: 41–124.

Cohen, B. 1971. *The Future of Sterling as an International Currency*. London: Macmillan.

———. 2012. "The Yuan Tomorrow? Evaluating China's Currency Internationalisation Strategy." *New Political Economy* 17 (3): 361–71.

———. 2014. "Will History Repeat Itself? Lessons for the Yuan." Asian Development Bank Institute Working Paper No. 453.

Cohen, B. and T. Benney. 2014. "What Does the International Currency System Really Look Like?" *Review of International Political Economy* 21 (5): 1017–41.

Cox, R. W. 1987. *Production, Power and World Order*. New York, NY: Columbia University Press.

De Cecco, M. 1974. *Money and Empire*. Oxford: Blackwell.

Deer, L. and L. Song. 2012. "China's Approach to Rebalancing: A Conceptual and Policy Framework." *China & World Economy* 20 (1): 1–26.

Dooley, M. P., D. Folkerts-Landau and P. Garber. 2004. "The Revived Bretton Woods System." *International Journal of Finance & Economics* 9 (4): 307–13.

Drezner, D. 2014. "The System Worked: Global Economic Governance during the Great Recession." *World Politics* 66 (1): 123–64.

Eichengreen, B. 2008. *Globalizing Capital*, 2nd ed. Princeton, NJ: Princeton University Press.

Falkus, M. E. 1971. "United States Economic Policy and the 'Dollar Gap' of the 1920s." *The Economic History Review* 24 (4): 599–623.

Flandreau, M. 1997. "Central Bank Cooperation in Historical Perspective: A Sceptical View." *Economic History Review* 50 (4): 736–63.

Fung, E. 2014. "More Than 1 in 5 Homes in Chinese Cities Are Empty, Survey Says." *The Wall Street Journal*, June 11. www.wsj.com/articles/more-than-1-in-5-homes-in-chinese-cities-are-empty-survey-says-1402484499.

Gambles, A. 1999. *Protection and Politics: Conservative Economic Discourse, 1815–852*. London: Boydell & Brewer Ltd.

Germain, R. 1997. *The International Organization of Credit*. Cambridge, UK: Cambridge University Press.

Germain, R. and H. Schwartz. 2014. "The Political Economy of Failure: The Euro as an International Currency." *Review of International Political Economy* 21 (5): 1095–122.

Gourevitch, P. A. and J. Shinn. 2005. *Political Power and Corporate Control: The New Global Politics of Corporate Governance*. Princeton, NJ: Princeton University Press.

Gruin, J. 2013. "Asset or Liability? The Role of the Financial System in the Political Economy of China's Rebalancing." *Journal of Current Chinese Affairs* 42 (4): 73–104.

Guevara, M., G. Ryle, A. Olesen, M. Cabra, M. Hudson, and C. Giesen. 2014. "Leaked Records Reveal Offshore Holdings of China's Elite." *International Consortium of Investigative Journalists*, January 21. www.icij. org/offshore/leaked-records-reveal-offshore-holdings-chinas-elite.

Guy, D. J. 1984. "Dependency, the Credit Market, and Argentine Industrialization, 1860–1940." *Business History Review* 58 (4): 532–61.

Helleiner, E. 1994. *States and the Re-emergence of Global Finance*. Ithaca, NY: Cornell University Press.

———. 2014. *The Status Quo Crisis*. Oxford, UK: Oxford University Press.

Helleiner, E. and J. Kirshner, eds. 2009. *The Future of the Dollar*. Ithaca, NY: Cornell University Press.

Hobsbawm, E. 1975. *The Age of Capital*. London: Weidenfeld and Nicolson.

Houthakker, H. S. and S. P. Magee. 1969. "Income and Price Elasticities in World Trade.' *The Review of Economics and Statistics* 51 (2): 111–125.

Hung, H. F. 2013. "China: Saviour or Challenger of the Dollar Hegemony?" *Development and Change* 44 (6): 1341–61.

IMF. 2009. *Global Financial Stability Report*. October 2009. Washington, DC: IMF.

Ingham, G. K. 1984. *Capitalism Divided? The City and Industry in British Social Development*. London, UK: Macmillan.

Ito, T. 2010. "China as Number One. How about the Renminbi?" *Asian Economic Policy Review* 5 (2): 249–76.

Jenkins, P. and J. Zelenbaba. 2012 "Internationalization of the Renminbi: What It Means for the Stability and Flexibility of the International Monetary System." *Oxford Review of Economic Policy* 28 (3): 512–31.

Kindleberger, C. 1981. *International Money: A Collection of Essays*. Boston, MA: George Allen & Unwin.

Kirshner, J. 2014. *American Power after the Financial Crisis*. Ithaca, NY: Cornell University Press.

Langley, P. 2002. *World Financial Orders*. London: Routledge.

Norloff, C. 2014. "Dollar Hegemony: A Power Analysis." *Review of International Political Economy* 21 (5): 1042–70.

Offer, A. 1991a. *The First World War: An Agrarian Interpretation*. Oxford: Oxford University Press.

———— 1991b. "Farm Tenure and Land Values in England, c. 1750–1950." *Economic History Review* 44 (1): 1–20.

Pettis, M. 2014. *The Great Rebalancing: Trade, Conflict, and the Perilous Road Ahead for the World Economy*. Princeton, NJ: Princeton University Press.

Prasad, M. 2012. *The Land of too Much: American Abundance and the Paradox of Poverty*. Cambridge, MA: Harvard University Press.

Ricardo, D. 1817. *On The Principles of Political Economy and Taxation*. London, UK: John Murray.

Scannell, K. and S. Bond. 2012. "Audit Firms Face SEC China Crackdown." *Financial Times*, December 3, www.ft.com/cms/s/0/6ee44ace-3d6d-11e2-9f35-00144feabdc0.html.

Schumpeter, J. A. 1939. *Business Cycles*. 2 vols. New York, NY: McGraw-Hill.

Schwartz, H. 1989. *In the Dominions of Debt: Historical Perspectives on Dependent Development*. Ithaca, NY: Cornell University Press.

————. 2009. *Subprime Nation: American Power, Global Finance and the Housing Bubble*. Ithaca, NY: Cornell University Press.

————. 2010. *States versus Markets*, 3rd ed. New York, NY: St. Martin's Press.

Schwartz, H. 2015 (forthcoming). "Banking on the FED: QE123 and the Rebalancing of the World Economy." *New Political Economy*.

Seabrooke, Leonard. 2006. *The Social Sources of Financial Power*. Ithaca, NY: Cornell University Press.

Shambaugh, D. 2015. "The Coming Chinese Crack-up." *The Wall Street Journal*, March 6, www.wsj.com/articles/the-coming-chinese-crack-up-1425659198.

Sinclair, T. J. 2005. *The New Masters of Capital: American Bond Rating Agencies and the Politics of Creditworthiness*. Ithaca, NY: Cornell University Press.

Stokes, D. 2014. "Achilles' Deal: Dollar Decline and US Grand Strategy after the Crisis." *Review of International Political Economy* 21 (5): 1071–94.

Strange, S. 1971. "The Politics of International Currencies." *World Politics* 23 (2): 215–31.

SWIFT. 2015. "RMB Strengthens Its Position as the Second Most Used Currency for Documentary Credit Transactions." www.swift.com/ about_swift/shownews?param_dcr=news.data/en/swift_com/2015/PR_ RMB_second_most_used_currency.xml.

Thimann, C. 2008. "Global Roles of Currencies." *International Finance* 11 (3): 211–45.

Triffin, R. 1960. *Gold and the Dollar Crisis: The Future of Convertibility.* New Haven, CT: Yale University Press.

US Bureau of Labor Statistics. 2015. Consumer Price Index for All Urban Consumers: All Items [CPIAUCSL], Consumer Price Index for All Urban Consumers: Apparel [CPIAPPSL], and Consumer Price Index for All Urban Consumers: Nondurables Less Food and Beverages [CUSR0000SANL11]. FRED, Federal Reserve Bank of St. Louis. https://research.stlouisfed.org/fred2. March 5.

Van der Pijl, K. 1998. *Transnational Classes and International Relations.* London, UK: Routledge.

Wang, D., Y. Huang and G. Fan. 2015. "Will the Renminbi Become a Reserve Currency?" *China Economic Journal* 8 (1): 55–73.

Wang, X. and R. Herd. 2013. "The System of Revenue Sharing and Fiscal Transfers in China." OECD Economics Department Working Papers No. 1030. Paris: OECD.

Weber, M. 1978. *Economy and Society: An Outline of Interpretive Sociology,* 2 vols., edited by G. Roth and C. Wittich. Berkeley, CA: University of California Press.

World Bank. 2014. World DataBank. Washington, DC: World Bank Group. http://databank.worldbank.org/data/home.aspx.

Wong, C. P. 2000. "Central-local Relations Revisited: The 1994 Tax-sharing Reform and Public Expenditure Management in China." *China Perspectives* 31: 52–63.

Veblen, T. 1978. *The Theory of Business Enterprise.* Rutgers, NJ: Transaction Publishers.

Yu, Y. 2013. "China's Capital Account Liberalization." Australian National University, Pacific Trade and Development Working Paper Series, Paper No. 36-07, Canberra.

———. 2015. "Understanding China's External Imbalances." *China Economic Journal* 8 (1): 40–54.

Part Two

China's Financial
Internationalization

6

Constraints of Currency Intervention on China's Monetary Policy

Hailong Jin, Domenico Lombardi and Coby Hu

Since the 2008 global financial crisis (GFC), the Chinese government has emphasized financial reforms at the centre of its agenda and has taken steps to internationalize China's financial markets in response to the changing dynamics of the international monetary system (Zhou 2009; Dorrucci and McKay 2011). The ongoing financial reform in China can be divided into three parts: domestic market deregulation, capital account liberalization and renminbi (RMB) internationalization. While the normal sequence of financial reform would typically entail deregulation of the domestic financial market first, liberalization of the capital account next, and then internationalization of the currency, instead, "China, uniquely, reversed this conventional order by launching an ambitious currency internationalization program in 2009 despite maintaining draconian capital controls and heavily regulated domestic interest rates" (Kroeber 2013, 1).

This chapter explores some issues behind RMB internationalization for the People's Bank of China (PBoC) by focusing on the costs associated with its currency intervention policy in the foreign exchange market. The currency intervention policy relates to Beijing's goal of maintaining RMB exchange rate stability. The PBoC achieves this goal by issuing RMB funds outstanding for foreign exchange, or FX funds to purchase foreign exchanges in order to sustain the undervalued RMB against key currencies, such as the US dollar. The opposite would occur if the RMB faced depreciation pressures. However, such a policy is not without risks and costs.

To better understand some of these risks and costs, the chapter explores a two-country (China and the United States), two-period currency intervention model to investigate the RMB exchange rate dynamics and the costs associated with the PBoC's exchange rate stability regime. We assume that China, the foreign exchange intervening country, adopts a sterilization policy to mitigate the effects on the domestic money supply from foreign assets purchases or sales in the first period. The international currency issuer, the United States, issues special bonds to retrieve the PBoC's foreign exchange back to US circulation. In the second period, however, China substantially revalues its currency and achieves external balance in terms of US dollars. We assume price levels remain fixed for both countries in the benchmark model.

Drawing from the model, we first show the dependency of the yuan interest rate on the US interest rate following the interest parity condition. We show that the US interest rate effect on the RMB interest rate can be represented by China's current account (CA) elasticity to its exchange rate. Here, a higher CA elasticity to the exchange rate implies that the Chinese and US economies are more closely connected. Based on historical data, it can be inferred that China's CA elasticity is large enough that a US interest rate effect is positive. In other words, the Chinese interest rate tends to move together with the US rate, and in the same direction.

The chapter further show that monetary neutrality does not hold well in the Sino-US economy as a whole under the PBoC's currency intervention policy, as monetary policies in these countries have long-term effects. Specifically, a contractionary monetary policy in China and an expansionary monetary policy in the United States will expedite China's economic development, while an expansionary monetary policy in China and a contractionary monetary policy in the United States will impede it. The shrinking output from a domestic monetary expansion implies China will also face inflation risks. Thus, the PBoC's monetary policy becomes ineffective for the purpose of stimulating the economy.

The results also show that excessive depreciation or appreciation of the yuan from the balanced exchange rate generates a large wealth transfer effect from China to the United States.[1] The US dollar enjoys a "premium" by serving as the reserve currency, which is generated when the PBoC deliberately reduces its government credit by sterilizing its US-denominated foreign assets. Similarly, we show there is a high cost for the PBoC to continue its currency intervention policy, stemming from the yuan's appreciation against the US dollar, the primary denomination of its reserve assets. In fact, earlier studies estimated this cost to

---

1   The balanced exchange rate in the model is the exchange rate that equates the CA to 0.

vary between US$180 billion (Jin and Choi 2014) to US$238 billion (Gagnon, Lardy and Borst 2011) for 2011.

These results are based on the assumption that China uses a sterilization approach for currency intervention. In turn, the United States also issues bonds to China to nullify the influence of the PBoC's mounting foreign assets on each country's domestic money supply. The results can be reversed if China does not sterilize or the United States does not expand its money supplies.

The chapter is organized as follows. The second section introduces the background of China's currency intervention and sterilization policies. The third section constructs the associated benchmark framework of the exchange rate overshooting model as well as the external constraint to the PBoC's balance-of-payment account. The application of the interest parity condition and monetary neutrality is explored in the fourth and fifth sections, respectively. The PBoC's losses due to its currency intervention policy are further investigated in the sixth section. Finally, the seventh section concludes.

Background: China's Currency Intervention and Sterilization

The PBoC's currency intervention policy refers to the systematic purchase, or sale, of foreign exchange currency to stabilize the RMB external value around a target level. Historically, this policy was implemented through the issuance of yuan, either by selling the PBoC's assets or by borrowing in the local markets to purchase foreign assets (Gagnon, Lardy and Borst 2011). As the extra yuan in circulation can induce inflationary pressures on the RMB, the PBoC conducts a "sterilization" policy to negate these pressures. Therefore, the PBoC can pursue exchange rate stability by first intervening in the foreign exchange market and then address the resulting inflationary pressures via monetary sterilization.

Such policies have generally been controversial. In principle, currency intervention may represent an indirect tax subsidy for China's export-oriented firms, thus contributing to export-oriented growth. In practice, the currency intervention policy required large purchases of foreign assets, such as US Treasury bills, from the PBoC. This has led to the accumulation of the largest foreign exchange reserves in the world valued at over US$4 trillion in 2014. For comparison, Japan, the second-largest holder of foreign reserves, boasts about US$1 trillion, while the United States holds a mere US$0.12 trillion, according to the International Monetary Fund (IMF).

The large accumulation of foreign reserves is not without risks and costs, however. The immediate risk associated with the PBoC's foreign reserve accumulation is the foreign exchange risk. Due to the continued appreciation of the RMB, its foreign reserve assets have symmetrically depreciated in value since its assets are denominated in other currencies. This chapter focuses on the direct as well as the indirect costs related to the PBoC's monetary policy. Before doing so, however, we briefly discuss China's currency intervention and sterilization policies.

China's Currency Intervention

The Chinese mainland initiated its currency intervention policy in 1994. Prior to that, the RMB was under a dual-track system where both an official rate, determined mostly by trade-related transactions, and a swap market rate existed. In 1994, the PBoC closed the swap market and began to manage its currency by moving the official exchange rate to the then prevailing swap market rate. It then informally pegged the RMB to the US dollar in order to integrate both markets (Kanomori and Zhao 2006). Under this currency exchange policy, all domestic firms and individuals were required to sell their foreign exchange earnings to banks and were only permitted to purchase the foreign exchange needed for trade transactions (Neftci, Yuan and Zu 2007; Goldstein and Lardy 2009).

Some experts point out that by keeping a fixed exchange rate, China has gained an unfair competitive advantage in the global market since this rate was below the competitive, equilibrium value (McKinnon and Schnabl 2009; Cheung, Chinn and Qian 2012; Bonatti and Fracasso 2013). From 1994 to 2005, the Chinese government maintained a relatively stable RMB exchange rate, trading at around RMB 8.3 per US dollar, despite a burgeoning CA surplus. However, in 2005, the PBoC overturned the previous policy by allowing the yuan to "float" within a small margin against a basket of currencies. Since then, the RMB has appreciated steadily against the US dollar at around three to five percent per year.

Figure 1 illustrates China's CA surpluses and exchange rates from 1994 to 2013. China's CA surplus was only around one percent of GDP in 1994. It increased to 2.5 percent in 2002 after China joined the World Trade Organization (WTO), and then hit its historical high of US$420.6 billion, about 10 percent of GDP, in 2008. Following the GFC, China's CA surplus dropped to US$243.3 billion,

Figure 1: China's CA Surpluses and Exchange Rates

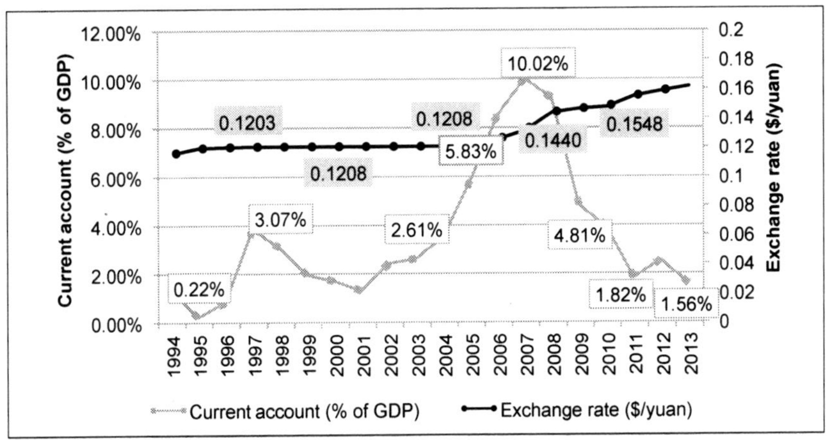

Source: The State Administration of Foreign Exchange (SAFE) and CEIC.
Note: The CA is measured in billions of nominal US dollars. The exchange rate is the nominal exchange rate between the US dollar and the yuan in terms of the dollar value of one yuan.

US$136.1 billion and US$215.4 billion, which correspond to 3.9 percent, 1.8 percent and 2.5 percent of GDP for 2010, 2011 and 2012, respectively. Given the large magnitude of these figures, China's exchange rate policies came under increasing scrutiny.

China's Sterilization to Foreign Assets

To keep the RMB from appreciating, each year the PBoC issued a large amount of RMB funds to purchase foreign exchange currencies (FX funds). At the same time, the Chinese government adopted a contractionary monetary regime to deal with the expected inflation from the FX funds issuance. Figure 2 illustrates the proportions of the FX funds (FX_t) in China's monetary base or reserve money (M_t) and FX funds (FX_t) from 1994 to 2014. The FX funds-to-monetary-base ratio was only 25 percent in 1994. It then increased steadily, first reaching 49 percent in 2002 and then nearly 100 percent in 2005. This points to high sterilization costs originating from foreign exchange purchases for the PBoC. In 2006, the PBoC began to rely on the reserve requirement ratio (RRR) — the fraction of customer deposits or capital that must be held as reserves at the central bank — to sterilize currency intervention. Figure 3 shows that, since 2006, the RRR has nearly tripled for large financial institutions and more than doubled for medium and small institutions.

Figure 2: Proportions of FX Funds to Monetary Base, 1994–2014

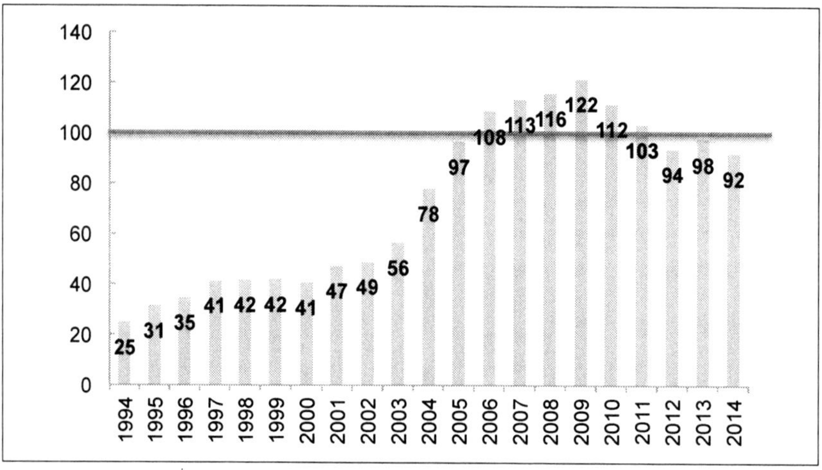

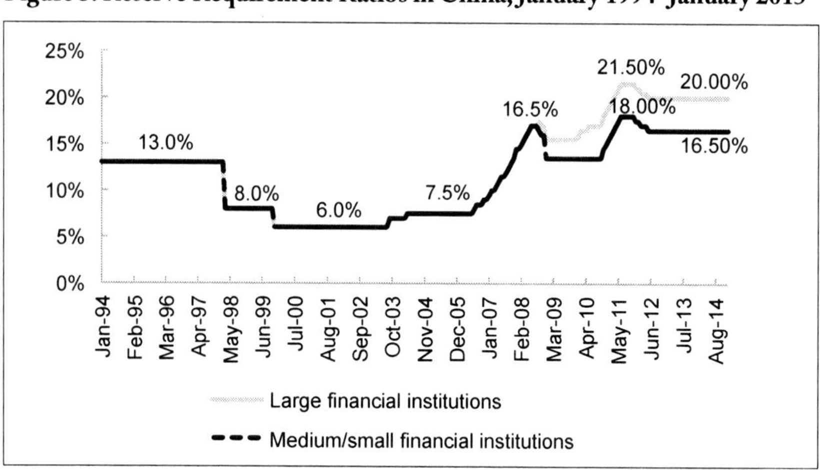

Source: Authors' calculations; PBoC.

Figure 3: Reserve Requirement Ratios in China, January 1994–January 2015

Source: PBoC.

External Constraint to the Balance-of-Payment Account

In this section, we build a two-country, two-period currency intervention model to investigate the external constraints of China's macroeconomic policies in the rest of the chapter.

CA Surplus Function

Assume that China is an open Keynesian economy, where prices are rigid and output is less than the full potential output, and that China trades only with the United States. The US dollar is an international currency that is widely used to denominate international contracts, while the RMB, with the unit yuan (¥), can only be used for domestic circulation. The PBoC pursues exchange rate stability through currency intervention policy. Due to the large income gap, the Chinese output is under its full potential in the Sino-US economy, and any changes in the dollar–yuan exchange rate affect its GDP, Y_{CN}.

Let $X(E_{S/¥}, Y_{US})$ be China's exports in dollars and $q(E_{S/¥}, Y_{CN})$ be its imports in yuan in the initial period, where $E_{S/¥}$ is the indirect exchange rate, i.e., the dollar price of yuan, and Y_{US} and Y_{CN} are GDPs of the United States and China, respectively.

China's GDP, expressed in yuan, can be defined as:

$$Y_{CN} = C + I + G + S_S / E_{S/¥},$$

where S_S is China's CA surplus in dollars; C, I and G are domestic consumption, investment and government spending respectively, all measured in yuan.

If we write China's GDP as a function of its CA surplus in yuan, i.e., $Y_{CN} = y(S_S / E_{S/¥})$, then China's CA surplus measured in dollars can be expressed as:

$$S_S = X(E_{S/¥}, Y_{US}) - E_{S/¥} q(E_{S/¥}, y(S_S / E_{S/¥})).$$

China's exchange rate can be defined as a function of its CA around the neighbourhood of the balanced exchange rate, or the exchange rate that balances out the CA to 0, by

$$E_{S/¥} = f(S_S). \tag{1}$$

Although in reality a depreciating currency may temporarily decrease the CA and generate a J-curve effect in the short run — the propensity for trade balance (CA) to decline as a result of increased cost of imports and decreased value of exports — our focus is on a much longer time horizon. Hence, we assume that the J-curve effect exerts little influence on China's CA, and RMB depreciation will improve China's CA so that $f' < 0$.[2] Equation (1) reflects the fact that the CA can lead to pressures on the exchange rate. As China's trade balance (CA) increases, it implies that the country is lending abroad more than it is borrowing to finance trade. This leads to excess supply of foreign exchange currencies (in this case, the US dollar), which appreciates the RMB exchange rate. In contrast, if China runs a CA deficit, then it is spending more on trade. Accordingly, as it must borrow from foreign sources to finance this deficit, more foreign currencies (US dollar) are demanded and the RMB depreciates (Figure 4).

Figure 4: Exchange Rate and Trade Surplus

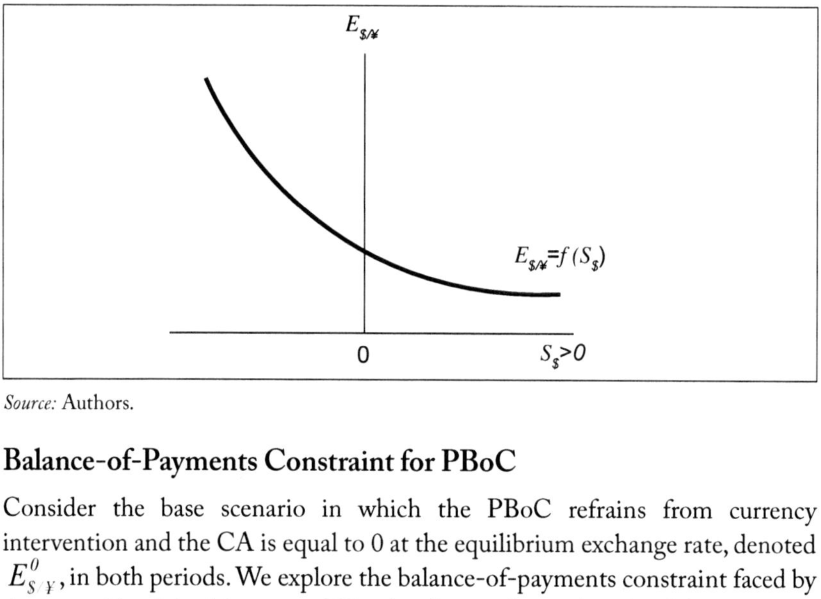

Source: Authors.

Balance-of-Payments Constraint for PBoC

Consider the base scenario in which the PBoC refrains from currency intervention and the CA is equal to 0 at the equilibrium exchange rate, denoted $E^0_{S/Y}$, in both periods. We explore the balance-of-payments constraint faced by the central bank in this setting. We relax the condition that the CA must equal to 0 in each period by allowing a CA surplus or a deficit in the first period (i.e., so as the CA in period 1 is non-zero). However, as the CA must be balanced in the international currency (US dollar) over the two periods, when China incurs

---

2   Jin and Choi (2013) show that if the sum of elasticity of imports and exports with respect to the indirect exchange rate (dollar price of yuan, $E_{S/Y}$) is less than one, which can be treated as a transformation of the Marshall-Lerner condition, then the dollar price of yuan and CA in China move in opposite directions.

a CA surplus in period 1 it must have a CA deficit in the next period so that its dollar-valued CA is balanced over the aggregate of the two periods.

Next, assume that the PBoC pegs the yuan below the equilibrium rate in the first period so that $E^1_{S/Y} < E^0_{S/Y}$, and China incurs a CA surplus, $S^1_S > 0$, which is purchased by the PBoC with FX funds to invest in US dollar-denominated assets. In the second period, the PBoC's FX reserve will accrue to $R_S S^1_S$ US dollars, where R_S is the gross interest rate on US assets. That is to say that the PBoC invests its CA surplus in US dollars and earns the US rate of return. To achieve a balanced CA over the two periods China must appreciate its exchange rate in the second period to achieve a CA deficit that depletes its FX reserves back to 0. This implies the condition where $S^2_S = -R_S S^1_S$, or

$$R_S S^1_S + S^2_S = 0. \tag{2}$$

In the long run, a country's FX reserves cannot accumulate indefinitely. Equation (2) can be understood as the equation capturing this basic *external constraint* to the PBoC's balance-of-payments account. In other words, the PBoC cannot simply increase its FX purchases to absorb the CA surplus. There will be *reactionary* economic pressures for the PBoC to ease its policy, stemming, for example, from higher opportunity costs associated with continued purchase of US dollar-denominated assets. This is consistent with Figure 2, where the FX to monetary base ratio was at an all-time high in 2009, but has steadily declined since then.

Constraint to Capital Market

The interest rate is usually treated as the prime instrument for monetary policy. After maintaining its yuan-to-dollar peg, the PBoC needs to manage the interest rate in China's capital market to avoid speculative attacks. In this section, we will focus on the implication of the non-arbitrage condition for the PBoC's interest rate management under currency intervention policy. In doing so, we first examine the interest parity condition and then discuss its properties under currency intervention policy.

The Interest Parity Condition

Speculators can make profits through foreign exchange futures on the undervalued or overvalued currency when arbitrage opportunities arise from interest rate differentials. As a result, under a floating exchange rate policy, exchange rates continuously adjust to satisfy the interest rate parity condition. Under currency intervention policy, however, the exchange rate is managed and less flexible. Accordingly, the PBoC needs to make additional efforts to avoid speculative attacks.

The PBoC faces pressure to adjust the yuan interest rate to avoid large arbitrage opportunities.[3] This relationship can be approximately expressed as:

$$R_Y = R_S - \frac{E^2_{S/Y} - E^1_{S/Y}}{E^1_{S/Y}}, \tag{3}$$

where R_Y and R_S are gross interest rates (1 plus net interest rate) on the yuan and dollar respectively, and $E^1_{S/Y}$ *and* $E^2_{S/Y}$ are dollar–yuan exchange rates in the first and second periods. Equation 3 implies that the interest rate difference between the yuan and dollar must offset the yuan depreciation against the dollar. From this condition, we may readily see that if the RMB is expected to appreciate against the dollar, then the RMB deposits should offer a lower return than the one offered on dollar deposits to avoid speculations on yuan-denominated assets, and vice versa.

Properties of the Yuan–Dollar Interest Parity Condition

We now investigate how the PBoC manages interest rates in China's capital market under the interest parity constraint.

Impact of Dollar Interest Rate

If we combine the exchange rate function (1), the external constraint to the PBoC's balance-of-payments account (2) and the interest parity condition (3), we get the following equation for the yuan interest rate:

$$R_Y = R_S - \frac{f(S^2_S) - f(S^1_S)}{f(S^1_S)} = R_S - \frac{f(-R_S S^1_S) - f(S^1_S)}{f(S^1_S)}. \tag{4}$$

---

3   Although in the short run the PBoC may discourage currency speculation by controlling the capital account, it still has to intervene in the yuan interest rate. On the one hand, the long-term arbitrage opportunity in Sino-US financial market cannot be completely ruled out. On the other, even in the short run, international market participants may still "use 'leads and lags' in trade invoicing and settlement and relabel short-term capital flows as long-term flows to evade remaining restrictions" (Eichengreen and Kawai 2014, 11).

Differentiating the yuan interest rate equation (5) with respect to the US interest rate R_S, we have:

$$\frac{dR_Y}{dR_S} = 1 - \frac{-f'(-R_S S'_S)S'_S}{f(S'_S)}$$

$$= 1 - \frac{f'(-R_S S'_S)(-R_S S'_S)}{f(-R_S S'_S)} \frac{f(-R_S S'_S)}{R_S f(S'_S)} \tag{5}$$

$$= 1 - \frac{E^2_{S/Y}}{R_S E'_{S/Y}} \eta_{E^2_{S/Y},S^2_S}$$

$$= 1 - \frac{E^2_{S/Y}}{R_S E'_{S/Y} \eta_{S^2_S,E^2_{S/Y}}},$$

where
$$\eta_{E^2_{S/Y},S^2_S} = \frac{f'(S^2_S)S^2_S}{f(S^2_S)} \quad \text{and} \quad \eta_{S^2_S,E^2_{S/Y}} = \frac{1}{\eta_{E^2_{S/Y},S^2_S}}$$

are the elasticity of the exchange rate with respect to the CA and the elasticity of the CA with respect to the exchange rate in the second period, respectively.

The sign o f dR_Y / dR_S in (5), which describes the impact of US interest on the Chinese interest rate, is positive when China's CA elasticity with respect to the exchange rate is negative, or $\eta_{S^2_S,E^2_{S/Y}} < 0$. In contrast, the interest rate relationship, described by dR_Y / dR_S, is uncertain when the CA elasticity is positive, or $\eta_{S^2_S,E^2_{S/Y}} > 0$. The actual relationship depends on the magnitude of China's CA elasticity to exchange rate changes in this case.

It should be noted that the US interest rate effect, dR_Y / dR_S, is an increasing function of the elasticity $\eta_{S^2_S,E^2_{S/Y}}$, and we have a positive relationship between US and Chinese interest rates if $\eta_{S^2_S,E^2_{S/Y}} > E^2_{S/Y} / (R_S E'_{S/Y})$. Accordingly, if the CA surplus elasticity is sensitive enough to the exchange rate, then the Chinese and the US interest rates need to move in the same direction under currency intervention. However, if the CA surplus sensitivity to the changes in the exchange rate is small, then the respective interest rates can move in opposite directions under currency intervention. The second scenario describes China as a relatively closed country where its international trade is limited. Thus, it is reasonable to assume that China's CA elasticity is large enough so that $\eta_{S^2_S,E^2_{S/Y}} > E^2_{S/Y} / (R_S E'_{S/Y})$ and $dR_Y / dR_S > 0$ for all S'_S. This implies the yuan interest rate is positively related to the dollar interest rate.

Under the balanced exchange rates, the CA is equal to 0 and the expected change in the dollar–yuan exchange rate is zero, so that $S_S^1, S_S^2 = 0$, and $E_{SY}^1 = E_{SY}^2$. However, for exchange rates near the equilibrium, then

$$0 < dR_Y / dR_S < 1, \tag{6}$$

whenever the elasticity is small. By maintaining a sustainable level of CA surplus, the PBoC also successfully creates an absorber to the external interest rate shocks.

The intuition is that if the US interest rate increases, China's foreign exchange reserves also increase. To rebalance its balance-of payments account, the RMB must appreciate more against the dollar. As a result, the yuan interest rate would increase less than the dollar interest rate under the interest parity condition. Figure 5 illustrates the comparison of the annual average interest rates of the three-year treasury bonds between the United States and China.[4] As it can be seen, between 2000 and 2007, the interest rate in China generally moved in the same direction as the US interest rate.

Figure 5: Yuan and Dollar Interest Parity

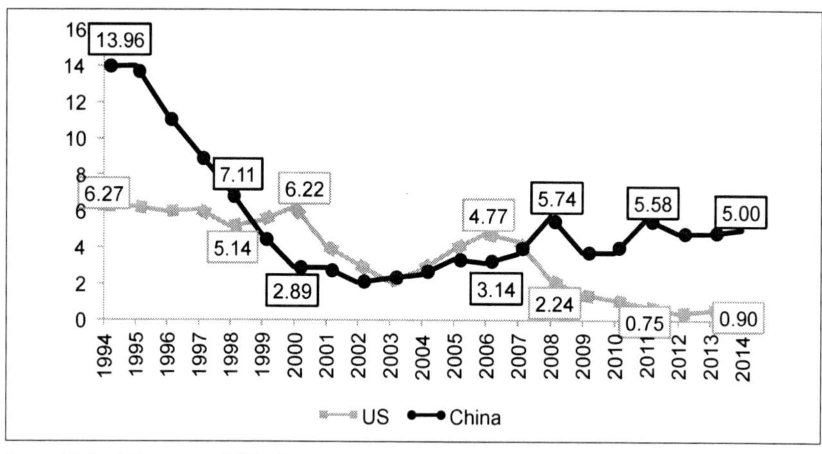

Source: Federal Reserve and PBoC.

---

4   The three-year treasury bonds have been among the most frequently issued bonds in China.

Effect of the Exchange Rate

From the two-period foreign exchange balance equation stating that the aggregate CA must balance in period 2, or $S_S^2 + R_S S_S^1 = 0$, we can express the second period's exchange rate as:

$$
\begin{aligned}
E_{S/Y}^2 &= f(S_S^2) \\
&= f(-R_S S_S^1) \\
&= f(-R_S f^{-1}(E_{S/Y}^1)),
\end{aligned}
\tag{7}
$$

where f^{-1} is the inverse function of f. This function describes the level of China's CA balance as a function of the RMB exchange rate.

Differentiating with respect to $E_{S/Y}^1$ yields

$$
\frac{dE_{S/Y}^2}{dE_{S/Y}^1} = -R_S \frac{f'(-R_S f^{-1}(E_{S/Y}^1))}{f'(f^{-1}(E_{S/Y}^1))} < 0.
\tag{8}
$$

Under currency intervention, the exchange rate in the second period is a decreasing function of the exchange rate in the first period. The more the exchange rate in the first period devalues from the balanced exchange rate, the larger CA surplus for China relative to the United States is generated. In response to that, the PBoC needs to appreciate the RMB more in the second period so as to generate a larger CA deficit to achieve the two-period CA balance.

Furthermore, differentiating the RMB exchange rate appreciation (depreciation) rate, $(E_{S/Y}^2 - E_{S/Y}^1)/E_{S/Y}^1$, with respect to the first period exchange rate, $E_{S/Y}^1$, and recalling that $E_{S/Y}^1, E_{S/Y}^2 > 0; dE_{S/Y}^2/dE_{S/Y}^1 < 0$, we have:

$$
\frac{d\left((E_{S/Y}^2 - E_{S/Y}^1)/E_{S/Y}^1\right)}{dE_{S/Y}^1} = \frac{E_{S/Y}^1 dE_{S/Y}^2/dE_{S/Y}^1 - E_{S/Y}^2}{(E_{S/Y}^1)^2} < 0.
\tag{9}
$$

Equation (9) implies that *the exchange rate appreciation is negatively related to the first-period RMB exchange rate*. The more the exchange rate in the first period deviates from the balanced exchange rate and is undervalued, the more the exchange rate in the second period must be appreciated, and vice versa.

Moreover, from (3) it follows that the change in the yuan interest rate due to changes in the dollar–yuan exchange rate is:

$$\frac{dR_Y}{dE^1_{S/Y}} = -\frac{d\left((E^2_{S/Y} - E^1_{S/Y})/E^1_{S/Y}\right)}{dE^1_{S/Y}} > 0. \tag{10}$$

This means that the yuan interest rate is an increasing function of the first period's exchange rate (see Figure 6). In turn, this implies that if the PBoC revalues its currency in the first period, then it may also need to increase the yuan interest rate to reduce speculative risks.

Figure 6: Yuan Revaluation on Yuan Interest Rates

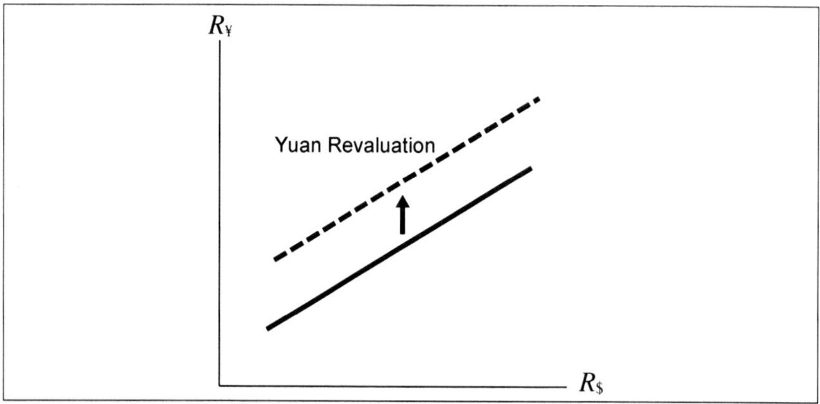

Source: Authors.

Technology Improvement

For over two decades, China's total factor productivity (TFP) growth has played a central role in its economy (Curtis 2013). Figure 7 shows TFP growth for the Group of Seven (G7) nations, and Brazil, Russia, India and China (BRIC) for the period between 1994 and 2013. China's TFP growth rate is clearly an outlier. The average TFP growth for China is 2.5 percent while the average is only 0.2 percent for G7 nations and 1.22 percent for Brazil, Russia and India. This implies that technology improvements played a large role in GDP growth for China relative to other countries. Accordingly, it is helpful to investigate their impact on China's surplus function and capital market constraint.

Figure 7: TFP Growth Rate: BRIC and G7 Nations

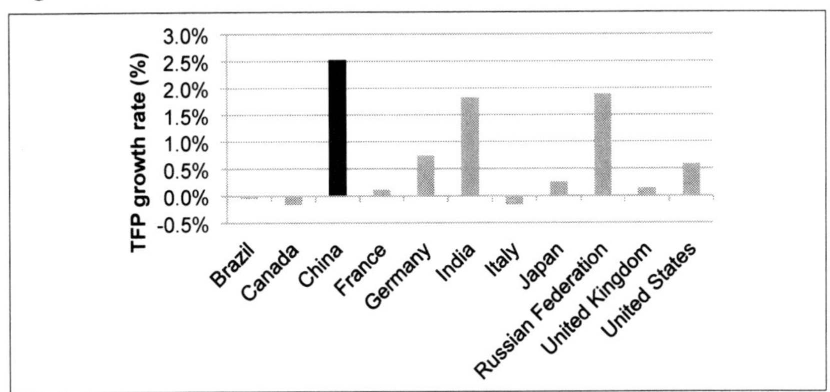

Source: Conference Board.

Figure 8: Technology Improvements on Exchange Rates

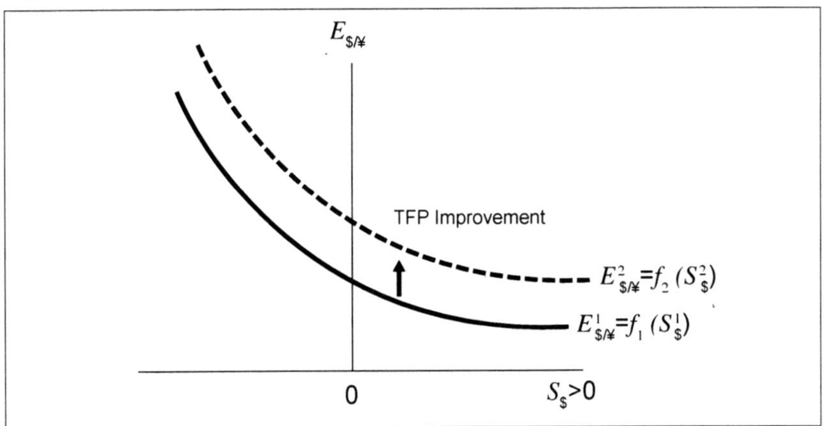

Source: Authors.

Suppose there is a TFP improvement in the second period relative to the first period. In this case, the same exchange rate will yield more CA in the second period than that in the first period. Thus, the exchange rate curve in the second period will shift rightward compared to that in the first period (see Figure 8).

In turn, in the second period, the RMB exchange rate will appreciate more than in the no-TFP growth case, which will shift the interest curve downward (see Figure 9). This result is similar to having more currency devaluation in the first period in the no-TFP growth case. In other words, technology improvements can also protect the economy by mitigating the impact of external shocks on the domestic interest rate.

Figure 9: Technology Improvement on Interest Rates

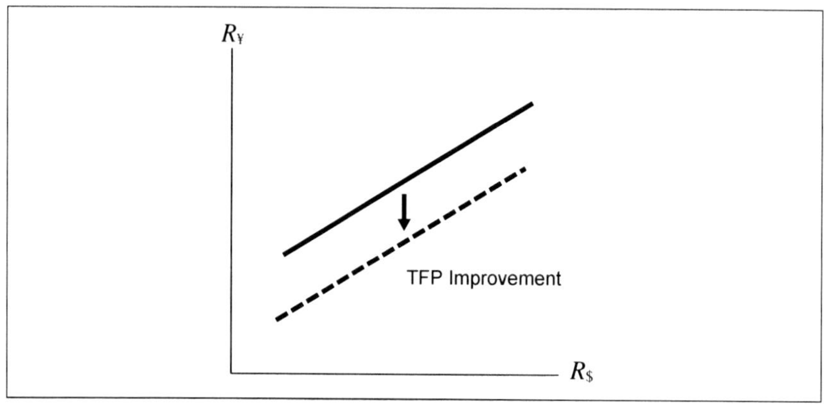

Source: Authors.

Implication of Monetary Neutrality

Monetary neutrality, the assumption that changes in the money supply only affect nominal variables in the economy (for example, prices and exchange rates) and not real variables such as real GDP ("units" of output), is an important underpinning of our model. We extend our analysis by investigating the implication of monetary neutrality in the Sino-US economy under the PBoC's currency intervention policy.

Money Neutrality in the Sino-US Economy

Consider the money market equilibrium. We assume that China's money supply, M^S, is controlled by its central bank through monetary policies such as open-market operations, changes in required reserve ratios, and the discount rate for loans and deposits. We assume the aggregate money demand, M^D, is the total demand for money from all agents in China's economy. M^D follows the classic *money-demand* function in the LM (liquidity preference and money supply) model:

$$M^D = P \times m(R, Y^d),\qquad(11)$$

where P, R and Y^d denote the country's price level, interest rate and real disposable income (Y less CA), respectively; $m(R, Y^d)$ is the aggregate real money demand function related to real disposable income and interest rate. The condition for equilibrium in the money market can be defined as the intersection of money supply and demand so that $M^S = M^D$.

Dividing both sides by the price level P yields:

$$\frac{M^S}{P} = m(R, Y^d). \tag{12}$$

Suppose that there is a relative monetary expansion in China or a monetary contraction in the United States in the first period. This implies that the PBoC accommodates the inflationary effects of FX funds issuance on China's economy, or the US Federal Reserve purchases more bonds through open market operations. Since the PBoC pegs the nominal yuan–dollar exchange rate, this monetary change actually appreciates the real exchange rate of yuan against dollars.

Figure 10 illustrates the impact of this monetary policy on the Sino-US economy under the interest rate parity condition. First, assume that monetary neutrality still holds in the United States. In other words, the US economy is under full employment and any monetary variation will be offset with a proportional rise (or decline) in prices. As a result, the real money demand and supply curves remain unchanged and the equilibrium interest rate is still at R_S (quadrant IV).

Quadrant I shows the interactions of the yuan and dollar interest rates, R_Y and R_S, under the interest parity condition. Recall that a yuan revaluation in the first period closer to the balanced exchange rate that equates China's CA to 0 will reduce the appreciation needed for the yuan against the US dollar in the second period, assuming that the yuan is still undervalued and the CA is in surplus. Under the interest parity condition, the RMB interest rate should increase to cover the exchange rate loss of the yuan against the US dollar, thus shifting the yuan-dollar interest rate curve upward. As a result, for the same dollar interest rate, the yuan interest rate in the second period increases from R_Y^1 to R_Y^2.

Suppose China's economy is a Keynesian economy. In the money market, an uptick in the yuan interest rate decreases real money supply and reduces real output, which shifts both the real monetary supply and demand curves leftward. As a result, the equilibrium moves from C1 to C2 and the real output in China decreases from Y_{CN}^1 to Y_{CN}^2.

Figure 10: Monetary Effects under Currency Intervention

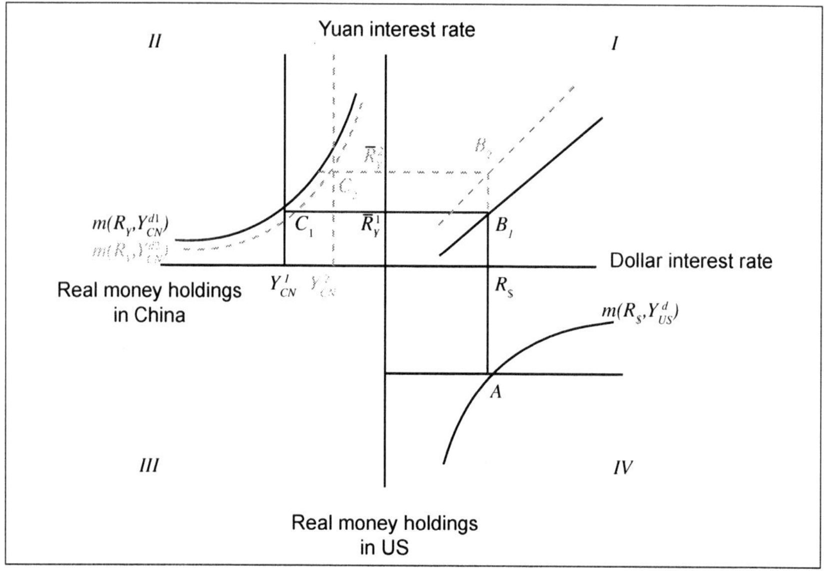

Source: Authors.

It should be noted that if the total money supply increases, the shrinking output implies that China will also incur inflation risks. Therefore, monetary expansion policy is an inefficient tool to stimulate the domestic economy in the long run.

This result is consistent with China's recent economic history. Just prior to the GFC, the Chinese economy experienced both high growth and low inflation under contractionary monetary policy. However, thereafter the Chinese authorities faced painful trade-offs between low inflation and high growth rate (see Figure 11). Yu Yongding (2013, 1-2) labels this growth pattern as a "groundhog day" phenomenon: "Since the global financial crisis, the Chinese economy has followed the familiar cyclical pattern of the past two decades: high investment supported by expansionary policy drives growth; inflation follows after lag; policy is tightened; growth drops away, but inflation is still high; more tightening; inflation falls at last, but growth falls away more than desired at the same time; policy is shifted from tight to expansionary; again, led by investment, growth rebounds. And a new economic cycle."

Figure 11: China's Real GDP Growth Rate and Inflation (%), 1979–2014

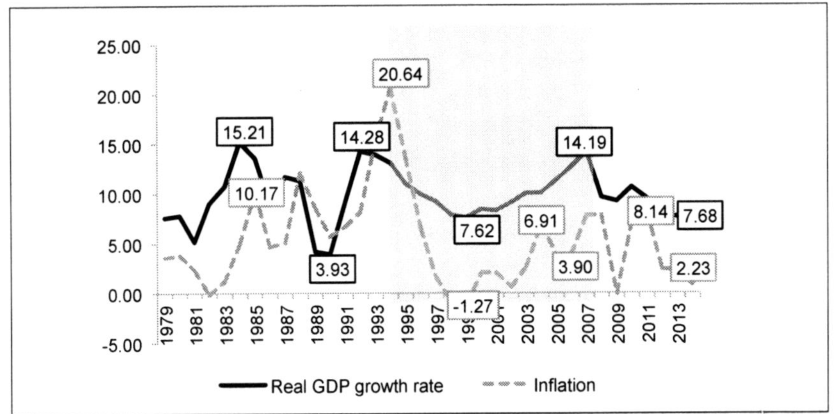

Source: World Bank WDI Database.

In contrast, if the US economy is not under full employment, then a monetary expansion in the United States, or monetary contraction in China, will induce inflation spikes with output shrinking in the United States. We have the following proposition: under currency intervention policy, money may not be neutral globally. A domestic monetary expansion or foreign monetary contraction will bring adverse effects to long-term financial stability and output growth, and vice versa. In other words, assuming local monetary neutrality in our model, the results show that money neutrality may not hold for both the United States and China simultaneously when China pursues a managed exchange rate policy.

China's Unsterilized Currency Intervention

Suppose the total money supply in China, MB_t, satisfies the following law of motion

$$MB_t = (1+\varsigma_t)MB_{t-1} + \Delta FX_t \tag{13}$$

Where ς is an index of the monetary policy: a higher ς is associated with a looser monetary regime. Here $\varsigma_t < 0$ implies the PBoC sterilizes the FX funds, while $\varsigma_t \geq 0$ implies that those issuances are not sterilized. Jin, Hu and Lombardi (2015) show that if ς is constant, then the long-run price level will also be constant under unsterilized currency intervention. From this perspective, controlling the exogenous expansionary rate (EER) and controlling the inflation rate can be fundamentally equivalent. Following Jin, Hu and Lombardi (2015), we also call this index the EER.

From (14), we can use the following way to calculate the EER:

$$\varsigma_t = \frac{MB_t - \Delta FX_t}{MB_{t-1}} - 1. \tag{14}$$

Figure 12 illustrates the EERs based on (14) from 2002, the year following China's joining of the WTO, to 2014. Typically, the EER varied from minus 19.1 percent to minus 6.7 percent until 2009, which indicates that the PBoC adopted a FX funds sterilization policy. However, in 2010 the rate spiked to 6.7 percent and the PBoC has maintained the EER at this level since then. This evidence suggests that the PBoC has not only discontinued the FX funds sterilization, but has reversed this policy by expanding its money supply, thereby switching into a new regime of unsterilized currency intervention.

Jin, Hu and Lombardi (2015) show that under unsterilized currency intervention policy, the long-run CA-to-output ratio will be positively related to the technology growth rate, g, but will be negatively related to the EER, ς. Figure 13 compares China's CA-to-GDP ratios with the EERs from 2002 to 2014 and shows that the former ratio moves in the opposite direction as the monetary expansion rate, ς. Prior to the GFC, the PBoC sterilized newly issued FX funds in China's total money supply. Accordingly, the gross exogenous monetary expansionary rate shrank $(\varsigma < 0)$. Benefitting from this contractionary money-supply policy, China's CA-to-GDP ratio kept increasing up to 10.1 percent in 2007. In contrast, the expansionary monetary policy pursued after the GFC has reduced the CA-to-GDP ratio to only about two percent.

Figure 12: EERs of China's Money Supply, 2002–2014

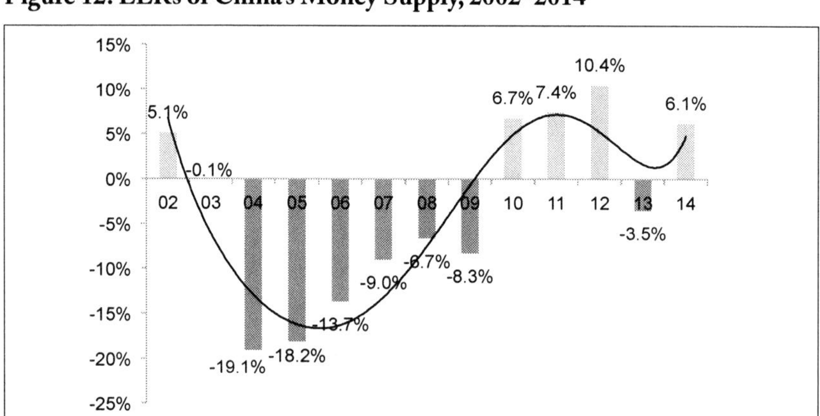

Data source: "Balance Sheets of Monetary Authority 2002-14" by PBoC and authors' calculation.

Since 2006, the PBoC has relied more on the RRR to sterilize the newly issued FX funds. Therefore, it becomes harder to approximate the actual policy just from observing the EER. We adjust the EER according to the variations of the RRR to precisely measure the magnitude of the PBoC's sterilization policy. Let RRR_t and RRR_{t+1} denote RRRs in period t and $t+1$ respectively. Then the theoretical (maximum) money multiplier in period t and $t+1$ will be $1/RRR_t$ and $1/RRR_{t+1}$. This means that one unit of reserve currency or monetary base (MB) can generate $1/RRR_t$ and $1/RRR_{t+1}$ units of currency to the total money supply in period t and $t+1$, respectively. Thus the MB in period t, MB_t will be equivalent to $\dfrac{RRR_{t+1}}{RRR_t} MB_t$ in period $t+1$.

Accordingly, using $\dfrac{RRR_t}{RRR_{t-1}} MB_{t-1}$ to replace in (15), we can get the following adjusted EER function:

$$\varsigma_t^{adj} = \frac{RRR_t}{RRR_{t-1}} \frac{MB_t - \Delta FX_t}{MB_{t-1}} - 1. \tag{15}$$

Figure 13 also contains the adjusted EER. We observe a negative relationship between the adjusted EER and CA-to-GDP ratio. While the adjusted EER decreased substantially before 2007, the CA-to-GDP ratio climbed up. Similarly, while the adjusted EER increased after 2007, the CA-to-GDP ratio went down. Note that the money multipliers used in (15) were the theoretical maximal multipliers. The actual multipliers were smaller in practice and the gap might also vary over time. Therefore, the fluctuations in the adjusted EER can be interpreted as the impact of the biases from the theoretical and actual money multipliers.

Moreover, although Figure 13 shows that the sensitivity of China's CA-to-GDP ratio to EER at the current stage remains unchanged, the PBoC does not have the same tools available to sterilize FX funds while managing its exchange rate stability to bolster China's export-led growth pattern.

Figure 13: Adjusted EER, EER and CA-to-GDP Ratio

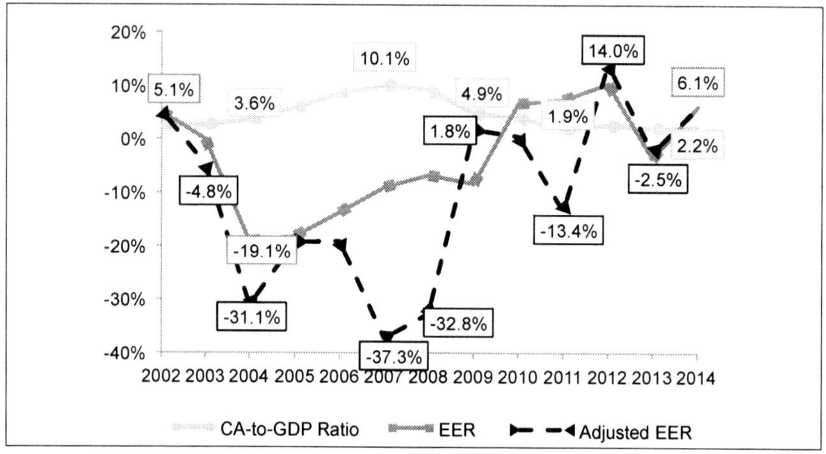

Data source: Authors' calculations and SAFE, and the National Bureau of Statistics (China).

Reserve Accumulation Costs

There are at least two major costs stemming from the large accumulation of FX reserves for the PBoC: the exchange rate risk of holding assets denominated in other currencies and the interest rate cost of holding large reserves when a higher rate can be earned elsewhere. Gagnon, Lardy and Borst (2011) examine these costs. They first assume that the PBoC must fund these FX purchases by either selling assets, borrowing in the local markets or raising the required reserve ratio for banks. They estimate the capital loss to the PBoC to be US$172 billion due to the appreciation of the RMB against the currencies held in its reserves, while the interest rate cost is estimated to be US$77 billion. In aggregate, for the 12-month period from mid-2011 to mid-2012, they estimate the total cost of China's foreign exchange policy to be US$238 billion, assuming that the PBoC earned an annual interest of US$11 billion on its reserve.

In reality, the economic cost associated with the PBoC's currency intervention policy may be substantially higher than the accounting losses it incurs from depreciating reserves. As the same authors point out: "The low rates paid to banks on required reserves and central bank bills represent an implicit tax on banks who would be earning much more at market interest rates. Ultimately this tax is passed along to Chinese households who earn meager rates (often negative in real terms) on their savings accounts in order to subsidize the profitability of the banks" (ibid.).

In order to examine these issues in more detail, we extend our analysis to an accounting profit function of the PBoC in the following section. Similar to Gagnon, Lardy and Borst (2011), we show that the PBoC has been incurring large accounting losses from its currency intervention, to the order of billions of US dollars, but this result does not take into account the economic interactions between the PBoC's policy and China's overall financial system, including its banking sector.

Accounting Profit Function

Under currency intervention, the PBoC issues FX funds to manage the exchange rate stability of the yuan against the international reserve currency, the US dollar. In the long run, however, the PBoC needs to adjust the exchange rate level to achieve the dollar-valued FX reserve balance, which equals 0.

Consider the accounting profit function in the PBoC's balance-of-payment account under currency intervention. Assume that the PBoC pegs the yuan below the equilibrium rate that equates the CA to 0 so that $E^{1}_{\$/\yen} < E^{0}_{\$/\yen}$ in the first period and incurs a CA surplus where $S^{1}_{\$} > 0$. To maintain this surplus, the PBoC issues $S^{1}_{\$} / E^{1}_{\$/\yen}$ amount in FX funds to purchase the CA surplus and invest this amount in US assets. In the second period, the PBoC's FX reserve will accrue to $R_{\$}S^{1}_{\$}$ US dollars, where $R_{\$}$ is the gross interest rate including the principal. To achieve the FX reserves level so that they balance in the aggregate by the end of the second period, the PBoC must appreciate the RMB exchange rate to achieve a CA deficit that will deplete its FX reserves so that $S^{2}_{\$} = -R_{\$}S^{1}_{\$}$, which brings $R_{\$}S^{1}_{\$} / E^{2}_{\$/\yen}$ in revenue in yuan to its FX funds reserve.

Thus the total profit in yuan realized by the PBOC's FX funds is:

$$\pi(S^{1}_{\$}) = \frac{R_{\$}S^{1}_{\$}}{E^{2}_{\$/\yen}} - \frac{S^{1}_{\$}}{E^{1}_{\$/\yen}} = \left(\frac{R_{\$}}{f(-R_{\$}S^{1}_{\$})} - \frac{1}{f(S^{1}_{\$})} \right) S^{1}_{\$} \qquad (16)$$

Jin and Choi (2013) show that:

1. If $R_s = 1$, then the optimal CA surplus that yields the highest profit to the PBoC's FX funds account is 0. That is, neither a trade surplus nor a deficit in the first period is optimal.

2. If $R_s > 1$, then the PBoC can make a positive profit by pegging a first period's exchange rate below the balanced exchange rate.

3. However, there is an upper bound in the devaluation rate for the PBoC to gain positive profits. An excessive deviation from the balanced exchange rate may bring huge losses to PBoC's balance-of-payments account (see Appendix I).

There is a lower bound for the optimal exchange rate in case 3 above, when the *actual* RMB exchange rate deviates from the exchange rate that equates the CA to *0* (balanced exchange rate). This lower bound can be characterized by

$$E_{S/Y}^{1} > \frac{E_{S/Y}^{0}}{R_s}.$$

That is to say that the dollar return for the optimal exchange rate in period 1, $E_{S/Y}^{1}{}^{*}R_s$, must yield exchange rate, $E_{S/Y}^{0}$. It is worth noting that this lower bound can be easily violated. For example, we may rewrite the lower bound as:

$$\frac{E_{S/Y}^{0} - E_{S/Y}^{1}}{E_{S/Y}^{0}} < \frac{E_{S/Y}^{0} - E_{S/Y}^{1}}{E_{S/Y}^{1}} < R_s - 1. \tag{17}$$

The first expression of (17) is the devaluation rate of the first-period exchange rate from the balanced exchange rate, while the final expression is the US net interest rate (gross interest rate less *1*). If this condition is violated, that is, if the devaluation rate in the first period is greater than the US net interest rate (usually less than five percent in recent history), then the PBoC may experience losses from its currency intervention policy (see Figure 14).

Figure 14: Profits and CA Surplus

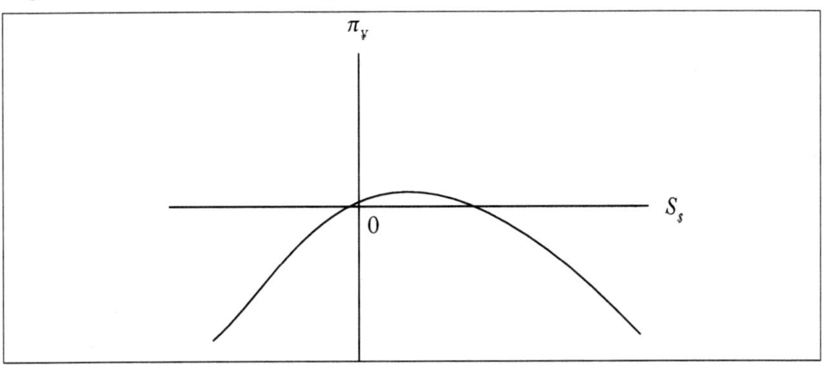

Source: Jin and Choi (2013).

Negative Profits to the PBoC

Figure 15 displays the cumulative accounting profits for the FX funds from purchasing CA surplus since 1994, when the PBoC started its current currency intervention policy. Although a central bank can make a profit on its FX funds through currency intervention, this is not the case in China's recent history. Let CS_i denote the amount of cumulative CA surpluses invested in US Treasury bills in period i. Assume that the stock of cumulative CA in the initial period is zero ($CS_0 = 0$). If we define the accounting profit in period i, which is to be known in period $i+1$, as $\pi_i = \dfrac{CS_i \times R_i}{E_{i+1}} - \dfrac{CS_i}{E_i}$, then it can be shown that the

cumulative profit in period i equals to $\Pi_i = \sum_{t=0}^{i} \pi_t$. (See Jin and Choi [2014].)

Figure 15: Profits for FX Funds Purchases of CA (billion RMB)

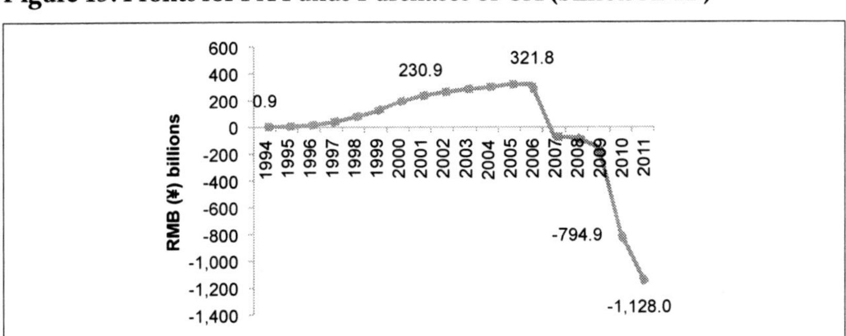

Data source: Jin and Choi (2014).

Figure 15 illustrates Jin and Choi's (2014) calculations of the PBoC's cumulative profits from purchasing CA surpluses between 1994 and 2011.[5] In the early years, cumulative profits in yuan from currency intervention steadily increased, reaching a peak value of RMB 321.8 billion in 2006. Due to the RMB appreciation, however, the PBoC began to lose money in 2007 when its cumulative profits were wiped out. The PBoC has since found it difficult to recover from the mounting losses, which reached RMB 1,128 billion, or about US$180 billion, in 2011. Such losses are expected to rise further as the yuan appreciates. Clearly, the PBoC's pegging of the RMB exchange rate against the US dollar exceeded the lower bound suggested in the section Accounting Profit Function.

Conclusion

China maintained exchange rate stability between 1994 and 2005 when the exchange rate remained broadly unchanged at around US$0.12 per yuan. This was achieved by the PBoC through the systematic purchase or sale of foreign assets to meet its targeted RMB exchange rate peg. This policy was eased by the PBoC since 2005, in favour of a "soft" peg, where the yuan was permitted to float against a basket of currencies within a small margin. The RMB has appreciated against the US dollar by three to five percent per year in response.

This chapter investigates the implications of the currency intervention policy implemented by Beijing by proposing a two-country (China and the United States), two-period currency intervention model to investigate the constraints of the currency intervention policy for China. We assume that the PBoC adopts a sterilization policy to minimize the monetary impact of foreign asset purchases. Since the CA surplus cannot increase indefinitely, we impose the assumption in the model that the Chinese CA must balance in aggregate over the two periods.

We first examine the effect of the US interest rate on China. Through the interest rate parity condition, we express the relationship between the Chinese and US interest rates as a function of the Chinese CA elasticity to the yuan–dollar exchange rate. The results show that a positive relationship between the Chinese and US interest rates exists when China's CA is sensitive enough to the changes in the RMB exchange rate. This implies a positive US interest rate

---

5   Here the initial period is 1994. China's foreign exchange reserve, current account and yuan–dollar data is obtained from the SAFE. The US Treasury bill interest rate data is from the Federal Reserve website. Since the annual interest rates are not available in certain years, the six-month interest rate data is used.

effect where any exogenous changes in the US interest rate will cause similar movements in the Chinese interest rate in the same direction.

We also elaborate on the costs of Beijing's currency intervention policy. The direct cost represents the capital (accounting) losses to the PBoC's foreign reserve due to the appreciation of the RMB. Since the assets held in its foreign reserve are mostly denominated in other currencies, an appreciation of the RMB implies a depreciation of its reserve assets. In addition, the PBoC can incur a portfolio loss if the value of its foreign-denominated assets, such as US Treasury bills, declines. The cost associated with the PBoC's foreign reserve holdings ranges from US$180 billion (Jin and Choi 2014) to US$238 billion (Gagnon, Lardy and Borst 2011) for 2011.

There are, of course, additional economic costs associated with China's currency intervention policy. One example is the implicit tax imposed through the PBoC's high RRR in its banking sector. Indeed, the RRR for China's large financial institutions has continued to increase — from 7.5 percent to 20 percent between 2005 and 2014. In turn, the high RRR prevents the financial sector from shifting part of its available capital to pursue a higher rate of return. Similarly, the currency intervention policy imposes constraints on the PBoC's monetary policy. From the model, while the PBoC pursues a stable external value for the RMB, it needs to fully adjust the interest rate in response to any interest rate changes in the United States. Therefore, China's central bank loses some monetary policy independence.

These considerations challenge Beijing's currency intervention policy. Along similar lines, in 2013, PBoC Deputy Governor Yi Gang stated, "it's no longer in China's favor to accumulate foreign-exchange reserves" (Gang quoted in BloombergBusiness 2013). Similarly, Zhou Xiaochuan, the PBoC governor, outlined the bank's aim to end its normal foreign exchange interventions and to let the RMB float more freely in the foreign exchange market (ibid.). Over time, as the PBoC reduces its interventions, the RMB exchange rate will become more flexible. In turn, China will be in a much better position to move toward the liberalization of its capital account, and thus to further internationalize its currency.

Appendix I

Proof: 1) If $S_S^l = 0$, then $\pi(S_S^l) = 0$. This means that non-intervention in the foreign exchange market yields zero profit for the PBoC. If China chooses to have a CA surplus in the first period, then $E_{S/Y}^l < E_{S/Y}^0$, and $S_S^l > 0$.

Since $E_{S/Y} = f(S_S)$ is a decreasing function of S_S and $S_S^l > 0$, we have $f(-S_S^l) > f(0) > f(S_S^l)$ or $E_{S/Y}^2 > E_{S/Y}^0 > E_{S/Y}^l$, and

$$\frac{1}{f(-R_S S_S^l)} - \frac{1}{f(S_S^l)} < 0.$$

Thus, $\pi(S_S^l) < 0$ for all $S_S^l > 0$.

Similarly, if $S_S^l < 0$, then $f(-S_S^l) < f(0) < f(S_S^l)$ and $\dfrac{1}{f(-R_S S_S^l)} - \dfrac{1}{f(S_S^l)} > 0$.

Thus, $\pi(S_S^l) < 0$ for all $S_S^l < 0$. Therefore, zero CA surplus is the *highest profit for the PBoC's FX funds account.*

2) Differentiating with respect to S_S^l gives

$$\pi'(S_S^l) = \frac{R_S}{f(-R_S S_S^l)} - \frac{1}{f(S_S^l)} + S_S^l \left(\frac{R_S^2 f'(-R_S S_S^l)}{f^2(-R_S S_S^l)} + \frac{f'(S_S^l)}{f^2(S_S^l)} \right).$$

Evaluating the above at $S_S^l = 0$, we get

$$\pi'(0) = \frac{R_S}{f(0)} - \frac{1}{f(0)} > 0.$$

This implies that profit is increasing in S_S^l when evaluated at $S_S^l = 0$.

Since $\pi(0) = 0$ and marginal profit is increasing in S_S^l at $S_S^l = 0,$, there exists a positive surplus that yields positive profits for the PBoC. Moreover, when $S_S^l < 0$, we have $E_{S/Y}^2 < E_{S/Y}^l$, and $\pi(S_S^l) = \dfrac{R_S S_S^l}{E_{S/Y}^2} - \dfrac{S_S^l}{E_{S/Y}^l} < 0.$

Therefore, the optimal policy that yields the highest profits to the PBoC must be a CA surplus.

3) From the profit function, the optimal level of CA surplus is positive where

$$\pi(S_S^{l*}) = \left(\frac{R_S}{f(-R_S S_S^{l*})} - \frac{1}{f(S_S^{l*})} \right) S_S^{l*} > \pi(0) = 0.$$

Since $S_S^{l*} > 0$, this implies that,

$$R_S f(S_S^{l*}) = R_S E_{S/Y}^l$$
$$> f(-R_S S_S^{l*}) = E_{S/Y}^2$$
$$> f(0) = E_{S/Y}^0,$$

or

$$E_{S/Y}^l > \frac{E_{S/Y}^0}{R_S}.$$

This implies that there is a lower bound for the optimal exchange rate.

Works Cited

BloombergBusiness. 2013. "PBOC Says No Longer In China's Interest to Increase Reserves." BloombergBusiness. November 21. www.bloomberg.com/news/articles/2013-11-20/pboc-says-no-longer-in-china-s-favor-to-boost-record-reserves.

Bonatti, L. and A. Fracasso. 2013. "Hoarding of International Reserves in China: Mercantilism, Domestic Consumption and US Monetary Policy." *Journal of International Money and Finance* 32, 1044–78.

Cheung, Yin-Wong, Menzie D. Chinn and Wingwang Qian. 2012. "Are Chinese Trade Flows Different?" *Journal of International Money and Finance* 31, 2127–46.

Curtis, C. Chadwick. 2013. "Economic Reforms and the Evolution of China's TFP in the State and the Private Sectors." www.economicdynamics.org/meetpapers/2013/paper_1023.pdf.

Dorrucci, Ettore and Julie McKay. 2011. "The International Monetary System after the Financial Crisis." European Central Bank Occasional Paper Series No. 123.

Eichengreen, Barry and Masahiro Kawai. 2014. "Issues for Renminbi Internationalization: An Overview." ADBI Working Paper No. 454.

Gagnon, Joseph E., Nicholas R. Lardy and Nicholas Borst. 2011. "The Internal Cost of China's Currency Policy." *RealTime Economic Issues Watch* (Peterson Institute for International Economics blog). http://blogs.piie.com/realtime/?p=2427.

Goldstein, M. and N. R. Lardy. 2009. *The Future of China's Exchange Rate Policy.* Washington, DC: Peterson Institute for International Economics.

Jin, Hailong, Coby Hu and Domenico Lombardi. 2015. "China's CA Balance Under Currency Intervention." Draft paper.

Jin, Hailong and Eun-Kwan Choi. 2013. "Profits and Losses from Currency Intervention" *International Review of Economics & Finance* 27, 14–20.

———. 2014. "China's Profits and Losses from Currency Intervention, 1994–2011." *Pacific Economic Review*, 19, 170–83.

Kanamori, Toshiki and Zhijun Zhao. 2006. *The Renminbi Exchange Rate Revaluation: Theory, Practice, and Lessons from Japan.* Tokyo: ADB Institute. www.adb.org/sites/default/files/publication/159375/adbi-renminbi-exchange-rate.pdf

Kroeber, Arthur. 2013. "A Chinese Trilemma: Renminbi Internationalization, Capital Account Opening, and Domestic Financial Liberalization." Concept paper for Harvard Law School Program on International Financial Systems China-US Symposium, September 11–13, Chicago, IL.

McKinnon, R. and G. Schnabl. 2009. "China's Financial Conundrum and Global Imbalances." *China Economist* 21 65–77.

Neftci, S. N., M. Yuan and M. Xu (eds.). 2007. *China's Financial Markets: An Insider's Guide to How the Markets Work.* Amsterdam; Boston: Elsevier Academic Press.

Yu, Yongding. 2013. "China's Groundhog Day Growth Pattern." *East Asia Forum*, Feburary 10.

Zhou, Xiaochuan. 2009. "Reform the International Monetary System." Speech delivered March 23. www.bis.org/review/r090402c.pdf.

7

China's Rise as an International Creditor: Sign of Strength?

Stuart S. Brown and Hongying Wang

After growing by an average of 10 percent annually over three decades, China's economy emerged as the world's second largest in 2012. In December 2014, the International Monetary Fund (IMF) claimed that on a purchasing power parity basis, China's GDP had already surpassed that of the United States. Meanwhile, China's international financial clout seems to have increased as well. Its official foreign reserves reached almost US$4 trillion in 2014, the largest in the world by far. Its net foreign assets amounted to US$2 trillion, more than any other country except Japan. In contrast, US net external liabilities have continued to soar. While the latter is regularly reported as a harbinger of US national decline, China's net creditor status, for many, epitomizes its increasingly dominant stature within the world economy.[1]

This perspective draws support from historical precedent. For example, a positive association between net creditor status and global economic-cum-geopolitical power has often been struck in contrasting the respective trajectories of Great Britain and the United States during the twentieth century. Britain's move from international creditor to debtor, paralleling the evolution of the United States to a position of net creditor, epitomized, for many, the hegemonic transition

---

1   Not everyone agrees that growing (net) external liabilities augur US national decline. Setser and Roubini (2005a), Setser and Roubini (2005b) and Setser (2008) are early attempts to relate the US international investment position to its — purportedly waning — global influence. But Levey and Brown (2005a and 2005b) argue that the US external position suggests underlying economic strength. See also Brown (2013, chapter 4) and Drezner (2009).

from the one to the other. In his book *Eclipse*, for instance, Arvind Subramanian (2011) captures this development with a recounting of the US power play over Britain during the 1956 Suez crisis. Subramanian suggests that China can amass similar leverage over the United States (and others) in the not-too-distant future. He constructs an index of national economic power in which net debtor (creditor) status is incorporated and quantified as a decided vulnerability (strength).[2]

In this chapter we offer an alternative perspective. China's net international creditor position has neither yielded unambiguous financial gains nor has it translated *pari passu* into expanded political influence. China's creditor status, in any case, reflects an unsustainable development model. Were China to manage to transition to a healthier economic structure — one based less on the repression of household income and consumption growth — its international creditor position could weaken and potentially disappear altogether. As we will argue, however, such a development — a progressive decline in China's net external assets — may be more conducive to the longer-term stability of the Chinese economy, higher living standards for the median Chinese household and the ability of the Chinese state to wield greater geopolitical muscle on the world stage. More generally, this chapter cautions against drawing broad inferences about leverage and influence from a country's net creditor (or debtor) status alone. Examining the composition of the main gross asset and liability positions underlying the headline net creditor (debtor) figure appears imperative. It is also essential to evaluate a country's external asset position within the context of the prevailing global economic governance and power structure.

The first part of the chapter dissects the sources of China's international creditor status and explains why it has garnered China fewer financial gains and less political influence than is often assumed. The second part describes how China's net creditor status mirrors its underlying economic development model, discusses China's limited success in transitioning toward a more consumption-centred system, and looks ahead at how such structural change may affect its international influence. The concluding section summarizes the findings and highlights the utility and limitations of a country's creditor status in shaping its international clout.

---

2   It is notable that as one of only three variables comprising Subramanian's measure of national economic power, net international investment position (NIIP) receives only a five percent weight. For his measure of national economic power, Subramanian attaches the largest weight to openness (captured by the volume of overall imports and exports) and secondarily to GDP.

The Limited Influence of an International Creditor

In assessing the health of a country's external finances, its NIIP should receive careful attention. NIIP measures the difference between a country's gross external assets and liabilities. It thus compares the country's financial claims on residents in the rest of the world with the rest of the world's financial claims on domestic residents. Since 2004, the first year such data were released, China's NIIP has been positive. The ratio of China's NIIP to its economy peaked just under 35 percent in 2007, stabilizing in more recent years at just above 20 percent of GDP (see Figure 1). This contrasts markedly with the situation in the United States, whose NIIP has been negative since the late 1990s, its trend accelerating downwards since 2007 (see Figure 2). What is the source of China's positive NIIP (net creditor position)? Has it brought China economic gains and political influence?

Figure 1: China's Current Account and NIIP

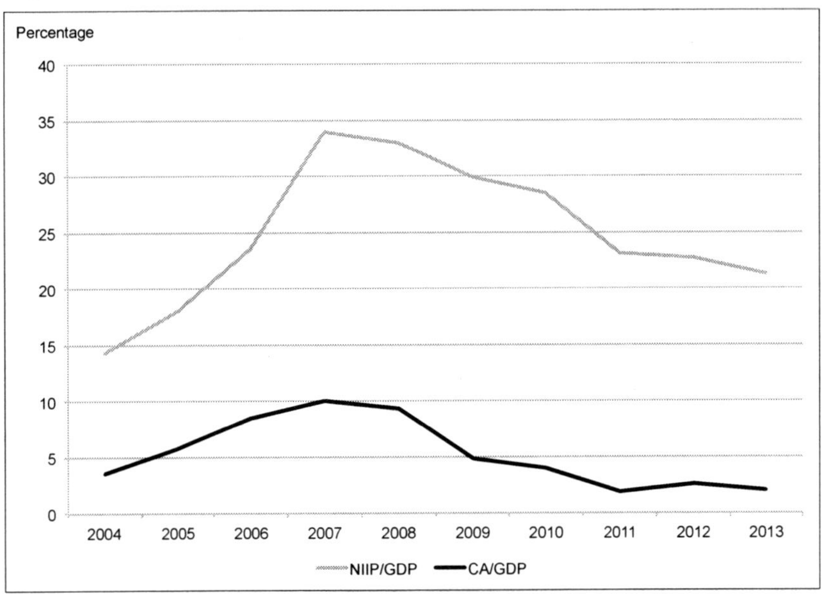

Data sources: State Administration of Foreign Exchange (SAFE) (2015a); SAFE (2015b); World Bank (2015).

Figure 2: US CA and NIIP

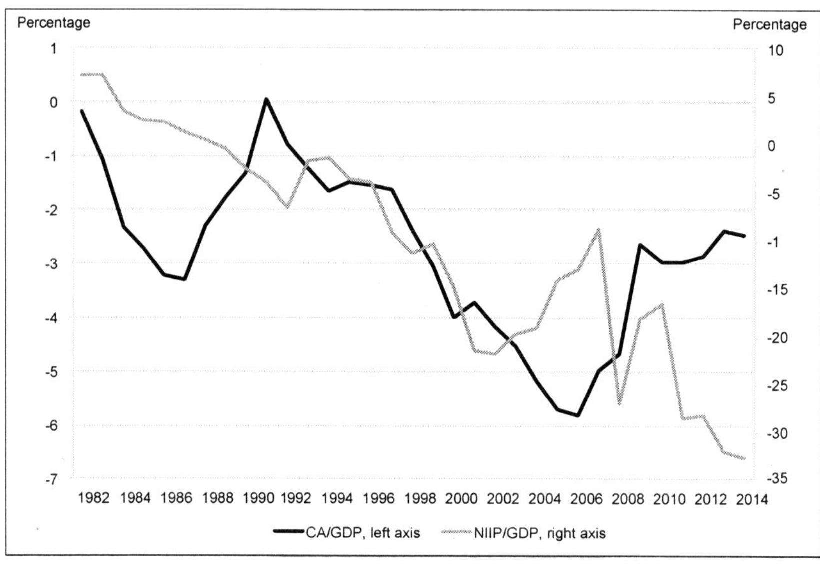

Data source: US Bureau of Economic Analysis (2015).

Since 1994, China has consistently run a current account (CA) surplus. Achieving a surplus on current account is equivalent to being a net exporter ("lender") of capital.[3] This largely explains China's rising NIIP (in absolute terms) during this period, as the increase in China's gross external financial claims outpaced the increase in gross foreign financial claims on China (Figure 1). In addition, during the same period, China consistently ran a (non-official) capital account surplus.[4] China's official foreign reserve buildup, in turn, mirrors the sum of its current account and (non-official) capital account surpluses.[5]

---

3   As the balance-of-payments statement must sum to zero, a current account surplus requires a capital account deficit, i.e., the export of excess domestic savings (capital) to the rest of the world. The term "lender" should be used advisedly because it need not involve the accumulation of **debt** claims. It can also involve foreign direct investment or acquisition of portfolio **equity** positions.

4   By the non-official capital account balance, we mean capital inflows less capital outflows **net of** official capital (central bank net purchases of foreign exchange [FX]).

5   China's non-official capital account surplus reflects consistently high net inward foreign direct investment and at times high, speculative capital inflow driven often by expected renminbi (RMB) appreciation. In managing its exchange rate (mainly against the US dollar), the combined inflow of FX on current and capital accounts requires regular FX intervention and a rapid pace of official reserve accumulation.

In the rest of this section, we turn to examining whether China's net creditor status has brought economic and political benefits to the country. We demonstrate and explain the limited financial gains associated with China's positive NIIP, followed by a discussion of the limited political influence China has achieved.

China's Limited Financial Gains

To evaluate the economic returns associated with China's creditor status it is useful to examine China's net investment income (NII) from abroad Intuitively NIIP and NII — known equivalently as the net factor services balance — should be correlated. In particular, if a country is a large international creditor — it possesses many more foreign assets in comparison with its foreign liabilities — one tends to assume a priori (and assuming all other things equal) that its residents receive a larger annual flow of income from abroad in the form of profits, dividends and interest than they collectively pay out. This expectation for NII follows because foreign assets and liabilities must be serviced; and one would expect that more sizeable assets would generate a higher flow of income related to the capital "services" they generate, than a much smaller stock of gross liabilities would require in payments. In contrast, a large net debtor, presumably, would face the opposite situation: its NII, ceteris paribus, would be expected to be negative, reflecting the need to service a much larger stock of external liabilities.

In light of the popular perception of China's (economic and geopolitical) rise and of America's parallel decline, a comparison of the two countries in terms of NIIP and NII is instructive. As Figure 3 demonstrates, its leading net creditor status notwithstanding, China's recent annual flows of NII have been negative. NII was in balance during the early 1990s, but declined moderately in 1995, mirroring a modest net debtor position at the time. By 1997, however, as NIIP began its steady ascent, NII remained moderately negative until 2005. During 2006–2008, China experienced a sharp improvement in NII, briefly entering positive territory in the run-up to the global financial crisis, before plummeting by some US$100 billion during 2008–2011. By 2013, China's NII had rebounded somewhat, but remained at negative US$60 billion, in stark contrast to a positive NIIP of virtually US$2 trillion.

Figure 3: China's Net Foreign Assets and Net Investment Income Flows, 1991–2012

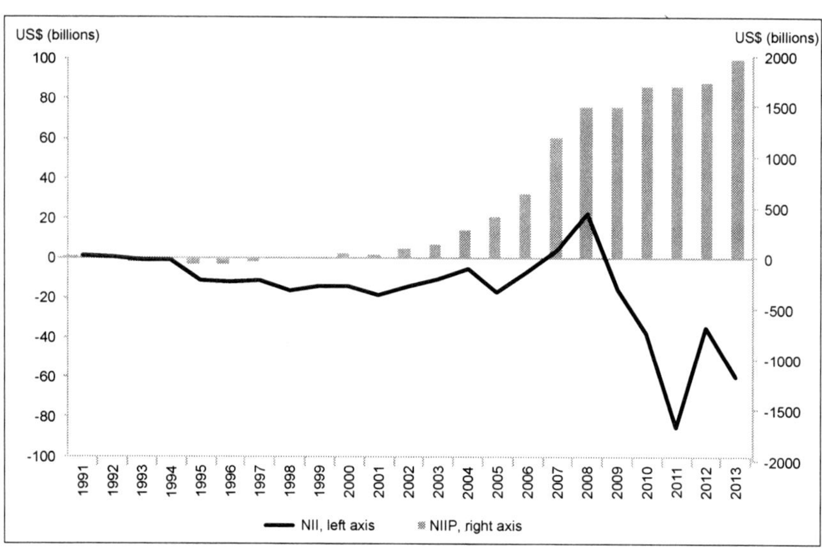

Source: People's Bank of China (PBoC), SAFE and Rhodium Group; historical data before 2004 based on the Global Wealth dataset by Lane and Milesi-Ferretti. Data provided by Rhodium Group; version of figure appeared in Hanemann (2014).

The relationship between the dramatic drop in China's NII receipts and the Great Recession is hardly coincidental. Indeed, this relationship underscores the enduring structural financial power of the United States, its steadily worsening net debtor position notwithstanding.[6] This structural power lies in the dollar's role as the world's dominant reserve currency, the ability of the United States to attract a consistent net inflow of capital and, thus, the willingness and, indeed, necessity, to run persistent current account deficits. It likewise involves the ability to "finance" the excess of national spending over income (or investment over savings) via expanded issuance of its own currency. The latter equally presupposes the rest of the world's willingness to hold increasing quantities of these dollar-denominated financial claims. Such willingness, in turn, reflects the depth and liquidity of US financial markets, the protection of property rights, superior product and process innovation and, arguably, even US military power (Norloff 2010).

---

6   "Structural power" (Strange 1987; Helleiner 2006) refers to an indirect form of power derived from the making or manipulation of the rules of game or otherwise shaping the environment in which others have to operate.

Even as the epicentre of the worldwide Great Recession — a dubious achievement that no doubt diminished its reputation qua metropolis of global capitalism and cheerleader for worldwide structural reforms — the United States subsequently attracted an avalanche of global capital. That is, rather than abandon the prime precipitator of the crisis, foreign (official and private) capital flocked to the United States in droves, embracing US government debt as the safest asset to hold, particularly during trying and uncertain times. Certainly this phenomenon — the ability of the United States to borrow in its own currency at low rates even as the epicentre of a global financial crisis — captures better than most other statistics the enduring clout of the United States within the global economy. Like many other emerging market countries, the Chinese government maintained its purchases of low-yielding US debt, a leading factor depressing China's NII. (See further discussion below.)

The US experience contrasts markedly with that of China (see Figure 2). Owing to a string of current account deficits since the early 1980s — with the sole exception of a modest surplus in 1991 — US NIIP has steadily descended into increasingly negative territory — i.e., the United States transitioned from a large net creditor to a large net debtor — beginning with the Reagan presidency. This transition has hardly been linear, however. Persistent current account deficits notwithstanding, NIIP for the United States improved dramatically from a negative 22 percent of GDP in 2002 to a negative 8.8 percent of GDP by 2007 before again sharply retreating. After another positive rebound during the financial crisis, US NIIP had declined to negative 32 percent of GDP by the end of 2013.

Certain NIIP volatility lies in valuation effects. In particular, because US liabilities are denominated almost exclusively in dollars, a depreciation of the dollar against foreign currencies, *ceteris paribus,* raises the NIIP. This follows because US liabilities do not alter in response to dollar depreciation — foreign creditors are still paid in the same dollars — while its foreign assets increase in dollar equivalent terms. In addition, if (foreign-held) US assets underperform (US-held) foreign assets, US NIIP also improves. (Of course, the opposite is the case when the dollar appreciates and US assets outperform foreign assets, as has been the case recently.) The upshot is that such valuation effects involving currency movements and differential asset performance affect the NIIP in addition (and sometimes in opposite directions) to annual current account balances.[7]

---

7   In particular, when the dollar depreciates and US assets underperform foreign assets, everything else being equal, this slows the pace at which the US current account deficit needs to correct, hence the size of the required real dollar depreciation.

Figure 4: Net Foreign Assets and Net Investment Income Flows of the United States, 1999–2013

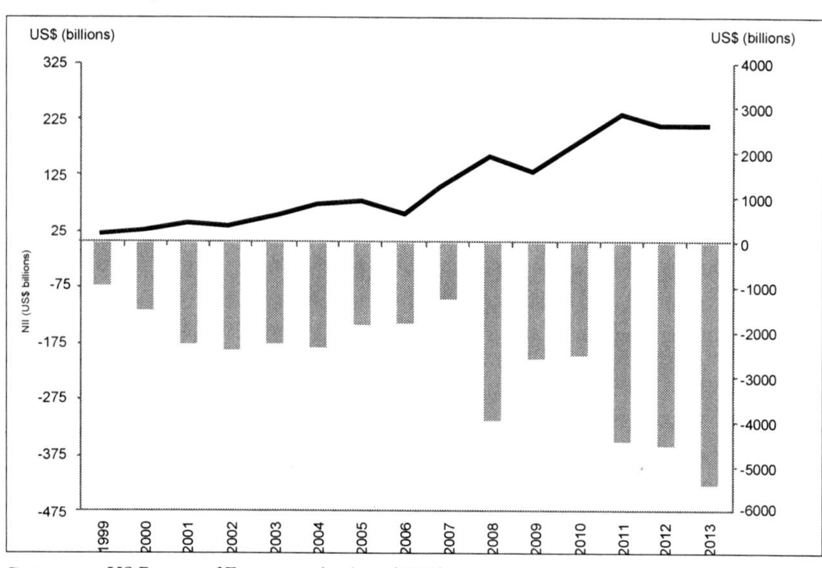

Data source: US Bureau of Economic Analysis (2015).

Most strikingly, over the entire period during which NIIP has been consistently negative, the United States has managed to maintain a positive balance on NII (Figure 4). By the end of 2013, US NII remained at 1.2 percent of GDP. To explain this apparent puzzle, particularly in relation to the opposite situation for China (as seen in Figure 3), one needs to probe beneath the headline NIIP figure and examine the composition of each country's gross assets and liabilities, respectively.

A breakdown of China's principal external assets and liabilities is shown in Figure 5. Dominating the asset side of China's external balance sheet are its official FX reserves. By the end of 2013, these totalled US$3.9 trillion, representing as much as 65 percent of China's gross external assets. Well in excess of the amount recommended for any country's needs according to traditional FX adequacy criteria, China's holdings represent no less than 30 percent of global official reserves.[8]

---

8   Conventionally, FX adequacy is measured in terms of months of import coverage, coverage of short-term external debt, and (partial) backing for the money supply. The standard recommendation for import coverage ranges between three and six months. According to the so-called Greenspan-Guidotti rule, a country should have enough reserves to cover 100 percent of its short-term external debt (under one year in maturity) and sometimes including the total debt maturing in a given year. The final, less definitive measure encapsulates a country's ability to sell sufficient FX reserves to contend with episodes of capital flight (captured by bank deposit withdrawals and conversion into FX).

Figure 5: China's International Investment Position, 2004–2013

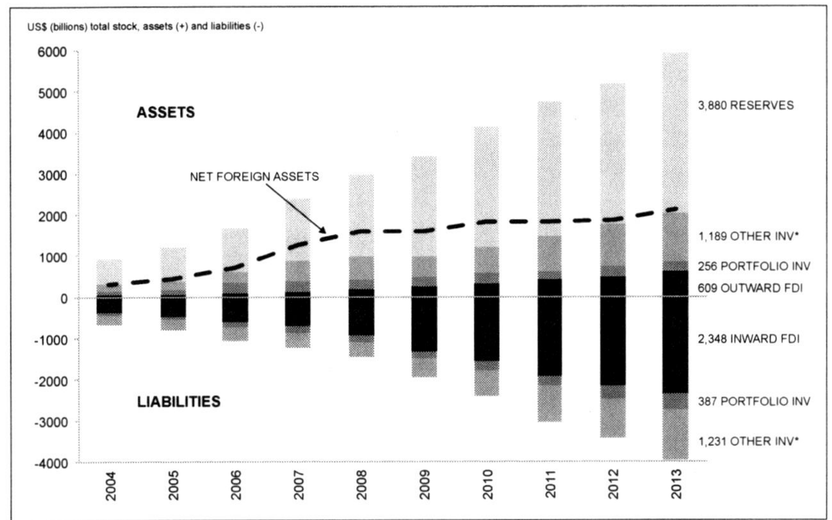

Source: PBoC, SAFE and Rhodium Group. Data provided by Rhodium Group; version of figure appeared in Hanemann (2014).

Note: Other investments include mainly trade credit, loans, currency and deposits in financial institutions.

Another sizeable asset category for China is other investments, representing mostly shorter-term loans and trade credits China has extended as well as foreign currency deposits. This category totals approximately US$1.2 trillion, comprising roughly 20 percent of gross external assets. China also has a little over US$600 billion in foreign direct investment (FDI) by Chinese enterprises abroad as well as US$256 billion in (equity and debt) portfolio investment. All of these categories have witnessed sizeable increases over the last decade.

On the liability side of China's ledger, the largest component by far at some US$2.3 trillion is inward FDI, representing about 60 percent of China's gross external liabilities. Compared with other countries at varying levels of development, China's FDI to GDP ratio has exceeded that of other developing countries and indeed exceeds that of advanced countries such as Korea and Japan while being roughly comparable to that of Germany and the United States (Rosen and Hanemann 2014). Such inward FDI has no doubt generated sizeable flows of profit income to the foreign multinational corporations

(MCNs) involved, in the process lowering China's NII.[9] Rounding out its external liabilities are foreign portfolio investments in China representing some 10 percent of China's total liabilities abroad and, finally, other foreign investments in China, which are roughly balanced by China's other investments abroad.

It seems apparent that one of the keys to China's puzzle — running a negative annual NII despite a sizeable, positive NIIP — lies in the relatively low rates of return earned on China's official FX reserves. These reserves are overwhelmingly invested in official assets issued in the developed countries, such as US Treasuries and agency paper as well as non-US government securities. Interest rates have been depressed throughout the advanced industrialized world, except for short periods in crisis-prone European peripheral countries such as Italy and Spain. But even in the peripheral countries of the European Monetary Union yields have come down dramatically in recent years.

Aside from official reserves, the leading driver of the (negative) NII appears to be net inward FDI, which typically generates far higher returns for foreign investors than the returns China garners from its official FX reserves. However, it is critical to recognize that given the advanced technology, managerial expertise and improved corporate governance embodied in many of the FDI projects, China has gained faster total factor productivity growth, propelling per capita national income higher.[10] Moreover, a sizeable proportion of China's exports are the product of foreign-owned MNCs. Thus, inward FDI has markedly increased employment and wages in China's tradable sector. One is considerably less concerned about such (longer-term equity) liabilities notably as compared to foreign currency-denominated short-term debt in the form of bank loans and (government and corporate) bonds. Put more positively, any contribution inward FDI makes toward (temporarily) depressing NII should be more than compensated in the longer run by the direct contribution and positive externalities of inward direct investment for the Chinese economy.

Meanwhile, much research has attempted to uncover the reasons for a positive NII despite a negative NIIP in the United States. Some have argued,

---

9   It should be noted, however, that a significant portion of FDI flow into China is so-called "round-tripping" FDI, i.e., Chinese capital exiting China through various channels of capital flight and later returning to China as foreign capital in order to escape FX controls, to take advantage of tax benefits and better property rights protection, and to diversify domestic risks (Huang 2003). A careful study a decade ago estimated that round-tripping FDI accounted for about 40 percent of the total FDI flowing into China (Xiao 2004).

10   It will be interesting to see whether China follows the pattern of those countries such as Australia and Canada, which have raised their level of development in line with FDI increasing its role in the economy, or rather follow the experience of Korea, Japan and Germany, which have seen an earlier levelling off of FDI's share in GDP.

controversially, that the United States somehow garners a higher rate of return on all of its assets relative to what it pays on its comparable liabilities. That is, its government has traditionally borrowed for less than other advanced countries[11] and the returns on its foreign equity portfolio and FDI regularly exceed foreign countries' returns on their equity portfolio and FDI in the United States, and so on (for example, see Forbes 2008). Less controversial is the conclusion that the driving force behind its positive NII lies in the different composition of US assets and liabilities, respectively. In particular, gross US capital exports tend to be relatively more concentrated in riskier assets, yielding a higher expected average annual return, in comparison with US capital imports. The latter are relatively more concentrated in lower-yielding fixed-income assets, in particular official US government bills, notes, and bonds and agency (government-sponsored enterprise) paper.

The underlying factor on the liability side of the US national balance sheet relates to its leading reserve currency status and the persistent perception of US government debt as the world's leading "safe asset." In contrast, on the asset side, the depth of US capital markets and US-headquartered MNCs facilitate the export of sizeable portfolio (debt and equity) capital and direct investment to the rest of the world, including the emerging economies, which themselves invest disproportionately in the official (lower-yielding) assets of the United States and other developed economies.

China's Limited Political Influence

Understanding the political influence that may or may not come with China's creditor's position, just like understanding its financial outcome, requires looking beneath the headline figure. As a large net creditor, China has accumulated sizeable foreign assets, which significantly exceed its foreign liabilities. In principle, these financial claims can vary by type and issuer. Given the dominant position of the United States within the international financial system, a disproportionate share of China's foreign assets is unsurprisingly held in US assets, especially those of the US government and government-sponsored agencies. Therefore, China's net creditor position largely reflects its claims on the United States, especially its lending to the US government. Being a creditor to the United States is quite different from being a creditor to other countries. For instance, there has been much discussion about Chinese lending and aid to Asia, Africa and Latin America (Bräutigam 2009; Gallagher, Koleski

---

11 Recent years have marked an exceptional period in which certain European governments have been able to borrow at lower rates than that of the United States. But these lower rates are more a sign of relatively depressed economic conditions in Europe today.

and Irwin 2012). Certain observers claim that such loans provide China with strong political leverage over the borrowing countries, while securing for China special access to their resources. The politics of China's foreign lending to the developing countries is an important and controversial issue, but beyond the scope of this chapter.[12] Instead, our focus here is on whether China's creditor status is a source of influence over the leading global power, the United States.

China's massive holding of US debt has generated suspicion that it accords China enhanced leverage over the United States.[13] Some evidence suggests that China may have indeed tried to exploit this purported financial leverage. According to diplomatic cables released by WikiLeaks, for instance, following the outbreak of the global financial crisis, China pressed American regulators to accelerate the approval of its US$1.2 billion equity investment in Morgan Stanley. Although American officials did not respond to the request openly, China's purchase of Morgan Stanley shares was announced quickly, suggesting the plausibility of Chinese leverage (Flitter 2011). On the other hand, it is questionable just how effective China's leverage is in pushing for its business interests in the United States. In 2012, President Obama blocked a Chinese company from building wind turbines near a Navy facility in Oregon. Subsequently, Congress released a report declaring that Huawei and ZTE, major Chinese equipment companies, should be blocked from investing in the United States because they posed a threat to national security (Roberts 2012). Such cases illustrate the ongoing obstacles faced by Chinese entities that seek to invest in the United States. Unsurprisingly, during recent years China has invested relatively more in Europe than in the United States (Hanemann and Lysenko 2013).

Beyond individual deals, China may have tried to use its creditor position to gain policy influence. For instance, in the aftermath of the global financial crisis, officials in charge of China's foreign reserves raised the issue of American weapon sales to Taiwan as potentially undermining public support for China's continued purchases of US debt. Indeed, during 2009, when tension rose in bilateral relations, China's holdings of US Treasuries temporarily fell (Flitter 2011). Moreover, Chinese government officials intensified their criticism of expansionary monetary policy in the United States, decrying its depressive

---

12   With regard to China's motivations for lending to developing countries, a recent study of Chinese policy banks' loans to Latin American countries (Gallagher and Irwin 2015) argues that China's lending in the region is about neither soft power nor "extractive diplomacy;" it is primarily commercially driven. There are also signs of late that China is becoming more cautious in making loans to other developing countries (see, for example, Arnold and Hinshaw 2014).

13   For support of this proposition see, for example, Thompson (2007) and for the opposing view see, for example, Drezner (2009).

impact on the RMB value of Chinese-held US dollar-denominated assets (Drezner 2009; Wang 2014b).

However, there is little evidence that Chinese pressure has actually altered US policy. At the height of the global financial crisis, for example, the Chinese government expressed serious concern over the safety of its Fannie Mae and Freddie Mac debt holdings. China (along with Russia) tried to pressure the US government into guaranteeing this agency debt, backing it with the full faith and credit of the US government. The United States opted only for conservatorship, something it would have done without any prodding from the creditors of these government-sponsored organizations (Drezner 2009; Flitter 2011).

While the short-term fiscal outlook in the United States has since improved owing to the economic recovery, little has changed on the long-term entitlement front where the debt trajectory remains unsustainable. Notwithstanding periodic indications or speculation that the Chinese would look to significantly diversify the composition of their FX holdings away from Treasuries and US dollar holdings more generally, it does not appear that any such moves to date have exerted a material impact on US policy. In the event, Chinese exhortations and admonishments have driven neither the reversal of real effective dollar depreciation nor the recent cyclical narrowing in the US fiscal deficit. Rather, given the more rapid US recovery relative to that in Europe and Japan — owing in no small part to aggressive US counter-cyclical policies — the US dollar has appreciated to multi-year highs.

In the longer run, it has been widely suggested that the global capital markets could eventually become seized by the conviction that the US political system would fail to act to avoid a fiscal Armageddon. Such realization would spur a sharp reduction in the willingness of all investors — domestic and foreign residents alike — to hold Treasuries and agency paper. Some have speculated that for economic, if not political, reasons, China could eventually decide to tip the balance (see, for example, Roach 2014). In so doing, China would be progressing beyond its rhetorical anti-US profligacy stance and "voting with its feet" over the perceived recklessness of US macroeconomic policy.

But most observers believe that a threat to "dump" US Treasury holdings is not credible for the foreseeable future because it would cement financial losses for the Chinese themselves. So far, the Chinese government has not exhibited any readiness to disturb what Lawrence Summers (2004) calls a "balance of financial terror." Although more and more Chinese analysts have voiced concerns over the safety of Chinese assets in the United States and urged the

Figure 6: China's Holding of US Government Debt Securities

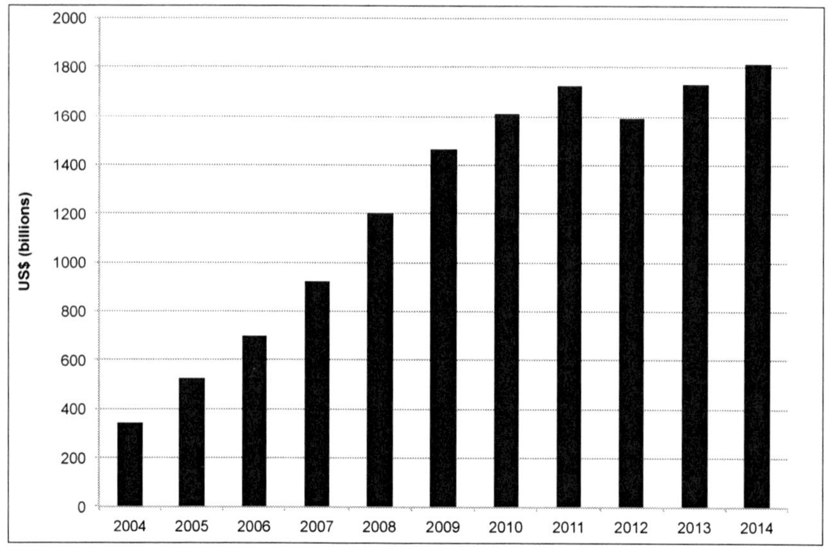

Data source: US Department of Treasury. www.treasury.gov/resource-center/data-chart-center/tic/Pages/ticpress.aspx#2.

government to reduce its holdings of US government debt, by the end of 2014 China had not decreased its stock of US debt securities (see Figure 6).[14]

Not only has China been unable to coax the United States into altering its macroeconomic policy framework, its net creditor status in fact renders it dependent on US structural power within global capital markets. Although China does not divulge the asset and currency composition of its FX reserves, US data indicate that China holds over US$1.2 trillion in Treasury securities alone. This does not include investment in agency paper and long-term equity investments in the United States. A conservative estimate would be that China holds some 60 percent of its official reserves in US dollar-denominated assets.[15]

In this context, it is useful to review how Chinese official views on its international investment position have evolved over time. From 2001 to 2012, China's official reserves rose rapidly from about US$200 billion to over US$3 trillion. For a while, this trend met with unreserved enthusiasm. By the end of 2006, China's foreign reserves had exceeded the symbolic threshold of US$1 trillion. For many inside and outside the government this represented an historical accomplishment. They argued that "foreign reserves are a manifestation

---

14   These numbers are most likely an underestimate of China's actual holdings, as they reportedly purchase Treasuries through third parties.

15   It is probably also the case that a substantial share of China's sovereign wealth funds and banking system's foreign assets is held in US dollars.

of the accumulation of a country's wealth and of its comprehensive power. The huge reserves of over $1 trillion mean that our country has abundant international payment capacity. To some degree this highlights China's economic power, which is strong enough to influence the world" (Xinhua 2007).

Emerging from decades of chronic FX shortage, China was understandably eager to build up its reserves. Chinese policy makers' belief in the crucial role of large foreign reserves in safeguarding national power and national security deepened after the Asian financial crisis in the late 1990s. However, not everyone within the Chinese economic policy establishment agreed. For example, in 2007, the head of the SAFE, Hu Xiaolian, noted that sustained huge trade surpluses had rendered macroeconomic management exceedingly complex. He argued that China should gradually achieve a more balanced international payment structure (Hu 2007). In fact, almost as soon as China began to publish its NIIP data, SAFE officials conceded that net foreign assets did not accurately mirror a country's financial power. Instead, a country's financial strength might rest more on the maturity of its financial markets, the international competitiveness of its financial institutions and the internationalization of its currency. Certain officials pointed out that even though the United States was the world's largest international "debtor," its overall global financial influence remained dominant (Xinhua 2006).

Voices of concern over the quality of China's net foreign asset position grew progressively louder in subsequent years. Some analysts have complained that China's holding of Treasuries has cost it dearly because their returns compare poorly with China's inward FDI-related income payments abroad, a factor raised above (see, for example, Wang 2007). Some have attributed China's (disappointing) NII to US structural power, including the dominance of the dollar in the international financial system (Ba 2010). They argue that China should diversify the currency composition of its reserve holdings and increase the scope of private assets relative to official assets through gradual capital account liberalization (see, for example, Zhang 2012).

This concern appeared to become more pressing with the introduction of quantitative easing in the United States and other advanced countries. Chinese analysts argue that such reflationary policies threaten China's interests and rights as an international creditor (Wang 2014b). For instance, a Chinese official once made the following, unusually candid comment: "We hate you guys. Once you start issuing $1 trillion–$2 trillion…we know the dollar is going to depreciate, so we hate you guys but there is nothing much we can do" (quoted in Prasad

2014).[16] In the event, concerns over inflationary finance in the United States were never realized. If anything, by spurring the US recovery, quantitative easing proved positive for the global economy, including China.

For Chinese authorities to disparage the United States over notional losses on their FX reserves seems disingenuous. China's export-led growth strategy has required it to manage the external value of the RMB. China's unprecedented accumulation of FX reserves mirrors this tightly managed exchange rate regime. In the context of a US-dominated financial system, such a policy choice has made China subject to eventual losses owing to the expected trend appreciation of the RMB (against the US dollar and other currencies).[17] But this "cost" has to be measured against the economic and social gains associated with higher employment and economic growth, achieved, in part, thanks to repressed (nominal) currency appreciation.

To summarize, China's net creditor status has failed to deliver the financial gains or tangible political influence one might have expected. At least with respect to its holdings of US government assets, China has been unable to leverage its creditor status into significant political or economic concessions. One such concession, presumably, would have been a US macroeconomic stance that facilitated a secular appreciation (as distinct from mere cyclical rebound) of the dollar. Instead, Chinese policy makers and analysts increasingly have come to view China's large holdings of US debt as a burden, effectively rendering China a prisoner to US policy diktat. Yet, the key factor underlying China's vulnerability concerns China's choice of development model (including exchange rate regime) against the backdrop of US structural power within the global economy.[18]

---

16   Of course, the current US economic cycle renders this concern somewhat less compelling as the dollar's effective exchange rate had reached new multi-year highs in 2014 and early 2015 with the prospects of tighter US monetary policy.

17   Future RMB real appreciation would reflect the well-known Balassa-Samuelson effect for a rapidly growing developing country. We are also persuaded by the view, articulated in particular by Michael Pettis (2014), that the losses the Chinese have long feared on their official reserves have already been incurred at the moment of FX intervention.

18   Chin and Helleiner (2008) compare China's vulnerability to American structural power with Japan's in the 1980s and argue that China is less vulnerable in that the Chinese state (rather than private actors) controls most of its external assets and that China does not depend on the United States for its national security. Nevertheless, they agree that China has been subject to the structural power of the United States, which limits its own financial power.

Creditor Status and Development Model

As noted above, China's positive NIIP has resulted principally from its persistent current account surplus over recent years. The greatest contributor to this surplus has been its favourable trade balance, which has in turn resulted from China's export-led development strategy. In this section, we explore in depth the relationship between China's net creditor status and its development model. We also discuss why China has been slow in abandoning this model despite a clear recognition of its costs, including the dilemma of the "dollar trap" (Prasad 2014). But before that, it is useful to situate China's net export of capital in a comparative context.

As a net capital exporter with nearly US$4 trillion in official reserves, disproportionately in the government assets of developed countries, China is a leading example of capital flowing "uphill." This violates conventional economic logic that predicts that capital will flow "downhill" from rich to poor countries. The presumption here is that the marginal productivity of capital invested in developing economies typically should exceed the rate of return on capital projects in the United States, Europe and other parts of the developed world. Because China remains a relatively poor country — per capita income (adjusted by purchasing power parity [PPP]) stood under US$12,000 in 2013, ninetieth in the world — China should be a net capital importer, hence a current account deficit country.

Nevertheless, China's example as a developing, large net creditor country is not unique, nor is the United States the sole example of a rich, large net debtor country. Economists have identified factors such as human capital differentials and political and credit market risks (Lucas 1990; Reinhart and Rogoff 2004) as factors that explain a net flow of capital to developed countries. Moreover, some empirical work supports the view that current account *surpluses* are statistically associated with higher economic growth in emerging economies. One interpretation is that emerging market countries are less constrained by an inadequate supply of domestic savings and more constrained by an inability to locate high-return investment projects (Prasad, Rajan and Subramanian 2007). Still, China appears to be a veritable outlier regarding the extent to which it exports capital. No other large emerging market country has run a string of current account surpluses as large as China has run over the last decade. And in a region now known for the rapid accumulation of central bank reserves held in US Treasuries, China overshadows all of its neighbours, with the sole exception of Japan (see Figure 7). Meanwhile, (much richer) Japan is the only country in the world that rivals China in the size of its net creditor status.

Figure 7: Asian Economies' Holdings of US Treasuries

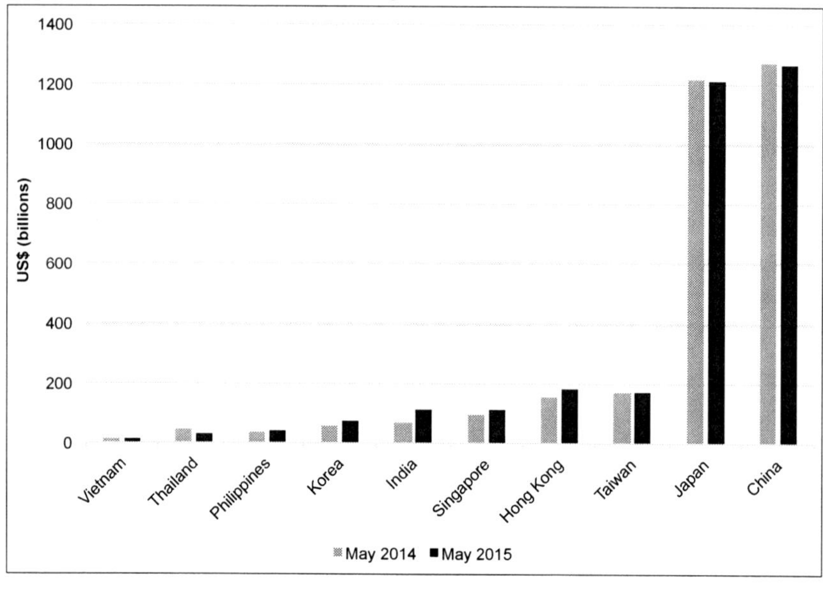

Data source: US Department of Treasury (www.treasury.gov/ticdata/Publish/mfh.txt).

A significant factor underlying China's uphill capital flow phenomenon concerns its repressed financial system. As we saw in the last section, the composition of China's gross international assets and liabilities is rather revealing. In particular, while it is a net exporter of financial capital (notably including FX reserves), China is actually a net importer of fixed capital — that is, direct investment. This feature reflects the discrepancy between the (relatively low) return on financial assets in China versus the relatively high marginal product of capital, particularly for those investment projects that attract foreign interest. Both the reliance on imported FDI (including the managerial acumen, advanced technology and intangible capital that accompany it) and the large net export of financial capital are a function of the (underdeveloped and policy-repressed) domestic financial system. Epitomizing these shortcomings of the financial (and political) system are a heavily borrowing-constrained household and private enterprise sector. Given their lack of ready access to credit, coupled with the paucity of reasonably well-yielding savings vehicles, households have a strong propensity to save more to meet certain core goals, even in low-interest bank accounts. Despite additional worthy projects promising high economic returns, private enterprises cannot secure ready access to the ample savings of Chinese households. When not being taxed to fund (generally less productive) state-owned enterprise (SOE) investment, excess household savings are effectively recycled abroad in the form of FX reserves.[19]

An accounting truism is that a country's current account balance equals its national savings-investment balance. A current account surplus country, therefore, would be one in which national savings exceed domestic investment. As shown in Figure 8, China's national savings rate has been significantly higher than that of the United States (and most other countries) for the last quarter of a century. Although China's investment has also been very high, its savings rate has been even higher. Consumption in China has been extraordinarily constrained even in comparison to other, high-savings East Asian countries at comparable stages of development (see Figure 9).[20] This pattern has supported China's export-led strategy, driving, in turn, its current account surplus and net creditor position.

Figure 8: Gross National Savings — China vs. United States

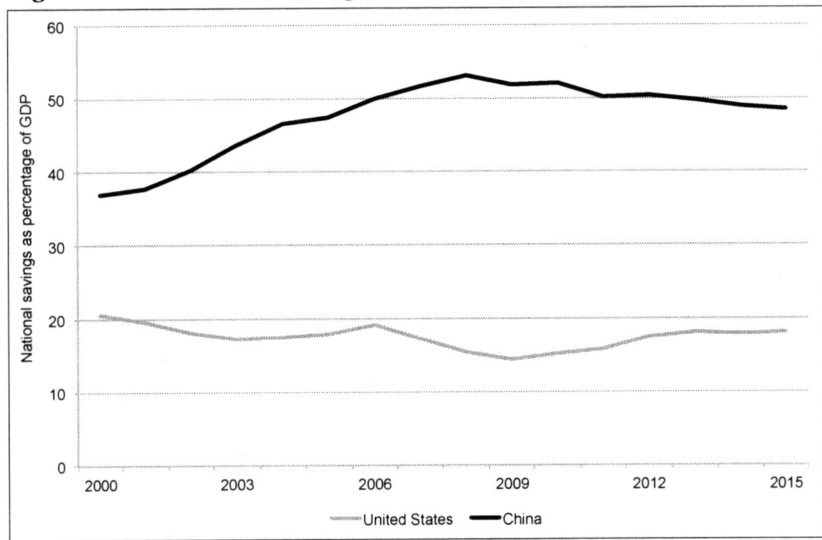

Source: IMF (2015).

---

19   For a mathematical model featuring some of these institutional characteristics of the Chinese economy, see Wang, Wen and Xu (2015).

20   Few observers dispute the comparatively low consumption share of China's GDP. Yet, it should be pointed out that at the same time that the consumption/GDP ratio fell below 40 percent, China's real average annual consumption growth was demonstrably robust. This no doubt reflects the positive externalities of China's outsized economic growth. For a sharp statement of this perspective, see Subramanian (2011).

Figure 9: Consumption–GDP Ratio in Selected East Asian Economies

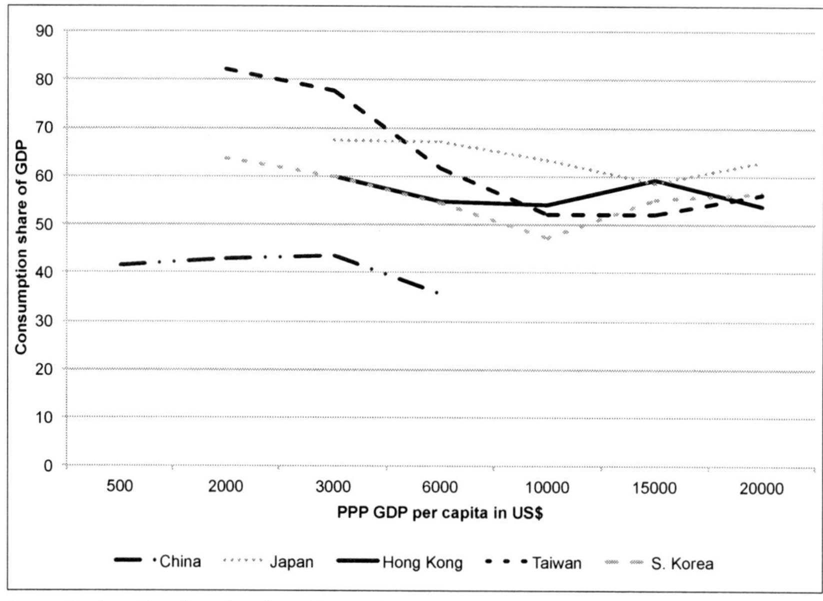

Source: Authors; based on data from Heston, Summers and Aten (2012).

This high-savings model has worked well in supporting economic growth, but it has been otherwise problematic. In particular, the sustained trade surplus has been a source of economic friction between developed and many emerging countries. And the growing size of the Chinese economy will make it increasingly difficult for the world to accommodate a sustained export surplus. Since the beginning of the Hu Jintao-Wen Jiabao administration in 2003, Chinese leaders have called for "changing the development model" to one based more on domestic consumption. After the global financial crisis in 2007-2008, the Chinese government came to recognize more clearly the vulnerability of China's economic growth to conditions abroad. Accordingly, the 18th Party Congress under the leadership of Xi Jinping re-stressed the urgency of economic restructuring.

Over the last decade, the Chinese government has adopted various policies aimed at boosting domestic consumption. For instance, it has tried to bolster household income by abolishing agricultural taxes and increasing wages for the urban work force. It has also expanded the provision of welfare in order to reduce precautionary savings. As a result, the household savings rate has stopped growing in recent years. Nevertheless, household consumption as a share of GDP actually declined to a low of 34 percent in 2013.

China's high savings rate reflects not only household savings, but also corporate savings (essentially corporate profits) and government savings (budgetary balance). China ranks near the top globally in all three components of savings — household, corporate and government. This combination elevates China's overall savings well above that of most countries. In recent years, the growth of corporate and government savings has been a major source of the rapid growth of national savings (Ma and Wang 2010; Prasad 2011). While corporate savings have gone up in many Asian countries since the Asian financial crisis, the rapid increase of government savings seems to have been especially notable in China. According to a report by the China International Capital Corporation, as of September 2014, total bank deposits held by government agencies and public institutions reached 30 percent of GDP (Li 2014). It is no wonder that policies focusing only on reducing household savings have been ineffective in reducing national savings.

Why have efforts to revamp China's economic growth model progressed so slowly? To be sure, the answer lies partially in economic factors.[21] But the most crucial factors are political, including the institutional framework and the power of vested interests, as discussed in the following section.

Political Obstacles for Reform

China's development model has proven resilient because many of its core features have been institutionalized. More than 30 years of economic reforms created a mixed economy best described as state capitalism. This system is characterized by limited use of market mechanisms combined with state ownership of the largest enterprises and state control of the most strategic and profitable sectors of the economy (Pearson 2005). Chinese state capitalism features a close symbiotic relationship between the government and businesses at every level. An "entrepreneurial state," "local state corporatism" and "capitalism with Chinese characteristics" are a few labels scholars have used to capture the political essence of the system (Duckett 1998; Oi 1999; and Huang 2008).

One prominent institutional feature of China's state capitalism is its state-controlled financial system featuring systemic financial repression. Although the Chinese government has introduced certain reform measures to diversify bank ownership, for example, publicly listing large state-owned commercial banks, creating joint stock banks and local government-backed banks, and allowing foreign banks to enter the Chinese market in limited ways, the financial

---

21   Paul Bowles (2012) argues that China's economic structure makes it a profit-led growth regime rather than a wage-led one. The introduction of wage-led growth policies in a profit-led growth regime is not likely to succeed in promoting economic growth.

system remains heavily state-dominated. As of 2010, state-owned banks and banks where the national government holds controlling shares accounted for 57 percent of total banking assets (Martin 2012). Indeed, the government enjoys significant influence over the operation of all types of banks regardless of their ownership. While the government has taken steps toward liberalizing interest rates and exchange rates since 2012 (see chapter 3 of this volume), bank lending continues to privilege SOEs at the expense of other enterprises. And by manipulating deposit and lending rates, Chinese banks have effectively transferred substantial wealth from households to large SOEs (Lardy 2012). One estimate puts this transfer in the neighbourhood of five to seven percent of GDP each year (Pettis 2011). This has enabled many large, inefficient SOEs to remain highly profitable, contributing strongly to corporate savings.

Expanded financial liberalization would go a long way toward raising exceedingly negative real interest rates that have served SOEs at the expense of consumers. In principle, this would help reduce excessive (household and corporate) savings, which in turn should, *ceteris paribus*, reduce China's current account surplus. Moreover, the liberalization of interest rates will directly raise the costs of sterilization, incenting a deceleration in official reserve accumulation (see further discussion below).

Another institutional feature of China's state capitalism is a bureaucratically dominated public finance system, which has extracted more and more of the national wealth and allocated less and less of it to enable household consumption. From 1999 to 2011, government revenues grew from RMB 1 trillion to over RMB 10 trillion, at an average annual growth rate of about 20 percent, well above the growth rate of GDP and household income. Various commentators criticized this trend as being part of the general phenomenon of *guojin mintui* (advancement of the state and retreat of the society) (see, for example, Tang 2012). Officials argue that it is necessary for the government to have adequate fiscal flexibility in order to implement counter-cyclical policy, redistribute wealth and build up the national defence (Xiang 2011).

Concentration of national wealth in the hands of the government, in principle, could serve to boost consumption through redistribution and welfare spending. However, China's fiscal system has a built-in bias against such policies. At the national level, although the National People's Congress (NPC) is authorized to approve the government's budget, its function has been little more than that of a rubber stamp. Instead, the main actors are the National Development and Reform Commission (NDRC) and the Ministry of Finance (MoF). Local government spending is even less transparent than that of the central government, consisting of large amounts of "extra-budget" items (Wong 2007).

Government bureaucracies at every level are motivated to invest in infrastructure and manufacturing because they contribute to economic growth, the leading criterion for political advancement. Large infrastructure projects also offer ample opportunities for officials to enrich themselves. In contrast, social welfare programs are unlikely to produce as many political and economic benefits in the near term. Without accountability to the public, government officials have few incentives to increase such spending.[22]

Reforming the public finance system would mark an important step toward rebalancing savings and consumption. With more public input and oversight, the government would be more constrained and accountable in its collection of revenues. Furthermore, a public finance system more responsive to public needs would place greater priority on social welfare spending relative to the traditional emphasis on GDP growth. As a result, government savings are likely to decline. More government spending on social programs should also reduce household precautionary savings. These factors can help decrease national savings, and *ceteris paribus* shrink China's current account surplus.

Thus far, the pace of financial liberalization and the democratization of public finance has been very slow. Although the government has called for a change of development model and knows what needs to change for that to happen, actual policies have been constrained by the power struggle between the defenders of the current model and the beneficiaries of reform.

The defenders of the existing model of development include powerful government and corporate actors, such as the NDRC, the MoF, the State Asset Supervision and Administration Commission (SASAC), large SOEs and local governments in the coastal provinces. The NDRC and MoF derive their power from the allocation of state-controlled resources through planning, guidance and budgeting. The SASAC and large SOEs owe their influence to the dominant position of the state sector in China's economy. For local governments in the coastal region, the export-oriented development strategy has brought jobs, revenues and political advances for their officials. They have strong incentives to maintain an export-oriented development strategy. All such winners from the existing system are politically powerful actors, whose vested interests lie in preserving the current development model, the very same model that supports China's net creditor status.

---

22   The allocation of the government's RMB 4 trillion stimulus package after the global financial crisis in 2008 offers a good illustration of how public money is spent in China. According to the plan made by the NDRC, the vast majority of the funds went to infrastructure. In contrast, social welfare spending only constituted eight percent of the package.

Systemic reform would serve the interests of many groups, including private entrepreneurs, labour, and the general population, all of whom have suffered from financial repression and an investment-focused system. With financial liberalization private entrepreneurs and households would gain greater access to credit, and the general public would earn higher returns on their savings. A public finance system more accountable to the people would pressure the state to implement its promise to increase social spending, improve average living standards and moderate savings. However, in China's political system today, these groups have little influence. They are largely excluded from the policy-making process and have few channels through which they can voice their preferences and advocate for their interests (Wang 2014a).

Nevertheless, the reformist agenda has found support within the Chinese government, with the impetus coming from the bureaucratic interests as much as a vision of national well-being. The NPC has long been a weak branch of the Chinese government, whose role has been to rubber stamp Party policy. Yet in recent decades, the NPC has adopted a somewhat independent stand on certain policy issues (O'Brien 2008). For instance, in shaping and promulgating the Social Security Law in 2010, the NPC faced much resistance from powerful employer groups and influential bureaucracies. The lawmakers worked hard to win more generous welfare provision for workers. As a key participant said, "we argued all the time against officials in the Ministry of Finance and the Ministry of Labor and Social Security. We told them they are too un-generous toward the workers. They didn't argue back because they knew we were right."[23]

Another institutional base for reform is the PBoC. As David A. Steinberg and Alex He point out in this volume, the PBoC cares principally about inflation. Preventing the RMB from appreciating too rapidly has required systematic FX intervention. Meanwhile, to avoid an overly expansionary money supply on the basis of more and more central bank-held FX assets has required sterilized intervention. But sterilization has proved increasingly costly, given the interest rate differential between domestic and foreign bonds (held as FX reserves). While ceilings on rates were designed to limit the costs of sterilization, the latter policy imposed additional burdens on the banks whose assets included sizeable quantities of domestic bonds. Therefore, the PBoC tended not to favour RMB undervaluation. And it increasingly believes that it can better control inflation (while preserving banking system stability) via a more market-based exchange rate regime.

As a bastion of reform-minded officials, the PBoC has taken steps toward liberalizing the financial system, including allowing greater scope for market

---

23   Author interview, 2012.

forces to influence interest rates and exchange rates. Some observers argue that the PBoC's recent push for RMB internationalization is "reform by Trojan Horse," aimed at pushing the liberalization of China's financial system (see chapters 2 and 8 of this volume). After all, in order for the RMB to become a credible international currency, China must advance domestic financial reforms, expand capital account liberalization and allow greater exchange rate flexibility.[24]

Overall, the interest and power configuration in China have posed serious obstacles to a fundamental alteration of development strategy. For instance, the government began to consider a plan to reform income distribution in 2004, and it was not until 2013 that the State Council even issued an opinion on the matter. In October 2014, Premier Li Keqiang presided over a State Council meeting, calling for government agencies to develop concrete plans to reform income distribution. It is not hard to imagine the amount of political resistance and struggle behind this protracted process of reform, which will likely continue for years, complicating the shift toward a domestic consumption-based growth model.

Looking Ahead

In rebounding from the US balance-sheet recession, Americans have reduced debt obligations — household debt as a share of real disposable income has declined significantly — and the US current account deficit as a share of GDP has shrunk to the range of two percent. In parallel, China has likewise reduced its current account surplus to the range of two percent. The IMF projects that China's and the United States' current account balances will not return to the elevated levels of 2005–2008. Yet, the IMF also forecasts that (stock) NIIP imbalances will continue to expand even as global current account imbalances narrow and essentially stabilize. This makes sense since even modest (positive and negative) current account balances will continue to move NIIP in the same directions, respectively (Lane and Milesi-Ferretti 2014).

As long as current account surpluses persist, China's NIIP would continue to trend upward. Under these conditions, China would presumably continue to bid for US assets, given the paucity of viable alternatives and provided that the United States does nothing substantial to damage its creditworthiness. This will perpetuate the eventual losses China must recognize owing to its systematic FX intervention. If Chinese leaders seriously embark on the transition, however,

---

24   One might draw a parallel with the earlier efforts by reformers in the Chinese government to use China's accession to the World Trade Organization to speed up domestic economic reforms (Kim 2002).

over time one would anticipate an increase in national welfare as household income rises relative to national production.[25] Meanwhile, increasing household income and consumption, and more generally expanding domestic demand-led growth, will decelerate the buildup in China's net external assets and may, in the long run, be associated with a modest net debtor position.

Would such an eventuality — a gradual transition from net creditor to (eventual) net debtor — materially reduce China's leverage in international affairs? It need not. A more decisive factor concerns the pace and depth of Chinese economic reform. Under a progressive reform strategy, the stabilization and eventual reversal of China's NIIP (mirroring more domestic demand-led growth) would coincide with a more efficient allocation of capital and more sustainable economic growth.[26] Ultimately, a country's influence in international affairs is positively related to its material capabilities and general economic performance.

This chapter has focused on China's net creditor status — its lending to the US government being the most important contributor to this. Nevertheless, its net creditor status represents only one, albeit crucial, dimension of China's role in the international financial system. China has also rapidly increased its bilateral lending to developing countries in recent years, raising alarms over the growing influence that may ensue. Furthermore, with its substantial financial resources, China is poised to play a leading role in various minilateral financial institutions, such as the New Development Bank and the Asian Infrastructure Investment Bank. Yet, China is discovering that many of its debtors may prove unable to repay (*The Economist* 2015; Kynge and Wildau 2015). And whether China's various minilateral initiatives threaten to seriously challenge or even undermine the international financial institutions remains to be seen (Wang, Wen and Xu 2015). Finally, as its remaining capital controls are progressively dismantled in the coming years, China's growing exposure to the vagaries of international capital movements will accelerate. This increasing international financial integration will bring economic and political consequences. A broader discussion of China's creditor status would address such issues more comprehensively, but they lie beyond the scope of the present chapter.

---

25   Besides being equal to the savings-investment balance, a country's current account also equals the difference between national production and the absorption of (spending on) domestic resources. A falling current account balance, therefore, implies that the growth of production must slow down relative to the growth of income (and spending).

26   It is important not to overstate China's reliance on extensive growth. In particular, in addition to an elevated rate of investment, China's labour productivity has vastly outpaced that of the advanced countries, something one would expect from a reasonably run emerging market economy that is able to exploit the "low-hanging fruit" that underpins productivity growth at lower development levels. Even today, China's productivity growth, although considerably lower, still exceeds that of the advanced economies.

Conclusion

In assessing global economic power, how much weight should one attach to a country's net international investment position? Does international creditor status translate unambiguously into economic gains and geopolitical influence? This chapter has argued that NIIP is an exceedingly noisy indicator. Nevertheless, weakly substantiated conclusions abound concerning the global power implications of net creditor (debtor) status for China and the United States, in particular.

For starters, one needs to deconstruct China's international financial position into its constituent subcomponents. After this exercise has been performed in this chapter, the purportedly positive contribution of net creditor status for China's international influence and leverage seems less obvious. In particular, China's ongoing accumulation of disproportionately US dollar-denominated FX reserves has involved increasing economic costs. Scant evidence of greater leverage over economic and/or geopolitical policies in the United States has accompanied this increasingly expensive policy stance. In contrast, its greatest gross foreign liability — FDI — has probably done more to strengthen China's economic fundamentals than any other single factor.

Second, China's international asset position must be assessed in the context of the country's broader development challenge. If successful, China's transition to more domestic consumption-led growth, alongside other core structural reforms, should slow the increase and eventually reduce China's net creditor position. In the process, China's economic system will become more balanced and more conducive to greater national prosperity, providing a firmer material foundation for global influence.

Finally, the implications of creditor versus debtor status should be explored within the context of the existing power structure that underpins the international monetary system. The overriding feature of this system today seems clear: the United States continues to predominate via the overwhelming depth and liquidity of its capital markets, the Federal Reserve's effective functioning as the global lender of last resort and the uncontested reserve currency status of the dollar. In comparison, China's financial system appears rudimentary, major capital controls remain in place and the currency has far to go to achieve advanced internationalization. That progress along these lines can be achieved only via a fundamental transformation of China's development model places its current creditor status in perspective.

Works Cited

Arnold, W. and D. Hinshaw. 2014. "China Takes Wary Steps Into New Africa Deals." *The Wall Street Journal*, June 6. www.wsj.com/articles/SB1000142 40527023036472045795458131948736 56.

Ba, S. 2010. "Ruhe Kandai Zhongguo Dangqian De Zhaiquanguo Diwei." ["How to View China's Current Creditor Nation Status."] http://finance.sina.com.cn/review/20100906/14488609766.shtml.

Bowles, P. 2012. "Rebalancing China's Growth: Some Unsettled Questions." *Canadian Journal of Development Studies/Revue canadienne d'études du développement* 33 (1): 1–13.

Bräutigam, D. 2009. *The Dragon's Gift: The Real Story of China in Africa*. New York, NY: Oxford University Press.

Brown, S. 2013. *The Future of US Global Power: Delusions of Decline*. Basingstoke, UK: Palgrave Macmillan.

Chin, G. and E. Helleiner. 2008. "China as a Creditor: A Rising Financial Power?" *Journal of International Affairs* 62 (1): 87–102.

Drezner, D. 2009. "Bad Debts: Assessing China's Financial Influence in Great Power Politics." *International Security* 34 (2): 7–45.

Duckett, J. 1998. *The Entrepreneurial State in China*. London: Routledge.

Flitter, E. 2011. "Special Report: China Flexed Its Muscles Using US Treasuries." www.reuters.com/article/2011/02/17/us-wiki-china-treasury-idUSTRE71G47920110217.

Forbes, K. 2008. "Why Do Foreigners Invest in the United States?" NBER Working Paper 13908. Cambridge, MA: National Bureau of Economics Research. www.nber.org/papers/w13908.

Gallagher, Kevin P. and Amos Irwin. 2015. "China's Economic Statecraft in Latin America: Evidence from China's Policy Banks." *Pacific Affairs* 88 (1): 99–121.

Gallagher, K. P., K. Koleski, and A. Irwin. 2012. *The New Banks in Town: Chinese Finance in Latin America*. Washington, DC: Inter-American Dialogue.

Hanemann, T. 2014. "China's International Investment Position: 2014 Update." http://rhg.com/notes/chinas-international-investment-position-2014-update.

Hanemann, T. and A. Lysenko. 2013. "Chinese Investment: Europe vs. the United States." http://rhg.com/notes/chinese-investment-europe-vs-the-united-states.

Helleiner, E. 2006. "Below the State: Micro-Level Power." In *International Monetary Power*, edited by D. Andrews. Ithaca, NY: Cornell University Press.

Heston, Alan, Robert Summers and Bettina Aten. 2012. "Penn World Table Version 7.1, Center for International Comparisons of Production, Income and Prices at the University of Pennsylvania, July.

Hu, X. 2007. "Cujin Guoji Shouzhi Jiben Pingheng, Shixian Guomin Jingji Youhao Youkuai Fazhan." ["Promote a Basic Balance in the International Balance of Payments, Achieve Good and Rapid Development of the National Economy."] Speech at the national conference on foreign exchange management in Beijing, January 21. http://news.xinhuanet.com/politics/2007-01/21/content_5633601.htm.

Huang, Y. 2003. *Selling China: Foreign Direct Investment during the Reform Era.* New York, NY: Cambridge University Press.

———. 2008. *Capitalism with Chinese Characteristics.* Cambridge: Cambridge University Press.

IMF. 2015. World Economic Outlook database. www.imf.org/external/pubs/ft/weo/2015/01/weodata/index.aspx.

Kim, I. 2002. "Accession into the WTO: External Pressure for Internal Reforms in China." *Journal of Contemporary China* 11 (32): 433–58.

Kynge, J. and G. Wildau. 2015. "China: With Friends Like These." *Financial Times*, March 17. www.ft.com/intl/cms/s/0/2bb4028a-cbf0-11e4-aeb5-00144feab7de.html#axzz3W5SIvxAr.

Lane, P. and G.M. Milesi-Ferretti. 2014. "Global Imbalances and External Adjustment after the Crisis." Washington, DC: IMF.

Lardy, N. 2012. *Sustaining China's Economic Growth after the Global Financial Crisis.* Washington, DC: Peterson Institute for International Economics.

Levey, D. and S. Brown. 2005a. "The Overstretch Myth: Can the Indispensable Nation Be a Debtor Nation?" *Foreign Affairs* (March April): 2–7.

———. 2005b. "'Levey and Brown Reply,' A Rejoinder to Brad Setser and Nouriel Roubini, 'How Scary Is the Deficit': American Power and American Borrowing." *Foreign Affairs*, July/August: 198–200.

Li, X. 2014. "Surge in Govt Savings to Weigh on Growth." *China Daily USA*, November 6. http://usa.chinadaily.com.cn/epaper/2014-11/06/content_18879855.htm.

Lucas, R. 1990. "Why Does Capital Flow from Rich to Poor Countries?" *American Economic Review* 80: 92–96.

Ma, G. and Wang Y. 2010. "China's High Saving Rate: Myth and Reality." *International Economics* 122: 5–39.

Martin, M. 2012. *China's Banking System: Issues for Congress.* Washington, DC: Congressional Research Service.

Norloff, C. 2010. *America's Global Advantage: US Hegemony and International Cooperation.* New York, NY: Cambridge University Press.

O'Brien, K. J. 2008. *Reform without Liberalization: China's National People's Congress and the Politics of Institutional Change.* New York, NY: Cambridge University Press.

Oi, J. 1999. *Rural China Takes Off.* Berkeley, CA: University of California Press.

Pearson, M. M. 2005. "The Business of Governing Business in China: Institutions and Norms of the Emerging Regulatory State." *World Politics* 57 (2): 296–322.

Pettis, M. 2011. "The Contentious Debate over China's Economic Transition." Carnegie Endowment for International Peace. http://carnegieendowment.org/2011/03/25/contentious-debate-over-china-s-economic-transition/37hy.

———. 2014. *The Great Rebalancing: Trade, Conflict, and the Perilous Road ahead for the World Economy.* Princeton, NJ: Princeton University Press.

Prasad, E. 2011. "Rebalancing Growth in Asia." *International Finance* 14 (1): 27–66.

———. 2014. *The Dollar Trap: How the US Dollar Tightened its Grip on Global Finance.* Princeton, NJ: Princeton University Press.

Prasad, E., R. Rajan, and A. Subramanian 2007. "Foreign Capital and Economic Growth." *Brookings Papers on Economic Activity*, spring: 153–230.

Reinhart, C. and K. Rogoff. 2004. "Serial Default and the 'Paradox' of Rich to Poor Capital Flows." *American Economic Review Papers and Proceedings* 94 (2): 53–58.

Roach, S. 2014. *Unbalanced: The Codependency of America and China.* New Haven, CT: Yale University Press.

Roberts, D. 2012. "Huawei, ZTE, and Chinese Investment in the U.S." Bloomberg Business. www.bloomberg.com/bw/articles/2012-10-08/huawei-zte-and-chinese-investment-in-the-u-dot-s-dot.

Rosen, D. and T. Hanemann. 2014. "New Realities in the US-China Investment Relationship." http://rhg.com/notes/new-realities-in-the-us-china-investment-relationship.

Setser, B. 2008. "Sovereign Wealth and Sovereign Power." *Council Special Reports.* No. 37, September, Washington, DC: Greenberg Center for Geoeconomic Studies at the Council for Foreign Relations.

Setser, B. and N. Roubini. 2005a. "How Scary Is the Deficit? American Power and American Borrowing." *Foreign Affairs,* July/August, 194–98.

————. 2005b. "The Kindness of Strangers, A Reply to Levey, David and Stuart Brown, 'How Scary is the Deficit: American Power and American Borrowing." *Foreign Affairs,* December, Special Edition for the Ministerial Meeting of the World Trade Organization's Doha Round, Hong Kong.

SAFE. 2015a. "Zhongguo Guoji Shouzhi Pingheng Biao Shijian Xulie Shuju [Chinese Balance of Payment Time Series Data]." www.safe.gov.cn.

————. 2015b. "Zhongguo Guoji Touzi Toucun Biao shijian Xulie Shuju [Chinese International Investment Position Time Series Data]." www.safe.gov.cn.

Strange, S. 1987. "The Persistent Myth of Lost Hegemony." *International Organization* 41: 551–74.

Subramanian, A. 2011. *Eclipse: Living in the Shadow of China's Economic Dominance.* Washington, DC: Peterson Institute for International Economics.

Summers, L. H. 2004. "The United States and the Global Adjustment Process." Speech at the Institute for International Economics, March 23, 2004. www.iie.com/publications/papers/paper.cfm?researchid=200.

Tang, Y. 2012. "Zhengfu Shouru Guodu Kuozhang De Fumian Xiaoying Yu Zishen Liyi De Goujian" [The Negative Effect of the Excessive Expansion of Government Revenues and the Construction of Self-interest Curtailing Mechanisms]. *Shijie jingji qingkuang* [*World Economic Situation*] (10): 61–65.

The Economist. 2015. "China's Financial Diplomacy: Rich but Rash." *The Economist,* January 31.

Thompson, H. 2007. "Debt and Power: The United States' Debt in Historical Perspective." *International Relations* 21 (3): 305–23.

US Bureau of Economic Analysis. 2015. "Table 1.2. U.S. Net International Investment Position at the End of the Period, Expanded Detail." www.bea.gov/iTable/iTable.cfm?ReqID=62&step=1#reqid= 62&step=6& isuri=1&6210=5&6200=144.

Wang, X. 2007. "China as a Net Creditor: An Indication of Strength or Weakness." *China & World Economy* 15 (6): 22–36.

Wang, H. 2014a. "Global Imbalances and the Limits of the Exchange Rate Weapon." In *The Great Wall of Money: Power and Politics in China's International Monetary Relations*, edited by Eric Helleiner and Jonathan Kirshner, 99–126. Ithaca, NY: Cornell University Press.

———. 2014b. *China and Sovereign Debt Restructuring.* CIGI Papers No. 45. www.cigionline.org/publications/china-and-sovereign-debt-restructuring.

Wang, P., Y. Wen and Z. Xu. 2015. "Two-Way Capital Flows and Global Imbalances." Working Paper 2012-016B. Research Division. Federal Reserve Bank of St. Louis. February http://research.stlouisfed.org/ wp/2012/2012-016.pdf.

Wong, C. 2007. "Budget Reform in China." *OECD Journal on Budgeting* 7 (1): 1–24.

World Bank. 2015. http://data.worldbank.org/indicator/NY.GDP.MKTP.CD.

Xiang H. 2011. "Zhongguo Caizheng Tizhi Gaige Liushinian" [Sixty Years of Reform of the Chinese Fiscal System]. www.chinareform.org.cn/ economy/tax/practice/201112/t20111202_129043.htm.

Xiao, G. 2004. "People's Republic of China's Round-tripping FDI: Scale, Causes and Implications." Asia Development Bank Institute Discussion Paper7. https://openaccess.adb.org/bitstream/handle/11540/3595/2004.06. dp7.foreign.direct.investment.people.rep.china.implications. pdf?sequence=1.

Xinhua. 2006. "Waihui Guanliju: Ruhe Kandai Zhongguo Guoji Touzi Toucun Zhuangkuang" ["SAFE: How to view China's NIIP]?" http://news.com/ fortune/2006-05/25/content_4600146.htm.

———. 2007. "Zhongguo Waihui Chubei Yu'e Tupo Wanyi Meiyuan." ["China's Foreign Reserves Surpass One Trillion Dollars."] http://news.xinhuanet.com/fortune/2007-01/15/ content_5609476.htm.

Zhang, C. 2012. "Zhongguo waihui chubei duoyuanhua guanli yanjiu [A Study of the Diversification of the Management of China's Foreign Reserves]." Ph.D. dissertation, Wuhan University. http://cdmd.cnki.com.cn/Article/ CDMD-10486-1013029251.htm.

8

The Domestic Political Sources of China's International Financial Policies

David A. Steinberg

ew countries are as important to the global monetary and financial system as China. As the world's second-largest economy and its biggest exporter of goods, China's monetary and financial policies inevitably have profound impacts throughout the global economy.[1] Moreover, China's international financial policies are far from ordinary. China continues to impose stringent controls on international capital flows, even though most other countries have reduced restrictions on cross-border capital flows in recent decades. China also holds far more foreign currency reserves than any other country. These interventions in the foreign exchange market are a form of "exchange rate protectionism" that suppresses the value of China's currency, the renminbi (RMB). C. Fred Bergsten (2010), a former undersecretary of international affairs in the US Treasury Department, has suggested that China's currency policies represent "the largest protectionist measure maintained by any major economy since the Second World War."

This chapter examines why China's international monetary and financial policies differ dramatically from most other nations. In other words, my objective is to illuminate the political origins of China's international monetary and financial policies. As Eric Helleiner and Jonathan Kirshner (2014b, 2) recently pointed out, "the study of China's increasingly important role in the international monetary system has focused primarily on economic questions

---

1   According to the World Bank (2014), China's GDP was second only to the United States in 2013. The World Trade Organization (2014, 32) reports that China exported a larger volume of goods than any other country in 2013.

and technical issues, with much less detailed attention given to the *politics* of China's international monetary relations." Following Helleiner and Kirshner's (2014a) lead, this chapter explores how political considerations influence China's decisions about international monetary policies.

My central argument is that China's international monetary and financial policies strongly reflect China's unique domestic political and economic structures. China's political elites have incentives to adopt international financial policies that benefit the country's most powerful interest groups, namely politically connected firms and the export-oriented manufacturing sector. The interests of these powerful interest groups go a long way toward explaining why China retains capital controls, keeps its exchange rate relatively fixed and undervalued, and has accumulated foreign reserves at an unprecedented pace. To be sure, there are a variety of other factors that also influence China's international monetary and financial policies. Rather than attempt to provide a comprehensive account of this issue, my goal in this chapter is to demonstrate that interest group politics are one important — and often underappreciated — force behind China's international monetary and financial policies.

I develop this domestic political argument in three main steps. The first section is theoretical. There, I explain why domestic politics is likely to influence various facets of international financial policy. In the second section, I describe China's domestic political and economic system, and explain how it empowers certain interest groups at the expense of others. The third section summarizes key facets of China's international financial policies and shows that Chinese leaders selected these policies in large part because of the benefits that they provided to powerful interest groups. The final section summarizes my findings and discusses their implications for the future.

Why Domestic Politics Influences International Financial Policies

How do governments choose which international monetary and financial policies to adopt? Economic considerations undoubtedly matter. However, these economic considerations tend to be insufficient on their own. It is often unclear which international financial policies are optimal from the standpoint of the nation as a whole. As Jonathan Kirshner (2003, 4) reminds us, for most facets of financial policy, "the aggregate benefits of various policy decisions are ambiguous, modest, and dwarfed by their political and differential effects." Simply put, international financial policies create clear winners and losers. This section examines the distributional effects of various aspects of international financial policy and explains how political battles between winners and losers of various policies shape policy choices.

To support this argument, I examine four facets of international financial policy: capital account policy; the degree of exchange rate stability; the level of the exchange rate; and foreign reserve holdings. For each of these four issue areas, there is no single choice that is best for the nation as a whole. Each policy, however, has powerful distributional effects. Table 1 lists the winners and losers of each of these four policies.

Several caveats are in order before proceeding. First, these are surely not the only relevant facets of international financial policy, but they represent several of the most important decisions that countries must make vis-à-vis the global financial system. Second, although my discussion analyzes these four policies separately, they are not entirely independent of one another. These policy choices are at least partially interrelated. For this reason, when I discuss the Chinese case later in the chapter, I integrate the discussion of several of these policy issues. Nevertheless, for analytical purposes, it is useful to treat these policies as distinct. As shown in Table 1, each policy issue creates somewhat distinct groups of winners and losers.

Table 1: The Distributional Effects of International Financial Policies

Policy	Winners	Losers
Capital Controls	Politically connected firms	Non-politically connected firms, savers
Fixed Exchange Rate	Internationally oriented industries	Domestically oriented industries
Undervalued Exchange Rate	Export-oriented firms, import-competing firms	Firms with foreign-currency debts, non-tradable firms, labour
Foreign Reserve Accumulation	Export-oriented firms, import-competing firms	Financial sector

Source: Author.

Capital Controls

Countries must choose whether to maintain capital controls — defined as regulations, taxes and other barriers to cross-border investment flows — or to remove impediments to international capital flows. Neither policy choice is optimal for all citizens or countries. Instead, the distributional effects of capital account policy often swamp the aggregate welfare effects. Hence, government decisions regarding capital controls are driven as much by political considerations as by economic ones.

In theory, open capital markets should enhance welfare because they allow investment funds to flow to the location where they will earn the highest rate of return. Capital account openness should, therefore, lead to a more efficient allocation of capital. In reality, however, it is not clear that these aggregate efficiency gains are very large. Previous studies have failed to uncover strong and consistent support for the proposition that capital account openness increases economic growth (see Eichengreen 2001; Kose et al. 2009).

Moreover, from a macroeconomic standpoint, capital account openness is no free lunch. The theory of the "open economy trilemma," due originally to Mundell (1963) and Fleming (1962), explains why. According to this theorem, countries are able to attain only two of the following three outcomes: free flow of capital across borders; a fixed exchange rate; and monetary policy independence. Thus, capital controls help countries maintain a stable exchange rate and enhance their ability to use monetary policy for domestic purposes, such as to smooth out the business cycle. By contrast, when countries open themselves up to international capital flows, it is more difficult for central banks to adjust interest rates for purely domestic purposes. This can be an important cost of open capital markets: the loss of monetary policy independence makes it more difficult for governments to respond to economic downturns. Consequently, open capital markets may increase macroeconomic volatility (Tornell, Westermann and Martinez 2004). The very existence of a trilemma suggests that there is no single level of capital controls that is optimal when it comes to macroeconomic outcomes.

Another reason that capital account openness intensifies economic instability is that international capital flows tend to be pro-cyclical. Countries with open capital markets are more vulnerable to "surges" in capital inflows that are often followed by equally rapid reversals in capital flows (Ahmed and Zlate 2014; Ghosh et al. 2012; Rey 2013). Capital controls are a potentially valuable policy tool because they can reduce countries' vulnerability to rapid swings in capital flows.

Overall, then, the decision to adopt or remove capital controls poses difficult trade-offs between various goals, including between efficiency and volatility. From the standpoint of national welfare, it is unclear how intense or loose capital controls should be (see also Kirshner 2003, 4–6). There is no single choice that is optimal for all citizens or countries.

The distributional effects of capital account policy often swamp the aggregate welfare effects. Capital account policy creates clear winners and losers.[2] Politically connected firms are one group that often benefits from the imposition

---

2   This discussion of the distributional effects of capital controls borrows from Nelson, Steinberg and Nguyen (2014).

of capital controls — at least in political and economic contexts where rulers have incentives to cater to these firms. Many developing countries have used capital controls as part of a general strategy of "financial repression" (Giovannini and De Melo 1993; Leblang 1997). Developing countries frequently use capital controls to help keep domestic interest rates below international interest rates and/or below their market levels. Excessively low interest rates, in turn, generate an excessive demand for credit and the need for credit rationing. In such conditions, the allocation of credit typically becomes politicized, and the government channels subsidized credit to politically connected firms. Since governments often use capital controls-cum-financial repression to channel cheap credit to politically connected firms, these firms have much to gain from the imposition and retention of capital controls. Evidence from Malaysia supports this intuition: Johnson and Mitton (2003) show that the imposition of capital controls in the 1990s increased the stock prices of firms with strong ties to the prime minister.

On the other hand, capital controls are anathema for several interest groups. Firms that lack political connections — typically small, private sector firms — tend to have difficulty obtaining credit from local banks and are harmed by capital controls as a result. Capital account liberalization benefits these firms because it reduces the government's role in allocating credit — a role that, more often than not, starves them of credit. In addition, capital account openness makes it easier for firms to borrow from abroad, thus opening up new avenues through which they can obtain funding.

Savers also benefit from capital account openness. Capital controls hurt savers for the same reason that they help connected firms: this policy allows governments to suppress interest rates. Consequently, when governments restrict capital flows, savers often earn low, or even negative, real returns on their savings. Below-market interest rates serve as a form of implicit taxation on savers. Capital controls facilitate this type of financial repression because they ensure that depositors are unable to move their funds abroad to escape this type of taxation and earn better rates of return. Open capital markets thus benefit savers because it makes it harder for governments to tax their savings in this way. It also enables individuals to move their savings abroad and earn potentially higher returns in the process. Moreover, capital account liberalization allows savers to construct internationally diversified portfolios, which reduces their exposure to downturns in local financial markets (Freeman and Quinn 2012).

In short, some domestic groups benefit from capital controls while others are better off without such controls.[3]

Capital controls clearly illustrate why domestic politics matters for international financial policy. From the standpoint of national welfare, it is unclear whether governments should retain capital controls or liberalize them. It is therefore improbable that policy choices in this realm are driven entirely by economics. Since capital controls have strong distributional effects, it is likely that political considerations, such as the balance of political power between competing social groups, influence capital account policy.

Fixed Exchange Rates

The exchange rate regime, which refers to the arrangements by which a currency's foreign exchange value is determined, is a second important facet of international financial policy. In essence, the decision about the exchange rate regime is a decision about the degree of exchange rate stability or flexibility (Frieden 1991). At one extreme, countries may keep the exchange rate fully fixed in value against a foreign currency. At the other end of the spectrum, countries may adopt a floating exchange rate, in which authorities allow the exchange rate to regularly fluctuate in response to market conditions. Many countries also adhere to intermediate arrangements, such as "managed floating" systems, where central banks permit market forces to influence the value of the currency but they intervene in the exchange rate market to prevent excessive volatility.

The choice between fixed and flexible exchange rates is strongly influenced by domestic politics. Each policy option involves costs and benefits, and it is difficult to make a strong case that either fixed or flexible exchange rates are unambiguously superior. Similarly to the case of capital controls, research often fails to find any systematic relationship between the exchange rate regime and economic growth rates (Ghosh et al. 1997; Rose 2011). As Jeffrey Frankel (1998) put it, "no single currency regime is right for all countries or at all times."

Whether a fixed or flexible exchange rate is appropriate depends on various national attributes, which are often referred to as the "optimum currency area" criterion (Mundell 1961; McKinnon 1963). For instance, fixed exchange rates

---

3   It should be noted that some interest groups have more mixed and ambiguous interests. The local banking sector is one example. On the one hand, capital account liberalization benefits local banks because it enables them to expand their overseas operations and to obtain cheaper capital from abroad. On the other hand, liberalization intensifies competition because it makes it more likely that foreign financial institutions enter the national financial market (Pepinsky 2013).

are more beneficial to economies that are closely integrated with the economy of the anchor-currency country. Thus, economic theories, such as optimum currency area theory, have the potential to provide useful prescriptions about when countries should fix their exchange rates. On the other hand, optimum currency area theory has a poor track record when it comes to explaining actual policy choices. Policy makers regularly ignore the prescriptions of this theory. The European monetary union is one clear example: countries adopted the euro in spite of the fact that most academic economists believed that the euro zone was not an optimal currency area. Consequently, there was "widespread skepticism about the desirability of a monetary union in Europe" (De Grauwe 2006, 712).

Rather than national welfare, it is the distributional effects of exchange rate regimes that have the strongest impact on whether countries maintain fixed or flexible exchange rate arrangements. Jeffry Frieden (1991) points out that internationally oriented industries benefit from fixed exchange rate arrangements. Fixed exchange rate systems reduce the risks and costs of international economic transactions and, in turn, increase the volume of international trade (Klein and Shambaugh 2006; Lee and Shin 2010; López-Córdova and Meissner 2003; Rose 2000). Hence, firms and individuals heavily engaged in international trade and investment should favour a fixed exchange rate.

Fixed exchange rates also create losers. Domestically oriented industries are one such group (Frieden 1991). For any given level of capital controls, fixed exchange rates reduce monetary policy independence. Because fixed exchange rates tend to make it more difficult for governments to use interest rate adjustments to smooth out the business cycle, they tend to increase economic volatility (di Giovanni and Shambaugh 2008; Levy-Yeyati and Sturzenegger 2003). Economic volatility is especially costly for those citizens whose fortunes are tied to the performance of the national economy — that is, those employed in domestically oriented sectors of the economy. Whether governments maintain fixed or flexible exchange rates should depend greatly on the relative political influence of domestically oriented industries and internationally oriented ones.[4]

---

4   Bearce and Hallerberg (2010), Blomberg, Frieden and Stein (2005), Frieden (2002) and Steinberg and Malhotra (2014) present cross-national evidence that fixed exchange rate regimes are more (less) likely in countries where internationally oriented (domestically oriented) industries are powerful.

Undervalued Exchange Rates

The level of the exchange rate is a third aspect of international financial policy that is influenced by domestic political considerations. The issue at stake here is whether governments keep their foreign exchange rate near its "equilibrium value," defined here as the level that equalizes domestic and foreign prices.[5] Many governments intervene in the foreign exchange market to push their exchange rates away from their equilibrium values. Some governments keep their exchange rates more depreciated than the equilibrium rate, which is known as an "undervalued" exchange rate. Other governments do the opposite and maintain appreciated, or "overvalued," exchange rates.

It is difficult to explain government decisions toward the exchange rate level on the basis of purely economic criterion. Most economists agree that overvalued exchange rates are highly problematic. One problem is that they increase the risk of financial crises. Overvaluation reduces exports relative to imports, and countries eventually run out of foreign exchange to pay for imports, leading to currency and sovereign debt problems. Previous research reveals that an overvalued real exchange rate is one of the strongest predictors of the onset of a financial crisis (see, for example, Kaminsky, Lizondo and Reinhart 1998; Frankel and Saravelos 2012). And yet, despite the widespread recognition that overvalued exchange rates are economically suboptimal, many governments overvalue their exchange rates. Many countries in Africa and Latin America have overvalued their exchange rates since the 1960s and a number of Eastern European countries have done so during their transitions from Communism. The frequent adoption of overvalued exchange rates is not driven by considerations of aggregate economic welfare. As Huizinga (1997, 273) points out, "real exchange rate overvaluation…[is] puzzling, because it can hardly be the case that developing country policy makers do not know how to reverse overvaluations, or that they believe that real exchange rate overvaluation generally improves economic efficiency and welfare."

Economics also fails to provide clear guidance for policy makers trying to decide whether to keep the exchange rate undervalued or keep it at its equilibrium rate. There is no consensus among economists as to whether an undervalued exchange rate or a market-valued one is better for economic performance. Economic orthodoxy maintains that exchange rates are best kept at their market

---

5   This condition is known as "purchasing power parity." There are several alternative definitions of the equilibrium real exchange rate, but I focus on purchasing power parity because it is the simplest and most widely used benchmark.

rates, for any distortion is problematic.[6] On the other hand, a large number of recent studies have found that countries with undervalued exchange rates grow more rapidly than both those with overvalued exchange rates and those whose exchange rates are close to their equilibrium values (Béreau, Villavicencio and Mignon 2012; Berg and Miao 2010; Levy-Yeyati, Sturzenegger and Gluzmann 2013; Gluzmann, Levy-Yeyati and Sturzenegger 2012; Mbaye 2013; Rodrik 2008).[7] However, some other recent studies call this evidence, and the wisdom of undervaluation, into question. Haddad and Pancaro (2010) find that undervaluation has positive short-run effects, but more negative long-term effects on growth. Nouira and Sekkat (2012) fail to find any evidence of a positive association between undervaluation and growth while Schröder (2013) presents evidence that growth is most rapid when the exchange rate is near its equilibrium rate. In short, economic research does not currently provide unequivocal evidence in favour of an undervalued exchange rate strategy.

As with other facets of international financial policy, decisions about the exchange rate level are influenced by distributional considerations. Although it is unclear whether undervaluation promotes or hinders economic growth, it is quite clear which groups within the economy benefit from an undervalued exchange rate. Firms that export their products and those that compete against foreign producers are the strongest beneficiaries of an undervalued exchange rate (Frieden 1991). Keeping the exchange rate undervalued reduces the costs of domestically produced goods in international markets. As a result, undervalued exchange rates are associated with "export surges" (Freund and Pierola 2012). Undervalued exchange rates also make imported goods more expensive, which encourages local consumers to shift their expenditure from foreign goods to locally produced ones. Thus, firms that produce goods that are internationally tradable, such as agricultural and manufacturing goods, benefit from an undervalued exchange rate.

At the same time, undervalued exchange rates inflict substantial harm on other groups. Undervalued exchange rates raise the costs of imports, which is problematic for businesses and consumers that rely on imported products

---

6   According to Williamson (1990), a "competitive," or non-overvalued, exchange rate is one of the 10 principles of the "Washington Consensus." He summarizes the consensus view as follows: "the real exchange rate needs to be sufficiently competitive to promote a rate of export growth that will allow the economy to grow," but it "should not be more competitive than that, because that would produce unnecessary inflationary pressures and also limit the resources available for domestic investment."

7   A number of explanations have been offered for this finding. Some economists believe that undervaluation promotes growth because it reduces real wages, which increases aggregate investment rates (Levy-Yeyati, Sturzenegger and Gluzmann 2013). Others argue that undervaluation is beneficial because it encourages production in tradable industries, which tend to have higher productivity rates than other industries (Rodrik 2008).

(Frieden 1991). Firms that produce non-tradable goods, such as those in the service and construction sectors, are examples. Since non-tradable firms, by definition, do not compete against foreign producers, an undervalued exchange rate provides them with few benefits. However, many non-tradable firms rely upon imported intermediate inputs.[8] Thus, undervaluation is problematic for firms in the construction and service sectors because it raises their operating costs without improving their competitiveness.

Workers are another group that tends to be harmed by an undervalued exchange rate. Undervaluation of the exchange rate makes imported consumer goods, such as food and clothing, more expensive. As a result, an undervalued exchange rate reduces workers' real wage rates and their purchasing power (Broz and Frieden 2001; Huizinga 1997; Levy-Yeyati, Sturzenegger and Gluzmann 2013).

An undervalued exchange rate also harms financial institutions, firms and individuals with debts that are denominated in foreign currency. In developing countries, it is common for firms and individuals to have unhedged foreign currency debts, meaning that their debts must be repaid in foreign currency, typically dollars, while their revenues or earnings are denominated in local currency (Eichengreen and Hausmann 2005). An undervalued exchange rate is very costly to actors with unhedged foreign currency debt: currency depreciations increase the value of their foreign debts relative to their earnings (Pepinsky 2009; Walter 2013; Woodruff 2005). Since an undervalued exchange rate creates clear winners and losers, the balance of power between these opposing political forces is likely to impact whether governments undervalue their exchange rates.

Foreign Reserve Accumulation

Central banks must choose how large a stockpile of foreign reserves to hold.[9] Many developing countries have acquired large quantities of foreign reserves since the Asian financial crisis of the late 1990s. However, there is dramatic variation in the size of reserve holdings across countries today. Here, I explain why the size of a country's foreign reserve stockpile has more to do with domestic politics than with economics (see also Steinberg 2014).

Economists have put forth two main explanations for the rapid accumulation of foreign reserves in developing countries. The first explanation, known as the

---

8   Using firm-level survey data from the World Bank, Steinberg (2015, 39) reports that the average firm in the service and construction sector in the developing world exports just five percent of its production but imports 29 percent of its inputs from foreign countries.

9   In addition to deciding on the quantity of foreign reserves, governments must also choose how to allocate their foreign reserves across different currencies. I do not tackle that question in this chapter. For political-economy analyses of this issue, see Bowles and Wang (2008), Helleiner and Kirshner (2009), and Shih and Steinberg (2012).

"precautionary theory," asserts that countries accumulate reserves because they want to enhance financial stability. Holding large quantities of foreign reserves reduces countries' vulnerability to financial crises (see, for example, Frankel and Saravelos 2012). Since financial crises are costly events, this argument suggests that it can be rational for welfare-maximizing governments to accumulate large quantities of foreign reserves, especially when countries have opened themselves up to international capital flows (Aizenman and Lee 2007; Aizenman and Marion 2003; Obstfeld, Shambaugh and Taylor 2010; Steiner 2013).

A second popular explanation, often referred to as the "mercantilist theory," maintains that countries accumulate reserves as a means to promote exports (Dooley, Folkerts-Landau and Garber 2003; 2004). According to this argument, central banks purchase foreign reserves to prevent their exchange rates from appreciating, and thus promote exports. Michael Dooley, David Folkerts-Landau and Peter Garber (2004, 2) argue that reserve accumulation is a "sensible" development strategy because it encourages investment in export-oriented industries, which results in a "superior" domestic capital stock.

These economic theories of reserve accumulation highlight two important benefits of reserve accumulation — financial stability and export-led growth — but it remains far from clear that it is optimal for countries to acquire large quantities of foreign reserves. The costs of foreign reserves are also quite substantial. First, foreign reserves are an unprofitable asset for central banks to hold. Most foreign exchange reserves are held in the form of US Treasury securities, which yield a very low rate of interest. Dani Rodrik (2006) estimates that the low returns earned on foreign reserves reduce many countries' income by as much as one percent of GDP. Increased inflationary pressures are a second cost of large-scale reserve accumulation (Pineau et al. 2006; Roubini and Setser 2005). Foreign reserve accumulation can increase inflation because it increases the amount of liquid assets in the economy.[10] While reserve accumulation undoubtedly brings about some economy-wide benefits, it also has several negative effects. It is far from clear what the optimal level of foreign reserves is, and many scholars believe that China and other countries have accumulated excessive amounts of foreign reserves (Calvo, Izquierdo and Loo-Kung 2012; Green and Torgerson 2007; Jeanne 2007; Rodrik 2006; Summers 2006).

While governments surely consider these macroeconomic effects when choosing their reserve policies, their decision about the level of foreign reserve holdings is likely to hinge at least as much on whether foreign reserve accumulation helps

---

10   While central banks can reduce the inflationary effects of foreign reserve accumulation via "sterilized" interventions — selling bonds to offset the increase in liquidity — their ability to effectively sterilize foreign currency inflows is often limited (Calvo 1991).

or harms particularistic interest groups. As with the previous three policy issues, rapid accumulation of foreign reserves creates concentrated winners and losers. Since reserve accumulation contributes to the undervaluation of the exchange rate, and undervaluation benefits export-oriented and import-competing industries, these groups should favour reserve accumulation.

The financial sector is one interest group that is harmed by reserve accumulation. As mentioned earlier, reserve accumulation tends to increase inflationary pressures, and the financial sector typically dislikes inflation with passion (Kirshner 2003, 19-20; Posen 1995). Another problem is that large-scale foreign reserve accumulation often requires an intensification of domestic financial regulations and controls, which directly reduces the profitability of financial institutions (Cruz and Walters 2008, 671). Whether governments rapidly accumulate reserves or not is likely to depend in large part on the political influence of groups that are helped and those that are harmed by this policy.

Summary and Implications

In sum, domestic politics is an important driver of international financial policies. Policies toward the international financial system — such as whether to impose capital controls, maintain a fixed exchange rate, undervalue the exchange rate and accumulate foreign reserves — are not determined solely by economic considerations. Each of these policy choices creates winners and losers. Consequently, decisions about international financial policy are heavily influenced by distributional considerations. International financial policies are likely to reflect the preferences of powerful domestic groups.

China's Domestic Political System

This section describes the balance of political power between various economic interest groups within China. In China, as elsewhere, power is not equally distributed across all social groups. This uneven power distribution creates incentives for leaders to select certain types of international financial policies over others.

Which interest groups are privileged in China's political and economic system and which groups are disadvantaged? Assessing the distribution of power is an inherently difficult task. Nevertheless, it is clear that concentrated business groups tend to control far more political, economic and organizational resources than diffuse groups, such as savers or workers. Moreover, some business groups have more political power than others. The export-oriented manufacturing sector is an especially privileged sector of the economy. Across firms, those with politically connected owners have a greater ability to influence Chinese economic policy than firms whose owners lack such connections.

The organization of China's domestic political system is a major reason why organized interests have advantages over more diffuse interest groups. China has been ruled by one party, the Communist Party of China, since 1949. This authoritarian single-party structure has profound effects on the distribution of power within China. In comparison to democratic governments, authoritarian regimes such as China are responsive to a smaller segment of the population (Bueno de Mesquita et al. 2003). The absence of elections means that the general public and unorganized social groups have few ways of getting their voices heard, and are less likely to influence policy (Bearce and Hallerberg 2011). Consequently, authoritarian governments such as China's have less of a political incentive to adopt international financial policies that benefit savers, the working class and other broad-based groups.[11]

China's system of labour relations further curtails workers' ability to influence government policy (see also Wang 2014, 122-123). Chinese workers are not able to organize into independent labour unions. The country's only legal labour union, the All China Federation of Trade Unions, is effectively controlled by the Communist Party (Chen 2009; Taylor and Li 2007). Similarly, China's constitution does not provide workers with the legal right to strike, and the government retains the ability to declare strikes to be illegal — an ability that it frequently exercises (Chan and Nørlund 1998; Chen 2007). These sorts of restrictions on workers' rights to organize and strike reduce the capacity of the working class to advocate for its economic interests (Anner and Caraway 2010; Mosley 2010). Thanks to a repressive labour system, Chinese policy makers have few incentives to adopt international financial policies that benefit labour.

While producers are generally better positioned to influence Chinese financial policy than consumers or labourers, some businesses are better placed to do so than others. An abundance of evidence shows that Chinese firms with political connections are more likely to win favourable financial policies than firms that lack political connections. Firms that are owned, in whole or in part, by the state obtain better access to finance (Brandt and Li 2003; Firth et al. 2009). Similarly, firms whose owners have joined the Communist Party have an easier time obtaining loans than other firms (Bai, Lu and Tao 2006; Li et al. 2008).

---

11   Previous cross-national studies find that, compared to democracies, authoritarian governments tend to retain stricter capital controls (Eichengreen and Leblang 2008; Eichengreen and Rose 2014; Milner and Mukherjee 2009) and higher degrees of exchange rate stability (Broz 2002; Bearce and Hallerberg 2011; Leblang 1999). As discussed in the previous section (see Table 1), both of these policies tend to benefit special interests relative to the mass public.

Yunling Chen, Ming Liu and Jun Su (2013) demonstrate that firms that have larger entertainment and travel budgets — an indication of their capacity for bribing officials — are rewarded with larger loans from the Chinese banking system. Political connections bring large benefits in China. One would therefore expect politically connected firms to have a greater impact on international financial policy.

Lastly, some business sectors are more politically powerful than others. China's export-oriented manufacturing sector is particularly powerful in China. There are at least three reasons for this. First, even though the export-oriented manufacturing sector is comprised of a large number of relatively small private firms, they have considerable capacity to pressure Party leaders. Most manufacturing production occurs along China's eastern coast, and their geographic concentration makes it easier for firms in this sector to overcome collective action costs and lobby (Kaplan 2006). Second, close ties to key political decision makers enhance this sector's power. Two central ministries, the Ministry of Commerce (MoC) and the National Development and Reform Commission (NDRC), represent the manufacturing sector and advocate for policies that benefit this sector (Foot and Walter 2011, 117; Freeman and Wen 2011; Wright 2009, 182–85). China's manufacturing industries also have ties to political representatives from China's coastal provinces, who have been overrepresented in key Party bodies, such as the Central Committee, Politburo and Politburo Standing Committee, for most of China's era of reform and opening (Li 2005; Shirk 1993). Third, the fact that China's manufacturing sector accounts for a large share of the economy's production and employment makes it difficult for policy makers to ignore this group's preferences.[12] Even if the manufacturing sector does not actively lobby for policies, their economic importance provides them with "structural power" over policy makers — an indirect form of power than enables them to win favour without directly lobbying officials (see Hacker and Pierson 2002).

To summarize, China's political system privileges businesses in the manufacturing sector and those with political connections. By contrast, non-tradable industries, the working class and small savers have little ability to shape China's international financial policies. In the words of Hongying Wang (2014, 122), "private entrepreneurs, labor, and the general population as savers and consumers…are largely excluded from the policymaking process and have few channels to effectively voice their preferences and push for their interests." The next section shows that, over the past decade, China has maintained international financial policies that are largely consistent with the interests of

---

12   Manufacturing production accounts for over one-third of China's total production in most years (Steinberg 2015, 86-87).

the country's most powerful economic interest groups. The evidence also reveals that government officials paid close attention to the distributional consequences of international financial policies. China would probably have adopted different international financial policies if the country's domestic political system allocated political power in a different manner.

The Influence of Domestic Politics on Chinese Financial Policy

When it comes to international financial policy, China has adopted policies that differ substantially from most other nations. This section has two main goals: first, to describe China's international financial policies, and, second, to examine whether and how China's domestic political arrangements influence these policies. As in the earlier sections of this chapter, I focus here on four facets of China's international financial policies: capital controls, the degree of exchange rate stability, exchange rate undervaluation and foreign reserve accumulation.

To help put China's international financial policies in context, Table 2 presents some quantitative indicators of China's international financial policies in the year 2010. The table also compares China with several comparator groups: all other countries; China's peers within the region of East Asia; fellow countries with a history of socialism; and countries at a similar level of development. The quantitative data, as well as my more qualitative description that follows, show that, compared to most of its peers, China adopts more intense capital controls, maintains a more stable exchange rate, keeps its exchange rate more undervalued, and holds more foreign reserves.

Table 2: China's International Financial Policies in Comparative Perspective

	Capital Account Openness	Exchange Rate Stability	Exchange Rate Undervaluation	Foreign Reserves (months of imports)
China	0.16	0.65	0.17	20.70
All Countries	0.49	0.60	0.02	5.97
East Asia	0.53	0.41	0.11	6.51
Socialist or Former Socialist	0.56	0.48	0.22	5.05
Upper Middle Income	0.51	0.56	0.04	6.42

Note: All data are based on the year 2010. Capital account openness and exchange rate stability are from Aizenman, Chinn and Ito (2008). Exchange rate undervaluation was calculated by the author using the approach of Rodrik (2008) and data from Heston, Summers and Aten (2012). Foreign reserve data are from World Bank (2014). The classification of East Asian countries follows the World Bank (2014). The classification of socialist countries is from La Porta et al. (1999). Following the most recent World Bank definition, upper middle income countries are defined as those with per capita GDP between US$4,086 and $12,615; GDP per capita data were obtained from Heston, Summers and Aten (2012). Countries without their own currencies are excluded.

Each of these four facets of Chinese international financial policy benefits some of the country's most powerful interest groups. This is no mere coincidence. One of the main reasons that China retains stringent capital controls, keeps the exchange rate stable and undervalued, and rapidly accumulated foreign reserves is to benefit politically powerful interest groups.

Capital Controls

China heavily regulates short-term capital flows.[13] Since the 1980s, most developing countries have abrogated capital controls, but China has not followed this trend. To be sure, over the past 20 years, China has moved in the direction of greater liberalism when it comes to capital account policy. But the shift in that direction has been fairly limited — especially when compared to most other nations.

China's government maintains intense restrictions on foreigners' ability to invest in China's financial system.[14] Foreigners are simply prohibited from participating in China's money market and derivatives market. Other types of foreign portfolio inflows are allowed but are heavily regulated. The qualified foreign institutional investor (QFII) mechanism, established in 2002, permits foreign portfolio inflows, but requires all transactions to gain the approval of China's State Administration of Foreign Exchange. By the end of 2010, only 97 foreign investors had received permission to enter China's domestic capital market. Moreover, the QFII program sets quotas for each foreign institution as well as quotas for the total amount of foreign portfolio investment.

Similar regulations apply to outflows of foreign portfolio investment. These financial flows are regulated by the qualified domestic institutional investor (QDII) scheme, which was created in 2006 to permit domestic financial institutions to invest abroad. The government approved 88 domestic investors to invest overseas by the end of 2010. However, as with QFII, quotas limit the amount that any single institution can invest abroad and the cross-border issuance of securities still requires government approval.

Overall, then, portfolio investment flows in China remain, in the evaluation of two International Monetary Fund (IMF) researchers, "severely restricted" (Bayoumi and Ohnsorge 2013, 4). Among the 40 types of capital account transactions classified by the IMF, only five were fully open by the end of

---

13   However, regulations on long-term capital flows, also known as foreign direct investment, are much less stringent.

14   Arora and Ohnsorge (2014), Bayoumi and Ohnsorge (2013), Lardy and Douglass (2011) and Zhang (2012b) present excellent descriptions of China's capital account regulations. This section borrows from those works.

2010 and another 25 had some restrictions, while another 10 were completely prohibited (Zhang 2012b, 85). These capital account restrictions are much more stringent than those utilized by most other developing countries (Lardy and Douglass 2011, 14; He et al. 2012, 30).

The data presented in the first column of Table 2 provides further evidence that capital account transactions are much more heavily regulated in China than in most of its peer nations. I use Aizenman, Chinn and Ito's (2008) measure of capital account openness, which ranges from a minimum of zero, for the most stringent capital controls, to a maximum of one if countries do not restrict capital flows. The average country scores above 0.5, but China receives a score of just 0.16.

While it is clear that China maintains unusually strong restrictions on capital flows, the question remains why. The fact that some of the beneficiaries of capital controls have more political clout than many of the groups that are harmed by capital controls contributes to this outcome. In China, politically connected firms strongly benefit from capital controls. One advantage of capital controls is that it makes it easier for governments to intervene in domestic financial markets and target credit toward preferred borrowers. As noted earlier, much evidence suggests that Chinese banks give firms with political connections more favourable treatment than non-connected firms (Bai, Lu and Tao 2006; Chen, Liu and Su 2013; Firth et al. 2009; Li et al. 2008). Capital controls make it much easier for the government to channel credit towards favoured firms. As a result, capital account liberalization would reduce the ability of politically connected firms to obtain these favourable domestic financial policies. In short, firms with political ties strongly benefit from capital controls. As Matthias Vermeiren and Sacha Dierckx (2012, 1656) point out, the "SOEs [state-owned enterprises] are the most important beneficiaries of financial repression…[and] arguably the strongest defenders of capital controls."

Groups that are harmed by capital controls are much more marginalized within China's political system. Small non-politically connected firms that have difficulty obtaining credit within China are one group that would benefit from liberalization of the capital account (ibid., 1655). Capital account liberalization would make it more difficult for the government to retain a non-market-based financial system that discriminates against them. An open capital account would also enable these firms to borrow funds on international capital markets, thus opening up new avenues for them to gain access to credit.

Households are a second group that is harmed by China's capital controls. One consequence of capital controls is that Chinese households have little choice but to deposit their savings in Chinese banks.[15] Unfortunately for them, Chinese banks pay them very low interest rates on their savings. Households actually suffered losses on their savings between 2004 and 2010: the real interest rate on deposits averaged −0.3 percent in this period (Lardy 2012, 78). As Nicholas Lardy (2012, 80) points out, "household interest earnings on average have been far less than they would have been in a more liberalized financial environment." Liberalization of the capital account would enable households to escape punitive taxation on their savings and to diversify their portfolios internationally. Several studies suggest that the removal of capital controls in China would lead to sizable increases in portfolio capital outflows as households shift their savings out of the country (Bayoumi and Ohnsorge 2013; He et al. 2012; Sedik and Sun 2012).

Chinese banks are another interest group that is affected by capital account restrictions, but their interests are less clear-cut than other groups. Capital controls are beneficial for China's banks in some ways. Since capital account liberalization is likely to lead to capital outflows, this could inflict damage on the Chinese banking system. In addition, capital controls ensure that Chinese banks do not have to compete with foreign banks for local market share. Capital controls, and the associated system of financial repression, also benefit banks because the government maintains a sizeable spread between deposit and lending interest rates, which ensures that banks remain profitable. Capital account liberalization would threaten these arrangements (Lardy and Douglass 2011; Vermeiren and Dierckx 2012). However, capital controls also harm Chinese banks in some ways. Certain facets of financial repression, such as extremely high reserve requirements, reduce banks' profits (Zhang 2012a). Capital account liberalization would also be a boon to banks by allowing them to capture a larger share of the global foreign exchange market (Eichengreen 2011). In the end, the interests of China's financial sector are decidedly mixed. This may explain why the financial sector's allies in the Chinese government are divided over capital account policy. Some of the financial sector's allies, such as the People's Bank of China (PBoC), have generally supported capital account liberalization (Vermeiren and Dierckx 2012, 1657). Other officials that are concerned about financial stability, including some scholars in the Chinese Academy of Social Sciences, have emphasized the need to avoid rapid liberalization (Gallagher et al. 2014).

---

15   The QDII program's quota system makes it nearly impossible for Chinese households to develop an internationally diversified investment portfolio. For example, the QDII investment quota was set at just 1.5 percent of total Chinese household savings in 2010 (Lardy and Douglass 2011, 12; He et al. 2012, 30).

The retention of stringent capital controls in China reflects a number of considerations, one of which is the balance of political power between various interest groups. The limited political power of households and small firms — two groups that are harmed by this policy — reduces the incentive to reform the capital account. The interests of politically connected firms are another reason why capital account liberalization has progressed so slowly in China.

Exchange Rate and Foreign Reserve Policies

China's exchange rate and foreign reserve policies also differ in striking ways from most other nations. This section describes China's policy toward the exchange rate regime, exchange rate level and foreign exchange reserves, and examines the political origins of these three policy choices. I integrate the discussion of these three issues because they were closely interconnected issues during the past decade. Broadly speaking, Chinese policy makers debated whether to continue accumulating foreign reserves to keep the exchange rate stable and undervalued, or if they should instead accumulate fewer foreign reserves and let market forces bring about an appreciation of the exchange rate. While there was some variation over time in these policies, the Chinese government largely stuck with the first, more interventionist, set of international financial policies.

Table 2 presents data on the degree of exchange rate stability, exchange rate undervaluation and the size of foreign reserve holdings. Column 2 presents Aizenman, Chinn and Ito's (2008) measure of exchange rate stability, which ranges from a low of zero to a maximum of one. The table shows that China's exchange rate was more stable than most other countries in 2010. The third column compares the degree of exchange rate undervaluation in China with various other groups of countries. This measure, following Rodrik (2008), is a continuous measure, with larger positive values indicating a larger degree of undervaluation of the real exchange rate. According to this measure, China's exchange rate was 17 percent undervalued in 2010. Most other groups of countries had less undervalued exchange rates in 2010, although the average former socialist country had an even more undervalued exchange rate than China in 2010; on the other hand, if one just goes back to 2008, China's exchange rate was considerably more undervalued than the typical socialist economy (22 percent versus 14 percent). China's exchange rate has been more undervalued than most, although perhaps not all, of its peers. The final column in Table 2 presents one measure of a country's foreign reserve adequacy: how many months' worth of imports can be purchased with current reserve holdings. By this metric, China has a far larger stockpile of foreign reserves than most other countries. Overall, the data presented in Table 2 demonstrate that China's exchange rate is more stable and undervalued than most countries and its foreign reserves are exceptionally large.

The Chinese government has shown little willingness to let market forces determine the RMB's value. Figure 1 presents data on the RMB-dollar exchange rate from January 2003 to June 2014. This figure shows that the exchange rate regime has changed several times during this period, but that flexibility has almost always been kept within strict limits. From 2003 to July 2005, China's new leaders, Premier Wen Jiabao and President Hu Jintao, continued their predecessor's policy of keeping the exchange rate fully fixed against the dollar. On July 21, 2005, the exchange rate was revalued 2.1 percent against the dollar. Following the July 2005 revaluation, the exchange rate was officially permitted to fluctuate, but the actual degree of flexibility was kept very minimal over the next two years. It was not until late 2007 that the government permitted the currency to appreciate at a faster pace, but this policy only lasted a few months. In July 2008, the government re-implemented a fixed exchange rate policy, and the RMB was fixed against the dollar for the next two years. Toward the end of 2010, the exchange rate was permitted to fluctuate again, and the exchange rate has been more flexible in the past four years than it was beforehand. Even in this period, however, China's exchange rate is nowhere near a fully flexible exchange rate system and the government continues to heavily intervene in the foreign exchange market.

China's authorities have kept the exchange rate stable by aggressively intervening in the foreign exchange market. There were market-based pressures for the RMB to appreciate against the dollar, but the PBoC, China's central bank, countered these pressures by intervening in the foreign exchange market to an unprecedented extent. The PBoC purchased dollar reserves, which helped keep the value of China's currency stable against the dollar. Figure 2 shows that China's holding of foreign reserves skyrocketed from less than half a trillion dollars in 2003 to over US$3 trillion by 2011 — a record for the largest stockpile of foreign reserves that the world has ever witnessed. These foreign reserve holdings are not just big in absolute value, but also relative to the size of China's economy. China's reserve holdings were worth over 40 percent of China's total GDP in 2012.

Figure 1: Exchange Rate Policy in China, 2003–2014

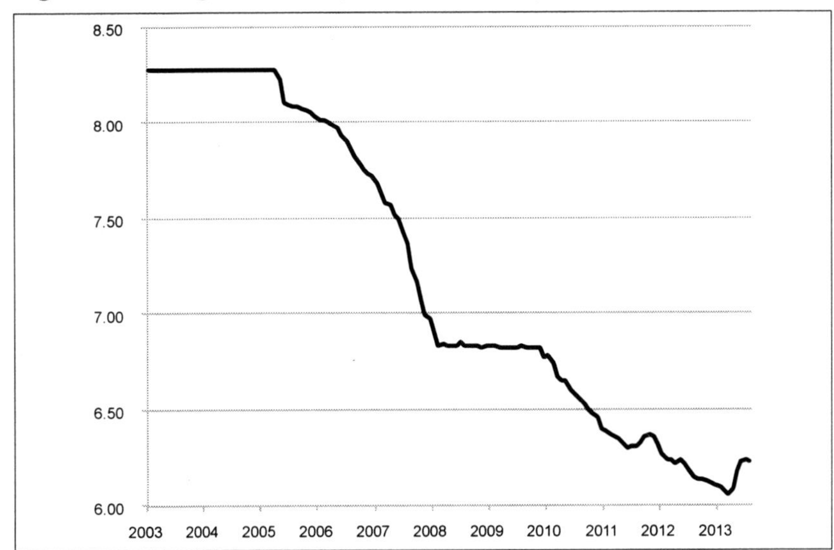

Data source: Federal Reserve Bank of St. Louis' FRED Database.

Figure 2: Foreign Exchange Reserves in China, 2003–2012

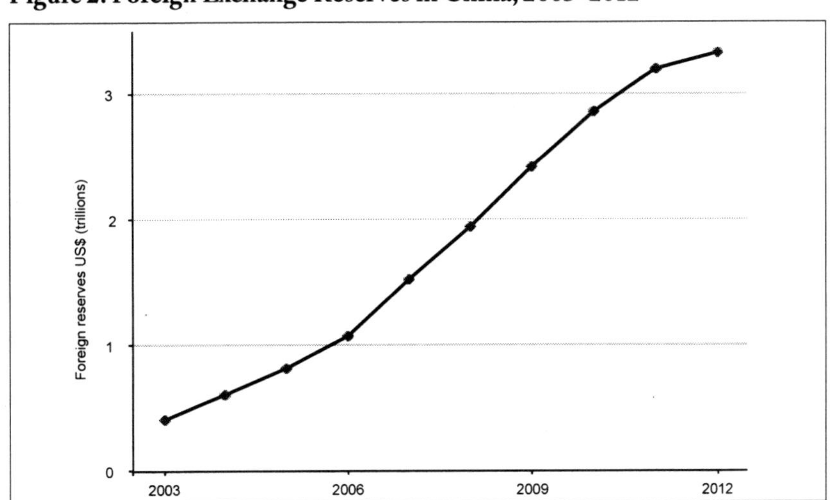

Data source: World Bank (2014).
Note: This figure displays non-gold foreign reserves.

This accumulation of foreign reserves had the effect of keeping China's exchange rate undervalued. Figure 3 presents the estimated degree of undervaluation in China, along with the 95 percent confidence interval of those estimates, for the 2003–2010 period. According to this measure, the exchange rate was 23 percent undervalued in 2003, and then became even more undervalued over the next several years. Although exchange rate appreciation contributed to a reduction in the degree of undervaluation between 2007 and 2010, the data indicate that the RMB remained undervalued in 2010. Unfortunately, my data only goes through 2010, but others scholars' estimates from the 2011–2013 period indicate that China's exchange rate continued to be undervalued throughout those years (Cline 2013; IMF 2013; Lipman 2011). More subjective evaluations accord with these conclusions. For example, the IGM Forum asked 41 prominent economists in October 2011 whether the "Chinese government pursues policies that keep the renminbi's exchange rate vis-à-vis the dollar lower than it would be if the currency floated without those policies." The consensus could hardly have been stronger: 17 percent responded that they were uncertain about the answer or did not know; 83 percent agreed or strongly agreed; and not a single surveyed economist disagreed.[16] Although estimating the degree of undervaluation of the currency is a tricky endeavour, there seems little doubt that the Chinese government has made extraordinarily strident efforts to keep its exchange rate weak and undervalued.

These policy choices did not reflect the preferences of China's top leaders. The gulf between China's international financial policies and the policy preferences of China's political leaders could hardly have been larger. President Hu and Premier Wen had backgrounds in the relatively poor rural inland regions of China. They came into office promising to improve the welfare of these less-well-off groups. To do so, they wanted to rebalance the economy away from investment and exports and toward greater consumption and domestic demand — objectives that would require an increase in exchange rate flexibility and appreciation (Kaplan 2006, 1196; Wright 2009). The top leadership did not appear to have clear ideas about foreign reserves when it came into office. However, after China's foreign reserves crossed the one trillion dollar threshold in 2006, a consensus emerged within the Chinese political elite that further accumulation of reserves would compromise the nation's financial stability (Bowles and Wang 2008, 346; Steinberg 2014, 93; Wright 2009, 256). China's top leaders have had surprisingly little success implementing their preferred international financial policies.

---

16   The results of this survey are available at www.igmchicago.org/igm-economic-experts-panel/poll-results?SurveyID=SV_3IWI6URnw6jxTla.

Figure 3: Exchange Rate Undervaluation in China, 2003–2010

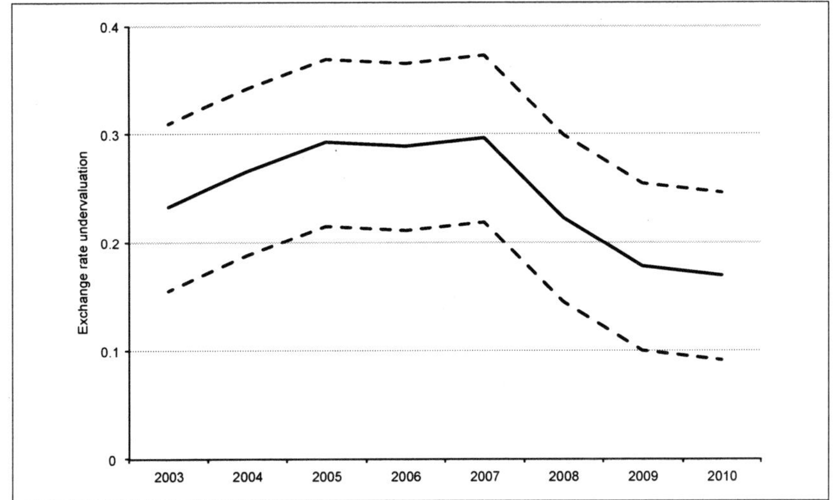

Note: The solid line presents the estimated degree of exchange rate undervaluation. The dashed lines present the 95 percent confidence intervals. Undervaluation was constructed by the author, using data for the 1960–2010 period from Heston, Summers and Aten (2012), and following the methodology of Rodrik (2008).

The preferences of powerful interest groups often trumped those of the president and premier. China's export-oriented manufacturing sector was one group whose policy preferences had a strong influence on China's foreign exchange rate policies. The industrial sector and its allies in the Chinese political system — particularly in the MoC, NDRC and provincial governments in coastal China — consistently lobbied against any government attempts to appreciate the exchange rate.[17] Their lobbying, in turn, was a crucial reason why China's government heavily intervened in the foreign exchange market throughout this period. While opponents of prevailing exchange rate policies started agitating for policy change as early as 2003, lobbying by the exporter coalition was able to delay revaluation until 2005, and was a major reason why appreciation was so limited over the next few years (Steinberg 2015, 102–07). The decision to abandon exchange rate appreciation in 2008 was also driven by intensifying pressures from the industrial sector. Manufacturing firms vocally registered their opposition to exchange rate appreciation in the spring of 2008, and their pressure on top Party leaders was a central reason that the government decided to return to a policy of a fixed undervalued exchange rate in the summer of

---

17   For more detailed descriptions of this lobbying, see Freeman and Wen (2011), Lardy (2012), Steinberg (2015), Steinberg and Shih (2012) and Wright (2009).

2008 (ibid., 110–12). Exchange rate policy makers in China have been very responsive to the preferences of China's manufacturing firms.

Other interest groups in China have been less pleased with the government's foreign exchange policies, but Chinese political elites have been much less concerned with their interests. The working class is one group that has been harmed by China's foreign exchange rate policies: an undervalued exchange rate raises the costs of imports, which reduces workers' real wages. However, because China's working class is not well organized, it has been largely invisible in debates over international financial policy.

The financial sector and the PBoC, which has been the financial sector's main ally within the central government, have been the strongest and most vocal opponents of the fixed undervalued exchange rate and of reserve accumulation.[18] The central bank has repeatedly argued that China should introduce a more flexible exchange rate regime. In the PBoC's view, a less rigid exchange rate system would be beneficial because it would enhance monetary policy autonomy and make it easier for the central bank to control domestic economic conditions.

The central bank also opposed the rapid accumulation of foreign reserves and the undervalued exchange rate for two main reasons. The PBoC's first concern was that these policies exacerbated inflationary pressures. Its desire to limit inflation caused them to lobby for a revaluation of the currency and for less rapid reserve accumulation. Secondly, the central bank worried that China's international financial policies were distorting the national financial system and reducing commercial banks' profitability. To ensure that the rapid increase in foreign reserves did not immediately lead to rising prices, the government sterilized its foreign exchange market interventions, meaning that they sold domestic government bonds to reduce liquidity. However, this sterilization imposed large costs on China's commercial banks, which earned a mere 1.7 percent to 2.5 percent on these bonds — far lower than the 7–8 percent interest they would have earned from lending out those funds.[19] Zhang (2012a) estimates that sterilization reduced the profits of Chinese commercial banks by over RMB 100 billion (about US$13 billion) in 2006 alone.

The central bank and financial sector won some small policy victories between 2003 and 2014. Their advocacy helped bring about some modest appreciation in 2005, 2007, and between 2010 and 2013 (Freeman and Wen 2011, 7; Steinberg

---

18   This discussion of the central bank's preferences borrows from Lardy (2012), Steinberg (2014; 2015), Wright (2009) and Zhang (2012a).

19   For this reason, oftentimes no willing buyers of these bonds came forth, and the central bank had to force the state-owned commercial banks to purchase them.

and Shih 2012, 1416–19; Wright 2009, 202–209, 247–251).[20] However, their relatively weak position in the Chinese political system has limited their gains, and meant that their successes have always been partial and fleeting.[21] The political weakness of groups that favour more market-based international financial relative to those that favour a fixed and undervalued exchange rate has been an important driver of China's international financial policies.

Conclusions and Implications for the Future

When it comes to a government's policies toward the global monetary and financial system, it is often unclear which policies serve the national interest. Most international financial policies — including capital controls, a fixed exchange rate, an undervalued exchange rate and foreign reserve accumulation — create some winners and some losers. The distributional effects of international financial policies are often much clearer than their effects on aggregate welfare. As a result, political considerations, rather than purely economic criteria, typically determine governments' decisions about international finance (Kirshner 2003).

China's government is no exception. This chapter showed that China's international financial policies impose large costs on workers, savers and firms in the non-tradable sector — groups that have limited political clout in China. Chinese leaders were aware of the detrimental effects of their international financial policies, and made some efforts to change policy as a result. However, lobbying by powerful interest groups — politically connected firms and the manufacturing sector — helped dissuade China's leaders from changing course. The evidence indicates that the balance of power within the Chinese political system has influenced China's international financial policies.

This analysis has important implications for our understanding of China's future role in the global monetary and financial system. A number of observers expect that China will ultimately adopt similar international financial policies to previous rising powers, such as promoting the international use of its currency (see, for example, Kirshner 2014; Subramanian 2011). There is no doubt that China has been making some efforts to turn the RMB into an international reserve currency. China has also started to implement various policies, such

---

20   An alternative explanation maintains that US pressure was the main reason for these appreciations. This argument has found little support in the data: quantitative studies reveal that foreign pressure on China to appreciate its exchange rate either had no effect or a *negative* effect on the pace of appreciation (Liu and Pauwels 2012; Ramírez 2013).

21   The central bank's case for appreciation has usually been strengthened during periods of rising inflation. However, this influence has had a tendency to evaporate quickly whenever inflationary pressures subside.

as reducing capital controls and increasing exchange rate flexibility, that are necessary for turning the RMB into an attractive reserve currency. However, as discussed earlier, these steps have been quite modest thus far. A crucial implication of this chapter is that, even if China's political and economic rise continues, China's international financial policies are unlikely to change drastically in the near future unless China's domestic political arrangements also change in meaningful ways.

Even the most optimistic prognosticators realize that the RMB's ability to become an international reserve currency "will be conditional on China undertaking far-reaching reforms of its financial sector and exchange rate policies" (Subramanian 2011, 9). Given the current balance of political and economic power within China, Chinese leaders are unlikely to adopt these "far-reaching reforms" any time soon. The actors within China that favour the government's current financial policies are powerful forces. These groups have been largely successful at blocking attempted financial reforms in the past. There is no obvious reason why their influence should wane over the coming years. Hongying Wang's (2014, 125) study of China's international financial policies echoes this view: "As long as the political foundations of the current model remain in place…it is reasonable to expect minor tinkering to continue without fundamental changes." China's international financial policies are likely to continue to evolve in the direction of greater liberalism and internationalization, but domestic political considerations are likely to hinder major policy changes. Since China's domestic political system differs radically from the domestic political systems of previous rising powers, it is doubtful that a rising China will follow the same policies as earlier rising states.

Works Cited

Ahmed, Shaghil and Andrei Zlate. 2014. "Capital Flows to Emerging Market Economies: A Brave New World?" *Journal of International Money and Finance* 48: 221–48.

Aizenman, Joshua and Nancy Marion. 2003. "The High Demand for International Reserves in the Far East: What Is Going On?" *Journal of the Japanese and International Economies* 17 (3): 370–400.

Aizenman, Joshua and Jaewoo Lee. 2007. "International Reserves: Precautionary Versus Mercantilist Views, Theory and Evidence." *Open Economies Review* 18: 191–214.

Aizenman, Joshua, Menzie D. Chinn and Hiro Ito. 2008. "Assessing the Emerging Global Financial Architecture: Measuring the Trilemma's Configurations over Time." National Bureau of Economic Research Working Paper Series No. 14533.

Anner, Mark and Teri Caraway. 2010. "International Institutions and Workers' Rights." *Studies in Comparative International Development* 45 (2): 151–69.

Arora, Vivek and Franziska Ohnsorge. 2014. "Capital Account Liberalization in China: Some Considerations." In *Capital Account Liberalization in China*, edited by Kevin P. Gallagher, 89–98. Boston, MA: Frederick S. Pardee Center for the Study of the Longer-Range Future.

Bai, Chong-En, Jiangyong Lu and Zhigang Tao. 2006. "Property Rights Protection and Access to Bank Loans." *Economics of Transition* 14 (4): 611–28.

Bayoumi, Tamim and Franziska Ohnsorge. 2013. "Do Inflows or Outflows Dominate? Global Implications of Capital Account Liberalization in China." IMF Working Paper 13/189.

Bearce, David H. and Mark Hallerberg. 2011. "Democracy and De Facto Exchange Rate Regimes." *Economics and Politics* 23 (2): 172-94.

Béreau, Sophie, Antonia López Villavicencio and Valérie Mignon. 2012. "Currency Misalignments and Growth." *Applied Economics* 44 (27): 3503-11.

Berg, Andrew and Yanliang Miao. 2010. "The Real Exchange Rate and Growth Revisited." IMF Working Paper WP/10/58.

Bergsten, C. Fred. 2010. "Protectionism by China Is Biggest Since World War II." *Economix* (blog), October 8. http://economix.blogs.nytimes.com/2010/10/08/biggest-protectionism-since-world-war-ii/.

Blomberg, S. Brock, Jeffry Frieden and Ernesto Stein. 2005. "Sustaining Fixed Rates." *Journal of Applied Economics* 8 (2): 203-25.

Bowles, Paul and Baotai Wang. 2008. "The Rocky Road Ahead: China, the US and the Future of the Dollar." *Review of International Political Economy* 15: 335-53.

Brandt, Loren and Hongbin Li. 2003. "Bank Discrimination in Transition Economies: Ideology, Information, or Incentives?" *Journal of Comparative Economics* 31 (3): 387–413.

Broz, J. Lawrence. 2002. Political System Transparency and Monetary Commitment Regimes. *International Organization* 56 (4): 861–87.

Broz, J. Lawrence and Jeffry A. Frieden. 2001. "The Political Economy of International Monetary Relations." *Annual Review of Political Science* 4: 317–43.

Bueno de Mesquita, Bruce, Alastair Smith, Randolph M. Siverson and James D. Morrow. 2003. *The Logic of Political Survival*. Boston, MA: MIT Press.

Calvo, Guillermo A. 1991. "The Perils of Sterilization." IMF *Staff Papers* 38 (4): 921–26.

Calvo, Guillermo A., Alejandro Izquierdo and Rudy Loo-Kung. 2012. "Optimal Holdings of International Reserves: Self-Insurance against Sudden Stop." National Bureau of Economic Research Working Paper Series No. 18219.

Chan, Anita and Irene Nørlund. 1998. "Vietnamese and Chinese Labour Regimes: On the Road to Divergence." *The China Journal* 40: 173–97.

Chen, Feng. 2007. "Individual Rights and Collective Rights: Labor's Predicament in China." *Communist and Post-Communist Studies* 40 (1): 59–79.

———. 2009. "Union Power in China Source, Operation and Constraints." *Modern China* 35 (6): 662–89.

Chen, Yunling, Ming Liu and Jun Su. 2013. "Greasing the Wheels of Bank Lending: Evidence from Private Firms in China." *Journal of Banking & Finance* 37 (7): 2533–45.

Cline, William R. 2013. "Estimates of Fundamental Equilibrium Exchange Rates, November 2013." Peterson Institute for International Economics Policy Brief 13–29.

Cruz, Moritz and Bernard Walters. 2008. "Is the Accumulation of International Reserves Good for Development?" *Cambridge Journal of Economics* 32 (5): 665–81.

De Grauwe, Paul. 2006. "What Have We Learnt about Monetary Integration Since the Maastricht Treaty?" *Journal of Common Market Studies* 44 (4): 711–30.

di Giovanni, Julian and Jay Shambaugh. 2008. "The Impact of Foreign Interest Rates on the Economy." *Journal of International Economics* 74 (2): 341–61.

Dooley, Michael, David Folkerts-Landau and Peter Garber. 2003. "An Essay on the Revived Bretton Woods System." National Bureau of Economic Research Working Paper Series No. 9971.

———. 2004. "The Revived Bretton Woods System." National Bureau of Economic Research Working Paper Series No. 10332.

Eichengreen, Barry. 2001. "Capital Account Liberalization: What Do Cross-Country Studies Tell Us?" *World Bank Economic Review* 15 (3): 341–65.

———. 2011. "What China is After Financially." East Asia Forum, January 30. www.eastasiaforum.org/2011/01/30/what-china-is-after-financially/.

Eichengreen, Barry and Ricardo Hausmann. 2005. *Other People's Money: Debt Denomination and Financial Instability in Emerging Market Economies.* Chicago, IL: University of Chicago Press.

Eichengreen, Barry and David A. Leblang. 2008. "Democracy and Globalization." *Economics and Politics* 20 (3): 289–334.

Eichengreen, Barry and Andrew Rose. 2014. "Capital Controls in the 21st Century." *Journal of International Money and Finance* 48: 1–16.

Firth, Michael, Chen Lin, Ping Liu and Sonia M. L. Wong. 2009. "Inside the Black Box: Bank Credit Allocation in China's Private Sector." *Journal of Banking & Finance* 33 (6): 1144–55.

Fleming, J. Marcus. 1962. "Domestic Financial Policies under Fixed and under Floating Exchange Rates." IMF *Staff Papers* 9 (3): 369–80.

Foot, Rosemary and Andrew Walter. 2011. *China, the United States, and Global Order.* New York, NY: Cambridge University Press.

Frankel, Jeffrey. 1998. "No Single Currency Regime Is Right for All Countries or At All Times." *Essays in International Finance* No. 215.

Frankel, Jeffrey and George Saravelos. 2012. "Can Leading Indicators Assess Country Vulnerability?" *Journal of International Economics* 87 (2): 216–31.

Freeman III, Charles W. and Wen Jin Yuan. 2011. "China's Exchange Rate Politics." A Report of the Freeman Chair in China Studies, Center for Strategic and International Studies.

Freeman, John R. and Dennis P. Quinn. 2012. "The Economic Origins of Democracy Reconsidered." *American Political Science Review* 106 (1): 58–80.

Freund, Caroline and Martha Denisse Pierola. 2012. "Export Surges." *Journal of Development Economics* 97 (2): 387–95.

Frieden, Jeffry A. 1991. "Invested Interests: The Politics of National Economic Policies in a World of Global Finance." *International Organization* 45 (4): 425–51.

———. 2002. "Real Sources of European Currency Policy." *International Organization* 56 (4): 831–60.

Gallagher, Kevin P., José Antonio Ocampo, Ming Zhang and Yu Yongding. 2014. *Capital Account Liberalization in China: A Cautionary Tale.* Global Economic Governance Initiative Policy Brief. Issue 002.

Ghosh, Atish R., Anne-Marie Gulde, Jonathan D. Ostry and Holger C. Wolf. 1997. *Does the Nominal Exchange Rate Regime Matter?* National Bureau of Economic Research Working Paper Series No. 5874.

Ghosh, Atish R., Jun Kim, Mahvash S. Qureshi and Juan Zalduendo. 2012. "Surges." IMF Working Paper No. 12/22.

Gluzmann, Pablo, Eduardo Levy-Yeyati and Federico Sturzenegger. 2012. "Exchange Rate Undervaluation and Economic Growth." *Economics Letters* 117 (3): 666–72.

Giovannini, Alberto and Martha De Melo. 1993. "Government Revenue from Financial Repression." *American Economic Review* 83 (4): 953–63.

Green, Russell and Tom Torgeson. 2007. "Are High Foreign Exchange Reserves in Emerging Markets a Blessing or a Burden?" Department of the Treasury: Office of International Affairs Occasional Paper No. 6.

Hacker, Jacob and Paul Pierson. 2002. "Business Power and Social Policy: Employers and the Formation of the American Welfare State." *Politics and Society* 30 (2): 277–325.

Haddad, Mona and Cosima Pancaro. 2010. "Can Real Exchange Rate Undervaluation Boost Exports and Growth in Developing Countries?" World Bank Economic Premise No. 20.

He, Dong, Lillian Cheung, Wenlang Zhang and Tommy Wu. 2012. "How Would Capital Account Liberalization Affect China's Capital Flows and the Renminbi Real Exchange Rates?" *China & World Economy* 20 (6): 29–54.

Helleiner, Eric and Jonathan Kirshner. 2009. *The Future of the Dollar.* Ithaca, NY: Cornell University Press.

———. 2014a. *The Great Wall of Money.* Ithaca, NY: Cornell University Press.

———. 2014b. "The Politics of China's International Monetary Relations." In *The Great Wall of Money*, edited by Eric Helleiner and Jonathan Kirshner, 1–22. Ithaca, NY: Cornell University Press.

Heston, Alan, Robert Summers and Bettina Aten. 2012. Penn World Tables Version 7.1, Center for International Comparisons of Production, Income and Prices at the University of Pennsylvania.

Huizinga, Harry. 1997. "Real Exchange Rate Misalignment and Redistribution." *European Economic Review* 41 (2): 259–77.

IMF. 2013. "People's Republic of China. 2013 Article IV Consultation." IMF Country Report No. 13/211.

Jeanne, Olivier. 2007. "International Reserves in Emerging Market Countries: Too Much of a Good Thing?" *Brookings Papers on Economic Activity* 38: 1–79.

Johnson, Simon and Todd Mitton. 2003. "Cronyism and Capital Controls: Evidence from Malaysia." *Journal of Financial Economics* 67 (2): 351–82.

Kaminsky, Graciela, Saul Lizondo and Carmen M. Reinhart. 1998. "Leading Indicators of Currency Crises." IMF *Staff Papers* 45 (1): 1–48.

Kaplan, Stephen B. 2006. "The Political Obstacles to Greater Exchange Rate Flexibility in China." *World Development* 34 (7): 1182–200.

Klein, Michael W. and Jay C. Shambaugh. 2006. "Fixed Exchange Rates and Trade." *Journal of International Economics* 70 (2): 359–83.

Kirshner, Jonathan. 2003. "The Inescapable Politics of Money." *In Monetary Orders: Ambiguous Economics, Ubiquitous Politics*, edited by Jonathan Kirshner, 3–24. Ithaca, NY: Cornell University Press.

———. 2014. "Regional Hegemony and an Emerging RMB Zone." In *The Great Wall of Money*, edited by Eric Helleiner and Jonathan Kirshner, 213–40. Ithaca: Cornell University Press.

Kose, M. Ayhan, Eswar Prasad, Kenneth S. Rogoff and Shang-Jin Wei. 2009. "Financial Globalization: A Reappraisal." IMF *Staff Papers* 56 (1): 8–62.

La Porta, Rafael, Florencio Lopez-de-Silanes, Andrei Shleifer and Robert Vishny. 1999. "The Quality of Government." *Journal of Law, Economics and Organization* 15 (1): 222–79.

Lardy, Nicholas R. 2012. *Sustaining China's Economic Growth after the Global Financial Crisis*. Washington, DC: Peterson Institute for International Economics.

Lardy, Nicholas and Patrick Douglass. 2011. "Capital Account Liberalization and the Role of the Renminbi." Peterson Institute for International Economics Working Paper No. 11-6.

Leblang, David A. 1997. "Domestic and Systemic Determinants of Capital Controls in the Developed and Developing World." *International Studies Quarterly* 41 (3): 435–54.

———. 1999. Domestic Political Institutions and Exchange Rate Commitments in the Developing World. *International Studies Quarterly* 43 (4): 599–620.

Lee, Jong-Wha and Kwanho Shin. 2010. "Exchange Rate Regimes and Economic Linkages." *International Economic Journal* 24 (1): 1–23.

Levy-Yeyati, Eduardo and Federico Sturzenegger. 2003. "To Float or to Fix." *American Economic Review* 93 (4): 1173–93.

Levy-Yeyati, Eduardo, Federico Sturzenegger and Pablo Alfredo Gluzmann. 2013. "Fear of Appreciation." *Journal of Development Economics* 101: 233–47.

Li, Cheng. 2005. "The New Bipartisanship within the Chinese Communist Party." *Orbis* 49 (3): 387–400.

Li, Hongbin, Lingsheng Meng, Qian Wang and Li-An Zhou. 2008. "Political Connections, Financing and Firm Performance." *Journal of Development Economics* 87 (2): 283–99.

Liu, Li-Gang, and Laurent Pauwels. 2012. "Do External Political Pressures Affect the Renminbi Exchange Rate?" *Journal of International Money and Finance* 31 (6): 1800–18.

Lipman, Joshua Klein. 2011. "Law of Yuan Price: Estimating Equilibrium of the Renminbi." *Michigan Journal of Business* 4 (2): 61–90.

López-Córdova, J. Ernesto and Christopher M. Meissner. 2003. "Exchange-Rate Regimes and International Trade." *American Economic Review* 93 (1): 344–53.

Mbaye, Samba. 2013. "Currency Undervaluation and Growth: Is There a Productivity Channel?" *International Economics* 133: 8–28.

McKinnon, Ronald I. 1963. "Optimum Currency Areas." *American Economic Review* 53 (4): 717–25.

Milner, Helen V. and Bumba Mukherjee. 2009. Democratization and Economic Globalization. *Annual Review of Political Science* 12 (1): 163–81.

Mosley, Layna. 2010. *Labor Rights and Multinational Production*. New York, NY: Cambridge University Press.

Mundell, Robert A. 1961. "A Theory of Optimum Currency Areas." *American Economic Review* 51 (4): 657–65.

———. 1963. "Capital Mobility and Stabilization Policy under Fixed and Flexible Exchange Rates." *Canadian Journal of Economics and Political Science* 29 (4): 475–85.

Nelson, Stephen C., David A. Steinberg and Christoph Nguyen. 2014. "The Institutional Sources of Financial Openness." Paper presented at the annual meeting of the American Political Science Association, Washington, DC.

Nouira, Ridha and Khalid Sekkat. 2012. "Desperately Seeking the Positive Impact of Undervaluation on Growth." *Journal of Macroeconomics* 34 (2): 537–52.

Obstfeld, M., J. C Shambaugh and A. M Taylor. 2010. "Financial Stability, the Trilemma, and International Reserves." *American Economic Journal: Macroeconomics* 2 (2): 57–94.

Pepinsky, Thomas B. 2009. *Economic Crises and the Breakdown of Authoritarian Regimes*. New York, NY: Cambridge University Press.

———. 2013. "The Domestic Politics of Financial Internationalization in the Developing World." *Review of International Political Economy* 20 (4): 848–80.

Pineau, Georges, Ettore Dorrucci, Fabio Comelli and Angelika Lagerblom. 2006. "The Accumulation of Foreign Reserves." European Central Bank Occasional Paper Series No. 43.

Posen, Adam S. 1995. "Declarations Are Not Enough: Financial Sector Sources of Central Bank Independence." *National Bureau of Economic Research Macroeconomics Annual* 10: 253–74.

Ramírez, Carlos D. 2013. "The Political Economy of 'Currency Manipulation' Bashing." *China Economic Review* 27: 227–37.

Rey, Helene. 2013. "Dilemma Not Trilemma: The Global Cycle and Monetary Policy Independence." Federal Reserve Bank of Kansas City Proceedings.

Rodrik, Dani. 2006. "The Social Cost of Foreign Exchange Reserves." *International Economic Journal*. 20 (3): 253-66.

———. 2008. "The Real Exchange Rate and Economic Growth." *Brookings Papers on Economic Activity* 2: 365–412.

Rose, Andrew K. 2000. "One Money, One Market: The Effect of Common Currencies on Trade." *Economic Policy* 15 (30): 7–46.

———. 2011. "*Exchange Rate Regimes in the Modern Era*: Fixed, Floating, and Flaky." *Journal of Economic Literature* 49 (3): 652–72.

Roubini, Nouriel and Brad Setser. 2005. "Will the Bretton Woods 2 Regime Unravel Soon?" Presented at the Symposium on the Revived Bretton Woods System, Federal Reserve Bank of Chicago, February 4.

Schröder, Marcel. 2013. "Should Developing Countries Undervalue Their Currencies?" *Journal of Development Economics* 105: 140–51.

Sedik, Tahsin Saadi and Tao Sun. 2012. "Effects of Capital Flow Liberalization — What Is the Evidence from Recent Experiences of Emerging Market Economies?" IMF Working Paper 12/274.

Shih, Victor C. and David A. Steinberg. 2012. "The Domestic Politics of the International Dollar Standard: A Statistical Analysis of Support for the Reserve Currency, 2000–2008." *Canadian Journal of Political Science* 45 (4): 855–80.

Shirk, Susan L. 1993. *The Political Logic of Economic Reform in China*. Berkeley: University of California Press.

Steinberg, David A. 2014. "Why Has China Accumulated Such Large Foreign Reserves?" In *The Great Wall of Money*, edited by Eric Helleiner and Jonathan Kirshner, 71–98. Ithaca, NY: Cornell University Press.

———. 2015. *Demanding Devaluation: Exchange Rate Politics in the Developing World*. Ithaca, NY: Cornell University Press.

Steinberg, David A. and Victor C. Shih. 2012. "Interest Group Influence in Authoritarian States: The Political Determinants of Chinese Exchange Rate Policy." *Comparative Political Studies* 45 (11): 1404–33.

Steinberg, David A. and Krishan Malhotra. 2014. "The Effect of Authoritarian Regime Type on Exchange Rate Policy." *World Politics* 66 (3): 491–529.

Steiner, Andreas. 2013. "The Accumulation of Foreign Exchange by Central Banks: Fear of Capital Mobility?" *Journal of Macroeconomics* 38: 409–27.

Subramanian, Arvind. 2011. *Eclipse: Living in the Shadow of China's Economic Dominance*. Washington, DC: Peterson Institute for International Economics.

Summers, Lawrence H. 2006. "Reflections on Global Account Imbalances and Emerging Markets Reserve Accumulation." L. K. Jha Memorial Lecture, Reserve Bank of India, Mumbai.

Taylor, Bill and Qi Li. 2007. "Is the ACFTU a Union and Does It Matter?" *Journal of Industrial Relations* 49 (5): 701–15.

Tornell, Aaron, Frank Westermann and Lorenza Martinez. 2004. "The Positive Link Between Financial Liberalization, Growth and Crises." National Bureau of Economic Research Working Paper No. 10293.

Vermeiren, Mattias and Sacha Dierckx. 2012. "Challenging Global Neoliberalism? The Global Political Economy of China's Capital Controls." *Third World Quarterly* 33 (9): 1647–68.

Walter, Stefanie. 2013. *Financial Crises and the Politics of Macroeconomic Adjustments*. New York, NY: Cambridge University Press.

Wang, Hongying. 2014. "Global Imbalances and the Limits of the Exchange Rate Weapon." In *The Great Wall of Money*, edited by Eric Helleiner and Jonathan Kirshner, 99–126. Ithaca, NY: Cornell University Press.

Williamson, John. 1990. "What Washington Means by Policy Reform." In *Latin American Adjustment*, edited by John Williamson, 7-20. Washington, DC: Institute for International Economics.

Woodruff, David M. 2005. "Boom, Gloom, Doom." *Politics and Society* 33 (1): 3-45.

World Bank. 2014. "World Development Indicators Database." http:// databank.worldbank.org/.

World Trade Organization. 2014. *World Trade Report 2014*. Geneva: World Trade Organization.

Wright, Logan. 2009. "The Elusive Price for Stability: Ideas and Interests in the Reform of China's Exchange Rate Regime." Ph.D. dissertation, Department of Political Science, George Washington University.

Zhang, Ming. 2012a. "Chinese Stylized Sterilization: The Cost-sharing Mechanism and Financial Repression." *China & World Economy* 20 (2): 41–58.

———. 2012b. "China's Capital Controls: Stylized Facts and Referential Lessons." In Regulating Global Capital Flows for Long-Run Development, edited by Kevin P. Gallagher, Stephany Griffith-Jones, and José Antonio Ocampo, 85–91. Boston, MA: Frederick S. Pardee Center for the Study of the Longer-Range Future.

9

Internationalization of China's Bond Market, Development of Offshore RMB Centres and Provision of Global Safe Assets

Liu Dongmin

n many countries, the bond market is the most important market for the financial system because it creates an interest rate benchmark for the domestic market, and provides the most powerful tool for direct financing. With its continuous and rapid economic growth, China has become a systemically important country; therefore, the development of China's bond market is not only an essential component of financial infrastructure for the nation itself, but also plays a significant role in the development of the international monetary and financial system.

Supply and Demand of Global Safe Assets after the 2008 Crisis

Global safe assets are assets that have little default risk in the global financial markets. According to the International Monetary Fund's (IMF's) (2012) analysis, global safe assets have many functions, including as a reliable store of value, collateral in the repurchase and derivatives markets, key instruments in fulfilling the prudential regulation and pricing benchmarks. In general, some developed countries' central government bonds and multilateral financial institutions' bonds, such as the bonds issued by the World Bank, which have an AAA rating, are typical global safe assets. Some other developed countries' central government bonds, some local governments' bonds and bonds issued by some cross-border financial institutions and companies, which have around an AA rating, are near global safe assets.

The global financial crisis and European debt crisis led to a decline in the supply of global safe assets. In order to save the financial market and prevent a severe economic depression, developed countries carried out large-scale bailout policies, transferring financial institutions' debt to sovereign debt. The governmental debt ratio has risen to a high level in many developed countries, creating serious debt risks in some. As a result, some advanced economies lost their AAA sovereign credit rating (see Table 1).

Table 1: Downgrade of Sovereign Credit Rating in Developed Countries

	US	UK	France	Austria
Sovereign credit rating before 2008	AAA	AAA	AAA	AAA
Current sovereign credit rating (by 12/2014)	AA+	Aa1	AA	AA+
Date of downgrade	Aug. 2011	Feb. 2013	Nov. 2013	Jan. 2012
Company that downgraded it	S&P	Moody	S&P	S&P
	Japan	Italy	Spain	Portugal
Sovereign credit rating before 2010	Aa3	Aa2	AAA	A1
Current sovereign credit rating (by 12/2014)	A1	Baa2	BBB	Ba2
Date of downgrade	Dec. 2014	Aug. 2014	May 2014	May 2014
Company that downgraded it	Moody	Moody	S&P	Moody

Source: Author.

Since a sovereign credit rating often represents the credit ceiling of a country, the downgrade of those sovereign credit ratings definitely damages the credit rating of local governments, companies and financial institutions. Take the United States as an example. With the downgrade of the US sovereign credit rating, at the same time Standard & Poor's (S&P) downgraded the rating of the Federal Deposit Insurance Corporation, the Federal Farm Credit Banks Funding Corporation, 10 Federal Home Loan Banks, Fannie Mae, Freddie Mac, the Depository Trust Company, three clearing corporations (National Securities Clearing Corporation, Fixed Income Clearing Corporation, Options Clearing Corporation), and about 11,000 municipal bonds. Soon after that, Moody's and Fitch also downgraded the credit rating of many large international banks and local governments in the United States (Chen 2013).

As a result, global safe assets and near safe assets decreased significantly after the 2008 crisis. According to the IMF's (2012) forecast, the supply of global safe assets will decrease by 16 percent by 2016, or around US$9 trillion.

On the other hand, global financial regulatory reform has resulted in a rising demand of safe assets. The issuance of Basel III aims to tighten the regulation, supervision and risk management of commercial banks. With the implementation of Basel III, banking sectors all over the world are facing higher capital adequacy requirements, lower leverage ratios and more rigid evaluations of risk-weighted assets. Under these measures, the banking sector now needs more low risk-weighted assets to meet the regulatory requirement. In other words, with the implementation of Basel III the demand for safe assets has increased. Moreover, many countries launched their own financial regulatory reform, which has also increased the demand for safe assets. For example, more and more over-the-counter derivatives' transactions require safe assets as collateral.

Consequently, for a relatively long time there will be an obvious mismatch between supply and demand of global safe assets. Traditionally, developed countries provided most global safe assets. Given that the sovereign debt problem of developed countries is difficult to deal with in the short to medium term, the shortage of global safe assets creates an opportunity for the emerging economies.

RMB Internationalization, China's Offshore Bond Market and Global Safe Assets

International Cases: The United States and the United Kingdom

One of the key indicators of currency internationalization is that the currency becomes an international reserve currency. To achieve this goal, bonds denominated in the currency must get a high credit rating and be considered as a global safe asset so that other countries can buy these bonds and use them as their foreign exchange reserve. The US dollar and the British pound are both good examples.

As the issuing country of the dominant currency and with comprehensive national strength, the United States has made its bonds the global safest asset. Despite the US loss of AAA sovereign credit rating in 2011, foreign holdings of US bonds increased from US$5.3 trillion in 2006 to US$9.3 trillion in 2013. Although the downgrading of the US sovereign credit rating meant that the security of the US bonds declined, other countries' bonds, such as German government bonds (AAA bonds), cannot replace the US bonds given their scale

Figure 1: Foreign Holdings of US Bonds

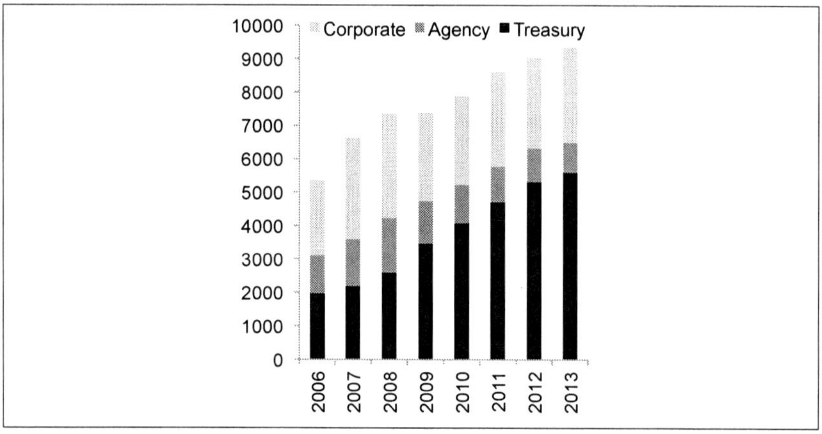

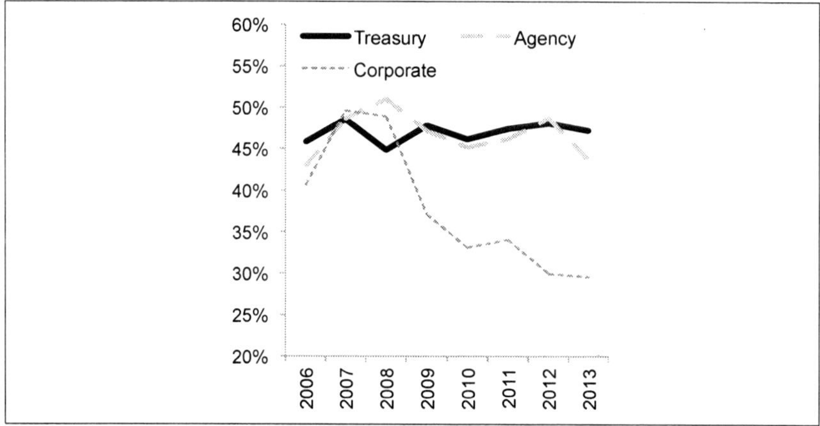

Data source: US Treasury.

Figure 2: Share of US Bonds Owned by Foreign Entities

Data source: US Treasury.

and liquidity. To a large extent, simply because of the strength of the US bonds market, the US dollar remains the number one international reserve currency (see Figure 1).

When looking at the foreign holdings of each kind of US bonds, it is clear that US Treasury bonds play the most stable and key role, followed by US agency bonds. Regardless of the crisis, about half of US Treasury bonds were held by foreign entities. But the share of the US corporate bonds' foreign holdings decreased dramatically from 49.6 percent in 2007 to 29.6 percent in 2013.

Figure 3: Share of UK Government Bonds in Foreign Holdings

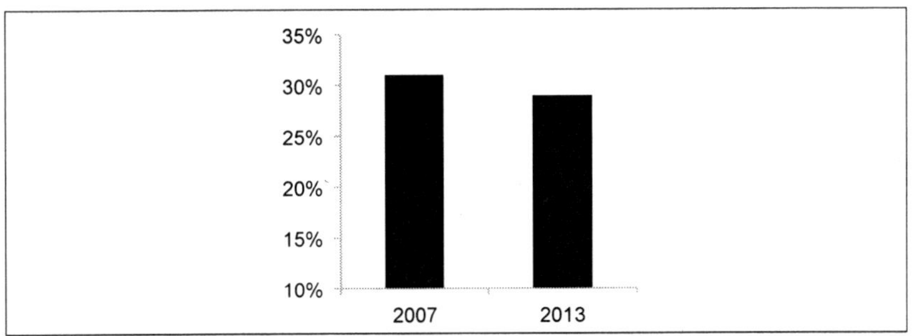

Data source: HM Treasury.

Compared with agency bonds and corporate bonds, US Treasury bonds are no doubt the safest asset (see Figure 2).

The pound sterling is another international currency. As in the United States, the share of government bonds has been stable in foreign holdings in the United Kingdom, despite the fact that the UK financial system suffered considerably during the 2008 crisis (see Figure 3). However, Figure 3 shows the appeal of the United Kingdom's government bonds for overseas investors is much smaller in comparison with that of the United States, indicating again that size and liquidity of a bond market matter a lot.

Up until now, it seems that the United States has achieved the most "successful" currency internationalization and has dominated the international monetary system. However, both economic theory (Triffin dilemma) and reality (2008 financial crisis) show that the current dollar-dominated system is vulnerable. Many investors are aware that, in the long run, the possibility of a weak dollar increases the risk of holding US bonds, but they currently have no other options. A multi-currency system is more stable and would be an important public good for global financial stability. China could learn from the experience of the United States and the United Kingdom to internationalize both its bond market and currency for the benefit of both itself and the world.

RMB Backflow Mechanism and Development of RMB Offshore Centres

By the end of 2014, seven RMB offshore centres (Hong Kong, Taipei, Singapore, London, Frankfurt, Paris and Luxembourg) had been established, with RMB deposits of RMB 1.6 trillion (see Table 2). Toronto became the first North American RMB offshore centre in March 2015.

Table 2: RMB Deposit in Offshore Centres (as of September 2014)

	Hong Kong	Taiwan	Singapore	Luxembourg	London	Total
Offshore RMB deposit (¥ billion)	944.5	300	257	79.4	14.5	1587.9

Data source: People's Bank of China (PBoC) (www.pbc.gov.cn) and the author's investigation at Hong Kong and London.

RMB holders in the offshore market are not able to find enough opportunities to invest with RMB in mainland China because China's capital account remains largely closed. This is a fundamental factor limiting the development of the RMB offshore market. In order to increase the investment opportunities for offshore RMB, the central government has gradually built some RMB backflow channels. Five channels have been opened so far: dim sum bonds, RMB qualified foreign institutional investor (RQFII), domestic interbank market, cross-border RMB loan and the Shanghai-Hong Kong Stock Connect (see Table 3). A dim sum bond is a bond issued at the offshore RMB market and denominated in RMB. An RQFII is a qualified foreign institutional investor that invests with RMB in China's financial market. The domestic interbank market is a market in the mainland of China where institutional investors can invest with RMB in notes, bonds, and so on. China's government now allows some foreign institutional investors to invest in the domestic interbank market. A cross-border RMB loan means that banks in Hong Kong can make loans to firms in some specific areas in mainland China. Currently, four areas are approved to carry out cross-border RMB loans: the Qianhai special zone in Shenzhen, free trade zone (FTZ) in Shanghai, Suzhou Industrial Park and Tianjin Eco-city. The Shanghai-Hong Kong Stock Connect enables investors in mainland China to invest in Hong Kong's stock market through the Shanghai Stock Exchange, and investors in Hong Kong to invest in Shanghai's stock market through the Hong Kong Stock Exchange.

However, these bank flow channels cannot meet the needs of offshore RMB holders. Even after China realizes its capital account convertibility, providing diversified and sound investment products for overseas RMB investors will still be a challenge. There are not yet enough investment tools available for China's domestic investors; as a result, many people invest in real estate, which, to some extent, leads to extremely high housing prices in major cities.

One of the big challenges for the central government in creating offshore RMB centres is how to further broaden the RMB backflow channel. Among current RMB backflow channels, dim sum bonds are the most effective and attractive tool for overseas investors. Based on the international experience discussed above, RMB-denominated bonds should be the largest channel for RMB

Table 3: Backflow Channel for Offshore RMB (as of end of 2014)

Dim Sum Bond (¥ billion)	RQFII (¥ billion)	Domestic Interbank Market	Cross-border RMB Loan	Shanghai and Hong Kong Stock Connect (RMB billion)
Hong Kong: 338.9 Taiwan: 8.7 London: 7.5 Singapore: 9.2 (by Jun. 2014)	Aggregate quota: 690 Confirmed quota: 97.4 (by Oct. 2014)	84 foreign banks, 34 RQFIIs, 7 QFIIs, 11 foreign insurance companies, and a few central banks are permitted to enter this market.	Qianhai special zone, Shanghai (FTZ), Suzhou Industrial Park and Tianjin Eco-city are permitted to get offshore RMB loans.	The initial quota is RMB 550.

Data source: PBoC.

backflow. Therefore, the question becomes how to increase the size of the asset pool of RMB-denominated bonds in the offshore market.

The Hong Kong Offshore RMB Bond Market

Hong Kong is presently the largest offshore RMB market in the world and it issues the most dim sum bonds.

Figure 4: Dim Sum Bonds in the Hong Kong Market (as of December 20, 2014)

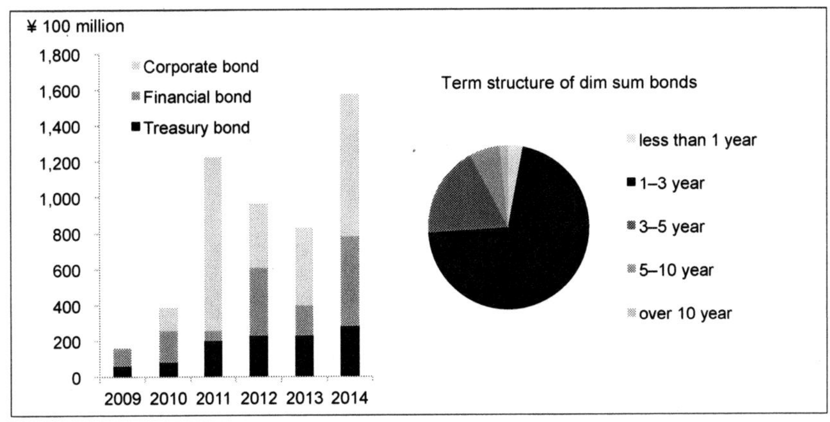

Data source: Wind Data.

Since the China Development Bank issued the first dim sum bond in Hong Kong in 2007, the Hong Kong dim sum bond market has developed quickly, issuing a total of RMB 514.4 billion as of December 20, 2014. However, comparing the dramatic rise of RMB deposits in Hong Kong to the issuance of dim sum bonds, there is a large discrepancy. The ratio of outstanding dim sum bonds to outstanding RMB deposits was 48.6 percent in 2009, which fell to 27.0 percent in 2014 (see Table 4).

Table 4: Dim Sum Bonds and RMB Deposits

	2009	2010	2011	2012	2013	2014
Outstanding dim sum bonds (RMB bn)	30.4	65.6	172.8	253.6	295.8	255.0
Outstanding RMB deposits (RMB bn)	62.7	314.9	588.5	603.0	860.5	944.5
Dim sum bonds/RMB deposits	48.6%	20.8%	29.4%	42.1%	34.4%	27.0%

Data sources: Wind Data, Hong Kong Monetary Authority and author's calculations.

Two factors account for the decreased ratio. First, the increase in the supply of dim sum bonds has been slower than the increase of RMB deposits in the offshore market.[1] Many firms in mainland China are not very interested in issuing bonds in offshore markets because it is more complex and difficult than issuing bonds at the onshore market (the section "Internationalization of China's Local Government Bonds and Provision of Global Safe Assets" gives a detailed explanation). Second, the gradual expansion of the RMB backflow mechanisms (such as RQFII and the domestic interbank market) provides more opportunities to overseas investors. However, according to the author's field investigation in Hong Kong, financial institutions and government officials in Hong Kong believe that dim sum bonds are still the most important and the most effective way to achieve RMB backflow.

The growth prospect for the issuance of dim sum bonds does not look very optimistic either. After a dramatic increase in 2011, the Hong Kong dim sum bond market experienced a two-year drop (see Figure 4). One reason is that the expectation of RMB appreciation has weakened since the end of 2011, which reduced the arbitrage opportunity for RMB holders in the offshore market, thereby lessening the demand for dim sum bonds. Meanwhile, the quantitative easing policy of the United States increased the liquidity of US dollars and reduced the interest rates of dollar-denominated bonds. This made many enterprises and financial institutions turn to issuing dollar-denominated bonds.

The maturity structure of dim sum bonds reflects the features of a less-developed financial market. The long-term government bonds of some developed countries, such as the United States and the United Kingdom, are a favourite product for foreign investors. But in the offshore RMB centres, most of the dim sum bonds are short-term bonds. Seventy-four percent of the total is under three years; only 1.7 percent is over 10 years (see Figure 4). On the one hand, the lack of long-term dim sum bonds is not unusual, because it is extremely challenging to

---

1   The year 2010 is a typical case demonstrating this. RMB deposits in the Hong Kong market experienced an explosion in 2010, which was far beyond the imagination of the central government, Hong Kong's administration and businesses. As a result, although the issuance of dim sum bonds increased greatly, the ratio of outstanding dim sum bonds to outstanding RMB deposits still fell significantly.

value a long-term financial asset in a less-developed financial market. But on the other hand, China has to make additional financial reforms so that it can build a long-term dim sum bond market if its bonds are to become global safe assets.

The composition of dim sum bonds poses yet another problem. In most periods, there are more corporate and financial bonds issued than treasury bonds on the Hong Kong offshore bond market. The highest percentage of treasury bonds issued was reached in 2013, amounting to 27.6 percent. In fact, China's treasury bonds are so welcomed by offshore RMB investors that the bonds have always been over-subscribed. The Hong Kong administration hopes that the central government will expand the scale of the treasury bonds. As mentioned above, the government bond is the most important and lowest default component of global safe assets. Since the demand is very high, the supply of China's government bonds in the offshore market should be enlarged.

If China wants to further expand the RMB backflow channel and continuously encourage the establishment of offshore RMB centres, it needs to address three challenges in the offshore bond market: the volume and growth rate of bonds issued, the maturity structure and the proportion of government bonds issued. A well-developed offshore bond market will help China make its government bonds global safe assets. Other factors also come into play to achieve this goal, including China's economic outlook, the government's ability and responsibility to pay back its debts and the credibility of the central bank. This chapter focuses on the relationship between the development of offshore RMB centres and the internationalization of China's bond market.

The Internationalization of China's Treasury Bonds and Provision of Global Safe Assets

Theoretically speaking, the internationalization of China's bond market involves increasing the issuance of China's bonds for overseas investors and attracting international bonds to the domestic market. This section discusses how to expand the issuance of China's treasury bonds for overseas investors.

Since 2008 the PBoC has signed currency swap agreements with 28 foreign central banks, with the swap quota reaching RMB 2.5 trillion. China's central government has already allowed foreign central banks to enter China's domestic interbank market so that central banks that have RMB could buy China's treasury bonds if they would like to make the RMB their reserve currency. In fact, some countries — such as Australia, Cambodia, Indonesia, Japan, Malaysia, Nepal, Nigeria, South Korea and Thailand — have already done so, although the exact size of RMB reserves in their central banks can not be determined.[2] The British government issued an RMB-denominated bond and made the RMB part of its reserves of foreign currency in October 2014. This was the first time that a foreign central government issued a treasury bond in RMB, and it is estimated that the British will invest in China's treasury bonds with the RMB fund. Although RMB-denominated treasury bonds have already entered the pool of global safe assets, they still play a tiny role compared with bonds denominated in dollars, euros, pounds, yen and Swiss francs.

Since 2009, China's central government has issued treasury bonds each year on the Hong Kong market in order to broaden the RMB backflow mechanism and, as mentioned above, the demand for these bonds is quite high. For example, the central government issued RMB 7 billion treasury bonds to institutional investors in the Hong Kong market in November 2013, while the subscription amounted to RMB 26 billion. In May 2014, RMB 14 billion treasury bonds were issued to institutional investors and the subscription amounted to RMB 41.9 billion.

One of the key factors for the shortage of treasury bonds is that China's central government is very prudent with respect to debt accumulation. Although the government debt ratio increased rapidly in China after the 2008 global crisis, China's fiscal deficit is still lower than many developed countries. In 2013, China's outstanding treasury bond to GDP ratio was 16.2 percent, while in the United States it was 70.7 percent, and in Japan it was 154.9 percent (see Figure 5). Even compared with Germany, one of the most fiscally prudent developed countries in the Group of Seven, China's issuance of long-term treasury bonds is much smaller (see Figure 6). As a result, in 2013, China's central government debt was only 15.3 percent and aggregate government debt is 53 percent, lower than that of many developed countries (see Figure 7).

China's central government has to change its view on the structure of the bond market if it wants to facilitate the internationalization of both the RMB and bond market. On the one hand, as mentioned before, a large-scale bond market is a key factor for currency internationalization; on the other hand, bond market development is one of the most significant components of a country's financial infrastructure. With respect to direct financing or building benchmarks for the market interest rate, the bond market plays the most basic and powerful role. The imbalance of China's financing structure is a long-standing problem. The proportion of the stock of direct financing is only 40 percent in China, while in

---

2   Strictly speaking, according to the IMF's definition, RMB in foreign central banks cannot be called foreign reserve currency because China has not realized total capital account convertibility. It is a problem of definition. In any event, RMB have already been put into the foreign currency reserve account of some central banks in the world.

Figure 5: Outstanding Treasury Bond/GDP

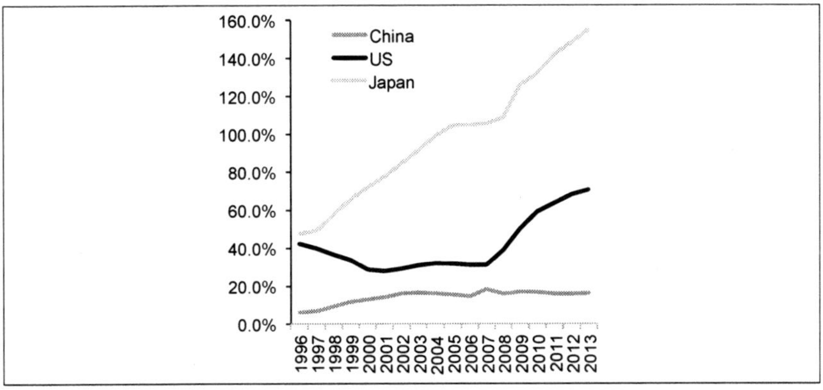

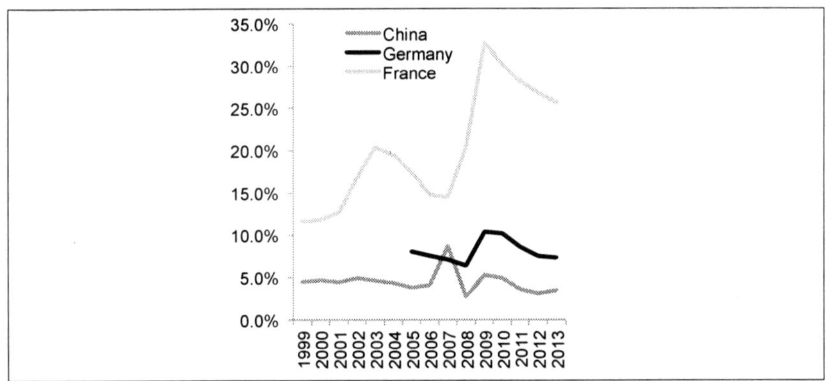

Data source: Wind Data.

Figure 6: Treasury Bond Issuance/GDP

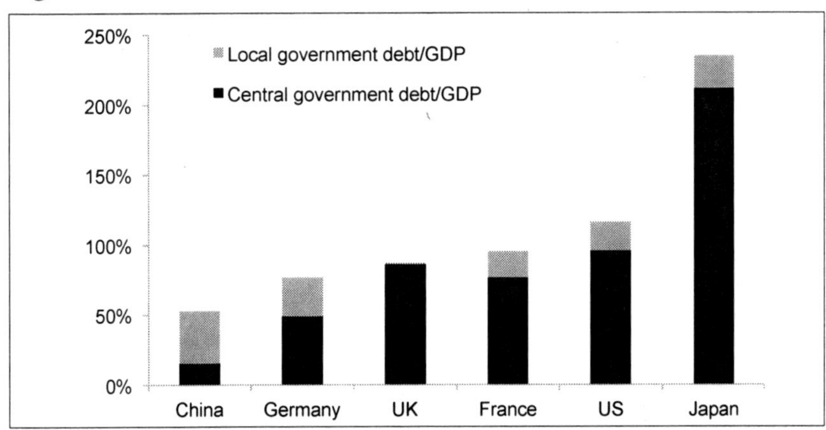

Data source: Wind Data.

Figure 7: Government Debt/GDP (2013)

Data sources: Wind Data, Chinese Academy of Social Sciences and author's calculation.

the United States, Japan and Germany it amounts to 70–90 percent. The bond market provides a very effective, flexible and diversified tool for direct financing and it will contribute greatly to China's interest rate liberalization. To achieve the above functions, the treasury bond is the key bond. Jia Kang, the former director of the Institute for Fiscal Science Research, Ministry of Finance (MoF), said in December 2014 that China should expand its public debt ratio. He argued that the central government could increase its deficit rate from 2.1 percent (a standard rate in recent years) to 2.6 percent, which means the issuance scale of the treasury bond could see an increase of several hundred billion yuan every year (Jia 2014b). The purpose for increasing the public debt ratio is to stimulate China's economic growth. The central government should enlarge the size of the treasury bond market, which will benefit domestic financial liberalization reform, capital market opening, RMB internationalization and even economic growth. It is clear that expanding the fiscal deficit too rapidly generates risks to financial stability, so the central government should also limit the speed of public debt accumulation according to the macroeconomic growth rate and the increase in the rate of fiscal revenue, so that the debt burden can be kept under a safe level.

In the short term, the most effective way might be to directly issue more of China's treasury bonds in the offshore market. Whenever the central government issued treasury bonds in the Hong Kong market, they were always oversubscribed. If more treasury bonds are issued, any investors in the offshore market can apply to purchase the bonds, which will immediately enlarge the supply of RMB-denominated financial products in an offshore market and contribute to the internationalization of China's bond market, the RMB backflow mechanism and the provision of global safe assets.

In addition to increasing the supply of treasury bonds in the onshore and offshore markets, the central government needs to undertake reforms on the sales, regulation and market entrance condition of bonds in order to internationalize the bond market.

To date, commercial banks have undertaken the key mission of underwriting the treasury bonds with insufficient transparency. The public auction of bonds should be enhanced to attract more international investors.

Currently, the market for treasury bonds in China has two components: the interbank market and the security exchange market. The former is regulated by the central bank — the PBoC — the latter is regulated by the China Securities

Regulatory Commission. The regulatory segmentation restrains the treasury bond market from forming a highly efficient transaction system, and limits its function as the market benchmark. If China creates a unified treasury bond market, more investors — including overseas investors — will participate in this market.

China should further open the interbank bond market to foreign investors. By the end of 2014, 84 foreign banks, 34 RQFIIs, seven QFIIs, 11 foreign insurance companies, and a few central banks and sovereign wealth funds were permitted to enter this market. These investors could invest in the interbank market within the quota confirmed by the PBoC. However, foreign investors have not been active in trading bonds in the interbank market. In contrast, foreign institutional investors are very active in buying Chinese treasury bonds in the offshore RMB market. Some experts believe this is because the PBoC's regulation results in a lack of foreign traders. This chapter argues that the PBoC should allow more foreign institutions to enter the interbank market and expand their quota to invest in RMB-denominated bonds.

Finally, in the long term, promoting the independence of the PBoC is very important. When a currency achieves international status, the country's monetary policy will have a powerful spillover effect. How to enhance the credibility of the monetary policy is a challenge facing any country that has an internationalized currency. Of course, countries pursue monetary policies on behalf of their own interest. However, central banks issuing international currencies must also aim to keep the currency and financial system stable in the long term. Financial history since World War II shows that a more independent central bank gives more weight to long-term targets than a less independent central bank does. Although it is not an independent institution, the PBoC, as a central bank of a rapidly developing country, has helped promote China's liberalization and protect the whole economic system from suffering a serious financial crisis. To some extent, the PBoC's achievement established relatively high credibility for the RMB so that its internationalization has proceeded very quickly. However, China still needs to strengthen the credibility of its monetary policy by institutional guarantee. The more independence the PBoC can realize, the more credibility the RMB would gain, and the more successful the internationalization of China's bond market will be in the long run.

Internationalization of China's Local Government Bonds and Provision of Global Safe Assets

Features and Current Situation of China's Local Government Bonds

According to China's Budget Law, "China's local governments have no right to issue local government bonds unless otherwise specified by the Law and the State Council." China's MoF has issued local government bonds on behalf of local governments since 2009.

Besides local government bonds, there are city investment bonds. Strictly speaking, city investment bonds are corporate bonds issued by local government-owned companies, and are often called local government financing vehicles. Most of these companies have names such as "Kunming Investment and Development Company" or "Nanjing Asset Operation and Management Company." Bank loans, city investment bonds and trust products are the three main financing tools that China's local governments are authorized to use at present. Of these three tools, only city investment bonds are explicitly or implicitly guaranteed by the local governments, so they are at least quasi-government bonds, reflecting local governmental credit.

Local Government Bonds and City Investment Bonds Are Crucial to China's Infrastructure Construction

The funds raised by both local government bonds and city investment bonds are mainly spent on infrastructure construction, so the two bonds typically provide public goods. Although the city investment bond is a corporate bond, the company that issues the bond always undertakes the local government's key projects in the infrastructure construction. As a large developing country, China still has a long way to go in infrastructure construction and local governments still have an important role to play in this area. Compared with bank loans and trust products, local government bonds and city investment bonds have longer maturity periods and lower costs, which gives them a comparative advantage for supporting infrastructure construction. Therefore, local governments are strongly inclined to issue these bonds, if they are permitted to do so.

The markets of both local government bonds and city investment bonds have developed quickly. As Figure 8 shows, before 2009 there were no local government bonds and the issuance of city investment bonds was tiny. The total amount of city investment bonds grew from only RMB 242.35 billion in 2008 to RMB 4,922.5 billion in 2014. This change is due to the 2008 financial crisis. In order to combat the global economic crisis, China's central government

**Figure 8: Outstanding Local Government Bonds and City
Investment Bonds**

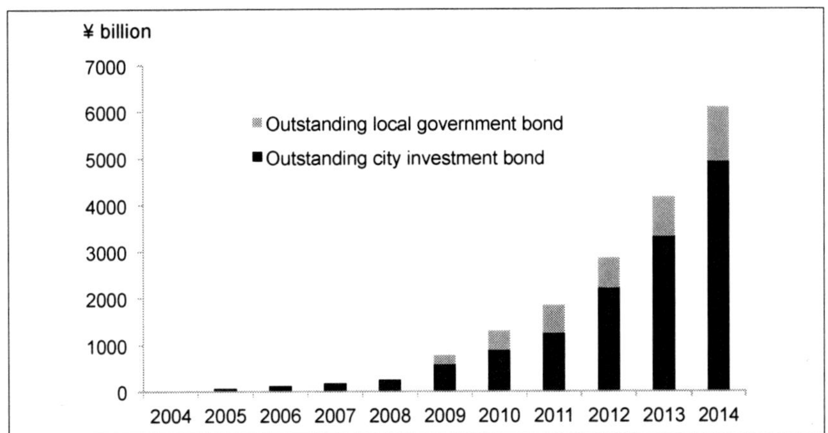

Data source: Wind Data.

carried out the RMB 4 trillion stimulus program to increase domestic demand.
As a coordinated measure, the MoF began to issue local government bonds
on behalf of local governments, and the National Development and Reform
Commission (NDRC) encouraged local governments to issue city investment
bonds, leading to a dramatic increase in both.

**Local Governments' Subsidies and Guarantees Make City Investment Bonds
Safe Assets**

A city investment bond cannot be issued without local government subsidy
and some kind of guarantee, because it is used for infrastructure construction
projects, which generate social benefits but few commercial profits. Local
governments have found ways to support the issuance of the city investment
bonds. Sometimes the government would grant the issuing company exclusive
privilege to develop a piece of land, so that the company could earn a high profit
from the land to repay the bond. At other times, the government would sign
a build-transfer agreement with the company and use future fiscal revenues to
repay the bond.

Whatever measures the local government chooses, it raises the credit rating of
the bond. In fact, there have been no defaults since the first issuance of the city
investment bonds in 1992. In addition, given China's rapid economic growth the
fiscal revenues of local governments are likely to enable them to support their
companies to repay the bonds. This is why most investors in China consider city
investment bonds as local government bonds. It is also why this chapter argues

China's local government bonds (including city investment bonds) could be global safe assets, provided China's central and local governments further reform the bond issuance system and regulation, expand capital account opening, and enhance the government's transparency and rule of law.

Local Government Bonds and City Investment Bonds Are Powerful Tools for Central Government's Macroeconomic Adjustment

For many years, the issuance of local government bonds has been controlled by the central government because they are issued by the MoF. In the near future, governments of the 32 provincial-level regions on the Chinese mainland will be allowed to issue bonds within a quota set by the State Council, so they will still be controlled by the central government. Even city investment bonds, which are issued by local governments at their own discretion, are completely under the control of the central government. Their issuance has to be examined and approved by the NDRC, which allows the NDRC to easily control the scale and speed of the issuance. In 2009, to cope with the global financial crisis, the NDRC rapidly approved and confirmed large volumes of city investment bonds, leading to an explosion of these bonds that year. The number and amount of city investment bonds issued in 2009 increased by 241 percent and 215 percent respectively compared to 2008 (see Figure 9). In order to prevent economic overheating, the NDRC then limited the issuance of city investment bonds, although local governments still had strong desires to issue more of them in 2010 and 2011, resulting in the fall of the bonds' issuance. In 2012, sustaining economic growth again became the most important task for the central government; therefore, the NDRC once more expanded the approval of city investment bonds, with the number and amount of bonds issued rising by 150 percent and 143 percent respectively (see Figure 9). It is clear that the central government has thorough control of the issuance of local government bonds, which is very different from bank loans and trust products. In China, the supply of bank loans and trust products is a commercial process in which the central government has only an indirect power to intervene. Since the central government can fully control the issuance of local government bonds and city investment bonds, the total volume of the outstanding bonds has been quite small compared to developed countries. Local governments have to rely on bank loans to support the economic growth model, so China's corporate debt (mainly composed of bank loans) to GDP ratio is high (see Figure 10).

Figure 9: New Issuance of City Investment Bonds

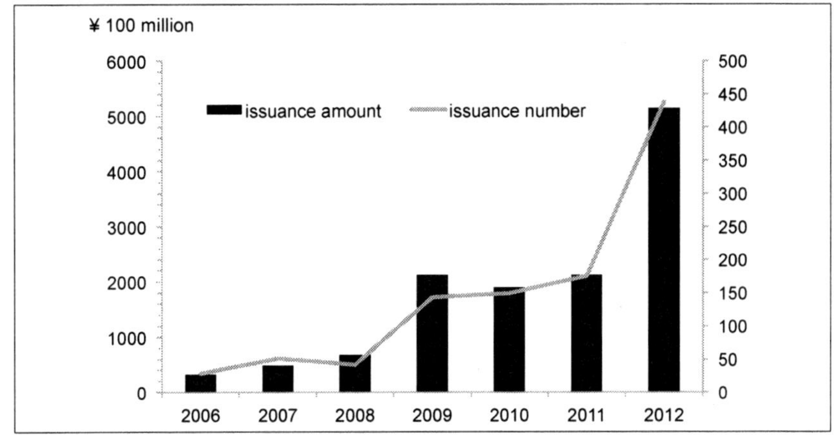

Data source: Wind Data.

Figure 10: Corporate Debt to GDP Ratio

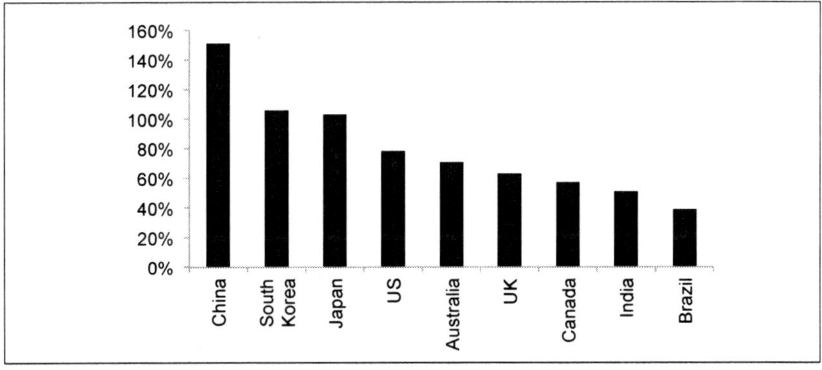

Data source: S&P and author's calculation.

Development Potential of China's Local Government Bonds

China's rate of urbanization — the most important engine of economic
growth — was 52.5 percent in 2013, and will undoubtedly continue to rise
for many years. Some experts argue that the central government should allow
local governments to increase their issuance of local government bonds and city
investment bonds in order to continuously promote infrastructure construction
and, therefore, encourage urbanization (Jia 2014a).[3] This would be good for both

---

3   In fact, Jia's remarks represent the opinion of the MoF.

economic growth and the internationalization of the bond market. However, the debt risk of local governments is also a sensitive issue. The burden of over-indebtedness of local governments will block sustainable economic growth in the long run and obstruct RMB-denominated bonds from becoming global safe assets. Through a comparison of local government bonds in China and the United States, this chapter argues that China's local government bonds are still safe and have great potential to develop internationally.

Municipal bonds are local government bonds issued by US states, cities and counties. The first municipal bond was issued in 1812 by New York for the construction of a canal. The municipal bond market in the United States is currently the largest local government bond market in the world. There are many similarities between municipal bonds in the United States and the local government bonds in China, based on their financing function and trustworthiness.[4]

Issuance Scale

By the end of 2012, the total for Chinese local government bonds and city investment bonds amounted to RMB 2.49 trillion (US$0.4 trillion), while the total for US municipal bonds amounted to US$3.72 trillion. The percentage of local government bonds plus city investment bonds in China is only 10.7 percent of that in the United States. In terms of bond to GDP ratio, China's was only 4.9 percent, while that of the United States was 24.5 percent. In terms of the ratio of bonds to local government fiscal revenues, China's was 42.2 percent while the United States was 111.1 percent (see Figure 11). It is clear that the bond market in China is much smaller than that in the United States. The ratio of bonds to local government fiscal revenues is a crucial indicator, which measures the debt-paying ability of a local government. US municipal bonds are now universally accepted as a near safe asset, although the ratio of bonds to local government fiscal revenues is over 100 percent. Therefore, with a relatively low debt ratio, China's local government bonds could at least become a near global safe asset if China could enhance its rule of law and risk surveillance system.

---

4   In terms of credit rating, the majority of US municipal bonds have credit ratings that, in general, are below US Treasury bonds but above most corporate bonds. A few US municipal bonds have no credit rating and they are still issued on the bond market. However, all the Chinese local government bonds and city investment bonds have to be rated before they can be issued. All local government bonds have the highest credit rating, like treasury bonds (AAA), and all city investment bonds' credit ratings are lower than treasury bonds but most are higher than the majority of corporate bonds.

Figure 11: Comparison of Issuance Scale between China and the United States (2012)

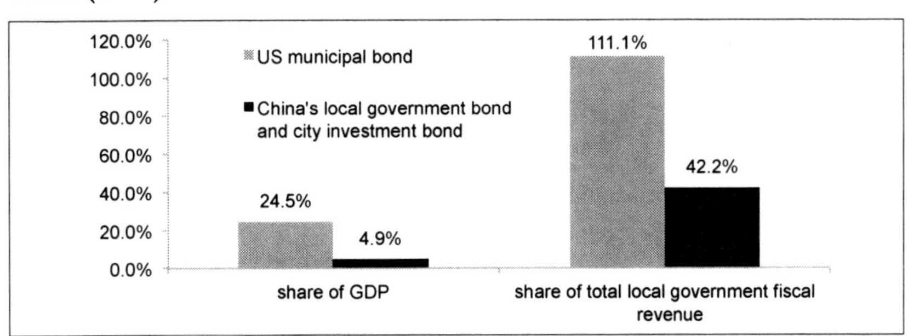

Data source: Wind Data, Securities Industry and Financial Markets Association (SIFMA) and author's calculation.

Maturity Structure

There is a big difference between the maturity structure of Chinese and US local government bonds. The maturity period of US municipal bonds ranges from one year to 30 years or longer. According to SIFMA data, the average maturity period of US municipal bonds at the end of 2012 was 16.5 years. The maturity period of China's local government bonds is three, five and seven years. The maturity period of China's city investment bonds is from five to 20 years (see Table 5). However, 82.7 percent of city investment bonds are shorter than eight years and the average maturity period is 5.7 years, only 35 percent of that of the United States in 2012.

Table 5: Maturity Structure of China's City Investment Bonds (2012)

Maturity Period (year)	5–8	10	11–20
Issuance Number	1194	209	41
Proportion	82.7%	14.5%	2.8%

Data source: Wind Data, author's calculation.

Two factors may account for the shortage of long-term local government bonds in China. First, the lack of long-term investors in the capital market is a typical problem in China. It is widely acknowledged that as an emerging economy, China's economic situation changes very fast and most investors do not have the patience to be a long-term investor. Many individual investors and institutional investors have a strong desire to make money quickly. Second, it also reflects the fact that many bonds in China do not have the confidence of investors, so even local government long-term credit is not widely accepted.[5]

Compared to other financial products, one of the most important advantages of bonds is that they are a powerful long-term financing tool that is particularly suited to financing infrastructure construction projects. In other words, improving the maturity structure of the local government bonds market is valuable for China's future economic development. In my view, the shorter maturity period of China's local government bonds does not necessarily indicate higher risks than bonds in the United States. Interestingly, China's local government bonds have not experienced a default since the first city investment bond was issued in 1992. However, this excellent performance has not increased the demand of China's investors for long-term bonds. This is characteristic of a rapidly growing market. Markets and regulations in China change so quickly that investors and local governments cannot have long-term and stable expectations for the future. When Xi Jinping became the new president of China, he declared that China was entering an era of "new normal," indicating that China's economic growth would experience a structural slowdown. With moderate economic growth, China will focus more on the quality than on the speed of growth, and will pursue deeper financial liberalization and stricter financial regulation. This will likely enhance the expectation of stability of both local governments and investors, thereby improving the maturity structure of the bond market.

Investor Structure

There is an obvious difference in the type of investor in local government bonds in China and in the United States. The largest holders of Chinese local government bonds (including city investment bonds) are banks, amounting to 31 percent of the total. In contrast, in the United States the largest holders are individual investors, amounting to 47.1 percent (see Figure 12). There are almost no individual investors who hold local government bonds in China. American individual investors buy local government bonds because the US government has a tax exemption policy for personal investments in municipal bonds. China does not have a similarly favourable tax policy, so personal investors have no incentive to buy local government bonds.

---

5   On the whole, China's credit system can be divided into three levels: central government; local government and state-owned enterprises; and private enterprises. The central government has an excellent reputation and provides the highest credit to Chinese people. Local governments and state-owned enterprises' reputation and credit are significantly lower than that of the central government. Private enterprises' reputation and credit are much lower. Therefore, China's treasury bonds are always welcomed by domestic investors, but private enterprises find it difficult to issue corporate bonds due to their credit rating.

Figure 12: Comparison of Investor Structure between China (left) and the United States (right), 2012

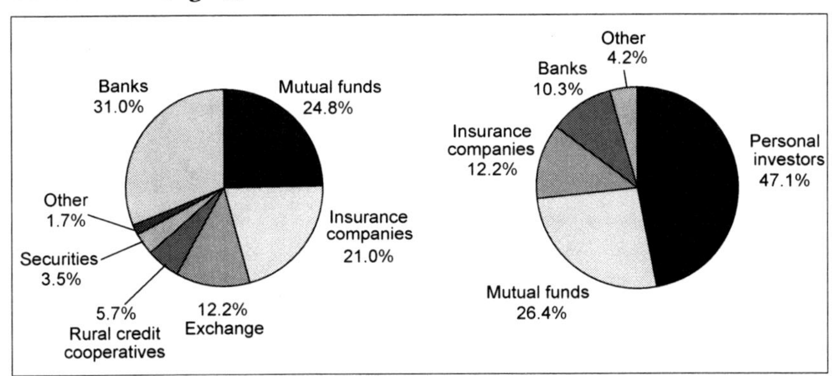

Data sources: China Bond Information Network and SIFMA.

Since 2012, China's central government has adopted stricter regulations to limit the expansion of local governments' debt so that banks are not allowed to issue more loans to local government-owned companies. However, at the same time, banks hold more and more city investment bonds. On the one hand, this shows that both banks and the regulators believe city investment bonds are safer than bank loans. On the other hand, it is helpful for local governments because, after all, bonds have a longer maturity period and lower interest rate than bank loans. This helps local governments manage the mismatch in term and rate of return in infrastructure construction.

With respect to the bank holding of Chinese bonds, it is interesting to note that foreign banks in the mainland of China hold few city investment bonds compared to Chinese banks (see Table 6). It would seem that foreign banks underestimate the ability of China's local governments to pay their debt from the bonds. In addition, it is clear that the credibility of China's local government bonds should be further enhanced by reforms (such as promoting transparency, rule of law and building an effective risk surveillance system) before they will be able to become global safe assets.

Table 6: Bank Holders' Structure

National Banks	City Banks	Rural Banks	Rural Credit Cooperatives	Foreign Banks	Village Banks
61.9%	20.1%	15.8%	1.1%	1.0%	0.1%

Source: China Bond Information Network.

Default Rate

The difference in the default rate may be the most significant difference between China and the United States. According to the Federal Reserve Bank of New York, the number of municipal bonds in the United States that defaulted from 1970 to 2011 amounted to 2,521, with 2,366 defaults from 1986 to 2011 (Appleson, Parsons and Haughwout 2012). Most of the defaults were municipal bonds that were not rated by a credit rating company. Among 2,521 defaults, 71 defaults bonds were rated (which means that the US credit rating system is highly effective). Commonly acknowledged as safe assets next to Treasury bonds, US municipal bonds still average 91 defaults per year. Since there is always some kind of risk in financial markets, a safe asset is one that has a very low default possibility, but there is always the possibility that it could default.

As noted above, China's local government bond market has not had any defaults since it was established in 1992. In 2011, two city investment bonds suffered from high-default risks. With the bailout of the local government and the intervention of the central government, the two incidents were safely resolved and the city investment bond market still maintains a zero default record. The absolutely safe status of China's local government bonds market is the result of two factors. First, China's high economic growth in the last three decades ensured that local government financing vehicles, which issued city investment bonds, earned enough profits to pay debt. Second, some local governments' bailouts also played a crucial role in preventing the defaults, although this situation was very rare. For the long-term development of the bond market, it is not beneficial to keep a zero default record. Today, the reason why China's institutional investors — banks, mutual funds and insurance companies — rush to buy city investment bonds is that they believe local governments will guarantee the payment of the bonds. This typically leads to moral hazard.

A tiny default rate has not prevented US municipal bonds from being safe assets alongside its Treasury bonds. Many large foreign banks hold US municipal bonds. In comparison, foreign banks hold few of China's local government bonds, even though the bonds have never experienced a default. Many factors account for the behaviour of foreign banks in China; however, it is clear that a zero default record is neither a sufficient nor a necessary condition for China's local government bonds to become global safe assets.

Future Development: Internationalization of China's Bond Market

This chapter argues that China's local government bonds still have a very promising future and could be global safe assets with the internationalization of the RMB and other liberalization reforms. As mentioned above, there are several factors facilitating the internationalization of China's local government bonds market. First, the lack of global safe assets; second, the scale of China's local government bond market is still very small and safe; third, the rapid progress of the internationalization of the RMB increases the demand of RMB-denominated bonds; and last, but not least, it is very likely that China will be able to sustain a relatively high GDP growth rate in the next 10 years (about a 6-7 percent growth rate per year) and local governments' fiscal revenue could, correspondingly, maintain a high rate of increase, which guarantees the payment for the debt of bonds. However, city investment bonds have some problems that prevent them from directly becoming global safe assets, unless some fundamental reforms are achieved.

Figure 13: Share of Credit Rating below AA and No Guarantee of City Investment Bonds

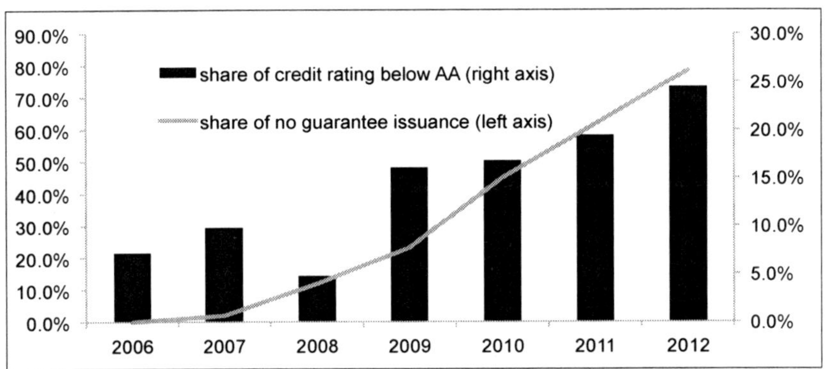

Data source: Wind Data.

Figure 13 shows the share of credit ratings below AA and no-guarantee issuance of city investment bonds. With more city investment bonds issued during the period shown, the credit rating of the newly issued bonds declined continuously. Only 4.8 percent of bonds issued in 2008 have a credit rating below AA while 24.4 percent of bonds issued in 2012 are below AA.[6] All bonds issued in 2006 were guaranteed by another entity (such as a firm or a financial institution), but 78.5 percent of bonds issued in 2012 have no guarantee. This would indicate that the bonds' credit risk has been accumulating. It is also a natural outcome

---

6   Credit ratings of local government bonds and city investment bonds are made by Sino-foreign joint-venture credit rating companies or domestic private credit rating companies.

of the evolution of the city investment bond market. The city investment bond market only became well developed after 2008 and all bonds issued must be approved by the NDRC. It is normal for the NDRC to allow the better local government financing vehicles, with a higher credit rating, to issue bonds first. Others followed afterwards, with a lower credit rating.

Although it is a normal market situation, the decline in credit rating and the rise in no-guarantee issuance will gradually pose a negative influence on the development of China's local government bonds, in particular on the internationalization of its bond market.[7] Generally speaking, foreign investors are more prudent than domestic investors in the Chinese financial market (see Table 6). With the debt problem becoming increasingly sensitive to the central government, local governments and investors, China's local government bond market has to make some basic changes in order to achieve sustainable development and internationalization.

The first reform should be for the central government to transfer the majority of city investment bonds into real local government bonds. Many researchers and officials support this idea. In fact, China's MoF declared in March 2015 that local governments are allowed to convert up to RMB 1 trillion worth of their debt (mainly bank loans and trust products) into lower-interest bonds. These bonds are typical local government bonds, which will be paid back by the fiscal revenues of local governments. Chinese local governments could not issue bonds by themselves before, so the debt swap in 2015 is the first time that all the provincial governments have the right to issue bonds. At the same time, the NDRC's approval of city investment bonds' issuance becomes more and more strict. Taking into account the two factors above, I consider that the debt swap is the beginning of the transformation of city investment bonds into real local government bonds, like municipal bonds in the United States.

There are two types of US municipal bonds. One is the general obligation bond, which needs no substantial guarantee and no corresponding project. The local government promises to pay the debt with its fiscal revenue, so the credibility of the general obligation bond is the credibility of the local government. Another is the revenue bond, which needs a concrete project that generates enough revenues to pay the debt. As a result, the credibility of the revenue bond rests

---

7   There are two kinds of guarantees on city investment bonds. One is a guarantee by another enterprise or a bank, which is an explicit guarantee. Figure 13 refers to this guarantee. Another is a guarantee by the local government, including an explicit guarantee and an implicit guarantee. So, although the first guarantee decreases, the local government's guarantee (in particular the implicit guarantee) still exists, making most domestic investors believe these bonds are still safe. But the implicit government guarantee leads to a severe moral hazard, which is bad for the sustainable development of the local government bond market.

on the credibility of the project. In light of this fact, the NDRC has already changed its requirements for approving the issuance of new bonds. In the past, most of the funds raised by city investment bonds were used in infrastructure construction projects. When the projects themselves could not pay the debt, local government-owned companies that issued city investment bonds made use of other projects' revenue and the government subsidies to pay the debt. This practice has been forbidden since 2014. The new issuance cannot be approved by the NDRC unless it can show that the company will invest the funds raised by the bond into a project profitable enough to pay the debt. This type of city investment bond is called a revenue bond in China, just as it is in the United States. According to the recent change in the NDRC's regulations, we can assume that the fundamental reform of city investment bonds is underway. I argue that the majority of city investment bonds should be turned into local government bonds, which are similar to general obligation bonds in the United States, while the minority of city investment bonds, which are similar to revenue bonds in the United States, could be kept unchanged.[8] After being changed into local government bonds in the strict sense, some of them will get a higher credit rating and move closer to safe assets.

The second reform should be that the central government allows all current local government bonds issued by the MoF for local governments since 2009 to be issued by local governments themselves. I believe this is becoming a very clear trend. Since 2011, a pilot program has allowed some provinces and cities to issue local government bonds by themselves. In 2014, four cities (Beijing, Shanghai, Shenzhen and Qingdao) and six provinces (Jiangsu, Shandong, Guangdong, Zhejiang, Jiangxi, Ningxia) were granted the power to issue their own local government bonds. The pilot areas could be enlarged in the future and eventually spread nationwide.

With these two reforms, China's local governments would have full autonomy to issue a large scale of local government bonds. After a few years, the asset pool of RMB-denominated bonds, which are guaranteed by local governments, would expand dramatically. If China could deepen its reform and sustain sound economic growth, government transparency and rule of law could be achieved and many local government bonds could receive relatively high credit ratings and will eventually become global safe assets.

A third reform should be for the central government to facilitate the issuance of more local government bonds in the offshore RMB market. At present, the

---

8   If the project is profitable, the corresponding city investment bond should stay unchanged because it can easily pay the interest to the bondholder. If the project is not profitable, which is the case for most projects, the bondshould be converted to a local government bond, which is guaranteed by the government's fiscal revenue.

central government allows all kinds of corporate bonds, financial institution bonds and government bonds to be issued in offshore markets. But there are actually few city investment bonds and no local government bonds issued in offshore markets. One of the reasons for this is that there are some limitations on issuing bond at offshore markets. For example, many offshore issuers (companies and financial institutions) are forbidden to take RMB back to mainland China after they have raised the funds. They can only use the RMB funds offshore. This is an unnecessary restriction. Compared to the huge monetary supply in mainland China, the amount of dim sum bonds issued is tiny and the funds raised by dim sum bonds are negligible. Even if most flow back to mainland China, their impact would be minimal. Another reason is there are some difficulties in issuing dim sum bonds in offshore markets. City investment bonds have to be rated by the three international credit rating companies (Moody's, S&P, Fitch) if they want to expand their issuance scale and reduce the financing cost in offshore markets. On the one hand, the international credit rating companies charge a lot; on the other hand, they are unlikely to rate the city investment bonds as high as the local credit companies do because they do not accept the idea that the implicit guarantee of local governments will prevent a default. This problem may be ameliorated once the city investment bonds are turned into real local government bonds with explicit guarantees from the local government. Finally, most companies have no desire to issue bonds in offshore markets because city investment bonds are popular in the onshore market and the offshore issuance is much more complex than onshore issuance.

Taking into account that China's local government bond market will increase a great deal, the dim sum bond market will experience a boom if the central government removes the limitations and encourages offshore issuance. For example, the NDRC should simplify the approval procedure to speed up the offshore issuance of city investment bonds. Most offshore RMB markets (such as Hong Kong, London, Paris, Frankfurt and Singapore) have strict market regulations, so there is no need for the NDRC to engage in a complex approval process. With the expansion of offshore issuance, the central government is sure to face new risks, such as exchange rate instability and interest rate pressure. The offshore market will increasingly affect the onshore market. To address this problem, the central government must further facilitate financial liberalization and promote macroprudential regulations.

Internationalizing China's Bond Market: The Benefits

The internationalization of China's bond market will bring many benefits to both China's domestic reform and to the transformation of the international monetary system.

Since President Xi Jinping took office, he has continued "to promote reform by opening up." In the 1980s, China took advantage of the inflow of foreign direct investment to help create a domestic market system. In 2001, China used its entrance into the World Trade Organization (WTO) to advance economic liberalization, in particular liberalizing current account items. At that time, many conservatives argued that entering the WTO would subject China to a large-scale invasion of foreign goods and its national industry would be destroyed. Instead, now it is goods made in China that occupy the world market, and it is Chinese enterprises that are undertaking mergers and acquisitions with foreign enterprises. China's entry into the WTO was a successful experience for the country to promote reform by opening up. Through long-term economic growth, many vested interest groups have been formed, and they exert great pressure on the government to hamper further reform. Reform-oriented politicians have to set up a "reverse pressure mechanism," forcing domestic change by bringing in foreign pressure. Many Chinese officials and scholars consider RMB internationalization a reverse pressure mechanism that would facilitate domestic financial reform. It is clear that if China wants to completely internationalize its currency, it has to liberalize capital control as well as the exchange rates and interest rates.[9] Therefore, the PBoC — the most reform-oriented agency of the Chinese government — actively pushes forward RMB internationalization in order to speed up China's financial reform.

Similar to RMB internationalization, the internationalization of China's bond market can be another powerful reverse pressure mechanism to force domestic liberalization.

First, in order to make RMB-denominated bonds global safe assets, China must greatly expand the size of its bonds market,[10] thereby fundamentally changing

---

9   An internationalized currency requires free convertibility, indicating that China has to completely open its capital account. If China only opens its capital account but still controls the exchange rate and interest rate systems, arbitrage between offshore RMB markets and the onshore RMB market will occur, leading to large-scale cross-border capital flow and thereby affecting China's financial stability. Therefore, China has to completely liberalize its exchange rate and interest rate systems at the same time as it opens its capital account and internationalizes its currency.

10   The size of a bond's market is not a necessary condition for a safe asset, but liquidity is a crucial condition for many investors (especially for central banks and commercial banks, which are the main buyers of safe assets).

the current financial development pattern where the banking sector has absolute dominance in the financial system. China must enlarge the treasury bond market to form the basic pool of global safe assets. China must also expand its local government bond market because excessive dependence on the treasury bond market is risky for China. The enormous size of the US Treasury bond market poses a major problem for the United States in that the fiscal deficit of the US federal government has led to a downgrade of its sovereign credit rating. This has a negative influence on the country's sustainable economic development. China should diversify its government debt risk to include local governments.[11] It is necessary to expand the local government bond market so that the treasury bond market and local government bond market can be integrated as a large pool of safe assets. In addition, some highly rated bonds of financial agencies and large companies could also become global safe assets. Therefore, by internationalizing the bond market, China will build a more diversified and more powerful direct financing system.

Second, internationalizing the bond market will force China's central government and local governments to build a more transparent, well-regulated and accountable fiscal system. China's central government is always prudent in its debt management. However, local governments do not do very well in this area. They have had strong intentions to promote GDP growth for many years. To some extent, "GDPism" has been good for China's development during the last three decades. But, after China becomes a middle-income country and local governments' debt has accumulated rapidly, fiscal and financial regulation of local governments will have to be stricter. The internationalization of the bond market provides an effective way to do that. Generally speaking, a governmental bond market is a tool of investors' oversight of the government. The international purchase of a government bond means an international "vote" of confidence. Since China wants its currency and bonds market to be internationalized, it must accept the oversight of the international market. Conversely, China will use the international market regulations to enhance the transparency, accountability and regulation of local governments' fiscal and financial systems.

If RMB-denominated bonds become global safe assets, it will greatly facilitate the internationalization of the RMB, which will profoundly change the

---

11   In China, the central government has a very strong control of the whole economy and most Chinese people deeply believe in the central government's will and ability to save the financial market if any risks break out. One of the reasons why city investment bonds are highly welcomed is that most investors believe that the central government will bail out this market if local governments cannot pay the debt, which leads to severe moral hazard and accumulates the risk on the central government. I argue that the central government should diversify the debt risks to local governments. Only when the central government allows a local government to go bankrupt, can the local government really take responsibility to manage its debt.

international monetary system. The US dollar has played a dominant role in the international monetary system since 1945. After the 2008 financial crisis, the world became aware of the fragility of the dollar system. Such a system led to a serious global imbalance. On the one hand, the United States has continuously exported dollars by keeping a trade deficit over a long period of time. On the other hand, many Asian countries have maintained trade surpluses and then invested their foreign reserves back in the United States. Such a global imbalance to some extent caused the 2008 financial crisis. But the global financial crisis has not changed the international monetary system so far. The United States became a highly indebted country after the crisis, but it has still been able to easily raise low-cost funds from the international bond market. At the same time, China's foreign reserve has grown to over US$4 trillion. Given the dominance of the US dollar, this situation is not likely to change.

When China fully internationalizes its currency and makes RMB-denominated bonds global safe assets, the international monetary system will be effectively diversified, considerably reducing the dependence of international investors on assets denominated in US dollars (these are mainly US Treasury bonds). That means the United States will no longer be able to raise low-cost capital to easily finance its current account deficit and fiscal deficit. When this occurs, the United States will have to seriously consider rebalancing its economy. As a result, the United States will have to shrink its consumption and increase its savings. Since the main trade deficit of the United States is with Asia, the rebalance will decrease its import from Asia. In that case, Asian countries cannot rely on the US market to support their economic growth, and will have to expand their domestic consumption.

In brief, the internationalization of the RMB and China's bond markets will create a more diversified international monetary system and lower the demand for US dollar-denominated assets, therefore pushing forward the global rebalance and promoting the stability of the global economy. RMB-denominated bonds along with other bonds, such as US dollar- and euro-denominated bonds, could form a large pool of safe assets to support better global financial governance in the long run.

Works Cited

Appleson, Jason, Eric Parsons and Andrew Haughwout. 2012. "The Untold Story of Municipal Bond Default." Federal Reserve Bank of New York Working Paper.

Chen, Hong. 2013. "Impact of Sovereign Credit Rating upon Other Ratings." [In Chinese.] *Tribune of Social Sciences*, 8.

IMF. 2012. *Global Financial Stability Report*. April.

Jia, Kang. 2014a. "Issuance of Local Government Bonds Will Significantly Rise in 2015." [In Chinese.] www.gw.com.cn/news/news/2014/0905/200000375831.shtml.

———. 2014b. "China's Government May Increase Its Debt Ratio in the Future." [In Chinese.] *Phoenix Finance*, December 22. www.rmlt.com.cn/2014/1222/362458_2.shtml.

Part Three

China in International Financial Governance

10

China at the IMF

Bessma Momani

hina's rising power and influence in international monetary relations are increasingly more visible in its provision of balance-of-payments finance, its growing influence as a creditor and the broader reach of its currency in international reserves and transactions (Helleiner and Kirshner 2014). This chapter considers how China has used its growing global power to shape debates at the International Monetary Fund (IMF), in particular, since the simultaneous increase of its regional and global power since the 2000s. The first section of the chapter focuses on the role of China in shaping debates about IMF governance and considers how China has leveraged its prestigious, single-seat representation at the executive board. Using its single-seat representation at the IMF executive board is a useful way to have its views heard in international economic debates, but China has also relied heavily on forming coalitions, particularly with fellow emerging market economies such as the BRICS (an informal coalition grouping composed of Brazil, Russia, India, China and South Africa) to build support for issues it seeks to promote and for raising broader concerns it has with Fund governance. China has also pushed for intellectual diversity in the IMF, including recruitment diversity in Fund staffing and in upper IMF management. Despite state media rumours favouring a Chinese managing director, China did not present a candidate for the coveted managing director position in 2011; however, it did succeed in getting the conciliation of a Chinese national appointed to a newly created deputy managing director position.

The second section of this chapter focuses on the role of China in reforming IMF surveillance. Chinese criticism of IMF failings to see broader systemic risks caused by the dominance of the US dollar has been a strong position advocated by Chinese officials in repeated fora. At the IMF, China has criticized the scope of the Fund's surveillance work, claiming that staff had spent more energy focusing on bilateral surveillance exercises, such as Article IV consultations, than examining multilateral risks and spillovers. China has also faced a great deal of IMF criticism for its exchange rate policy, and has often viewed IMF actions as a veil for US policy preferences. In some way, the international financial crises of 2008 reaffirmed long-standing Chinese positions on the problems associated with the IMF's prioritizing bilateral surveillance over multilateral surveillance. Meanwhile, the IMF has also had a difficult time prodding China to let its currency appreciate in response to US pressure to use IMF surveillance mechanisms to call out the Chinese for undervaluation of its currency.

The third section focuses on the IMF's unit of account, the Special Drawing Right (SDR), and the role that China has played over time in shaping the usage of SDRs. China has called for the IMF to make the SDR more available to countries, in order to diversify international holdings away from the US dollar. The Fund has also assessed the prospects of including the renminbi (RMB) in its own SDR basket, but this has not yet materialized.

China on IMF Governance

From the early days of the meetings at Bretton Woods in New Hampshire, United States, in 1944, the Chinese government (under the Kuomintang government), played a prominent role in negotiating the governance structure of the IMF (Helleiner and Momani 2014, 45). The People's Republic of China assumed its single seat at the IMF executive board in the early 1980s, and has used this position for decades to argue for increasing its own political and decision-making power at the executive board and for building the overall power and influence of other emerging market economies (Momani 2013). Having a single-seat representation at the executive board, where it does not represent other countries in its constituency, has given China a prestigious voice at the Fund. Its executive board seat has always provided China with a voice to call for enhanced and broadened IMF decision making. China has used its seat at the IMF to primarily call for reforming the board to allow for more emerging market economies and developing countries at the table. It has also called for changes to IMF policies that move beyond the neoliberal model the Fund currently adopts and preaches through its conditionality on countries that borrow money from it. Finally, China's position on governance reforms includes the call for diversifying the candidate pool used to select the IMF managing director and to increase hiring and recruitment of Chinese economists.

China has often argued that it wants to be a team player in the broader objectives of global governance reforms, in particular reforms at the IMF. In addition to its prominent role in fora such as the Group of Twenty (G20), China uses its place at the IMF to advocate for transferring political power to new economic players, such as emerging market economies, throughout the international economic architecture. China sees international governance reforms as a necessary part of taking account of the new global shift toward a multipolar world economy, one in which it and other emerging market economies contribute more to global economic growth than in the previous US-dominated unipolar world economy. China often argued that new economic players — developing countries and emerging market economies in the South — continue to hold a smaller share of decision-making power in the IMF voting distribution than they deserve. For example, the advanced economies' share of IMF voting shares is 60 percent (as of 2011), with the United States holding 17 percent of that; in contrast, all emerging market economies and developing countries hold 40 percent, with China having less than six percent of voting shares. The most overrepresented countries, in relation to their contribution to global GDP, are many of the European and Group of Seven countries, which collectively hold 45 percent of IMF voting shares despite their declining global economic influence and growth. China has argued that it must advocate for this position and perspective to correct this imbalance on behalf of other countries because it is the largest developing country in the world today (Ma 2013). The reforms at the IMF are part of creating a "more just system" (ibid.) Moreover, IMF reforms are also seen as part of a need for more "holistic" improvements, in the words of China's governor, to getting better coordination among the UN bodies, the G20 and other international institutions (ibid.), where US dominance has also characterized the international system, especially after the end of the Cold War.

In keeping with its position of wanting to see a shift in global institutional power to developing countries, China has spent a great deal of regional and international political and diplomatic energy to push for the implementation of the 2010 IMF quota and governance reform package. Despite its loud voice, in chorus with the G20 and other countries, the proposal has languished for years due to US Congressional hang-ups. In 2010, Zhou Xiaochuan, governor of the People's Bank of China (PBoC) and China's IMF governor, noted that "to establish an equal, inclusive, and orderly international financial architecture, the international community has placed great importance on reforming the International Monetary Fund and the World Bank, aimed at a thorough improvement of their governance structure with a significant increase of developing countries' representation and voices, and tangible progress in upgrading their ability to fulfill their mandates....This reform will significantly enhance the IMF's legitimacy and representativeness, which will ultimately benefit all the member countries. We call for understanding, support, and contribution to this reform" (Zhou 2010c).

The imperative of reforming the IMF to shift power and influence from developed economies to developing economies is strongly tied to what China views as an effort to return legitimacy to the Bretton Woods organization. Specifically, China had previously argued that the IMF lost legitimacy in its handling of the 1997 Asian financial crisis and in its prescription of austere conditionality to other developing countries throughout the 1980s and 1990s.

China argued that the Asian financial crisis demonstrated that the existing "international monetary and financial system can no longer accommodate the needs of international economic and financial development, and, therefore, the system needs to be reformed" (Dai 1999), and that the IMF and its political backers in the West had "forced [developing] countries to restructure their economies according to the developed countries' standards" (ibid). The dominant model of fiscal austerity prescribed by the IMF, which developing countries are obligated to follow in exchange for sorely needed finance, is a model that Chinese authorities have questioned at the IMF. To reform the international monetary and financial system, changes at the IMF need to be made and to prevent future crises, the IMF decision-making structure needs to be widened to include not just developed countries, but also developing countries. China sought to have an "automatic adjustment mechanism" that would be used to better keep up with changes in the global economic distribution of wealth and power (Xie 2009). Governance reform, the Chinese often argued, would improve the development models prescribed by the IMF, which has led its "dogmatist mentality" (Zhou 2004).

As the above quotes from Chinese governors indicate, while there are Chinese concerns with IMF governance structures, China has also felt under-represented in terms of ideas at the IMF. In tandem with governance reforms at the IMF, China wants the Fund to better reflect its views and opinions in the design of policy and programs. According to Ferdinand and Wang (2013, 899) China would "prefer a less intrusive IMF, one that is more akin to a clearing-house for ideas on economic cooperation and development and on financial regulation, more pragmatic and open-minded." Ideally, China envisions an IMF that is more tolerant of a system that allows "greater freedom for states to experiment in devising policies that are best suited to their particular circumstances, just as

China has done" (ibid.). Indeed, the view of how the IMF recruits and trains its staff into set development models and ideas is often a missing element in IMF reform debates (see Momani 2007). On this issue, China would like to see the Fund broaden its recruitment and "do much more to promote diversity of skills and experience among its staff" (Ferdinand and Wang 2013, 899).

Generally speaking, IMF economists who are educated in the developing world are clearly under-represented at the IMF and the Fund has a higher preference for US-trained economists (see Momani 2005). China is cognizant of this trend and has pushed for a broader IMF recruitment strategy. Ferdinand and Wang (2013, 899) point out that China is highly under-represented among IMF staff; moreover, Chinese Ph.D. and M.A. graduates are even more under-represented at the IMF, than, say, Chinese nationals with Ph.Ds. from outside China who work at the Fund. Specifically, "although China was also among the top ten countries in terms of level of education of Fund staff, only 0.6 per cent of PhDs, 1.1 per cent of Master's degrees, and 2.6 per cent of Bachelor's degrees were obtained from Chinese universities" (ibid.). In contrast, approximately 79 percent of all incoming economist program recruits at the IMF were educated at Anglo-American universities, and the IMF identified that most of its globally preferred university graduates were also Anglo-American (Momani 2005). This explains why Chinese nationals who do work at the Fund are mostly educated outside of China and are, therefore, less likely to reflect Chinese models and ideas. Nevertheless, the Chinese nationals who do work at the Fund, and these are low numbers to begin with, are still an under-represented percentage considering the country's economic heft in the global economy. By diversifying IMF recruitment to include more Chinese-educated economists, China had argued, the IMF would have less dogmatic development models (see Ferdinand and Wang 2013, 899).

At the third meeting of the newly formed G20 (leaders' level) summit in Pittsburgh in 2009, China and other like-minded states used the growing international consensus around the need to facilitate coordinated action that could restore global economic stability, as an opportunity to push for reforms that would reconfigure IMF quotas to better reflect emerging market economies' contribution to the world economy. China's Assistant Finance Minister Zhu Guangyao recommended transferring IMF voting weight from the developed countries to the developing countries. Specifically, he recommended that namely Organisation for Economic Co-operation and Development developed countries, which had 57 percent of voting rights at the IMF, transfer some of this power to developing countries. China and other emerging market economies wanted developed countries to transfer seven percent of their voting rights to the developing countries, which collectively had 43 percent at the IMF. China did not get the seven percent commitment, but the G20 agreed to shift five percent of developed country quotas to under-represented developing countries. Implementation of these quota revisions was set to be implemented by January 2011, but continued to be delayed for years, as the US administration did not want to confront a hostile US Congress.

After frustrating calls for the US Congress to pass the 2010 quota reforms (which still languish in Congress as of 2015), some of the strongest words used by China in its calls for IMF reform were found in an often-cited article by Xinhua, the official Chinese news agency, that declared, "Washington's political chaos proves it's time for a de-Americanised world. As this latest crisis reveals, the US is unfit to govern itself, let alone lord it over the rest of us. We need a new world order" (Chang 2013). The Xinhua article went on to lambast American leadership, suggesting that the destinies of many countries were in the "hands of a hypocritical nation [that] have to be terminated, and a new world order should be put in place, according to which all nations, big or small, poor or rich, can have their key interests respected and protected on an equal footing" (ibid.) To achieve a de-Americanized world, the Xinhua article noted the need for reforms at the United Nations and the IMF and World Bank, and the introduction of "a new international reserve currency that is to be created to replace the dominant US dollar, so that the international community could permanently stay away from the spillover of the intensifying domestic political turmoil in the United States" (ibid.). By challenging US leadership at the IMF and vocally criticizing IMF policies and prescriptions, this has arguably won China the added support of developing countries at the IMF.

China has often sought to use coalition building with developing countries to push its agenda and views forward. One of the most important fora used by the Chinese to build a coalition in favour of IMF reforms has been the BRICS. The BRICS first met in 2009, in Russia, and has continued to add political and financial heft behind the loose coalition of states. Through the BRICS, these leading emerging market countries continuously issue joint statements, often in parallel with other high-level meetings such as the G20, the IMF Annual Meetings, and so on, showcasing their views about global governance reforms. China is instrumental in using the BRICS meetings to have its positions known, while using the "caucus with other countries on matters of common interest" as an important way to signal that "they view multilateral cooperation as a means to larger ends" (Edwards 2011). In other words, by acting multilaterally in its quest for IMF reforms, China looks like the "responsible stakeholder" that is upholding a multilateral process and not using its growing economic heft to dictate new terms of engagement.

China is keen on not sounding dictatorial or unilateral in its views, a style that it often accuses the United States of exercising, particularly at the IMF. China, along with the other BRICS countries, also announced in 2009 that it would contribute funds to the IMF through a mechanism allowing the temporary purchase of SDR-denominated securities or quasi IMF bonds. Again demonstrating they were responsible stakeholders, the BRICS raised IMF capital by an added US$150 billion through purchases of these bonds at a time of a great shortfall in IMF finances and high demand after the international financial crisis. China demonstrated its strength among the BRICS countries when it purchased the largest share of IMF bonds, US$50 billion worth, while the other countries had each purchased US$10 billion. China was keen to ally with the BRICS to link the issues of both providing these additional funds to the IMF and the issue of transferring votes and quota to the developing countries (Glosny 2010). China's actions are meant also to underscore that it has no ambitions to "undermine and destroy the existing international order," on the contrary it is a responsible player in ensuring the endurance of the system by reforming its governance, returning legitimacy and contributing finances to the IMF (ibid.).

IMF leadership, in particular the role of the managing director, has historically been dominated by the Europeans. This "gentlemen's agreement" between the Europeans and the largest quota holder, the Americans, had allowed the United States to keep the president position at the World Bank for one of its own nationals. China has consistently argued against this quid pro quo among the Americans and Europeans at the Bretton Woods institutions and called for widening the selection process to include non-Europeans to hold the top post at the IMF. China has repeatedly called for the IMF managing director selection process to be "open, transparent and merit-based" (Xie 2009). When, in May 2011, then IMF Managing Director Dominique Strauss-Kahn resigned after a scandal in the United States, China called on the IMF to open the process to include emerging market economies. Specifically, China's central bank chief Zhou Xiaochuan told Agence France-Press that "the make-up of top [IMF] management should better reflect changes in the global economic structure and better represent emerging markets" (quoted in *China Economic Review* 2011). Taking this further, Chinese state media *People's Daily* reported they would like to see a Chinese national take the position: "It will be great sign of respect for a rising China and a symbolic step of optimizing the international financial order if the 24 executive directors who hold shares of the IMF can see this clearly and elect a Chinese president [*sic*] of the IMF" (*People's Daily* 2011). Chinese media noted that Min Zhu, a former deputy governor of China's central bank and a special adviser to Strauss-Kahn, would be a suitable candidate to fill the post (ibid.). Selecting a Chinese national to lead the IMF did not come to fruition, however.

Christine Lagarde courted China and many of the emerging market economies, such as Brazil, India and Russia, by personally visiting these countries and seeking support for her bid to lead the IMF. Despite China earlier voicing its reservations about having yet another European at the helm of the IMF, when votes were cast, China and other emerging market economies did support Lagarde's candidacy and not that of the Mexican candidate. Perhaps what Lagarde had promised to China was the creation of an added new position of a third deputy managing director, which Lagarde announced soon after taking office. At her first press conference, she noted "The world is going to continue to change…We have these tectonic plates that are moving at the moment, and that needs to be reflected in the composition of governance and employment at the fund" (quoted in Wroughton 2011). Min Zhu was accorded a new title and a third deputy managing director post was created by Lagarde for the Chinese. This new position for a Chinese national had effectively quelled Chinese demands for opening the managing director position to non-Europeans. But, it remains to be seen what will happen after Lagarde leaves the Fund, and whether the Chinese will mount a campaign to have one of its nationals take the helm.

China on IMF Surveillance

The purpose of IMF surveillance is to report on both the individual member countries and on the overall health of the global economy. In theory, the Fund's access to data, information and officials in its member countries allows it to have the insight and perspective to predict, warn and assess the global economy and potential crises. This has not always worked well in the past, as the IMF did not predict many of the major financial crises, including the 1997 Asian financial crisis and the 2008 international financial crisis. While there are great debates on the main causes and policy errors made in these crises, the IMF has had the unenviable burden of being the sole institution that is expected to be capable of providing the warning to its members of upcoming economic shocks and potential growth setbacks. Even prior to the international financial crisis, many academics and analysts noted the need for improving the efficacy of IMF surveillance (see Lombardi and Woods 2008; Eichengreen 2007).

China has also had strong criticism and reservations about the conduct and substance of IMF surveillance. For nearly a decade before the international financial crisis, China warned that too much of the IMF's surveillance resources, energy and study had been focused on developing and emerging market economies, while the IMF and its staff had too often ignored developments in developed countries. China had persistently called on the IMF to look at the systemic relevance of its members with advanced economies and to put more of its surveillance emphasis on those countries. China's rationale was that systemically important countries, such as the United States, have stronger spillover effects if there are risks or policy errors made, which can then reverberate in the global economy. Simply put, systemically important countries have a stronger chance of pushing contagion when and if they are unhealthy. Since the United States and European economies are the most interlinked to the global financial and economic system with their highly internationalized and liberalized capital markets, this means that these economies are riskier than others and can induce a negative domino effect in the global economy (see Xiao 2000).

China used the IMF Annual Meetings to highlight some of the concerns it had with the IMF surveillance mechanisms. PBoC Governor Xianglong Dai (2002b) noted: "We hope that, with close coordination and clear focus on the roles of the *World Economic Outlook* and the *Global Financial Stability Report* — the two major global surveillance tools — the Fund's multilateral surveillance will be more effective. At present, the Fund should strengthen its surveillance of the major industrial countries and important financial centers with a view to preventing large fluctuations among the major currencies, effectively monitoring international capital movements, ensuring the sound and efficient operation of international financial markets and promoting the healthy development of the world economy."

Urging the IMF to double its efforts on monitoring the US economy as opposed to focusing its surveillance efforts on other countries was a persistent theme of the Chinese governors' messages at the IMF Annual Meetings for several years. This criticism of IMF surveillance work came to a loggerhead in 2003, when China called out the IMF staff for its overly optimistic assessment of the US economy in its annual Article IV consultation report (see Li 2003). China was concerned with the United States' intervention in Iraq and the rising debt of its geopolitical gambles abroad and what these geopolitical adventures would mean for the global economy. Again calling out the IMF staff in particular, Chinese Governor Li (2003) stated "the IMF should now set priorities and focus on those areas that can really enhance the crisis prevention capabilities of member countries." To achieve better crisis prevention, Li added that "in light of the current situation in which the world economy is more dependent on the economies of the industrial countries, the IMF needs to tighten its surveillance of the macroeconomic and financial policies of the major industrial countries." Again for China, too little IMF emphasis and consideration were placed on studying the potential spillover effects of the US economy and its highly internationalized currency.

Some of China's frustration with the way the IMF conducted its surveillance activities was rooted in the belief that the IMF, backed and supported ideologically by the United States, was transcending its mandate in interfering with how countries chose to manage their exchange rates. China wanted the IMF's surveillance function to look at exchange rates, in so far as they pertained to the stability and health of the global economy. Countries should retain full sovereignty on choosing the type of exchange rate system that works for their economy, China often argued, and the IMF should not interfere in these choices, as long as those countries do not contribute to global financial vulnerability.

While China raised criticism of IMF lapses in monitoring the US economy, the United States was very concerned with Chinese undervaluation of its currency. Some had argued that China's RMB was potentially 25 to 50 percent undervalued in relation to the US dollar, which increased the US trade deficit, hurt US exports and aggravated high rates of US employment (see Sanford 2006). The IMF's Article IV makes clear that members, including China, are not allowed to manipulate and fix their currencies to achieve an unfair trade advantage. The US policy and academic community increasingly criticized the US government, generally, and the IMF, specifically, for not forcing the Chinese to readjust their currency (ibid.). Analysts continued to point to how Chinese government policies manipulated the exchange rate to prevent a natural appreciation of the RMB. While the IMF noted this as a concerning development, US analysts argued that the IMF was soft on China and did not forcibly call out the Chinese for manipulating its currency.

Hardline US commentators argued that the IMF was not doing enough to get China to become a more liberalized economy, particularly in its exchange rate policy. For example, pointing to the 2006 staff reports, Michael Mussa (2007) argued that the IMF staff were vague about wanting "greater flexibility" in China's exchange rate, instead of forcefully calling on China's currency manipulation. Mussa criticized the IMF's Asian and Pacific Department for not properly valuating the extent of China's currency manipulation. As a former Fund employee and chief IMF economist, Mussa (2007, 5) sharply criticized the IMF, stating: "Pointing out forcefully to Chinese authorities what they are obliged to do to fulfill their specific obligations or general obligations under Article IV — either in public, in discussions of the IMF Executive Board, or even in private — is not something that the Managing Director (or key IMF staff) appear to be prepared to undertake." Again, these were harsh words coming from a former and senior IMF employee, but Mussa was not alone in his criticism.

Morris Goldstein, a former Fund employee and deputy director of IMF research, also weighed in with his criticism. Like Mussa, Goldstein (2006, 150) accused the IMF of being "very timid and purposely noncommittal" on calling out Chinese currency manipulation. Goldstein said there was "overwhelming evidence" before the IMF, but that the Fund was "intimidated by the extreme sensitivity of the Chinese authorities to external criticism of their exchange rate policy" (ibid). Increasingly, US officials and commentators started to pressure the IMF to use its surveillance function as a means of shaming China to reform its currency policies.

The United States continued to search for policy options to counter the lack of movement and rising underappreciation of the Chinese currency. One option had been to raise the dollar-RMB dispute before the IMF or the World Trade Organization (Sanford 2006). In September 2005, US Treasury Under-Secretary Timothy Adams had criticized the IMF for not enforcing its own Article IV rule that members would not engage in currency manipulation. Adams charged that the IMF was "asleep at the wheel" and that it should challenge the Chinese directly for failing to live up to its agreement with the IMF's own articles of agreement (quoted in Blustein 2005). The IMF's Managing Director Rodrigo de Rato responded to Adams' accusation of being negligent, noting that the Fund had already investigated China's currency policy and did not feel further action was required (ibid). Rato responded to criticism that the Fund ought to increase its scrutiny over China by saying, "there is a trade-off between our role as confidential adviser in our surveillance work and our role as a transparent judge" (quoted in Giles and Guha 2006, 8). The United States' push for a reform of IMF surveillance was not just to identify global exchange rate and current account imbalances for some altruistic global good, but to confront China's growing trade surplus with the United States, which was a politically contentious issue in the US Congress (see Broome and Seabrooke 2007).

The United States did not let up in its criticism of China, however.[1] Most famously, in 2005, Deputy Secretary of State Robert B. Zoellick gave a defining speech in front of the National Committee on the United States and China Relations in New York, which had criticized China's relationship to the IMF. Zoellick (2005) said: "China is big, it is growing, and it will influence the world in the years ahead. For the United States and the world, the essential question is how will China use its influence? To answer that question, it is time to take our policy beyond opening doors to China's membership into the international system: We need to urge China to become a *responsible stakeholder* in that

---

1   Some analysts read Zoellick's speech as an invitation to China to get more involved in international affairs. They saw this largely as a positive signal rather than as criticism of China, but this author argues that it was interpreted as criticism by most analysts.

system. China has a responsibility to strengthen the international system that has enabled its success" (emphasis added).

The catch phrase that followed was that China needed to be a "responsible stakeholder" in the global economy and, importantly, at the IMF. For China to achieve its objectives of increasing its power at the IMF, the United States charged, it needed to also be a responsible stakeholder in its monetary policy choices. Simply put, China could not have its cake and eat it too. For China to be more powerful in an institution that puts exchange rate liberalization as the cornerstone policy tool in a healthy global economy and trading system, the Chinese needed to follow the IMF's mantra and liberalize its exchange rate. In the American view, China had no moral right to pursue increased economic and political power at the IMF if it continued to flagrantly dismiss the rules of the liberal economic system, such as flexible exchange rates. The view that the IMF was incapable or soft on China was shared by many within the United States, but many Chinese officials argued that the IMF was overly focused on its exchange rate regime, to the detriment of other, more pressing, surveillance issues.

At the Fund, the Chinese currency issue was being discussed among the IMF staff and the executive board. Some proposals to strengthen IMF surveillance were believed to be a means for increasing IMF power to reprimand countries that manipulated their currency, such as, perhaps, the Chinese. The IMF's focus on China's exchange rate in the mid-2000s was of great concern for Chinese leadership — they felt that the IMF was ignoring the United States' potential role in contributing to global economic and financial vulnerabilities. Governor Zhou (2006) spoke to this at the 2006 IMF Annual Meetings: "Exchange rate policy is only one component of macroeconomic policy. Each country is entitled to choose an exchange rate system consistent with its own economic development. If [IMF] surveillance is wrongly focused on an evaluation of the exchange rate level or an isolated judgment as to whether the exchange rate system is appropriate, it will hardly be objective and certainly miss more fundamental issues. This would be contrary to the maintenance of economic and financial stability and might even deviate from the Fund's mandate."

The issue of US dollar hegemony and the vulnerabilities this brought to the global economy was related to Chinese concerns that the IMF was overly focused on liberalization in China's currency to the determinant of examining the extent of the potential negative spillovers emanating from the US economy. China raised the use of the SDR as a remedy to this problem (discussed further in the next section), but China also objected to the IMF's efforts to reform its surveillance policy in 2007. Meanwhile, the IMF got tougher on China in its Article IV consultations.

The Fund staff produced an IMF Article IV consultation that called out China for its undervalued currency, arguing that this prevented Chinese officials from having a more independent monetary policy and produced higher real interest rates, both of which caused domestic and international economic distortions (see IMF 2006, 28). The IMF, however, was limited in what it could do to force the Chinese to implement regarding currency liberalization. Moreover, China did not agree to release its annually scheduled Article IV consultation reports until 2004, and then it blocked the release of the IMF staff's reports in 2007, 2008 and 2009 (Ferdinand and Wang 2013, 903). Chinese authorities most likely blocked the IMF staff Article IV surveillance reports because of increased criticism therein about the manipulation of China's currency and the need for re-evaluation of its exchange rate (ibid.) Despite IMF staff pressure on China, there has been a gradual increase in the value of its currency relative to the US dollar, indicating that perhaps some of this external pressure has had an effect on Chinese officials (ibid.)

In 2007, IMF staff decided to revise the long-outdated surveillance policy with its Decision on Bilateral Surveillance over Members' Policies (see Lavigne and Schembri 2009). The 2007 decision was meant to strengthen the capacity of IMF staff to discuss exchange rate policies with its members, particularly when and if the IMF staff believes it endangers external stability (Leckow 2007, 289). The 2007 decision also provided more clarity and guidance on what the IMF believes is currency manipulation that can lead to unfair competitive advantage. The decision clarified that "members are only prohibited from manipulating exchange rates for the purposes of preventing effective balance-of-payments adjustment or to gain an unfair competitive advantage over other members. Thus, to find a member in breach of this provision, it is necessary for the Fund to determine the purpose of the member's policies and the intent of the member in engaging in exchange rate manipulation" (ibid, 291). China saw both rationales for the 2007 decision as an attempt for greater intrusion and interference in its policy-making choices.

In response to the updated surveillance policy, China said it "regretted" the adoption of the 2007 decision and suggested that it was "rushed" and "lacked consensus of members," meaning China felt that the United States pushed through the policy changes at the IMF against the will of others at the executive board. China argued that the 2007 decision again missed the core issues that the IMF should be focusing on, that is, "whether a member country's exchange rate regime is consistent with its medium-term macroeconomic policies, rather than on its exchange rate level" (Wu 2007). China wanted less IMF bilateral surveillance and more multilateral surveillance; moreover, China believed that exchange rate choices were a domestic, sovereign matter that did not introduce international economic vulnerabilities. Governor Wu (2007) used the 2007 annual meetings to urge for a reform of the 2007 Surveillance Decision: "The Fund should also take concrete steps to address problems related to the 2007 Decision and its application. The aim of these efforts is to enable the Fund to conduct surveillance in a prudent, fair, and effective manner based on clear consensus so that, through its surveillance, the Fund will contribute significantly to financial stability and economic prosperity."

China wanted IMF surveillance to scrutinize the United States, as an issuer of the globe's reserve currency, because capital flow volatility and monetary policy in the United States would have greater ramifications than would China's currency, which is not liberalized. To improve IMF surveillance, China called on IMF staff to "give the surveillance priority to the ongoing financial turmoil, deepen its analysis, learn lessons, and listen to the opinions of member countries… so that the Fund can determine where the true risks lie, and adopt effective measures to maintain a stable and orderly global economic and financial system" (Yi 2008a). China felt that a lack of unanimous support for the 2007 decision had also "had an adverse impact on the effective implementation of surveillance" (Li 2007). Chinese officials noted that this "mis-focused surveillance hampers the discharge of the Fund's mandate in promoting global economic and financial stability, and damages its credibility" (Yi 2008b). China continued to call for a reversal or reconsideration of the 2007 decision until it was updated in 2012.

The 2008 international financial crisis validated many of the concerns of Chinese officials. China criticized IMF staff for focusing on the 2007 decision modalities instead of having a complete understanding of cross-border capital flows. China argued that if IMF staff followed its calls for increased scrutiny of the United States in its surveillance duties, then the Fund would have better predicted and managed the fallout of the international financial crisis. In a 2010 speech to the IMF governors, Zhou (2010a) stated: "The hastily introduced 2007 Decision contains many flaws, and cannot meet the demands on Fund surveillance posed by global economic and financial development. The Fund should face this reality, resolve the problems in its surveillance as quickly as possible, amend the 2007 Decision, adjust its surveillance focus, improve modalities, and strengthen surveillance over developed countries, mature financial markets, and cross-border capital flows, in order to avoid a recurrence of the crisis."

Providing this damning critique using some of the strongest wording of Chinese governors at the IMF Annual Meetings, China had ultimately said "we told you so." Using the same platform, Zhou asked Fund surveillance to specifically look at developed countries' public debt and its impact on global interest rates, capital flows, inflation and global trade. Moreover, China wanted the IMF to fix its early warning tools and better understand tail risks of financial crises (ibid.)

China was pleased with IMF efforts to reform surveillance in 2011 with the Integrated Surveillance Decision. The new surveillance decision allowed for the bilateral Article IV consultations to be an important feeder into the production of IMF multilateral surveillance; clarifications on modalities of surveillance and providing countries with more latitude and discretion on exchange rate policies were key improvements over previous IMF policies. Moreover, the new surveillance mechanism allowed the IMF to study and document the potential spillovers of risky country policies, by noting this in both its Article IV reports and its multilateral reports. Indeed, China argued that the new policy was better at "integrating" both the bilateral surveillance of Article IV consultations and the multilateral surveillance processes such as the publication of the *World Economic Outlook*. Chinese officials were hopeful that the new surveillance policy would better examine the macroeconomic policies, financial sector policies and capital flow volatilities that were potentially emanating from economies issuing a reserve currency, like obviously that of the United States (see Yi 2012).

Following the international financial crisis, the IMF enhanced its surveillance function to be more systemic in its analysis because the Fund staff used their "theoretical and organizational resources" from past financial crises to effectively push for enhancing the IMF's surveillance role (Moschella 2011). This enhanced surveillance role for the IMF was an approach that was also in keeping with the aims of many other international monetary and financial institutions' "holistic visions of risk"; a factor used by IMF staff to their advantage when pushing for an expansion of their scope of work (ibid.). The international financial crisis had created some urgency, but the IMF staff were strategic in not wanting to move too quickly with the types of changes they wanted to see (Moschella 2012). Specifically, IMF staff did not want to challenge state authority, as they had with the Chinese government in its contentious 2007 decision, by seeking an overhaul to IMF surveillance that would require executive board approval (ibid, 59). Instead, IMF staff pursued incremental changes to surveillance that is perhaps tempered by their own intellectual limitations in the study of financial markets after failing to warn of the international financial crisis. Appeasing growing Chinese influence at the IMF was undoubtedly a concern for the IMF staff, but they were also keen to study the potential spillover effects of systemically important countries and pushed for this broadened scope of work in the 2011 surveillance decision. IMF surveillance remains a difficult function for the Fund to perform, because of the political and technical challenges it brings. Striking a delicate balance between providing the depth of coverage that could prevent another crisis while refraining from being too intrusive in the domestic affairs of countries such as China that are sensitive to Western prodding are among the challenges the IMF faces. China is sensitive about its exchange rate and will most likely continue to resist Fund surveillance and advice that appears to benefit US economic and trading interests (see Momani and English 2014, 428; also see IMF 2011b).

China on SDRs

For more than a decade, the role of China's currency in the global economy has been a matter of great debate. How can it be expanded? What could the IMF do to help RMB internationalization? Other chapters in this volume take up the question of sequencing in the internationalization of Chinese currency, but this chapter will consider the IMF's role in facilitating this and how the IMF's SDR can play a role in these developments. China has also seen the increased use of the SDR as a new or alternative reserve currency as part of the need for broader reforms of the international monetary system, which the IMF plays a central role in managing.

China has often framed the issue of internationalizing its currency in the broader context of wanting to see the IMF's SDR take on a larger role in the world economy. As part of the increased trend toward multipolarity, be it in trade, finance or political power, China argues that the world also needs a new international reserve currency, most likely the SDR, instead of relying on the de facto use of the US dollar. As early as 2002, Governor Dai (2002a), stated to the International Monetary and Financial Committee (IMFC), "it is obviously beneficial to expand the use of SDRs as an international reserve currency. Conditions should be created to encourage such an effort." Similar statements were repeated to the IMFC in 2006 by Governor Zhou. The international financial crisis again spurred Chinese officials to push for the issue of increasing the role of the SDR. Seeing the international financial crisis as a moment for consensus about the need for change and reform, Chinese officials used the IMF as a forum to push through their country's visions for monetary system reform.

In one of the most detailed speeches by a Chinese governor to the IMF on the rationale for enhancing the role of the SDR, Zhou framed the issue in the broader reforms needed in the global monetary system. In 2010, Zhou reminded the IMFC that the SDR was created in the 1970s to address a crisis in the issuance of the US dollar as a global reserve currency. He argued that the subsequent adoption of floating exchange rates by developing countries had turned attention away from addressing or studying the potential role of the SDR in helping to preserve or uphold international monetary stability. The 2008 global financial crisis and subsequent economic recession, Zhou argued, should remind countries that the international monetary system needs to be reformed and the best way to do this would be to "strengthen the role of the SDR" (Zhou 2010b). Ma Zhaoxu, assistant minister of foreign affairs, added that in addition to expanding the use of SDRs, China wanted to "improve the currency basket of the special drawing rights and build an international reserve currency system with stable value, rule-based issuance and manageable supply" (Ma 2013).

Whether or not Chinese governors had one-off statements about increasing the role of the SDR in global trade, the question of expanding the use of SDRs has been a hotly debated issue in academic and punditry circles. Glosny (2010) argues that after the 2010 comments before the IMF, China had "slowly backed away from this challenge." According to Glosny, the Chinese governor had raised the SDR option in his statements, but this was not necessarily discussed or put on the agenda by Chinese officials at the G20 summit meetings. Chris Buckley (2009) argues that "China, by far the most powerful BRIC nation, was largely silent in Yekaterinburg [Russia]. It did not echo Russian and Brazilian calls for the BRIC powers to try to loosen the grip of the dollar on the world financial system." Glosny (2010) shows how Chinese officials both floated the idea, but continued to backtrack from claiming it was their official position to undermine the US dollar as a global reserve currency. For example, Vice Foreign Minister He Yafei claimed that the dollar was "the most important major international reserve currency of the day, and for years to come….That's the reality," while also adding that the issue was "now a discussion among academics. It is not the position of the Chinese government" (quoted in Glosny 2010).

Indeed, the issue of having the SDR take on a larger role as a reserve currency had gained steam among academics, pundits and officials. A Harvard professor, Dani Rodrik (2009), argued in favour of the idea of having the IMF issue SDRs in the wake of the international financial crisis:

> This one seems a no-brainer to me. The easiest and quickest way to create global liquidity and enable credit-starved emerging and developing countries to increase their spending is for the IMF to engineer a vast new SDR allocation. It can be done at the stroke of a pen, and it does not require the IMF to negotiate a program for every country that needs a loan… A generalized SDR allocation — in return for a commitment

> to spend a share of these resources in pursuit of a globally
> coordinated fiscal stimulus — would give countries the cover
> needed to do what is good for them and for the rest of the
> world without suffering a reputational penalty.[2]

Following the international financial crisis and calls for reform at the G20, China welcomed the IMF's plan to research the potential role of the SDR. The international financial crisis had led to a "drying up of dollar liquidity" that greatly concerned the Chinese, and therefore China sought to better internationalize its own currency in 2009 (Schmelzer 2014). The issue now turned to whether China's currency could be included in the SDR basket of currencies as a means of diversifying the world's holdings away from the US dollar. The IMF staff studied the question of China's currency being used in the SDR basket in 2010.

The 2010 IMF report looked at the 2005–2009 period to see if variables, such as exchange rates, exports of goods and services, investment flows and reserve holdings, had an effect on SDR valuation. In its report, the IMF noted that China was the world's third-largest exporter, but the Chinese currency was not, in its opinion, a "freely usable currency" and would not be qualified to be included in the SDR basket of currencies. IMF staff rejected, in essence, the notion that China's currency could be included in the SDR basket (IMF 2010, 3). China called IMF studies on the SDR "encouraging" and stated that the IMF had "offered a number of constructive recommendations" (see Yi 2011). The IMF did note some encouraging signs, such as the fact that 21 central banks engaged in swap agreements with China that now made the RMB more "widely tradeable." Chinese media took this as a sign that the Chinese RMB was indeed taking a "key step toward the hallowed status of becoming a reserve currency" (*China Daily* 2013).

Focus and attention now turned to whether China would indeed make its currency free and usable in global trade and transactions. Chinese officials continued to insist that internationalization of its currency needed to be slow and that domestic inflationary concerns were paramount. Continuing to point to its developing country status, China emphasized that it was indeed trying to internationalize usage of the RMB through currency swaps, but that this needed to be done in small, incremental steps. In 2013, the IMF showed that Chinese efforts to increase foreign governments' holdings of its currency were taking hold: in the first quarter of 2014, foreign exchange holdings of Chinese RMB across the globe amounted to US$11.86 trillion, up from US$11.69 trillion

---

2   Note that the IMF made a US$250 billion SDR allocation in August 2009 to boost
     international liquidity.

worth of Chinese RMB only a few months earlier (Schmelzer 2014). The IMF noted that international reserves were slowly diversifying away from the US dollar. In 2000, for example, 71.1 percent of the country's reserves were held in US dollars, 18.3 percent in euros and 6.1 percent in yen (of US$1.52 trillion in reserves) (ibid.). In the final quarter of 2014, international holdings of US dollars decreased to 60.9 percent, holdings of euros increased to 24.4 percent and holdings of yen decreased to 3.9 percent (of US$6.21 trillion in reserves) (ibid.). International reserves of Chinese RMB, however, remain understandably limited and weak in comparison to other currencies, as countries will not choose to hold RMB when faced with a potential debt crisis unless the currency is fully internationalized.

Beyond reserves, the usage of the RMB in international transactions is increasing, but remains overshadowed by other currencies. In August 2014, according to the global payments system Society for Worldwide Interbank Financial Telecommunication, which tracks and facilitates financial transactions among financial institutions, the Chinese RMB accounted for a mere 1.57 percent of interactions; this was up from 0.63 percent of interactions in January 2013 (ibid.). This, nevertheless, pales in comparison to other currencies. The dollar accounted for 42 percent in August 2014 (ibid.). So while China is making strides in internationalizing its currency, it is still far from being liberalized and the IMF will undoubtedly not give the green light for it to be used in the SDR basket valuation in the years to come. Nevertheless, the slow liberalization of China's currency is an issue that is of great importance to IMF policy making, and the future role of the SDR will continue to be studied and deliberated in halls of academia and power.

The positive role that the IMF can play in RMB internationalization is in adding its staff's intellectual heft and providing market confidence and legitimacy to the idea and policy. After the international financial crisis, the IMF was interested in studying the idea of diversifying the monetary system away from dollar hegemony. In one of its 2011 reports, for example, it stated that:

> Only a few currencies are truly global; this is efficient — given the network externalities that are generated when economic agents agree to use the same currency to carry out international transactions. But, as discussed above, it also contributes to systemic fragility. Currently, only four currencies are recognized by the Fund to be freely usable, that is, in fact, "widely used to make payments for international transactions and widely traded in the principal exchange markets," the U.S. dollar, Euro, British pound, and the Yen. Those four

currencies make up the bulk of global international reserves — 96 percent in 2010. The ability to trade, borrow, and invest internationally in domestic currency reduces exchange rate risk for domestic economic agents. Thus, *expanding the use of emerging market currencies internationally could provide a less uneven distribution of exchange rate risk across countries* (instead of countries issuing reserve currencies bearing none and the rest of the world all of it). In the process, domestic financial markets gain depth and liquidity, as demand for domestic currency and financial assets denominated in it increases. (IMF 2011a, 20; emphasis added)

While the IMF has studied the issue and scope of RMB internationalization and sees some progress on both increased cross-border trade settlement, such as currency swap lines in Asia, and increased RMB-dominated investment vehicles, the Fund sees some challenges as well. Despite potentially high demand for RMB, thanks to China's growing international trading presence, IMF staff in the Monetary and Capital Markets Department stated in a study that "there is still significant progress to be made on the supply side to allow non-residents access to the currency and to RMB-denominated assets as stores of value. To meet that latter requirement, there is scope for policy action to reform the exchange rate and interest rate regimes and lay the ground for financial sector development and deepening" (Maziad and Kang 2012, 12). They noted that this may also be subject to market discretion. Markets will want to see the RMB freely accessible, a more developed Chinese capital market, and allowing foreign traders, firms and markets to trade goods and services in RMB (ibid.). The Fund does not see Chinese policy makers being ready yet for RMB internationalization, but it has suggested that market forces will continue to push for this.

Conclusion

It is difficult to predict the future, but it is clear that many believe that China's influence in the IMF will continue to grow. Managing Director Lagarde once noted that as China's economy grows, the Fund rules of having its headquarters in the capital of its largest shareholder means that, as she said, "the way things are going, I wouldn't be surprised if one of these days the IMF was headquartered in Beijing for instance" (quoted in Rastello 2014). While few believe this will happen any day soon, clearly the rise of China at the IMF is evident in political, technical and diplomatic terms.

China's rise at the IMF is, however, a slow one. Whether this can be explained by the Chinese not wanting to assume more power or by China being denied increased power and influence by Western nations is a matter of debate. Chen Xiangyang (2013), affiliated with the China Institutes of Contemporary International Relations, aptly said in an article for *China Daily*: "One of the imminent diplomatic challenges facing China is derived from its continuing economic rise and its disputed status as a developing country. China has come under pressure from Western countries, and also its neighbors, to assume more responsibilities as a major economic power. They choose to ignore the fact that even though it is the world's second-largest economy, the IMF ranks China's GDP per capita 89th in the world."

China will need to manage this tension between wanting to be seen and understood as a developing country and the desire and expectation of China to act as a superpower. On the one hand, China wants to derive legitimacy as a developing country to shape its narrative at the IMF and other international economic and political fora. Indeed, the great strides that China has made to uplift many of its citizens from poverty and to modernize its economy are no small feats. It is true, however, that China still has a great deal of development ahead for much of its rural communities and disenfranchised populations. China is still a developing country, despite the wealth, influence and global trading power it has amassed.

In addition to China's multiple identities, it has clearly tried to balance various international and domestic interests. Its slower approach to the internationalization of the RMB is attributable to its fears of rising domestic inflation and what this would mean for control by the Chinese Communist Party. It balances this domestic factor with the need and likely desire to internationalize its currency to become one of the world's hard currencies. Undoubtedly, the United States plays an important role in either supporting or challenging Chinese policy choices. The United States has been reluctant to give up power to China at the IMF, while also cherishing its intellectual dominance at the Fund. As economic realities necessitate the rise of China at the IMF on governance issues, the question of whether China will increase its intellectual voice at the IMF through the kinds of lobbying it displayed against the 2007 Surveillance Decision is clearly yet to be determined.

Using this split personality or identity in shaping its position in the halls of the IMF has confused and confounded outside analysts. When China asks the IMF to move away from hiring another European managing director, it is confusing to see the Chinese vote for Christine Lagarde. When China pushes for more surveillance of systematically important countries, it is confusing that

China does not actually see its global trading position as a source of systemic risk. And finally, while China calls for decreasing international dependence on the US dollar, it has not liberalized its currency to be used as an international alternative. Political and economic analysts have both marvelled at and been bewildered by China, and its actions at and toward the IMF are no exception.

Works Cited

Blustein, Paul. 2005. "IMF Chief Pressured on Trade Imbalances." *The Washington Post*, September 29, D1.

Broome, Andre and Leaonard Seabrooke. 2007. "Seeing like the IMF: Institutional Change in Small Open Economies" *Review of International Political Economy* 14 (2): 576–601.

Buckley, Chris. 2009. "Much-Trumpeted BRIC Summit Ends Quietly." Reuters, June 17. www.reuters.com/article/2009/06/17/us-bric-summit-idUSTRE55G20B20090617.

Chang, Liu. 2013. "Commentary: U.S. Fiscal Failure Warrants a De-Americanized World." Xinhuanet, October 13. http://news.xinhuanet.com/english/indepth/2013-10/13/c_132794246.htm.

Chen, Xiangyang. 2013. "Diplomatic Balancing Act." China Daily.com.cn, March 7. http://europe.chinadaily.com.cn/opinion/2013-03/07/content_16286675.htm.

China Daily. 2013. "A Step toward RMB Internationalization." China Daily.com.cn, October 16. http://europe.chinadaily.com.cn/business/2013-10/16/content_17036765.htm.

China Economic Review. 2011. "China Says Emerging Nations Should Help Control IMF." *China Economic Review*, May 20. www.chinaeconomicreview.com/content/china-says-emerging-nations-should-help-control-imf.

Dai, Xianglong. 1999. "Statement by Mr. DAI Xianglong, Governor, People's Bank of China at the Fifty-Third Meeting of the Interim Committee of the Board of Governors of the International Monetary System." International Monetary Fund, September 26. www.imf.org/external/am/1999/icstate/chn.htm.

———. 2002a. "IMFC Statement by Mr. Dai Xianglong, Governor of the People's Bank of China, International Monetary and Financial Committee, Fifth Meeting, Washington, DC." IMF International Monetary and Financial Committee, April 20. www.imf.org/external/spring/2002/imfc/stm/eng/chn.htm.

———. 2002b. "Statement by Mr. Dai Xianglong, Governor of the People's Bank of China, IMFC Meeting, Washington, D.C." IMF, International Monetary and Financial Committee, September 28. www.imf.org/external/am/2002/imfc/state/eng/chn.htm.

Edwards, Martin S. 2011. "China an Active and Stable Force in Multilateral Organization." China-US Focus. June 2. www.chinausfocus.com/finance-economy/china-an-active-and-stable-force-in-multilateral-organizations/#sthash.ygVMXYNH.dpuf.

Eichengreen, B. 2007. "A Blueprint for IMF Reform: More Than Just a Lender." *International Finance*, 10 (2): 153–75.

Ferdinand, P., and J. Wang. 2013. "China and the IMF: From Mimicry towards Pragmatic International Institutional Pluralism. *International Affairs*, 89 (4): 895–910.

Giles, Chris and Krishna Guha. 2006. "Interview with Rodrigo de Rato." *Financial Times*, January 28.

Glosny, M. A. 2010. "China and the BRICs: A Real (but Limited) Partnership in a Unipolar World." *Polity* 42 (1): 100–129. www.palgrave-journals.com/polity/journal/v42/n1/full/pol200914a.html.

Goldstein, Morris. 2006. "Currency Manipulation and Enforcing the Rules of the International Monetary System." In *Reforming the IMF for the 21st Century*, edited by Edwin M. Truman, 150-151.Washington, DC: Institute for International Economics.

Helleiner, E., and J. Kirshner, eds. 2014. *The Great Wall of Money: Power and Politics in China's International Monetary Relations*. Ithaca, NY: Cornell University Press.

Helleiner, E., and B. Momani. 2014. "The Hidden History of China and the IMF." In *The Great Wall of Money: Power and Politics in China's International Monetary Relations*, edited by E. Helleiner and J. Kirshner. Ithaca, NY: Cornell University Press.

IMF. 2006. "IMF Article IV Consultation for the People's Republic of China." IMF Country Report 06/394.

———. 2010. "Review of the Method of Valuation of the SDR — Prepared by the Finance Department in Consultation with the Legal and Other Departments." IMF, October 26. www.imf.org/external/np/pp/eng/2010/102610.pdf.

———. 2011a. "Strengthening the International Monetary System: Taking Stock and Looking Ahead." IMF Policy Paper. www.imf.org/external/pp/longres.aspx?id=4548.

———. 2011b. "Consolidated Spillover Report." IMF: Washington, DC. www.imf.org/external/np/pp/eng/2011/071111.pdf.

Lavigne, R., and L. Schembri. 2009. "Strengthening IMF Surveillance: An Assessment of Recent Reforms." Bank of Canada Discussion Paper No. 2009-10.

Leckow, R. 2007. "The IMF and Crisis Prevention — The Legal Framework for Surveillance." *Kansas Journal of Law & Public Policy* 17 (2): 285–94. http://law.ku.edu/sites/law.drupal.ku.edu/files/docs/law_journal/v17/leckow.pdf.

Li, Ruogu. 2003. "IMFC Statement by Mr. Li Ruogu, Assistant Governor of the People's Bank of China." IMF, International Monetary and Financial Committee, April 12. www.imf.org/external/spring/2003/imfc/state/eng/chn.htm.

Li, Yong. 2007. "Statement by the Hon. Li Yong, Alternate Governor of the World Bank Group for People's Republic of China, at the Joint Annual Discussion – Press Release No. 34." IMF, October 22. www.imf.org/external/am/2007/speeches/pr34e.pdf.

Lombardi, D., and N. Woods. 2008. "The Politics of Influence: An Analysis of IMF Surveillance." *Review of International Political Economy* 15 (5): 711–39.

Ma, Zhaoxu. 2013. "Balanced World Community." China Daily.com.cn, February 20. http://europe.chinadaily.com.cn/opinion/2013-02/20/content_16238842.htm.

Maziad, S. and J. S. Kang. 2012. "RMB Internationalization: Onshore/Offshore Links." IMF Working Paper. IMF: Washington, DC. www.imf.org/external/pubs/ft/wp/2012/wp12133.pdf.

Moschella, Manuela. 2011. "Lagged Learning and the Response to Equilibrium Shock: The Global Financial Crisis and IMF Surveillance." *Journal of Public Policy* 31 (2): 1–21.

———. 2012. "IMF Surveillance in Crisis: The Past, Present, and Future of the Reform Process." *Global Society* 26 (1): 46–60.

Momani, B. 2005. "Recruiting and Diversifying IMF Technocrats." *Global Society*, 19 (2): 167–87.

———. 2007. "IMF Staff: Missing Link in Fund Reform Proposals." *The Review of International Organizations* 2 (1): 39–57.

———. 2013. "China at the International Monetary Fund: Continued Engagement in Its Drive for Membership and Added Voice at the IMF Executive Board." *Journal of Chinese Economics* 1 (1).

Momani, B., and K. A. English. 2014. "In Lieu of an Anchor: The Fund and Its Surveillance Function." In *Handbook of the International Political Economy of Monetary Relations*, edited by Thomas Oatley and W. Kindred Winecoff, 428–49. Cheltenham, UK and Northampton, MA: Edward Elgar Publishing.

Mussa, Michael. 2007. "IMF Surveillance over China's Exchange Rate Policy." Paper presented at the Conference on China's Exchange Rate Policy, Peterson Institute, October 19. www.piie.com/publications/papers/mussa1007.pdf.

People's Daily. 2011. "IMF's New Chief Should Come from China." *People's Daily*. http://en.people.cn/90001/90780/91421/7385729.html.

Rastello, Sandrine. 2014. "Beijing-based IMF? Largarde Ponders China gaining on US Economy." Bloomberg, June 6. www.bloomberg.com/news/2014-06-06/beijing-based-imf-lagarde-ponders-china-gaining-on-u-s-economy.html.

Rodrik, Dani. 2009. "Why Don't We Hear a Lot More About SDRs?" Debate: Macroeconomics, a Global Crisis Debate, . VoxEU.org, February 4. http://voxeu.org/debates/commentaries/why-dont-we-hear-lot-more-about-sdrs.

Sanford, J. E. 2006. "China, the United States and the IMF: Negotiating Exchange Rate Adjustment." Washington, DC: Congressional Research Service, April. http://digital.library.unt.edu/ark:/67531/metacrs9142/m1/1/high_res_d/RL33322_2006Mar13.pdf.

Schmelzer, Vicki. 2014. "Analysis: Dollar Still Premier Reserve Currency, For Now." MNInews.com, September 2. https://mninews.marketnews.com/index.php/analysis-dollar-still-premier-reserve-currency-now?q=content/analysis-dollar-still-premier-reserve-currency-now.

Wroughton, L. 2011. "Lagarde to Give China Senior IMF Job: Sources." Reuters, July 6. www.reuters.com/article/2011/07/06/us-imf-lagarde-china-idUSTRE7655JM20110706.

Wu, Xiaoling. 2007. "IMFC Statement by Madam Wu Xiaoling, Deputy Governor, People's Bank of China, International Monetary and Financial Committee Sixteenth Meeting." IMF International Monetary and Financial Committee, October 20. www.imf.org/External/AM/2007/imfc/statement/eng/chn.pdf.

Xiao, Gang. 2000. "Statement by Mr. Xiao Gang, Deputy Governor of The People's Bank of China and Alternate Governor of the Fund for China, to the International Monetary and Financial Committee." IMF, International Monetary and Financial Committee, April 16. www.imf.org/external/spring/2000/imfc/chn.htm.

Xie, Xuren. 2009. "Statement by the Hon. Xie Xuren, Governor of the World Bank Group for People's Republic of China, at the Joint Annual Discussion." IMF, October 6-7 . www.imf.org/external/am/2009/speeches/pr08e.pdf.

Yi, Gang. 2008a. "Statement by the Hon. Yi Gang, Governor of the IMF for People's Republic of China, at the Joint Annual Discussion – Press Release No. 16," IMF, October 13. www.imf.org/external/am/2008/speeches/pr16e.pdf.

———. 2008b. "IMFC Statement by YI GANG, Deputy Governor, People's Bank of China, International Monetary and Financial Committee Eighteenth Meeting." IMF International Monetary and Financial Committee, October 11. www.imf.org/External/AM/2008/imfc/statement/eng/chn.pdf.

———. 2011. "IMFC Statement by Yi Gang, Deputy Governor, People's Bank of China, People's Republic of China, International Monetary and Financial Committee Twenty-Third Meeting." IMF, International Monetary and Financial Committee, April 16. www.imf.org/External/spring/2011/imfc/state.

———. 2012. "Statement by the Hon. Yi Gang, Alternate Governor of the IMF for People's Republic of China – Press Release No. 19." IMF, October 12. www.imf.org/external/am/2012/speeches/pr19e.pdf.

Zhou, Xiaochuan. 2004. "Statement by the Hon. Zhou Xiaochuan, Governor of the Fund for the People's Republic of China, at the Joint Annual Discussion – Press Release No. 32." International Monetary Fund, October 3. www.imf.org/external/am/2004/speeches/pr32e.pdf.

———. 2006. "IMFC Statement by Zhou Xiaochuan, Governor, People's Bank of China, International Monetary and Financial Committee Thirteenth Meeting." IMF International Monetary and Financial Committee. April 22. www.imf.org/External/spring/2006/imfc/statement/eng/chn.pdf.

———. 2010a. "IMFC Statement by Zhou Xiaochuan, Governor, People's Bank of China, International Monetary and Financial Committee Twenty-First Meeting." IMF, International Monetary and Financial Committee, April 24. www.imf.org/External/spring/2010/imfc/statement/eng/chn.pdf.

———. 2010b. "IMFC Statement by ZHhou Xiaochuan, Governor, People's Bank of China, International Monetary and Financial Committee Twenty-Second Meeting." IMF, International Monetary and Financial Committee, October 9. www.imf.org/External/AM/2010/imfc/statement/eng/chn.pdf.

———. 2010c. "Statement by the Hon. Zhou Xiaochuan, Governor of the IMF for People's Republic of China – Press Release No. 47." IMF, October 8. www.imf.org/external/am/2010/speeches/pr47e.pdf.

Zoellick, Robert B. 2005. "Whither China: From Membership to Responsibility?" Remarks to the National Committee on the United States and China Relations, presented in New York City, September 21. www.disam.dsca.mil/pubs/INDEXES/Vol%2028_2/Zoellick.pdf.

11

China at the G20: Review, Expectation, Strategy and Agenda

Alex He

China's accelerating willingness to demonstrate its ability to act as a responsible international power in economic governance is illustrated by its growing role within the Group of Twenty (G20), which China views as the ideal platform for contributing to global governance. The 2008 global financial crisis (GFC) provided a very timely opportunity for China to rise to the occasion and actively cooperate in the post-crisis recovery efforts, most notably the United States' coordinated large-scale fiscal stimulus.

This chapter illustrates China's increasingly active and contributory role in the G20, and demonstrates that although 2010 and 2011 witnessed China briefly shift into a defensive stance — as a result of criticism over its exchange rate policy in light of global imbalances — the country's active role resumed in 2013 after it cautiously dealt with the European debt crisis as well as the pressure brought about by the criticism regarding global imbalances.

China's continued support toward maintaining the international relevance of the G20 is evidence of the country's intentions to positively participate in global governance. China does not intend to become a leading agenda-setter, but instead looks to be treated as an equal and respected partner. China acknowledges its comparatively weak position relative to the United States and other Western countries, and is using its standing in the forum to concurrently better its relationship with member countries — primarily the United States — and push domestic reform.

Primarily based on scholars' reviews of China's performance in the G20 summits since 2008, this chapter explores China's policy making as it relates to its participation in the forum, and highlights the primary factors shaping the country's actions. Additionally, it illustrates the triple union of the forum's primary agenda, China's own global economic governance goals and China's fundamental interests as the largest developing nation. Trade and development are two primary interest areas that China has a responsibility to promote because of its status as the largest trade power and biggest developing country. Further, on the subject of energy governance — an issue that has received minimal G20 attention — China, as one of the largest importers, would be a natural champion. A short re-evaluation of China's goals in the G20 is provided in the conclusion, expanding on a new foreign strategy proposed by China, as well as the country's priorities when it hosts the forum in 2016.

A Chinese Review of China in the G20 Summitry

An Ideal Platform for China

As one of the world's leading economies by trade volume and economic size, China, in the early twenty-first century, showed interest in participating in various global economic governance organizations to showcase its ability to act as a responsible superpower (Wang and Li 2012). In the early 2000s, the Group of Eight (G8) considered extending an invitation to China, effectively signalling the inevitable role China would play in global affairs. This idea was evaded by China because of the undesirable challenges it would face as a member of the G8. First, China would be the only developing country in the group, and in light of Russia's experience, believed it may be subject to unequal treatment. Second, China was concerned about being asked to bear responsibilities and risks that were well beyond its capacity as a developing nation, and could potentially endanger its rapid domestic development. For these reasons China decided on a reasonable alternative and instead became a dialogue partner for the G8.

The G20, however, provided a timely and ideal opportunity for China to play a larger role in international economic governance. It solved China's G8-related apprehension, and the quick ascension of the G20 (and not the G8) signified the rise of emerging economies as a whole — a reality that Western countries could no longer avoid (Chen 2009; Cui 2009; Li 2009). Chinese scholars interpreted this change as a confirmation of Western countries' acceptance of China's "peaceful development approach" — an approach that emphasizes integration into, rather than contestation of, the existing international economic order (Chen 2009).

2008 and 2009: "Saviour" of the World Economy

The focus of the inaugural G20 summit in Washington, DC, was to promote an international recovery from the GFC. As an active measure to push the global economy out of the recession, the United States encouraged major economies to join forces in employing a stimulus policy. The International Monetary Fund (IMF) also called for a large fiscal stimulus totalling two percent of global GDP. Prior to attending the summit, China introduced an RMB 4 trillion (approximately US$580 billion) stimulus plan. At the following G20 summit in London in 2009, China joined other members in declaring a US$1.1 trillion stimulus plan, and also committed US$50 billion to bolster the IMF's crisis-fighting capacity. Then US Treasury Secretary Timothy Geithner, among others,[1] praised Chinese efforts to boost domestic demand (Geithner 2009). The subsequent coverage by Chinese media portrayed the country as the "saviour" of the world economy (Yang and Chong 2013).

In addition to the large role played in stimulating the world economy, China became a member of three of the most exclusive international financial standard-setting bodies: the Financial Stability Board (FSB), the Basel Committee on Banking Supervision (BCBS) and the Bank for International Settlements' Committee on the Global Financial System. China's proactive role at the international level was instrumental in increasing the voting shares of emerging market economies in the governance of the IMF and World Bank.

A final point of importance to note is that these initial, apparently selfless acts from China do in fact follow the country's national interest. The stimulus package was introduced because top Chinese leaders were worried that the GFC would act as a drag on China's economic growth, and endanger its political and social stability.

2010: Frustration Overshadows Breakthrough

The 2010 Toronto G20 Summit was a blow to China's enthusiasm toward, and expectations for, the G20. As the focus shifted from crisis response to financial market reform, the voices of developing countries gradually lost relevance. In this sense, relative to previous G20 summits, the Toronto summit was more like a Group of Seven meeting (He 2010). Proposals from China, in particular those aimed at strengthening the voice of developing countries in the Bretton

---

1   Then Australian Prime Minister Kevin Rudd, IMF Managing Director Dominique Strauss-Kahn, US Under Secretary of the Treasury for International Affairs David McCormick, World Bank President Robert Zoellick and Brazilian Finance Minister Guido Mantego (China.com 2008; Xinhua News 2008).

Woods system, were neglected by the United States and European countries. Further, the issues of development and anti-protectionism — two of the most relevant for developing economies — struggled to gain the prominence afforded by developed nations to issues such as macroeconomic coordination and financial stability. The Toronto and Seoul summits in 2010 marked the end of the tentative détente between Washington and Beijing over the thorny issue of RMB valuation and global imbalances.

One week before the Toronto summit, with the support of the People's Bank of China (PBoC), the Chinese government announced a restart of exchange rate liberalization. This was in anticipation of the summit potentially turning into a platform to pressure China to appreciate its currency, the renminbi (RMB). It also was intended to complicate the United States' efforts to corral needed support from other G20 members that remained ambivalent over their own willingness to spend scarce political capital on pressuring the Chinese over such a sensitive issue. Following the June decision to exit the dollar peg, the RMB appreciated very little, prompting further criticism from the US Treasury. In response to the increasing pressure, the PBoC orchestrated a rapid 2.5 percent appreciation of the RMB against the US dollar in the period from September 1 to October 15 (see Figure 1), a move that was widely viewed as China pulling the rug out from under the United States. Not long after, the Federal Reserve announced a second round of quantitative easing (QE) to commence days before the Seoul summit. This provided the Chinese with additional political ammunition.

Figure 1: China/US Foreign Exchange Rate

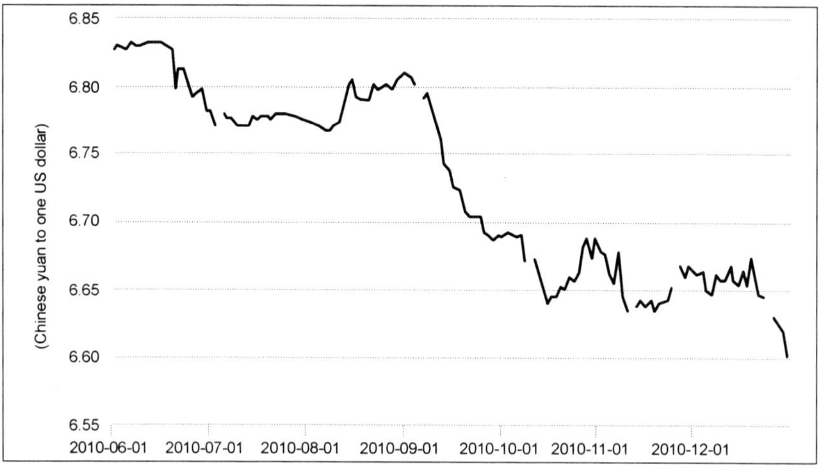

Source: Federal Reserve Economic Data (2014).

China's deputy finance minister Zhu Guangyao expressed his concern regarding the potential detrimental effects the Fed's unconventional monetary policy may have on financial and macroeconomic stability in emerging markets. He was not the only opposing voice; Germany too was concerned over the risk implications posed by excessive "money printing" (Dyer 2010).[2] The final leaders' declaration, however, included a vaguely worded commitment to "[move] toward more market-determined exchange rate systems, [and enhance] exchange rate flexibility to reflect underlying economic fundamentals."[3] The wording ensured that China could push exchange rate reform on its own terms.

Another attempt by the US Treasury to collect support from G20 finance ministers and central bank governors occurred in October 2010. Then Secretary of the US Treasury Timothy Geithner proposed setting a four percent of GDP limit on current account imbalances to be phased in by 2015. This was a convenient target, given that the United States' current deficit stood at three percent of GDP in 2009 and 2010. Even more convenient was that weeks earlier, Yi Gang, deputy governor of the PBoC, stated that "China [aimed] to reduce the surplus below four percent of its gross domestic product in the next three to five years, from 11 percent in 2007 and 5.8 percent in 2009" (Xie 2010). Relieved to find China on its side of Geithner's proposal, two weeks before the Seoul summit the United States reduced the volume of criticism over China's RMB policy. Additionally, the Treasury Department postponed the release of its biannual *Report to Congress on International Economic and Exchange Rate Policies*, which outlines its view on issues related to currency manipulation, and Geithner even publicly noted the strong appreciation of the RMB since the beginning of September. The proposed numerical current account limit appeared to have some potential, and even implied the United States' willingness to welcome external constraints on policy choices (Truman 2010; Walter 2012).

Other surplus countries such as Germany, Japan, Brazil and Australia strongly opposed the proposal, however. They were concerned with the potential repercussions of assigning a numerical target, specifically the negative pressure that may result from missing such a specific limit. After discussions with Germany, China refrained from its initial position, opening itself up to strong criticism from the United States (Walter 2012; Beattie 2010). In hindsight, China may have missed out on an important opportunity to arrive at an agreement with the United States (Guo 2013). As its current account imbalance has been below four percent since 2011, and is projected by the IMF to drop below three percent through 2019, China would have been fully compliant with Geithner's proposal without the need for additional macroeconomic

---

2   Ironically, Europe was pursuing its own QE program at the beginning of 2015.

3   See www.g20.utoronto.ca/2010/g20seoul-doc.html#framework.

adjustments. This, in turn, would have made it difficult for the US Treasury to argue that the RMB was undervalued to any meaningful degree.

2011 and 2012: From Defending Exchange Rate Policy to Assisting Europe

In January 2011, Chinese President Hu visited the United States and issued a joint statement in which he promised to promote the flexibility of the RMB. Months later, between the scheduled ministerial meetings in February and April of that year, French President Nicolas Sarkozy insisted on holding a G20 seminar on the reform of the international monetary system in China. Given China's resistance to the pressure and criticism from France and the United States, official ministerial statements by the G20 failed to directly target China, and instead generally stressed that emerging market economies "[enhance] exchange rate flexibility."[4] Further, regarding external imbalances, all decisions were to "take due consideration of exchange rate, fiscal, monetary and other policies."[5] Comments by IMF Managing Director Christine Lagarde highlighted the carefully chosen usage of the word "consideration" in the communiqué, so as to allow China to save face (Tongkui Chen 2011).

In 2011-2012, the primary focus of the G20 shifted from global imbalances to the eruption of the euro-zone debt crisis. China encountered and reluctantly managed it as an opportunity to further develop its international governance footprint, and to display its willingness and ability to act as a responsible international power.

Financial experts and the public advised China, as a poor and developing country, to proceed with caution, and to avoid overcommitting to assisting Europe (Wu and Li 2011, Bloomberg News 2011; *China News Week* 2011). China, in tacit agreement, entered the Cannes summit with a "wait-and-see" attitude toward the crisis. Chinese leaders expressed their readiness "to work with the international community [and] participate in resolving the European debt problem," but also conveyed their belief that Europe had the capacity to overcome the hardships and maintain economic stability and development (Wu and Li 2011).

As the crisis deepened in 2012, China experienced a drastic reduction in exports to Europe, which warranted a robust response. One potential means of

---

4   See www.g20.utoronto.ca/2011/2011-finance-110219-en.html.
5   Ibid.

assisting was by purchasing eurobonds.[6] This was promptly dismissed, however, as Europe was unable to meet China's purchasing requirements for two reasons: the acknowledgement of China's status as a market economy in various international fora (for example, the World Trade Organization [WTO]); and a relaxation of controls on high-tech exports to China. Alternatively, China opted to revisit the model used in response to the GFC and provide extensive resource contributions to the IMF. At the Los Cabos summit in June 2012, China announced its pledge of US$43 billion, a decision that had the approval of many Chinese scholars, but did not sit well with the public.

Contributing to the IMF provided a safer means of assisting Europe than purchasing sovereign debt directly. Additionally, it gave China an opportunity to reduce its relative share of foreign reserves invested in US Treasury bills, which was perceived by many as overly allocated. It was also argued that working with the IMF would help facilitate the RMB's internationalization, and increase China's role in the governance of the international monetary system.

Public opinion became an increasingly important factor in shaping China's policy toward Europe. The media began to highlight economic and social issues facing China, which increased public sensitivity toward assisting Europe (Jiang 2012).[7] The PBoC was put in a situation in which it was required to justify why China, a developing and impoverished country with widespread inequality, should help bail out European countries that enjoy high standards of living. On this subject, the PBoC explained that the US$43 billion contribution was a precautionary line of credit, of which not all was necessarily to be drawn. It stressed "the principal of the loan that China provided to the IMF through note purchase is safe with regular interest payment. Participation in the IMF resource increase is in China's interests, and proportionate to China's international status and responsibilities" (PBoC 2012).

---

6   According to statistics released by the General Administration of Customs of China, China's exports to the European Union in the first half of 2012 dropped by 0.8 percent and for the whole of 2012 dropped by 6.2 percent, compared to the same periods in 2011. Data available at www1.customs.gov.cn/tabid/49129/Default.aspx. Statistics from Eurostat cited by the Ministry of Commerce of China indicate that imports from China dropped by 9.7 percent from January to September in 2012. Available at http://countryreport.mofcom.gov.cn/record/view110209.asp?news_id=32682.

7   Surveys on Chinese public opinion on financial assistance to Europe are unfortunately not available. However, news reports on the subject are based on the tens of thousands of microblog posts that showed a high degree of sensitivity to the issue in China. For example, see Edwards and Kang Lim (2011) and Reuters (2011).

2013 and 2014: A New Start for the G20 and China?

By 2013, China's current account surplus had decreased dramatically and resulted in reduced sensitivity on the issue. The imbalance problem now needed to be addressed from a broader perspective, as greater dispersion in other countries now comprised a larger share of global imbalances.

China had resumed playing an active role in G20 discussions, and President Xi expressed China's objectives for the G20 moving forward as: to promote global macroeconomic coordination; maintain an open global trading system; continue to promote international financial reform (especially regarding emerging market economies' voting shares at the IMF); and put the RMB into the Special Drawing Right (SDR) basket. Xi admitted that domestically, China should adopt a set of structural adjustments aimed at shifting economic growth from export driven to consumption led.[8] This was in agreement with other G20 members, as the St. Petersburg Leaders' Declaration stressed the need for surplus economies to achieve stronger domestic demand-led growth, and for deficit economies to strive for more flexible exchange rates, increase savings and enhance competitiveness.[9]

At the 2014 Brisbane summit, G20 leaders promised in the Brisbane Action Plan to raise global growth to deliver better living standards and quality jobs, setting an ambitious goal to lift the G20's GDP by at least an additional two percent by 2018. This will continue to promote the G20's transition from a crisis-handling institution to a world economic steering committee to set the agenda for global growth. China proposed three suggestions at the summit: innovate on the development pattern; construct an open world economy; and improve global economic governance. The first suggestion is new — specifically, it suggests setting connectivity as one of the core topics, supporting the G20 in establishing a global infrastructure centre, making contributions to global infrastructure investment through the "One Belt, One Road" initiative,[10] the Asian Infrastructure Investment Bank (AIIB) and Silk Road Fund. For China, the biggest achievement at the Brisbane summit was the announcement that China will host the 2016 summit, which provides China the opportunity to lead the G20 in a variety of issue areas. China is expected to promote the forum to facilitate more cooperation in global governance.

---

8   President Xi's speech at an Asia-Pacific Economic Cooperation (APEC) CEO meeting in October 2013 discussed this point. His speech is available at http://news.xinhuanet.com/world/2013-10/08/c_125490697.htm.

9   See www.g20.utoronto.ca/2013/2013-0906-declaration.html.

10   Refers to the New Silk Road Economic Belt, which will link China with Europe through central and western Asia, as well as the 21st Century Maritime Silk Road, which will connect China with Southeast Asian countries, Africa and Europe.

Foreign Economic Policy Making in China and Its Impact on China's Participation in the G20

China's Foreign Economic Policy-making Model since the 1990s

Economic diplomacy in China was sparked in the 1990s, beginning with a negotiation to grant China's accession to the WTO. Since then, the importance of economic diplomacy has grown significantly as China has joined numerous international economic organizations.

Various ministries are responsible for the creation and execution of economic diplomacy in China. For example, the Ministry of Commerce is tasked with business diplomacy, whereas the Ministry of Finance (MoF) and the PBoC oversee financial diplomacy. Conducting economic diplomacy with numerous governing departments inevitably breeds problems, perhaps the most substantial of which are issues surrounding coordination and integration. These issues are tackled through assigning a vice premier to oversee all economic diplomatic affairs. This economic policy-making structure is best described as a collective decision-making process, embodied in a "dispersed-centralized"[11] governance model. It is characterized by a network of ministries, each with varying degrees of influence, creating their own policies, which often reflect the interest of primary stakeholders. Often these policies only affect the ministry's respective field and, as such, require minimal coordination. This is what comprises the "dispersed" component of the model.

The "centralized" portion of the decision-making model is used in major economic and monetary policies[12] such as adjusting interest rates, fighting inflation or stimulating economic activity, and reforming the RMB exchange rate, to name a few. These are discussed and debated by the State Council, before handing the final say to the Politburo.

Similar characteristics are exhibited in Western democracies; however, there exist distinct differences as well. Unlike the Fed or European Central Bank, the

---

11   "Dispersed-centralized" is a direct translation from Chinese. This term is a combination of a decentralized and centralized policy-making model. Most decisions are made at the ministerial level and coordination is usually absent. Major decisions with significant influence are made at the cabinet level in a coordinated way. Final decisions are made collectively by the highest leaders.

12   According to Article 22, chapter 5 of the Working Rules of the State Council, "Major policies and measures are those that involve plans for national economic and social development, the state budget, significant planning, macroeconomic control, as well as economic reform and opening up. These policies and measures are discussed by the executive or plenary meeting of the State Council." The original Chinese text of the Working Rules is available at www.gov.cn/zwgk/2013-03/28/content_2364572.htm.

PBoC is one of many ministries competing for influence over monetary and exchange rate policy. It may propose policies, but the State Council makes final decisions through executive or plenary meetings. That said, economic policies deemed to have considerable influence on China's future development — such as RMB exchange rate reform, opening capital accounts or marketization of interest rates — are in the hands of the highest decision-making body, the seven-member Politburo Standing Committee. It is important to note that although the premier and president do retain significant influence, final economic policy decisions fall on the consensus of the State Council or, in some cases, the Politburo Standing Committee (Hu 2013). When a decision warrants the involvement of the Politburo, its advisory group takes the initial lead, based on a principle that means, when roughly translated to English, to "lead collectively, and take responsibilities together."

In practice, the Politburo's advisory group in economic affairs — the Leading Group for Financial and Economic Affairs of the Central Committee of the Communist Party of China (CPC) — is the highest ranked policy-making body in China. Its membership consists of Politburo committee members, State Council leaders and ministers in major economic departments such as the National Development and Reform Commission (NDRC), Commerce, Finance and the PBoC. Headed by the premier or president, the Leading Group can be compared to the "White House's National Economic Council, [as it influences] decision-making by framing the options leaders' debate" (Davis and Wei 2013).

As potent as the Leading Group may be, all relevant ministries have their own means and channels in which to lobby the top decision makers — i.e., the premier of the State Council, the vice premier in charge of economic and financial affairs and other members of the Politburo Standing Committee. A noteworthy example occurred in 2011, when PBoC Governor Zhou lobbied top leaders in the Politburo Standing Committee and State Council for tighter monetary policy (Davis 2011).

China's Policy-making Process at the G20 Summit

When China initially joined G20 summitry, its policies concerning the G20 were made by several major economic departments in addition to the Ministry of Foreign Affairs (MoFA), then coordinated by Vice Premier Wang Qishan, and by Vice Premier Wang Yang since 2013. Until 2013, the final say on important policy decisions (on some occasions) was made by Premier Wen and President Hu. Premier Li and President Xi currently have the final say.

In most policy areas, the roles of the PBoC and MoF are relatively small. However, they play very large roles in the G20 due to the combination of their financial market expertise and the fact that the G20 structure accords the largest roles to the ministers of finance and central bank governors. Moreover, the two almost exclusively handle all the work on issues related to financial regulation, IMF and World Bank governance, and international macroeconomic coordination. The Ministry of Commerce is responsible for all trade-related issues, the NDRC for development, energy and climate-related policies, and the MoFA is responsible for bilateral relations with other leaders, such as BRICS (Brazil, Russia, India, China and South Africa) leaders.

The MoFA lacks financial and economics expertise and it is for this reason that it has gradually been marginalized in the economic diplomatic arena. In October 2012, the Department of International Economic Affairs was created within MoFA with the intent to give it more involvement in economic policy making, especially within the G20, as the platform was (and continues to be) regarded as an important diplomatic forum.

China's dispersed decision-making process requires a substantial degree of coordination among the various departments and responsibilities. For this reason, all involved entities engage in preparation work prior to G20 summits in order to coordinate policy goals, priorities and positions. In some cases this has yielded extensive results. For example, during the lead-up to the 2010 Toronto summit the PBoC announced an RMB reform restart, and the MoF (in conjunction with the State Administration of Taxation) cancelled the export tax rebate on over 400 categories of goods. These decisions were made in an effort to reduce expected criticism and pressure faced in the Toronto summit. Much still remains wanting, however, on coordination issues in the months prior to G20 summits. He (2004) states that a lack of effective communication is one of China's major handicaps in leveraging international negotiations for national interest. The protection of individual departments' interests and misleading information are further regarded as the reasons for coordination failures.

China's Goals and Expectations in the G20

China gained entry to the centre stage of global economic governance by participating in the leaders' summits, which are considered by China to be the ideal platform in which to play the role of a responsible power and maintain relations with other major powers. As the sole international governance forum in which China has the capacity to operate as a major power, the G20 has provided the opportunity for China to expand its institutional authority and influence in global economic governance. Additionally, the G20 acts as a valuable mechanism for fostering cooperation among elite factions in China, as China's foreign policy highly values the international prestige — namely, being seen as a responsible power — associated with participating in large-scale governing.

China's most authoritative document, the report of the CPC's 18th Party Congress, confirmed that the Chinese government places the greatest of emphasis on the G20. Released on November 8, 2012, the wording in the report specifies that China was hand-picked to "participate [in] international affairs with a more positive attitude, play as a responsible big country." The report also specified that "China will positively participate [in] multilateral affairs, support the UN, the G20, Shanghai Cooperation Organization and BRICS to play a positive role." This was the first time China expressed an overtly positive attitude toward participation in global governance.[13]

China has a strong interest in maintaining the status of the G20 as the premier forum for economic cooperation, and a vested interest in ensuring that it does not degrade into another "talk shop" of multilateral diplomacy. In line with this, Chinese scholars suggest a natural division of work between the G20 and the United Nations, arguing that China should promote the G20 as the permanent institution responsible for global economic affairs, while the UN remains responsible for managing international and political and security affairs (China 2020 Research Team 2013).[14]

Should China Play a Leading Role in the G20?

China has participated in all G20 summits, and Chinese leaders are beginning to see the imperative of carving out a clearer role for China in the forum. To a large extent, the country sits at a crossroad regarding its future degree of engagement, as decisions will likely have long-lasting impacts on Chinese foreign policy. On one hand, it can be argued that China already plays a crucial role, effectively acting as a bridge of communication between developed and developing nations. For example, China's involvement is paramount for maintaining strong lines of contact between the United States and BRICS countries (via the Strategic and Economic Dialogue and BRICS meetings, respectively).[15] On the other hand,

---

13   The full text of the 18th Party Congress report is available at http://news.xinhuanet.com/ english/special/18cpcnc/2012-11/17/c_131981259.htm.

14   For additional evidence illustrating China's views on this issue, see Associated Press (2012); and Jin, Xie and Hang (2013).

15   Of prominent status are Fengying Chen's comments, available at http://live.people.com.cn/ bbs/note.php?id=5713090412705_ctdzb_062.

internal constraints explain why China should perhaps not be leading the G20, and demonstrate why China is wary of overstepping into a leadership position.

Concerns regarding the optimal level of leadership China should strive for have grown in saliency since 2011, as some scholars from India, South Korea, Mexico, Turkey, France and Russia argue that China should speak on behalf of emerging economies.[16] Similarly, Barry Carin (2015) suggests that China's leadership is a necessary component required for the G20 to maintain relevancy. This is a crucial point, as between the hopeless stalemate in American politics and Europe's inward-looking tendency (highlighted by the euro-zone crisis), the G20's relevancy has come into question as of late. In considering China's optimal path, a crucial parameter to understand is the analytical gap that exists between Chinese and foreign experts that could hinder its ability to act as a leader in the G20. Chinese analysts have highlighted the following four primary internal constraints facing the country since 2008: China is still a low-income developing country, and is hampered by relative weaknesses; overcommitting to the G20 could obstruct domestic economic policy autonomy; China's lack of a "global vision"; and suspicions surrounding a potential "trap" set by Western countries intending to overburden China and hinder its growth.

First, these analysts indicate that Chinese elites view China as a low-income developing country, despite its large, rapidly growing economy. Chinese leaders, as well as the public, believe that China is not yet ready to take on a leadership role, largely because the country is impeded by weaknesses compared to developed countries — technological, financial and regulatory — and despite its rapid expansion, faces growing social problems, macroeconomic imbalances and inequality (Wang 2011).

Second, concerns regarding the possibility for G20 commitments to undermine domestic economic policy autonomy are a cause for China's hesitation toward embracing a leadership role. Such concerns were reflected in China's ambivalence over the Mutual Assessment Process (MAP) when it was proposed in 2009 — China believed the mechanism should be consultative in nature, whereas others thought it should contain strong compliance mechanisms targeting better policy coordination (Chen Dongxiao 2011).

Third, some Chinese scholars believe that China lacks a global vision (Li Minjiang 2011) and, while it learns how to conduct foreign policy in a multilateral setting, insists on making its national interest a top priority (irrespective of other countries' concerns in global governance regimes). For instance, China's decisions on whether it should step up the reform toward a

---

16   See Huanqiu.com (2013).

more flexible exchange rate system were driven mainly by domestic economic considerations rather than thinking of international obligations. China deems its decisions to be justified even if they are not always consistent with the so-called interest on global economic balance.

Fourth, and perhaps most prominent, is that strong voices in China — including senior officials and commentators — argue that the country should avoid the temptation of taking on responsibilities beyond its capacity to bear the associated costs and risks. They express doubt over the true intentions of the United States and other Western countries, and believe that the prospect and allure of a leading role in the G20 masks the malicious intent of Western nations. More specifically, they fear that US-led Western countries (where the United States is the leader or most influential country) intend to hamper the rise of China by overburdening it with excessive responsibilities such as liberalizing its capital account and exchange rate regime, reducing its large trade surplus and carbon emissions, transitioning into a consumption-driven economy and lowering its savings rate (Zhang 2012; Zhou 2013). Although it can be argued correctly that these goals are in the long-term best interest of the country, these events are largely regarded in China as a means by which Western countries hope to push international adjustment costs onto the country. For this reason, China remains vigilant against being asked to bear potentially excessive responsibilities.[17]

Overall, the consistent style of China's foreign economic policies over the past decade suggests that it is unlikely that it will promptly transition into a relatively more proactive or aggressive stance. Rather, it is likely that China will maintain its current stance — continue to actively engage while avoiding taking on responsibilities incommensurate with its status as a developing country, and avoid initiatives that may harm national interest — while illustrating its ability to act as a responsible power. This is consistent with the statement in the CPC's 18th Party Congress report.

Nevertheless, some scholars argue that it is not possible for China to avoid playing a leading role in international economic affairs, highlighting the historic opportunity China has been given in the wake of the euro-zone and global financial crises (see, for example, Pang and Wang 2013). Many of these scholars insist that these events crippled Western countries, and that China should jump at the opportunity to lead.

Alternatively, others perceive China to be the elephant that can no longer hide behind the cherry tree, suggesting that with its GDP projected to surpass that of the United States by 2020, it is impossible for China to avoid taking on greater

---

17   See Huo Jianguo's comments at http://finance.people.com.cn/GB/12255645.html and www.chinanews.com/gn/2013/07-20/5064630.shtml.

global responsibilities. These scholars speculate that China will be forced to take on a more active role in order to protect rapidly expanding overseas economic interests. Further, they suggest that China should push for the G20 to become a formal international institution that manages world economic affairs (China 2020 Research Team 2013), as opposed to the current forum-like platform.

Ultimately, the road China takes will largely depend on domestic debates regarding the country's international position. Since formulating the "reform and opening-up" policy in the late 1970s, China's ultimate foreign policy-related goal has been to support continued domestic economic and social development through forging a favourable international environment. More recently, this goal has transitioned into one of "maintaining national core interests" (Information Office of the State Council, People's Republic of China 2011) and "great rejuvenation of the nation" (Xinhua News 2012). With sustainable development still a fundamental interest, China's level of engagement within the G20 will depend on how the forum can best serve the country's national interests as a developing nation.

China's Strategies in the G20

Positively Participate, but Avoid Challenging the United States

The G20 provides a unique opportunity for China to coordinate, negotiate and cooperate with the United States and other large powers without direct confrontation. China benefits from the forum, as it coincides with China's foreign policy principles and promotes cooperation and relationship building among global powers.

Regarding the financial system, China does not seek a complete overhaul, but rather to strive for an equal share and further integration. Pang (2013) argues that "China's strong interest in raising the quotas at the IMF and putting the RMB into the SDR basket show that China is not seeking to create an alternative in global governance, but embracing strongly the existing regime."

Moreover, some scholars suggest that it is in fact the European countries, not the United States, that comprise the largest opposition to comprehensive governance reform at international bodies such as the World Bank and IMF. Therefore, regarding its relationship with the United States, China is better off seeking the "greatest common ground" rather than challenging or contending for power (China 2020 Research Team 2013). China has much to gain from its participation in the G20, so long as it can avoid being isolated on critical

issues and avoid being perceived to unilaterally challenge the United States —
in particular in the US-dominated area of international finance. Contrary to
popular Western opinion, China's attitude toward the US dollar hegemony is
not a case of China challenging the United States, but is instead a reflection
of China's efforts to positively participate in the G20. A prime example of this
is China's 2009 proposal to replace the US dollar with the SDR as the main
international reserve currency.

Prior to the London summit, Zhou Xiaochuan, governor of the PBoC, shocked
the international community with his article about replacing the US dollar with
the SDR.[18] The paper was initially interpreted as a call to terminate the US
dollar hegemony, and Chinese officials from the MoFA were quick to clarify
misinterpretation. The article merely looked to explore the roots of the GFC
and spur academic discussion, as evidenced by then Vice Foreign Minister
He Yafai's comments. According to He, replacement of the US dollar with
the SDR, or any currency for that matter, was at most a "discussion among
academics," and certainly not the "position of the Chinese government" (*China
Daily* 2009). Additionally, the director of the Institute of World Economics and
Politics at the Chinese Academy of Social Sciences (CASS) and one of China's
highly regarded economists, Zhang Yuyan, expressed the notion that the SDR,
as a reserve currency, is an ideal option with very little feasibility in the short
to medium term (Tan 2009). He's clarifying comments illustrate China's wish
that its desire to actively participate in the G20 not be misunderstood, as Zhou's
article was simply a reflection of China's unrest toward the US dollar's role in
the international monetary system and the consequent crises. It was not a step
toward concrete actions to challenge US dollar dominance.

China believes that a firm, but not inflexible *duo er bu po* (bend without breaking,
essentially) approach toward the G20 is the optimal way to contribute while
promoting healthy relations. China participates positively, building its acumen
for multilateral diplomacy while refusing unreasonable requests and avoiding
direct conflict. China's concurrent defence and compromise of its exchange rate
policy at the Toronto, Seoul and Cannes summits is a first-rate example.

Although efforts to participate in the G20 are among the highest goals of
Chinese foreign policy, when conflict arises, diplomacy in the G20 and other
multilateral regimes take a back seat to China's highest priority — relations
with the United States. This has been the case since the 1990s, and is the reason
that some Chinese scholars advise against both challenging the US dollar and
striving for a robust leadership role in the G20 (Pang 2013; China 2020 Research
Team 2013). China uses the *duo er bu po* approach on this front as well, most

---

18   See Zhou (2009).

notably in expressing its reservations toward the US dollar hegemony. Without challenging the United States, China has expressed its yearning for the United States to undertake responsible fiscal and monetary policies. That is, especially with regard to developing countries, to recognize global negative repercussions and consider the potential to promote trade and anti-protectionism.[19]

Cooperation with BRICS Countries Is Key for China in the G20

President Xi may have said it best, when he asserted that "the global economic governance system must reflect the profound changes in the global economic landscape, and the representation and voice of emerging markets and developing countries should be increased" (quoted in MoFA of the People's Republic of China 2013). China, as the largest developing country in the world, has an important role to play in representing other developing nations. Further, China has the opportunity to use its identity and economic strength to promote cooperation among emerging economies — in particular BRICS countries — in order to escalate their voice in global economic governance.

Western nations represent a considerable share of global economic governance influence, but as emerging economies grow, power is presumably going to gradually transition in favour of the East and South, as has occurred with the IMF and World Bank. The number of relevant parties in global governance has grown, and tackling major economic challenges requires active participation from all parties, including the emerging markets. Although this transition at the G20 is likely to be highly limited in the short run, the process can be expedited through a consolidated voice, representative of developing nations' interests. Investment in infrastructure construction with the support from the New Development Bank might be a suitable issue to strengthen the congruent interests. Forging a broad political consensus among diverse countries will be a key factor in this shift, and is one China can use to gain dominion in the G20.

The largest impediments to a joint strategy of this nature are the distinct interests voiced by the BRICS. Presently, there is no formal coordination mechanism for the five countries, only the largely unstructured BRICS summit and a coordinating meeting among BRICS countries during the G20 finance ministers and central bank governors meeting. Scholars[20] have recommended that China begin to institutionalize the BRICS mechanism by promoting

---

19   In the eyes of Chinese analysts, it is the US dollar hegemony and accompanying unconventional monetary policies (primarily QE2 and QE3) that have brought instability to the global economy. See *People's Daily Overseas Edition* (2013).

20   See Pang and Wang (2013) and Huang, Gong and Kai (2013).

communication, coordination, free trade and the finalization of the BRICS Development Bank and reserve fund.[21]

Acting as a Bridge between Developed Countries and Emerging Markets

In addition to China's approaches to maintaining relations with the United States and assembling a BRICS base, a third, complementary strategy is to operate as a bridge between developed and developing countries.[22] China is in a unique position to do so, as despite its status as a developing country, it possesses characteristics consistent with those of developed economies, namely, the size of its economy. This responsibility is consistent with the underlying reason for China joining the G20 and refusing admission to the G8 — developing countries are represented at the G20, whereas China views the G8 as a relatively illegitimate forum of wealthy states.

The G20 as a Tool for Pushing a Domestic Agenda

Chinese leaders, from the first generation of Chairman Mao to the current fifth generation leadership, all attached great importance to the shaping of China's national image on the international stage (Jin and Xu 2010; Xinhua 2013). Further, Chinese leaders feel that China's reputation will suffer if the country or its leaders are named and shamed in international fora such as the G20. Based on this, reformers have looked, and continue to look, to the G20 as a key source of leverage.

In recent years, liberal-minded elites in China have used international fora as tools to achieve domestic reform. Examples include China's entering the WTO in order to push for the otherwise politically impossible market-oriented reforms, the issue of the RMB joining the SDR basket by 2015 and top leaders' statements in the G20, all of which have been used as part of the strategies to advance difficult domestic reform.

Building a Community of Interests

American scholars Ian Bremmer and Nouriel Roubini (2011) describe the current state of international affairs as a "G-zero" world — one in which no

---

21   The BRICS Development Bank and reserve fund were created after the group of emerging economies signed the long-anticipated document on July 15, 2014, the first day of the sixth BRICS Summit held in Fortaleza, Brazil.

22   For discussion among Chinese scholars (in Chinese), see http://live.people.com.cn/bbs/note.php?id=57130904124705_ctdzb_062.

single country or bloc of countries has the economic capacity or political power to champion a truly global agenda. Further, it can be argued that under current circumstances, it is extremely difficult even for the G20, the primary forum for global economic governance, to effectively govern global issues such as macroeconomic coordination, financial regulatory reform, trade policy and climate change (ibid.). As a result, the preferred and perhaps most viable option is the piecemeal discussion of issues and gradual forming of a consensus. That said, it is becoming increasingly more evident that only at the height of systemically important crises will incentives align and real progress on core issues be made (the coordinated post-GFC response is an example of this dynamic).

Zheng Bijian, who proposed China's "peaceful development strategy," explains the underpinning of its foreign policy strategy as promoting the construction of a community of interests and eventually a convergence of said interests (Zheng 2013). As far as strong allies based on common interests, China does not have any among G20 members. Furthermore, China also does not currently have bilateral free trade agreements (FTAs) with G20 member countries (with the exception of Indonesia).[23]

Prioritizing the Sino-American relationship has remained China's overriding strategy since it participated in the G20 summit, despite the growing importance of other relationships. Chinese policy makers regarded the G20 as an important platform for engagement with the United States, which prevented any serious thoughts of China taking a significantly stronger leadership role in the G20. With China's hosting of the G20 summit in 2016 and the sign that China is shifting its diplomatic priority toward its neighbours and other rising powers, away from the United States and other great powers,[24] a more assertive strategy could be taken and the current prioritization of China-US relations in global economic governance could be relaxed. Whether this change will occur and, if it does, how beneficial to long-term Chinese interests it will prove to be, will depend on the wisdom in strategy design and the diplomatic acumen of Chinese leaders. The future success (or pitfalls) of continuing this arrangement will largely determine the future of the G20 as a fruitful and relevant platform of discussion for global governance issues.

---

23   The China–Association of Southeast Asian Nations FTA came into force on January 1, 2010. The China-South Korea FTA was signed on June 1, 2015, and is expected to be effective by the end of 2015. The China-Australia FTA is expected to be signed and come into force in 2015.

24   At the Central Work Conference held in November 2014, Chinese President Xi Jinping changed the order of the general framework for China's foreign relations, implying the elevation of the periphery and other major developing powers and logical downgrading in strategic priority of China's relations to the United States and other great powers.

China's Agenda in the G20

Macroeconomic Policy Coordination: The G20 MAP

The MAP was launched at the 2009 Pittsburgh G20 Summit as part of the G20's "Framework for Strong, Sustainable and Balanced Growth" — a document that serves as a quasi-charter for the forum. The MAP is a peer-review-based mechanism designed to promote and support macroeconomic policies among G20 nations.[25]

Along with Germany, China's opposition ensured that no common numerical benchmark for current account balances was set at the 2011 Cannes summit.[26] China and other developing countries also raised questions concerning the independence of the MAP and accompanying IMF staff analysis, against the backdrop of the easy monetary policies of the Fed and ECB (Chin 2011). Moreover, China firmly believed that the Fed's third round of QE in 2012 and Japan's unconventional monetary policy in 2013 were "beggar-thy-neighbour" policies, which served, in China's opinion, to discredit the MAP as a tool of peer review and pressure. Additionally, the MAP fails to acknowledge what emerging economies (including China) believe to be irresponsible policies of developed countries. This, in combination with the extensive emphasis on increasing domestic demand and exchange rate flexibility in emerging surplus economies, has led many Chinese elites to question whether the MAP is a tool for constraining the rise of emerging economies.

That said, China has slowly embraced the MAP as of late, as it aligns with its domestic objectives — China's external surplus contraction since the GFC continues to hold, and its current account imbalance is no longer a point of criticism in the G20. China still fights for a tightening of developed world monetary policy, but also continues to commit to promoting domestic demand (Xi 2013; Central People's Government of the People's Republic of China 2013), which is consistent with the MAP, IMF staff recommendations and its own goals (including intended transition toward more consumption-driven growth, as announced at the Third Plenum of the 18th Party Congress).

Further, Chinese scholars suggest that China propose a new comprehensive framework within the G20 by which to ensure stability and an efficient allocation of capital through managing international capital flows (Li Shicai

---

25   The MAP was enhanced at the 2010 Seoul summit through "indicative guidelines" developed by the Framework Working Group (headed by Canada and India), which was primarily designed to identify countries with systemically relevant macroeconomic imbalances.

26   In 2010, US Treasury Secretary Timothy Geithner floated the idea of symmetric common limits on current account positions at +/- four percent of GDP.

2011; He, Feng and Xu 2013). More specifically, the framework would be a global crisis prevention and response mechanism based on international coordination, surveilling the key reserve currency country's macroeconomic policy and working with the IMF and G20 central banks to prevent future unrestricted capital flow-related issues (Xu 2011; Huang, Gong and Kai 2013; Chen Weiguang 2014). The central targets of this proposal are the spillovers from the developed countries' loose monetary policies, which have contributed to dramatic US dollar exchange rate fluctuations, as well as short-term capital flows that frustrate attempts by the PBoC to liberalize the Chinese exchange rate framework.

Another primary focus of Chinese leaders since the GFC and euro crisis is sovereign debt sustainability. Some Chinese scholars highlight that unsustainable fiscal policies in developed countries, in addition to threatening (and likely continuing to threaten) China's development, jeopardize global macroeconomic and financial stability (Jin and Chen 2013; Chen Yulu 2014). These experts suggest constructing a formal framework for supervising and assessing the sustainability of all G20 countries' public finances in addition to revisiting options for improving the current sovereign debt restructuring approach (Jin et al. 2014).

Proposals of this nature may attract the approval of other large surplus countries, namely Japan and Singapore, as well as resource-rich countries such as Saudi Arabia, Brazil and Russia, as they too possess large amounts of US and European debt, and therefore share China's concern over the safety of foreign assets (ibid.). Although the support of other countries should help push the matter into G20 discussions, communicating with the United States on this, and related macroeconomic stability issues, would rapidly accelerate the process.

Promote the Reform of the International Financial and Monetary System

On the subject of international financial and monetary system reform, China has two central goals — to continue promoting the 2010 Seoul package of IMF quota and governance reforms, and to add the RMB to the IMF's SDR basket. China recognizes that compared with the IMF, the G20 is a favourable platform for advancing these goals, as its fewer members promote better coordination, and G20-agreed policies can be used to facilitate reforms at the IMF.

The reform package is highly regarded in China as an important foreign policy achievement (Xie and Qu 2010).[27] In addition to doubling the IMF's quota-

---

27   Also see Yu (2010).

based resources to US$720 billion, it will shift six percentage points of total quota shares to developing countries, effectively granting China the third-largest share of the board (while reducing Western Europe's representation). The United States, as the possessor of the sole veto, has continually failed to ratify the reform, with the most recent attempt taking place on March 25, 2014. China, together with other G20 members, has repeatedly criticized the United States and indirectly expressed its strong disappointment through its statements at IMF meetings.[28] This setback is being interpreted in China as a deliberate attempt to block the rise of emerging economies in global economic governance, despite the intense lobbying attempts by the Obama administration (led by the Treasury) to pass the necessary legislation. China sees the extensive delay as undermining the legitimacy and prestige of the IMF, as well as the credibility of US leadership of the institution (ibid.). An apparent option for China is to continue rallying support from emerging markets, however, the seemingly endless stalemate does not bode well for the possibility of an expedited reform, at least on this front.

China's second battle — placing the RMB into the SDR basket — follows on France's proposal at the 2011 Cannes summit to reform the currency composition of the SDR basket. Similar to the above reform proposition, this and subsequent motions have gained the support of China and other developing countries. Last revised in 2010, the criteria for revising the currencies (and relative weights) in the SDR basket are based on the value of exports of goods and services, and the amount of currency-specific reserves held by other IMF member countries (IMF 2014). China's choice international monetary system reform-related objective is to place the RMB into the SDR basket at the scheduled 2015 SDR IMF review, however, it has a considerable way to go in ensuring its currency meets the foreign exchange (FX) reserve requirement. In order to be considered for the SDR basket, China must accelerate the internationalization process of the RMB and accompanying capital account liberalization. This goal is therefore both a domestic and foreign policy-relevant issue.

International Financial Regulation: The FSB

Created at the London summit in 2009 as the successor to the Financial Stability Forum (FSF), the FSB's mandate is to promote and supervise financial stability. Since its implementation, the FSB has developed into the policy development arm of the G20 in terms of financial regulatory matters and, alongside the IMF's Financial Sector Assessment Program, serves to provide the G20 with its minimal degree of policy traction over members (Nolle 2012). In its current

---

28   See Reuters (2014).

state, the FSB is the central governing body of the global financial sector and is responsible for developing standards to which G20 countries (in theory) must adhere.

Chinese scholars recognize that the US is the driving force for development and enforcement of global financial standards (Li Minjiang 2011), and they see the FSB as a means by which the United States can maintain its dominance over the global financial system (Task Group of the Institute of Finance and Banking at the CASS 2009). Further, the adoption of the recent Basel Committee on Banking Supervision framework, Basel III,[29] although marking the successful creation of a new banking regulatory framework by the G20, allows the United States to realize one of its major foreign economic policy objectives.

On this front, China accepts reality, and does not seek to challenge US dominance, but instead sees itself engaged in the learning process of deepening its understanding and knowledge of international financial regulation. The popular Chinese phrase, *yu guo ji jie gui*, meaning to "catch up with the (modern) world" accurately describes China's reasoning behind, and approach toward its position in the FSB. China actively participates in the FSB and discussions with associated standard-setting bodies. The engagement provides China with an opportunity to learn international standards, and to apply them to the domestic financial sector reform it so craves.

Trade

A substantial share of China's economic growth since 2001 can be attributed to its entry into the WTO. Once a challenger of multilateral trade regimes, China has evolved into a sustainer, and has become one of the largest beneficiaries of economic globalization. China is the biggest country in the world by trade volume, and thus benefits from an open and stable world market. Further, it is in China's best interest to convince the world that an open multilateral trade arrangement is beneficial for all countries.

China's largest concerns regarding international trade are the Trans-Pacific Partnership and Transatlantic Trade and Investment Partnership, two regional FTAs spearheaded by the United States. China's concerns stem from the high intellectual property, labour and environmental standards associated with these agreements, as they effectively preclude the participation of China and most of the emerging economies. As such, some Chinese scholars stress the urgency for the further promoting of a comprehensive resolution to the Doha Round of

---

29   Basel III is a comprehensive international framework for strengthening bank capital and liquidity standards.

WTO negotiations[30] under the auspices of the G20 (Wang 2013; Huang, Feng and Kai 2013).

Relative to other involved parties, such as the IMF and World Bank in the G20, the WTO is fairly absent in global issues. China needs a resolute and assertive twenty-first century "version" of the WTO that affirms development and new issues in trade and investment, such as investor protectionism and competitive neutrality (ibid.). On the subject of anti-protectionism, both China and the United States share common interests, however, the two appear to accuse one another of protectionism more than they cooperate. Perhaps in the future the G20 can be used as a medium for exchange of information and promote coordination between the United States and China on these issues.

Development

China's interest and involvement in development issues at the G20 stem from its position as the largest developing country. Development was formally put on the G20 agenda at the 2010 Seoul summit through the creation and endorsement of the Seoul Development Consensus.[31] This marked the transition of the G20 from an emergency response mechanism to a global "steering body."

Effectively promoting development issues and coordination will inevitably require substantial mobilization of financial resources, as well as a certain degree of risk. Infrastructure — the first of the nine pillars[32] — would be a fitting field for China to champion through investment and multilateral financing. Infrastructure investment has become a critical policy concern for developed and developing countries alike. Further, China could realize substantial benefits should it take the lead in designing some form of infrastructure investment initiative within the G20, more specifically through providing an outlet for China's excessive savings and capacity as well as improving China's international image.

First, foreign investment from China is an alternative avenue for China's excessive savings, as instead of holding FX reserves and facing the associated

---

30   Officially launched in Doha, Qatar, in 2001, the Doha Round is the latest round of trade negotiations among the WTO membership, aiming to achieve major reform of the international trading system through the introduction of lower trade barriers and revised trade rules.

31   This consensus is a set of principles and guidelines to reduce inequality and tackle global poverty through sustainable, shared and equitable growth, as a complement to existing development commitments, for instance, the UN Millennium Development Goals.

32   The nine pillars are infrastructure, private investment and job creation, human resource development, trade, financial inclusion, growth with resilience, food security, domestic resource mobilization and knowledge sharing. See www.g20dwg.org/.

costs, China could invest (US dollars or Chinese RMB) internationally. This would also further the progress of the RMB internationalization process. Second, it would serve as a window for China to benefit through exporting equipment, labour and construction materials. Third, infrastructure investment as a form of foreign aid would positively promote China's international image, help guarantee resource and energy security, and strengthen economic and political connections (Jin 2012; An 2012).

Energy

The G20 has all the ingredients for strong global resource and energy governance, as its members include several of the major energy, food and commodity producers and consumers. The 2013 St. Petersburg summit put promoting stable global energy markets on the agenda, which committed the G20 to strengthen the Joint Organisations Data Initiative (JODI)[33] on oil. The summit also focused on promoting energy efficiency, inclusive green growth, energy security, phasing out inefficient fossil fuel subsidies, investment in energy infrastructure, and promoting renewable and/or nuclear energy. That said, energy is still a field that lacks a formal cooperation mechanism, in addition to receiving minimal attention from the G20.

China is among the top energy-consuming countries, and given its expected future growth rate, will continue to increase the size of its energy footprint. At the fifth World Future Energy Summit in Abu Dhabi in 2012, then Chinese Premier Wen Jiabao encouraged the idea of China leading a multilateral cooperative energy mechanism in the G20.[34] China hopes for a developed framework that, through consultation and dialogue, will lead to reasonable and binding international rules, as well as early warning mechanisms, price coordination and financial supervision. Such a mechanism could facilitate cooperation between major energy powers through a variety of pre-existing multilateral institutions: the Shanghai Cooperation Organization could facilitate coordination with Russia; the BRICS meetings for BRICS countries;

---

33   JODI was launched in 2001 by six international organizations — APEC, Eurostat, the International Energy Agency, the Latin American Energy Organization, the Organization of the Petroleum Exporting Countries and the United Nations Statistic Division — initially as the Joint Oil Data Exercise to address the lack of transparent and reliable oil statistics, which was identified as a key contributor to oil price volatility. It was formally born when the six organizations obtained agreement from their member countries to make the exercise a permanent reporting mechanism at the eighth International Energy Forum in 2002. It is a concrete outcome of the producer-consumer energy dialogue.

34   The transcript of Wen's speech is available at http://news.xinhuanet.com/world/2012-01/16/c_111442816.htm.

and the G20 for the United States and European member countries (Huang, Feng and Kai 2013).

Coordination between China and the United States on a global energy mechanism in the G20 would be in both parties' interest. China will need to revisit its overseas energy supply strategy and consider joining with the United States to contribute more actively to safeguarding the global energy supply — including through improving the security of the major sea routes for oil transportation.

Institutionalization of the G20

Some Chinese scholars suggest that the G20 could achieve greater legitimacy and enforcement capacity if it were formally institutionalized with a permanent secretariat.[35] Others agree, indicating that it would also give emerging countries a greater voice (Chen 2013). On the other hand, it is also argued that the G20's ability to form political consensuses rests on its informal character, and its ability to act as a node between various international institutions. They underscore that the G20's role is not to enforce, but to promote flexible discussion and hand enforcement responsibilities to other organizations such as the IMF, World Bank and WTO (Zhu 2013).

The latter viewpoint appears to be gaining traction, and although "official" Chinese opinions are scarce, He Jianxiong — director-general of the International Department of the PBoC — suggests that Chinese leaders may in fact be adapting to the informal characteristics of the G20 platform, particularly its ability to push vital international organizations (and their leaders and major stakeholders) into discussions that would otherwise be difficult to coordinate.[36]

Conclusion

Chinese leadership continues to place great importance on G20 summitry, and is expected to continue contributing to the G20's global economic governance. As the host in 2016, China will look to further push its primary goals, and perhaps use its agenda-setting responsibilities to begin playing a leading role in the areas of macroeconomic coordination, trade, energy, and development and institutionalization of the G20.

There is, however, a long way to go before China is capable of playing a leading role in global monetary governance, international financial supervision and

---

35   See Wang and Li (2012).

36   He's comments are available at http://jingji.21cbh.com/2013/8-24/1MNjUxXzc0ODg1Mg.html.

other traditional components of the primary G20 agenda. That said, en route to hosting the summit in 2016, China will continue to support the package of IMF quota and governance reforms, as well as push for the RMB to be added to the SDR basket in 2015. Further, China will retain its cautious approach toward transitioning into a leader, as the United States along with Western countries continue to dominate the international financial system.

The foreseeable future will likely consist of China's continued contribution to the G20 and potential leading roles in a handful of key areas. Then again, judging from its recent initiatives with the AIIB, the New Development Bank by the BRICS and the finally settled "One Belt, One Road" strategy in 2014, China will enhance bilateral and regional ventures, effectively improving its capacity to govern trade, energy and development-related issues in global governance. A two-track strategy for China's role in global governing is in progress. How China will coordinate new proposals and strategies with its capacity and willingness to lead on certain issues in the G20 remains to be seen. An area of interest could be how the infrastructure investment initiatives by China, with the support of the AIIB and the BRICS New Development Bank, could be coordinated with the Global Infrastructure Hub idea that was raised at the Brisbane G20 Summit.

Works Cited

An, Wenbo. 2012. "Guoji Jinrong Geju Tiaozheng ji Zhongguo Duice Yanjiu" ["A Study on Adjustment of the International Financial Regime and China's Strategy."]. Ph.D. thesis, Party School of the CPC Central Committee.

Associated Press. 2012. "Syria Should Not Be on Agenda at G20, Says Chinese Official." *The Independent*, June 11. www.independent.co.uk/news/world/politics/syria-should-not-be-on-agenda-at-g20-sayschinese-official-7835550.html.

Beattie, Alan. 2010. "US Shifts G20 Currency Focus to Trade Deficits." *Financial Times*, November 1. www.ft.com/intl/cms/s/0/13b5c364-e5fc-11df-af15-00144feabdc0.html#axzz2wd4sDjDc.

Bloomberg News. 2011. "China Can't Use Reserves to 'Rescue' European Countries, Minister Fu Says." Bloomberg News, December 3. www.bloomberg.com/news/2011-12-02/china-can-t-use-its-reserves-torescue-countries-vice-minister-fu-says.html.

Bremmer, Ian and Nouriel Roubini. 2011. "A G-Zero World: The New Economic Club Will Produce Conflict, Not Cooperation." *Foreign Affairs*, March/April.

Carin, Barry. 2015. "China and G20." In *China and the G20: The Interplay Between an Emerging Power and an Emerging Institution*, edited by Catrina Schläger and Dongxiao Chen, 3–17. Shanghai: Shanghai People's Publishing House. library.fes.de/pdf-files/bueros/china/11433.pdf.

Central People's Government of the People's Republic of China. 2013. "Xi Jinping Attends Informal Meeting of BRICS Leaders in St. Petersburg." [In Chinese.] September 6. www.gov.cn/ldhd/2013-09/06/content_2482275.htm.

Chen, Dongxiao. 2011. "China's Perspective on Global Governance and G20." *China-US Focus*, February 16. www.chinausfocus.com/political-socialdevelopment/china%E2%80%99s-perspective-onglobal-governance-and-g20/.

Chen, Fenying. 2009. "G20 Yu Guoji Zhixu Da Bianju." ["G20 and the Great Change of International Order"]. *Xiandai Guoji Guanxi* [*Contemporary International Relations*] no. 11: 8-9.

Chen, Jia. 2013. "Think Tank Seeks G20 Secretariat." *China Daily*, September 7. www.chinadaily.com.cn/china/2013xivisitcenterasia/2013-09/07/content_16950939.htm.

Chen, Tongkui. 2011. "G20 Wuchi, FaZhong Ruojiruoli" ["A Subtle France-China Relations in the G20"]. *Nanfengchuang* [*South Reviews*] no. 10.

Chen, Weiguang. 2014. "Qiuquan Zhili yu Qiuquan Jingji Zhili: Ruogan Wenti de Sikao" ["Global Governance and Global Economic Governance: Some Thoughts"]. *Jiaoxue yu Yanjiu* [*Teaching and Research*] no. 2.

Chen, Yulu. 2014. "Zhougguo Ke Jiji Shenban 2016 Nian G20 Fenghui" ["China Should Actively Bid to Host 2016 G20 Summit"]. *Huanqiushibao* [*Global Times*], April 8. http://opinion.huanqiu.com/opinion_world/2014-04/4957531.html.

Chin, Gregory. 2011. "What Next for China in the G20? — Reorienting the Core Agenda." CIGI Commentary, November 9. www.cigionline.org/publications/whatnext-china-g20-reorienting-core-agenda.

China 2020 Research Team. 2013. "2020: Zhongguo zai Shijie de Dingwei" ["Repositioning China in 2020"]. *Guoji Jingji Pinglun* [*International Economic Review*] no. 3: 9–43.

China.com. 2008. "Foreign Media Comment on China's 4 Trillion Fiscal Stimulus Plan: Greatly Boost the Global Economic Growth." China.com, November 11. www.china.com.cn/international/txt/2008-11/11/ content_16746528_2.htm.

China Daily. 2009. "China Reassures on Dollar Debate before G8." China Daily, July 6. www.chinadaily.com. cn/china/2009-07/06/content_ 8381924.htm.

China News Week. 2011. "Zhongguo Buyuan Chengwei Ouzhou de 'Shaqian' Laiyuan." ["China Won't Be the Source of 'Stupid Money' for Europe."] *China News Week*, November 3. http://newsweek.inewsweek.cn/ magazine.php?id=3262&page=3.

Cui, Liru. 2009. "G20 Kaiqu Le Tansuo Quanqiuzhili Xinlujing de Jihui zhi Chuang" ["G20 Started a New Window of Opportunity for a New Way of Global Governance"]. *Xiandai Guoji Guanxi* [*Contemporary International Relations*] no. 11, 1–3.

Davis, Bob. 2011. "Political Overlords Shackle China's Monetary Mandarins." *The Wall Street Journal*, April 15. http://online.wsj.com/news/articles/ SB10001424405274870341 06045762175535088212 90.

Davis, Bob and Lingling Wei. 2013. "Meet Liu He, Xi Jinping's Choice to Fix a Faltering Chinese Economy." *The Wall Street Journal*, October 6. http://online.wsj.com/news/articles/SB10001424052 7023049067045791114425665249 58.

Dyer, Geoff. 2010. "China Must Beware Scoring Own Goal with QE2 Criticism." *Financial Times*, November 10. www.ftchinese.com/ story/001035466/en/?print=y.

Edwards, Nick and Benjamin Kang Lim. 2011. "Beijing Risks Public Backlash if It Rescues Europe." Reuters, November 3. www.reuters.com/article/2011/11/03/us-china-europe-newspro-idUSTRE7A236S20111103.

Geithner, Timothy. 2009. "Press Briefing by Treasury Secretary Tim Geithner on the G20 Meeting." Pittsburgh, PA, September 24.

Guo, Xuejun. 2013. "Chapter One: Introduction." In *Jiyu G20 Shijiao de Woguo Guoji Jingji Jinrong Zhanlue Wenti Yanjiu* [*China's Economic and Financial Strategy Study in View of the G20*]. China Finance 40 Forum Research Report, September. www.cf40.org.cn/ uploads/PDF/20139163.pdf.

He, Fan. 2004. "Zhongguo Shifou Yao Jiaru Qiguo Jituan." ["Should China Join the G7?"]. *Guoji Jingji Pinglun* [*International Economic Review*] no. 5: 13–16.

———. 2010. "G20 Xiang Hechu Qu" ["Where Does the G20 Go?"] *Guoji Jingji Pinglun* [*International Economic Review*] no. 4: 149–51.

He, Fan, Feng Weizhuang and Xu Jin. 2013. "Quanqiu Zhili Mianlin De Tiaozhan Ji Zhongguo de Duice" ["Challenges for Global Governance Mechanism and China's Strategy"]. *Shije Jingji yu Zhengzhi* [*World Economics and Politics*] no. 4.

Hu, Angang. 2013. *Zhongguo Jiti Lingdao Tizhi.* [*China's Collective Leadership System*]. Beijing: China Renmin University Press.

Huang, Wei, Feng Gong and Kai Guo. 2013. "Chapter Three: Proposals for China's Agenda in the G20." In *Jiyu G20 Shijiao de Woguo Guoji Jingji Jinrong Zhanlue Wenti Yanjiu* [*A Study on China's Economic and Financial Strategy in View of the G20, China Finance 40 Forum Research Report*], edited by Jin Zhongxia. September. www.cf40.org.cn/uploads/PDF/20139163.pdf.

Huanqiu.com. 2013. "International Think-tanks Suggested China Play a Leading Role in the G20." [In Chinese.] http://world.huanqiu.com/exclusive/2013-09/4317903.html.

IMF. 2014. "Factsheet: Special Drawing Rights (SDRs)." March 25. www.imf.org/external/np/exr/facts/sdr.htm.

Information Office of the State Council, People's Republic of China. 2011. "China's Peaceful Development." September 6. http://news.xinhuanet.com/english2010/china/2011-09/06/c_131102329.htm.

Jiang, Shixue. 2012. "The European Debt Crisis in a Chinese Perspective." Working Paper Series on European Studies, Institute of European Studies, CASS 6 (3).

Jin, Minmin, Xie Peng and Hang Mo. 2013. "G20 St. Petersburg Fenghui De Zhenggui" ["The Right Track of G20 St. Petersburg Summit"]. Xinhuanet.com, September 6. http://news.xinhuanet.com/ world/2013-09/06/c_117258879.htm.

Jin, Zhengkun and Xu Qingchao. 2010. "Guojia Xingxiang de Suzao: Zhongguo Waijiao Xinketi." ["National Image Building: The New Task for China's Diplomacy."] *Journal of Renmin University of China* (2): 119–27.

Jin, Zhongxia. 2012. "Zhongguo de 'Marshall Jihua' — Tantao Zhongguo Duiwai Jichusheshi Touzi Jihua" ["China's Marshall Plan — A Discussion on China's Overseas Infrastructure Investment Strategy"]. *International Economic Review* no. 6.

Jin, Zhongxia and Chen Fengying. 2013. "Jing Zhongxia and Chen Fengying Interpret Highlights of the Eighth G20 Summit." [In Chinese.] http://live.people.com.cn/bbs/note.php?id=57130904124705_ctdzb_062.

Jin, Zhongxia et al. 2014. *Zhongguo Yu G20: Quanqiu Jingjizhili de Gaoduan Boyi* [*China and G20: High End Gaming in Global Economic Governance*]. Beijing: China Economic Publishing House.

Li, Yonghui. 2009. "G Shidai'de Guoji Xinzhixu: Bianju yu Bianshu" ["New International Order in the G Era: Change and Uncertainty"]. *Xiandai Guoji Guanxi* [*Contemporary International Relations*] no. 11: 11–13.

Li, Minjiang. 2011. "Rising from Within: China's Search for a Multilateral World and Its Implications for Sino-U.S. Relations." RSIS Working Paper, March 25. www.rsis.edu.sg/publications/WorkingPapers/WP225.pdf.

Li, Shicai. 2011. "Quanqiu Zhili Shiye Xia de G20 Yanjiu" ["The G20 Study with a Vision of Global Governance"]. Ph.D. thesis, Shanghai Academy of Social Sciences.

MoFA of the People's Republic of China. 2013. "President Xi Jinping Gives Joint Interview to Media from BRICS Countries." March 19. www.fmprc.gov.cn/mfa_eng/wjdt_665385/ zyjh_665391/t1023070.shtml.

Nolle, Daniel E. 2012. "Global Financial System: The Dodd Frank Act and the G20 Agenda." *Journal of Financial Economic Policy* 4 (2): 160–97.

Pang, Zhongying. 2013. "Quanqiu Zhili de 'Xinxing' Zuiwei Zhongyao: Xin de Quanqiu Zhili Ruhe Keneng" ["The 'New Modalities' of Global Governance Matter: On the Shaping of the Transformation of Global Governance"]. *Guoji Anquan Yanjiu* [*Journal of International Security Studies*] 31 (1).

Pang, Zhongying and Wang Ruiping. 2013. "Quanqiu Zhili: Zhongguo de Zhanlue Yingdui" ["China's Strategic Response to Global Governance"]. *Guoji Wenti Yanjiu* [*China International Studies*] no. 4.

PBoC. 2012. "China Announced Participation in IMF Resources Boost." www.pbc.gov.cn/publish/english/ 955/2012/201206281558050791715 79/20120628155805 079171579_.html.

People's Daily Overseas Edition. 2013. "US Dollar Overflow Will Pose a Danger to Global Economy." *People's Daily Overseas Edition*, November 29.

Reuters. 2011. "Political Deadlock Derails China's EU Aid Offer." Reuters, November 11. www.telegraph.co.uk/finance/financialcrisis/8883851/ Political-deadlockderails-Chinas-EU-aid-offer.html.

———. 2014. "China Urges IMF to Give More Power to Emerging Markets." Reuters, January 15. www.reuters.com/article/2014/01/15/us-china-imfidUSBREA0E1PT20140115.

Tan, Zhe. 2009. "Zhang Yuyan: G20 Shi Shijie yu Zhongguo de Zhuangzhedian." ["Zhang Yuying: The G20 Is the Turning Point for the World and China"]. *Zhongguo Shehui Kexueyuan Yuanbao* [*Chinese Academy of Social Sciences Review*], April 16.

Task Group of the Institute of Finance and Banking at the CASS. 2009. "Zonglun Quanqiu Jinrong Jianguang: Zhougguo Jinrong Chuangxin Buneng Yinyufeishi." ["On the Reform of Global Financial Regulation: China's Financial Innovation Cannot Stop for Fear of Possible Risk."] *Zhongguo Zhengquan Bao* [*China Securities Journal*], October 20. http://finance.ifeng.com/opinion/jjsh/20091020/1353703.shtml.

Truman, Edwin M. 2010. "The G-20 and International Financial Institution Governance." Peterson Institute Working Paper 10-13. www.piie.com/ publications/ wp/wp10-13.pdf.

Walter, Andrew. 2012. "Global Economic Governance after the Crisis: The G2, the G20, and Global Imbalances." Bank of Korea Working Paper. http://personal.lse.ac.uk/wyattwal/images/ Globaleconomicgovernanceafterthecrisis.pdf.

Wang, Ying and Li Jiguang. 2012. "China and the G20." *Contemporary International Relations* 22 (July/August).

Wang, Yong. 2011. "China in the G20: A Balancer and a Responsible Contributor." East Asia Forum, October 31. www.eastasiaforum.org/2011/10/31/ china-in-the-g20-a-balancer-and-a-responsiblecontributor/.

Wang, Yong. 2013. "The G20's Role in Addressing the WTO's Predicament: Seeking Political Compromise and Strengthening the Multilateral Trading System." In *Think20 Papers 2014: Policy Recommendations for the Brisbane G20 Summit*. Lowy Institute for International Policy. December 5.

Wu, Jiao and Li Xiaokun. 2011. "President Hu Confident in Europe." *China Daily*, November 1. http://usa.chinadaily.com.cn/china/2011-11/01/content_14012188.htm.

Xi, Jingping. 2013. "Speech in the First Session of the Eighth Summit of the G20 in St. Petersburg." Xinhua News, September 6. http://news.xinhuanet.com/ politics/2013-09/06/c_117249618.htm.

Xie, Shiqing and Qu Qiuying. 2010. "Shijieyinhang Toupiaoquan Gaige Pingxi" ["An Analysis on the Reform of Voting Share in World Bank"]. *Hongguan Jingji Yanjiu* [*Macroeconomics*] no. 8.

Xie, Ye. 2010. "China to Cut Current Account Surplus through Gradual Adjustment, Yi Says." Bloomberg News, October 9. www.bloomberg.com/news/2010-10-09/china-to-cut-current-account-surplus-throughgradual-adjustment-yi-says.html.

Xinhua News. 2008. "International Society Positively Praise China's Policy to Promote Economic Growth." Xinhua News, November 11. http://news.xinhuanet. com/world/2008-11/11/content_10339183.htm.

———. 2012. "Xi Pledges 'Great Renewal of Chinese Nation.'" Xinhua News, November 29. http://news.xinhuanet.com/english/china/2012-11/29/c_132008231.htm.

———. 2013. "Xi: China to Promote Cultural Soft Power." Xinhuanet.com, January 1. http://news.xinhuanet.com/english/china/2014-01/01/c_125941955.htm.

Xu, Hongcai. 2011. "Ershiguo Kuangjiaxia de Guoji Huobi Tixi Gaige" ["International Monetary System Reform under the G20 Framework"]. *Quanqiuhua* [*Globalization*] no 2. www.cciee.org.cn/NewsInfo.aspx?NId=2338.

Yang, Qingchuan and Dahai Chong. 2013. "China and the G20: From 'Savior' to Leading Actor." *International Herald Leader*, September 11. http://news.ifeng.com/shendu/gjxqdb/detail_2013_09/11/29512110_0.shtml.

Yu, Huifeng. 2010. "Only the First Step: China's Voting Shares in World Bank Enhanced." [In Chinese.] China.com.cn, April 28. http://news.china.com.cn/comment/2010-04/28/content_19922335.htm.

Zhang, Mingzhi. 2012. "Cong'Zhongguo Weixie Lun' dao'Zhougguo Zeren Lun': Xifang Lengzhan Siwei Dingshi Xia de Zhongguo Fazhan Anquan" ["From China Threat Theory to China's Reponsibility Theory: China's Development under the Western Countries' Cold-War Mentality"]. *Zhongguo Waijiao* [*China's Diplomacy*] no. 9.

Zheng, Bijian. 2013. "21 Shiji Di Er Ge Shinian de Zhongguo Hepingfazhan zhi Lu" ["China's Path of Peaceful Development in the Second Decade of the 21st Century"]. Guoji Wenti Yanjiu [*China International Studies*] no. 3.

Zhou, Xiaochuan. 2009. "Reform the International Monetary System." B*IS Review* 41, March 23.

Zhou, Xiaoyuan. 2013. "Zhongguo Tiaobudong Quanqiu Fusu 'Qianjindan'" ["'The Heavy Burden' of Global Recovery Is Too Heavy for China to Carry Alone"]. *People's Daily Overseas Edition*, July 20, section 2. http://paper.people.com.cn/rmrbhwb/html/2013-07/20/content_ 1271116.htm.

Zhu, Jiejin. 2013. "Fuhe Jizhi Moshi yu G20 Jizhihua Jianshe." ["The Compound Mechanism and the Institutionalization of the G20."]. *Guoji Guancha* [*International Review*] no. 3: 6–12.

12

China's Role in Financial Standard Setting after the 2007–2009 Financial Crisis: The Case of Basel III and Shadow Banking Reform

David Kempthorne

The 2007–2009 global financial crisis (GFC) was an important turning point in the governance of global finance. It facilitated the transition toward international financial standard-setting bodies (SSBs) — institutions that emerging markets were previously excluded from participating in — becoming more inclusive, representative and diverse. From the beginning of 2009, SSBs expanded their membership structure to include Group of Twenty (G20) member countries, including China. The expanded membership structure of SSBs helped address the "democratic deficit" (Porter 2001) that undermined the legitimacy and effectiveness of financial standard setting. Through these reforms, China and other emerging market powers finally occupied a seat at the table and would participate in the standard-setting process. Yet important questions remain about China's role in SSBs after the crisis. Although China has gained formal representation at SSBs, does it have sufficient power to influence the content of financial standards? And, perhaps more importantly, does China have a distinct set of regulatory preferences relative to its Group of Seven (G7) counterparts, or is it satisfied with the international regulatory status quo?

In order to analyze and understand the role of China in SSBs after the crisis, this chapter conducts an analysis of China's patterns of compliance with the Basel Committee on Banking Supervision's (BCBS) Basel III capital adequacy standards and the Financial Stability Board's (FSB's) shadow banking reforms. An analysis of these standards demonstrates that rather than meaningfully contesting financial standards after the crisis, China has pursued a series of domestic regulatory reforms aimed at complying with financial standards and addressing a number of regulatory gaps in China's regulatory framework. Financial standards have provided a valuable road map for reform at a time when China is seeking to liberalize its domestic financial system. At the same time, China has exercised its autonomy and diverged from financial standards on key issues, including the treatment of past-due loans and defaults on banks' balance sheets and corporate bond markets. China's divergence from financial standards demonstrates it has exercised a degree of autonomy from financial standard setting. But China has largely been compliant, even over-compliant, with financial standards since the crisis. Chinese regulators have utilized international financial standards as a tool to navigate the regulatory challenges of a growing and increasingly complex domestic financial system.

China's role as a status quo actor in SSBs after the crisis is explained by two factors. First, as international political economy (IPE) scholars have argued, representation does not guarantee influence (Chey 2015; Walter 2015). China's relative power within SSBs remains constrained by its limited financial power in the global financial system (Kapstein 1989; 1992; Simmons 2001; Drezner 2007; 2010; Bach 2010; Bach and Newman 2010; Helleiner and Pagliari 2011). Furthermore, the late development of China's domestic financial system and its commitment to restraining the size, influence and flexibility of domestic financial markets has contributed to a lack of regulatory capacity and expertise that is necessary to grant China the technical authority to influence the content of financial standards relative to G7 member countries (Baker 2009; Chwieroth 2008; Tsingou 2014).

Second, international financial standards have largely been consistent with its domestic political interests rather than China's preferences being directly in conflict with G7 member countries. In particular, China has made efforts to liberalize its domestic financial system to make it more competitive and flexible, which has the potential to threaten the safety and soundness of domestic financial markets. Financial standards have informed China's response to these domestic regulatory challenges. Through their participation in the standard-setting process and the implied obligation of compliance with financial standards, Chinese regulators have been able to mobilize further support for domestic reform. China's divergence from financial standards demonstrates that China's domestic regulatory regime continues to be shaped by domestic political interests. China's transition toward a more market-based system of finance is underway, but remains incomplete as the effects of China's industrial economic development model continue to impact financial regulatory preferences.

This chapter is structured as follows. The first section reviews the history of SSBs to identify the political dynamics of standard setting in the pre-crisis era and the political drivers of advanced industrialized economies' decision to expand the membership structure to include emerging markets. The second section analyzes existing IPE literature to identify the explanation for China's lack of influence over standard setting and pattern of compliance with financial standards after the crisis. The third and fourth sections analyze China's pattern of compliance with the BCBS Basel III Capital Adequacy Requirements and the FSB's shadow banking reforms respectively. The final section summarizes the major findings of this research and assesses the potential implications for China's future role in financial standard setting.

The History of Financial Standard Setting: From 1974 to the Post-crisis Standard-setting Regime

A key feature of financial standard setting since its emergence in the 1970s has been the exclusivity of SSBs and the disproportionate influence of advanced industrialized economies. Before the crisis, SSBs were regulatory clubs comprised of the Group of Ten (G10) member countries. The narrow membership structure of SSBs reflected a distinct set of historical developments in global financial markets and the disproportionate power of the United States, United Kingdom and European financial centres in global finance. The 2007–2009 GFC overturned the narrow membership structure of these institutions. Facing substantive domestic regulatory reforms at home, advanced industrialized economies needed to ensure that emerging markets were compliant with post-crisis reforms. For emerging markets, the crisis provided a unique opportunity to gain access to the standard-setting process to reflect their growing stature in the global economic and financial system. But as the following sections will demonstrate, representation did not ensure emerging markets would play an influential role in financial standard setting after the crisis.

Financial Standard Setting before the GFC

Financial standard setting first emerged in the 1970s in response to the breakdown of the Bretton Woods international monetary order and the impact of intensified national financial market integration and innovation on global financial stability. Having previously restricted cross-border capital flows under the Bretton Woods system that characterized the postwar international monetary order, national capital accounts and domestic financial markets were increasingly liberalized in the 1960s and 1970s. Subsequently, national financial markets became increasingly integrated and interdependent, causing financial instability to be rapidly transmitted across national borders.

Financial standards first emerged in response to the forced closure of German, UK and US banks in 1974. Foreign exchange market volatility and insufficient prudential regulation contributed to their collapse and the period of global financial volatility that followed (Alexander, Dhumale and Eatwell 2006, 22). In response, 13 central banks and banking regulators from G10 member countries established the BCBS to create a set of measures that addressed issues arising from the globalization of financial markets. The BCBS first developed the Basel Concordat in 1975 to assist in the supervision of cross-border financial firms and the Basel I Capital Adequacy standard in 1988 to coordinate prudential regulatory requirements for banks between national jurisdictions (see Kapstein 1989; Oatley and Nabors 1998; Wood 2005; Alexander, Dhumale and Eatwell 2006; Singer 2007). Over time, the international standard-setting regime expanded to include new SSBs that addressed other aspects of the financial system, including the Committee on Payment and Settlement Systems (CPSS) in 1980, the International Organization of Securities Commissions (IOSCO) in 1983, the International Association of Insurance Supervisors in 1994 and the International Accounting Standards Board (IASB) in 2001.

In the beginning, the narrow membership structure of financial standard setters reflected the nature of the governance challenges in the global financial system. These were largely specific to advanced industrialized economies that had liberalized their capital account and domestic financial systems in the 1970s and 1980s. For instance, the BCBS's capital adequacy standards were aimed at coordinating the requirements for banks in G10 member countries amidst intensified global competition and the threat of weakening prudential regulatory requirements to facilitate the expansion of internationally active domestic financial firms (Kapstein 1989). At IOSCO, securities regulators were primarily interested in addressing the threat of cross-border financial crime by creating governance mechanisms that helped overcome the legal barriers to investigating and prosecuting insider trading in foreign jurisdictions. These incidents largely occurred within and between advanced industrialized economies (Bach 2010; Kempthorne 2013). SSBs were predominantly created to address coordination and cooperation issues arising among developed financial centres. The issues in emerging and developing markets played a less prominent role.[1] This changed in the mid-1990s.

Emerging markets suffered a series of high-profile economic and financial crises in the 1990s, including the 1994 Mexican peso crisis, 1997-1998 East Asian financial crisis and 1998 Russian rouble crisis. These crises led world leaders, financial regulators and international financial institutions to give greater attention to the governance and regulation of financial markets in emerging economies. Facing economic and financial crisis, emerging markets received large bilateral and multilateral funding packages to stabilize their domestic economy and shore up their financial system. For instance, the US Treasury, US Federal Reserve, the Bank of Canada, and the IMF extended loans and credit facilities to Mexico to help stabilize its economy in 1994, while a number of East Asian economies received IMF assistance in 1997. These crises had widespread effects across the global financial system. A US-based hedge fund, Long Term Capital Management, nearly collapsed during the Russian rouble crisis, requiring a private bailout from US financial firms. The costs and consequences of financial crises in emerging markets for advanced industrialized economies and their domestic financial systems led the G7, international financial institutions and SSBs to strengthen the international standard-setting regime (Simmons 2001; Drezner 2007).

The policy process began in 1995 at the G7 leaders' summit in Halifax, Nova Scotia. The G7's communiqué stated: "With today's highly integrated financial markets, there is greater potential for the rapid transmission of financial disturbances. Close international cooperation in the regulation and supervision of markets is essential to safeguard the financial system and to prevent erosion of prudential standards" (G7 1995). Subsequently, the G7 directed SSBs to develop a set of core principles that could form a road map for the implementation of financial standards in 1995. After the East Asian crisis, the G7, in concert with the newly created Financial Stability Forum (FSF), the IMF and the World Bank, endorsed the creation of a monitoring and compliance program under the IMF's Financial Sector Assessment Program (FSAP) and the Report on the

---

1   IOSCO is an important exception. IOSCO was derived from the Inter-American Association of Securities Commissions, which was aimed at promoting the development of securities markets in the Americas through the creation of fair, effective and efficient regulatory frameworks for capital markets. Consequently, IOSCO has been relatively more sensitive to the interests and regulatory concerns of less developed financial centres, as reflected in a far more inclusive decision-making structure and the early establishment of committees dedicated to discussing issues in emerging and developing markets. Although financial standard setting remained heavily influenced by developed economies, which formulated and negotiated financial standards through IOSCO's Technical Committee, IOSCO's post-crisis IOSCO board has adopted one of the most diverse forms of representation in financial standard setting (see Sommer 1996; Kempthorne 2013).

Observance of Standards and Codes (ROSC). Through semi-regular missions to assess compliance with financial standards, the G7 believed the combination of external political pressure and market discipline would facilitate the adoption of domestic regulatory reforms in more peripheral financial centres in order to strengthen their national prudential regulatory and supervisory frameworks. The G7 also tried to make compliance with financial standards a condition of receiving IMF loans, but resistance from emerging and developing markets successfully defeated the measure (Helleiner 2014, 134).

The strengthening of the international financial architecture in the mid-1990s posed a problem. Financial standards had previously applied to G10 member countries that participated in the decision-making process. Non-participating states were able to voluntarily adopt financial standards to improve domestic regulation or attract foreign capital. For instance, Brazil voluntarily adopted capital adequacy requirements in line with Basel I in 1994. Brazil was not a member of the BCBS at the time, and its domestic banks were not internationally active, suggesting that Brazil's compliance with Basel I was driven by its own interests in strengthening its prudential regulatory and supervisory framework (Bandeira 2015, 5). However, from the late 1990s, emerging and developing markets were subjected to intensified external political pressure to adopt financial standards that they did not participate in developing or negotiating. Paul Martin, who was Canada's finance minister during the Mexican and East Asian financial crises, expressed his concern that the failure to include emerging markets in the development of financial standards would likely undermine their implementation. Martin argued that including emerging market economies from the recently created G20 would improve the regime's effectiveness, but opposition from other G7 members defeated the measure (Blustein 2013, 39).

Martin's assessment turned out to be prescient. Despite the strengthened monitoring regime, compliance with financial standards was uneven across countries and between financial sectors. Many countries, including China and the United States, refused to be assessed by the IMF. Ironically, the lowest participation rate in the IMF's FSAP and ROSC process in the pre-crisis period was among Asian economies (IMF 2009; 2012). A number of jurisdictions engaged in "mock compliance," meaning that they adopted financial standards through legislative reform but did not commit sufficient resources or expertise to meaningfully enforce them (Walter 2008). As Eric Helleiner argues, the G7's expectation that market discipline would reinforce compliance with financial standards did not materialize. Financial markets paid little attention to a country's record of compliance with financial standards in determining foreign investment decisions (Helleiner 2014, 135). However, emerging markets did strengthen their domestic prudential regulatory regimes, but this was largely driven by their collective experience of financial crises in the 1990s and a consequence of their interests in developing well-capitalized domestic financial systems as self-insurance against the volatility of global financial markets and the sudden reversal of international capital flows (Lane 2012; Helleiner 2014; Walter 2010).

The history of standard setting before the crisis outlines an important set of political dynamics that have shaped the post-crisis reform process. Critically, financial standard setting has historically been the exclusive domain of advanced industrialized economies with large, well-developed financial systems. G10 member countries have utilized the standard-setting process to export their domestic regulatory frameworks to more peripheral financial centres to mitigate the potential costs and consequences of under-regulated financial systems. Their exclusion has been an important source of frustration for emerging markets. The GFC provided a unique opportunity to change that.

The GFC and the Reform of Financial SSBs

In November 2008, Mario Draghi, who was chair of the FSF at the time, announced that the FSF supported "the call to broaden the FSF's membership to include key emerging market economies and will be working to rapidly achieve that objective" (FSB 2008). Draghi's announcement came a day ahead of the first G20 leaders' summit in Washington, DC, which was called to address the global economic and financial implications of the GFC. After Draghi's announcement, SSBs began reforming their membership structure to include China and other emerging market powers. As part of these reforms, China was granted three seats on the FSB's plenary and a seat on the FSB's influential steering committee. China was also invited to become a member of the BCBS, the CPSS, IOSCO's technical committee (now the IOSCO board) and the public oversight board of the privately governed IASB. Through these reforms, China gained representation on each of the main SSBs and occupied key positions of authority within these institutions.

Although it is possible that these reforms were aimed at addressing the "democratic deficit" (Porter 2001) that undermined the legitimacy of SSBs and the implementation of financial standards before the crisis, the events surrounding their accession suggest otherwise. Critically, the GFC originated in predominantly advanced industrialized economies. The United States, the United Kingdom and the European Union faced significant domestic political pressure to strengthen the prudential regulation of their domestic financial firms and markets in the wake of extensive and prolonged financial instability. The G7 was concerned that if foreign financial centres failed to follow suit, financial market activity could migrate to foreign financial centres with lower regulatory costs, affecting the profitability and competitiveness of their domestic financial markets. As Helleiner (2014, 111, 154) argues, the decision to extend membership to emerging markets was largely driven by the interests of G7 members in ensuring that post-crisis reforms were also adopted by emerging markets (also see Singer 2007).

Reforms to SSBs' membership structure are also explained by the political opportunism of emerging markets. In the days just prior to the first G20 leaders' summit, Brazil hosted the G20 finance ministers and central bank governors' meeting in Sao Paulo. The Brazilian hosts informed Mario Draghi that he was only able to speak in his capacity as the governor of Banca d'Italia and not as chairman of the FSF (Helleiner 2014, 138). Brazil clearly communicated emerging markets' belief that these institutions were no longer legitimate in its eyes and that it would no longer comply with a set of standards that it had no role in formulating. Chinese Premier Wen Jiabao also placed pressure on the G7 and SSBs to expand their membership structure. In October 2008, Premier Wen asserted that in order "to improve the functioning of the international financial organization so as to be more responsive in maintaining international and regional financial stability and strengthen financial regulation, emerging markets should be involved more in the decision making and rule making process" (quoted in Luo 2008). China and its emerging market allies were able to frame their inclusion in financial standard setting as a necessary next step in the governance of global finance in the wake of a financial crisis that originated in developed rather than emerging markets.

The events surrounding the decision to expand the membership structure of SSBs after the crisis suggests that developed and emerging market powers had a mutual interest in the initiative. For emerging markets, gaining representation in SSBs reflected their growing influence in the global economy and provided an opportunity to participate in the standard-setting process and shape the content of financial standards that had previously been dictated to them by G10-dominated SSBs. For developed economies, the participation of emerging markets was necessary to support the adoption of post-crisis reforms. Their exclusion could have contributed to a more fractured financial system and could have resulted in the migration of global capital toward more peripheral financial centres with less stringent prudential regulation. Although reforms to SSBs after the crisis were a critical first step in addressing the limitations of the pre-crisis standard-setting regime, questions remain about the extent to which it would meaningfully reform the standard-setting process. But, as Hyoung-kyu Chey (2015, 4) explains, emerging economies "have finally been given an *opportunity* to play meaningful roles in the establishment of international standards, as formal rule makers. Yet how much they can *actually* utilize this opportunity is another matter altogether" (emphasis in the original). As the following section argues, although China has gained formal representation, its ability to influence financial standards remains limited by its lack of structural power in the global financial system and a lack of regulatory expertise. Most importantly, China has largely been content to comply with financial standards and has not substantively contested advanced industrialized economies' regulatory preferences. China has largely acted as a status quo political actor in SSBs after the crisis.

The Power and Interests of China According to IPE

Since the emergence of financial standards in the 1970s and 1980s, IPE literature has investigated the political dynamics of financial standard setting, arguing that the creation and strengthening of financial standards are a function of the power and interests of competing stakeholders in the standard-setting process, including states, domestic political actors and financial regulators within SSBs. Although the literature has predominantly focused on the role and influence of political actors in the United States, the United Kingdom and Europe, it provides an important basis to understand the role of China.

Two bodies of literature are particularly relevant. First, state-centric literature has argued that the power of states to create and influence the content of financial standards is contingent on the size and structural power of their domestic financial markets. By controlling access to large, liquid and predominantly stable financial markets, and through the latent threat of exclusion, states with large advanced financial centres are able to enforce compliance with financial standards and obtain their preferences within standard-setting processes (Kapstein 1992; Simmons 2001; Singer 2007; Drezner 2007; Posner 2009; Bach 2010; Bach and Newman 2010; also see Helleiner and Pagliari 2010; Helleiner and Pagliari 2011; Chey 2015). Dominant states' interests in exercising control over the content and creation of financial standards help explain why G7 and G10 member countries have governed financial markets through regulatory clubs rather than multinational institutions. By restricting membership, the G7 and G10 have been able to ensure that the content of financial standards are consistent with their material and domestic political interests (Drezner 2007; Wade 2008). As Chey (2015, 6) argues, the lack of financial market power relative to advanced industrialized economies remains an important constraint on emerging markets' ability to influence financial standard setting and in utilizing their newfound position of power to advocate for reforms that are consistent with their interests.

China's financial power remains limited despite the growth of its domestic economy and foreign asset holdings. In recent years, China's foreign asset holdings have grown dramatically, rising from US$1 trillion in 2004 to US$5.93 trillion by the end of 2013 (Haneman 2014). However, the United States' total stock of foreign financial assets was US$24.6 trillion in the third quarter of 2014 (US Department of Commerce 2014). Furthermore, the European Union's total foreign asset holdings reached €9.45 trillion (approximately US$24.6 trillion) in the same time period (European Central Bank [ECB] 2015). China's position in global financial markets is not only small in absolute terms, but the composition of its foreign financial asset holdings further limits its power. At year-end 2013, US$3.8 trillion of China's US$6 trillion foreign financial assets were foreign currency reserves, while a mere US$865 billion were foreign direct or portfolio investments. These measures provide a snapshot of the extent to which foreign investment is contingent on Chinese capital. In contrast, in 2014, the United States and the European Union's total foreign direct and portfolio investment reached US$16.9 trillion (US Department of Commerce 2014) and €4 trillion (approximately US$17.7 trillion) (ECB 2015) respectively. These figures demonstrate that China's foreign financial asset holdings continue to be dwarfed by the United States and the European Union. Although China's power in global finance is likely to grow in the future, its position in global finance immediately after the crisis remains limited by its lack of integration into the global financial system.

The second body of literature, transgovernmental network theory, argues that the power to influence financial standards is contingent on technical authority and expertise. Early scholarship de-emphasized the contested nature of financial standards, arguing that financial standards were a function of the principled and professional interests of regulators in maintaining financial stability (Porter 2005a; 2005b). However, recent literature has argued these networks are exclusionary and that the preferences of regulators within transgovernmental networks are shaped by common educational backgrounds, professional norms and technocratic expertise (Baker 2009; Chwieroth 2008; Tsingou 2014). This suggests that regulatory networks privilege certain ideas and knowledge and that the ability of regulators to influence the content of financial standards is a function of the "expertise, material resources and the power of ideas" (Tsingou 2014, 4). For emerging markets, the lack of regulatory expertise remains an important constraint (Chey 2015; Walter 2015; Bandeira 2015). As Fernanda Martins Bandeira (2015, 3) emphasizes, despite the material benefits of participating in the international reform process, emerging market regulators remain constrained by a lack of "independence and powers as well as... availability of information, tools and human resources." Andrew Walter (2015,

6) argues that "knowledge and resource constraints" impact the "still low levels of emerging country actor voice in international standard setting." For instance, a participant of a working group at the Institute for International Finance, a powerful interlocutor between private finance and the BCBS, said, "emerging country bank participants rarely participate and appear to be 'on a very steep learning curve' on most issues" (quoted in ibid., 6-7).

China's lack of regulatory expertise, funding and experience relative to its G7 counterparts continues to be a constraint on its influence in SSBs. Although individual members of the People's Bank of China (PBoC), the China Banking Regulatory Commission (CBRC) and other regulatory bodies have demonstrated knowledge and expertise on key issue areas, China's financial regulatory system remains underfunded and suffers gaps in expertise on important areas such as risk management and auditing (IMF 2011; 2012). Furthermore, having maintained a closed economy until the late-1970s and 1980s, China had only a handful of banks at the time of Basel I's creation in 1988 and the PBoC was only four years old (Knaack 2015). Consequently, China has been late in developing the necessary expertise and institutional development to ensure it has an effective and influential voice on key regulatory issues.

Existing literature suggests that China's power to influence financial standards is still limited. But it remains to be seen whether China will seek to influence financial standards or whether its preferences substantively diverge from advanced industrialized economies. State-centric theory contends that it does. These scholars have argued the creation of financial standards has been driven by the interests of advanced industrialized economies, their regulators and the interests of powerful domestic political actors in exporting their national regulatory frameworks to foreign financial centres. Financial standards export regulatory adjustment costs to other financial jurisdictions to create a level playing field between national jurisdictions that enable dominant financial centres to maintain their dominant position in global finance (Oatley and Nabors 1998; Singer 2007; Wood 2005; Helleiner 2014). Alternatively, financial standards have historically been used as a governance mechanism to address the economic costs and consequences of financial market instability in emerging and developing market economies rather than a mechanism to improve the stability, efficiency and effectiveness of financial markets in foreign jurisdictions (Simmons 2001; Drezner 2007; Bach and Newman 2010). Dan Drezner (2007, 122) has argued that emerging and developing markets were required to absorb the high adjustment costs of reform while developed economies enjoy the benefits of improved coordination.

IPE scholars have also emphasized that financial standards fail to reflect the specific local circumstances in emerging markets. Financial standards reflect the Anglo-Saxon model of financial regulation that places emphasis on market-centric systems of risk measurement and disclosure and the separation of state from finance and investment (Walter 2008; Rodrik 2009; Helleiner 2010). More recently, scholars and non-governmental organizations have argued that international financial institutions and SSBs should apply the principle of proportionality in assessing compliance with financial standards and in making regulatory recommendations to emerging and developing markets (de Sousa 2015, 5; Global Partnership for Financial Inclusion 2014). These developments further emphasize that developed and emerging markets have competing preferences due to the fact that their respective financial systems are at different stages of development. Competing preferences help to account for why emerging markets were non-compliant with financial standards in the pre-crisis era (see Walter 2008).

State-centric literature suggests that China will oppose financial standards and seek to use its expanding power to pursue an alternative set of standards. Summarizing the position of realists, John Ikenberry (2008, 23) says realists expect "China will try to use its growing influence to reshape the rules and institutions of the international system to better serve its interests, and other states in the system." Representative of the realists' position on the issue, Drezner (2010) argues that China's expanding structural power will likely lead to the creation of rival standards to advance industrialized economies and the fragmentation of international regulatory regimes. Benjamin J. Cohen (2008, 456) provides an alternative perspective in emphasizing the power of autonomy rather than the power of influence. Cohen argues that emerging markets' dramatic growth before the crisis has led to the increased importance of autonomy, defined as the ability "to act freely, insulated from outside pressure." Subsequently, China (and other emerging market powers) may exercise its autonomy, as a function of its degree of financial self-reliance, to not comply with financial standards. In fact, China leveraged its autonomy to resist external political pressure to assess compliance with financial standards, refusing to undergo an IMF FSAP and ROSC assessment before becoming a member of the FSB.

IPE literature has also questioned these assertions. Ikenberry (2008) argues that China has grown and succeeded as a consequence of the existing international order and that the growing interdependence of national economies means that China has an incentive to integrate into rather than contest the existing international liberal order. For financial standard setting, Andrew Walter's (2010) and Peter Knaack's (2015) analyses of China's position on Basel II and

Basel III capital adequacy standards argue that, rather than contesting financial standards, China has been an enthusiastic adopter of reform. Walter (2010, 163) argues that China has traditionally embraced financial regulatory standards from Western economies and that Chinese regulators have leveraged financial standards to promote domestic regulatory reform. Knaack (2015) provides a different explanation, contending that Chinese regulators have aggressively pursued reform to cement China's reputation as a responsible and reputable financial regulatory jurisdiction to gain influence in financial standard setting in the future. A Hong Kong regulator stated: "I think they have a case to be keen on implementing those international standards domestically to be treated more seriously than other developing jurisdictions in order to gain [a position for] the country as a major player in international forums" (quoted in Knaack 2015, 16). Andrew Baker also questions whether China will pursue alternative sets of financial standards. Baker (2009, 211-12) says finance ministries and central banks from emerging markets have often adopted common regulatory preferences "in order to be taken seriously by their colleagues from the G7." This suggests that rather than being a regulatory spoiler, China is more likely to accept the regulatory status quo.

Existing literature suggests that China's power to influence financial standards remains limited and that, even if China were a powerful actor, it is not immediately apparent that it would seek to meaningfully influence the content of financial standards. An analysis of China's patterns of compliance with post-crisis financial standards provides further evidence for this perspective. China has been largely compliant with financial standards, but has argued that these standards should respect meaningful differences between national financial systems. China has also been non-compliant on key issues. In particular, it remains a laggard on the treatment of default, past-due loans on banks' balance sheets and the corporate bond market.

Domestic politics theory's emphasis on the domestic sources of international financial standards or state behaviour in financial SSBs helps explain China's patterns of compliance with financial standards. In particular, David Singer's (2007) theoretical framework argues that financial regulators are bureaucratic political actors whose decisions are shaped by their interests in maintaining their autonomy, prestige and future career opportunities. The bureaucratic political interests of regulators explain why regulators increase prudential regulatory requirements during periods of financial market instability. Other scholars have emphasized that domestic legislatures and regulators increase regulatory requirements on financial firms in response to the demands of their domestic constituents (Oatley and Nabors 1998; Helleiner and Pagliari 2010). Others have also argued that the ability of financial regulators or policy makers to pursue reforms is a function of the balance of power between competing domestic interest groups and that regulatory outcomes reflect the balance of power between pro-reform and status quo political actors (Helleiner and Pagliari 2010; Fioretos 2010; Walter 2008). This set of literature emphasizes that the competing interests and relative power of different domestic political stakeholders often explain financial regulatory outcomes. Financial regulatory reform and compliance with financial standards also have important distributive effects among certain interest groups.

As the following section demonstrates, reforming China's financial markets has been supported by financial regulators and the PBoC, and has received the backing of the Chinese government through its endorsement of a measured approach to financial market liberalization. Rather than viewing financial standards as posing an unnecessary regulatory burden with high adjustment costs, China has viewed them as a valuable road map for reform. China's compliance with Basel III and shadow banking reforms reflects the fact they are consistent with its domestic political interests. Complying with financial standards helps ensure that China's financial markets are made more resilient and supports financial market liberalization. At the same time, China's non-compliance with financial standards also demonstrates that financial regulation continues to be shaped by domestic political pressures and the continuation of a state-centric industrial development model.

China's Compliance with Basel III

After the crisis, the BCBS was tasked with reforming international capital adequacy standards. Through Basel III, the BCBS strengthened the quality and quantity of capital held by banks and reformed risk management requirements in response to new developments in the financial system. Rather than opposing Basel III reforms, China supported the United States, the United Kingdom and Switzerland, and other emerging markets, in strengthening capital adequacy requirements in the face of opposition from France and Germany (Bair 2012; Drezner 2014, 95; Helleiner 2014, 104). Emerging markets' support for higher prudential regulatory requirements is explained by the fact that they did not face significant adjustment costs because they had adopted higher capital adequacy requirements before the crisis.[2] China leveraged the crisis and its participation in the BCBS to pursue an aggressive set of domestic reforms that addressed gaps in China's domestic regulatory regime and strengthened the resiliency of its corporate banks.

Beginning in September 2008, Chinese regulators proposed a series of reforms that brought its regulatory framework in line with Basel II. Before China was invited to become a member of the FSB and the BCBS, the CBRC issued eight draft supervisory guidelines that required Chinese banks to strengthen internal controls and risk management procedures, and increase their capital adequacy requirements (KPMG 2009). After the completion of Basel III, the CBRC pursued further reform. In June 2012, China's banking regulator issued capital rules that reformed domestic capital adequacy and risk measurement requirements that were largely consistent with or above the regulatory requirements outlined in Basel III. Corporate banks were required to implement the measures by January 1, 2013 (CBRC 2012). The CBRC also issued notices to improve disclosure requirements and provide further areas of clarification to ensure consistency with Basel III over the course of 2012 and 2013 (BCBS 2012, 6). Through these reforms, China's corporate banks became compliant, even over-compliant, with Basel III. In the BCBS assessment of China's compliance with Basel III, it concluded that China was fully compliant with 13 of its 15 main categories and largely compliant with the remaining two. Chinese banks maintained an average total capital ratio of 13 percent and a tier 1 capital ratio of 10 percent, well above the minimum required capital ratio of eight percent and six percent respectively (BCBS 2012, 7).

At the same time, China imposed stricter regulatory requirements as a tool of economic policy rather than risk management. For instance, the BCBS peer review of China's prudential regulatory regime highlights that the CBRC's capital rules applies a 1250 percent risk weight to equity investments in commercial entities. Basel III requires only a 100 percent risk weight (BCBS 2012, 69-70). High risk weights incentivize banks to provide finance through direct credit lending rather than equity-based lending. China has also used higher risk weights to reduce the risks of mortgage and housing markets. The

---

2   In contrast, German and French regulators faced domestic political pressure to weaken regulatory requirements because of the heavy concentration of lending in the banking sector and the reliance on small to medium-sized enterprises on bank intermediated credit as a source of funding and investment. The EU would later weaken liquidity and risk measurement requirements under Capital Requirements Directive and Regulation IV (CRD IV). As the BCBS (2014, 4) identified in its assessment of compliance with Basel III, CRD IV gave "concessionary risk weights…[for loans] to small and medium-sized enterprises (SMEs)." This and other aspects of CRD IV made the EU "materially non-compliant with the minimum standards prescribed under the Basel Framework."

CBRC applies a 50 percent risk weight to mortgage lending in comparison to the 35 percent risk weight under Basel III (BCBS 2012, 69-70).

China's adoption of financial standards is explained by the interests of Chinese regulators and policy makers in strengthening the resilience of its corporate banks through the introduction of high capital adequacy requirements and the conservative treatment of credit risk weights. These reforms were driven by the interest of Chinese regulators in strengthening prudential regulatory requirements and domestic policy makers' interest in liberalizing its financial system. In 2011, China issued its 12th Five-Year Plan, indicating its intention to liberalize interest rates and promote private investment in Chinese banks (Xinhuanet 2012). Basel III provided a useful mechanism to strengthen the risk measurement, internal controls and capital adequacy requirements for China's corporate banks to foster a more market-based financial system and to navigate the challenges posed by financial liberalization for financial stability. Lifting deposit and lending rate controls will intensify competitive pressures on corporate banks and place downward pressure on interest rate spreads, and could cause capital adequacy levels to fall, making corporate banks more susceptible to risks in China's financial system. By reforming risk measurement and internal control requirements, Chinese regulators are able to foster a more transparent banking system that will both encourage private investment in Chinese banks and promote stronger market discipline. Doing so will make Chinese banks more efficient and flexible at a time when China's leaders are seeking to identify how the country can transition away from export-led growth toward building a stronger and more sophisticated domestic economy. This is reflected by the CBRC's discussion of Basel III with the Chinese press in 2011: Compliance with Basel III is "a necessary measure to facilitate the transformation of banks' development mode, improve the capability of the banking sector to tackle external impact, ensure the banking sector's long-term robust operation, and fend off systematic financial risks. Besides, it is also necessary to do so if we are to drive the banking industry to implement the 12th Five-Year Plan, improve the efficiency of financial resources configuration, and support strategic economic restructuring and sustained development of China's economy" (CBRC 2011).

The CBRC views Basel III as a useful blueprint to promote the development of China's banking system and ensure the continuing resiliency of its corporate banks as part of a broader strategy aimed at improving the flexibility and readjustment of its economy away from its reliance on industrial economic growth.

The use of crises and the leveraging of international financial standards to promote reforms is nothing new. As Walter (2010) highlights, China leveraged the Asian financial crisis to push through a set of domestic reforms to address gaps in its domestic regulatory framework. Financial standards helped overcome domestic political resistance to the adoption of a more market-based and risk-sensitive regulatory regime (Walter 2010, 162). The reforms led to a dramatic decline in non-performing loans (NPLs) as a percentage of total loans, falling from 22.4 percent in 2000 to 2.5 percent in 2008 (Asian Development Bank 2009, 63).

The BCBS peer review also highlights weaknesses in China's legal and regulatory framework for the treatment of defaults and past-due loans. The BCBS concludes that China remains non-compliant in regard to provisioning requirements for past due loans. Supervisors are not required to assess banks whose definition of default deviates from its established definition (2012, 65). China has historically used state-owned asset management companies (AMCs) to purchase non-performing loans from China's commercial banks, improving the health of Chinese banks while obfuscating losses from poor investments. *The Wall Street Journal*'s Carl Walter and Fraser Howie (2014) state: "AMCs are being enlisted in the Party's struggle against financial losses of all kinds. That includes not just bank loans, but also junk bonds and illiquid wealth management products (WMP)." The presence of AMCs and lack of transparency surrounding the treatment of NPLs in the Chinese banking sector demonstrates the extent to which the relationship between corporate banks and the state remains closely intertwined. China is still willing to provide implicit support for state-owned enterprises and Chinese industry.

China has also been vocally critical of Basel III, reiterating the importance of adapting financial standards to China's special circumstances. For instance, in 2010, the CBRC's chairman, Liu Minkang, critiqued the Basel III process:

> The design of supervisory standards in these two documents [Basel III consultation documents] mainly takes into consideration the banking practices in the European and US economies, while does not concern much about the actual situation of the emerging market economies like China. Therefore, considering that different economies are quite varied in terms of the structure of the financial system and maturity of financial market, we suggest that the BCBS should not make too rigid and prescriptive rules for these standards. Here, the issue is how to well balance the international convergence and national discretion, so that national supervisory authorities have more flexibility to reflect

the banking practices of their own country and enhance effectiveness of banking supervision. (CBRC 2010, 1)

Chinese banks have also critiqued Basel III for granting zero risk weights to sovereign bonds from developed economies. Basel III requires banks to hold a large amount of sovereign bonds as highly liquid assets. In granting preferred status to the sovereign bonds for Western economies, Basel III reduces the cost of funding for banks in advanced industrialized economies while imposing additional costs on Chinese banks despite the low likelihood of government default (Chen 2010). The BCBS did announce that it would review the zero risk weighting for Western sovereign debt and consider making sovereign bond risk weights more sensitive to sovereign debt risks in January 2015 (Reuters 2015a). This suggests that China and other emerging markets may have exercised a degree of influence over financial standards after the crisis.

After the crisis, China took aggressive steps to reform its domestic regulatory regime during and after the GFC. Chinese regulators seized the opportunity to promote domestic regulatory reforms that promoted higher prudential regulatory requirements and improved risk management systems. At the same time, China has diverged from financial standards, maintaining an opaque system for the treatment of defaults and past-due loans. It has also criticized the BCBS for failing to take account of the unique differences between national financial markets and advocated for less prescriptive financial standards to grant emerging markets greater flexibility to comply. Yet China has not proposed an alternative for financial standards, choosing to exercise its autonomy and maintain the domestic regulatory status quo on core issues in the same manner that a number of advanced industrialized economies have done over the course of the post-crisis reform process. There is little evidence that China has substantively changed the content of its financial standards. Instead, Basel III has been utilized as a road map for domestic reform, supporting China's efforts to liberalize its domestic financial sector.

China's Compliance with Shadow Banking Reforms

Shadow banking reform was an important issue in the post-crisis regulatory reform process. Shadow banking is defined by the FSB (2014a) as "credit intermediation involving entities and activities outside of the regular banking system," but particular emphasis is placed on those entities that "perform bank-like functions" by transforming short-term funding into long-term credit. Many believed that non-bank credit intermediation and the shadow banking system's interconnectedness with the traditional banking sector played an instrumental role in the 2007–2009 GFC. The shadow banking system doubled in size before the crisis, growing from just under US$30 trillion in 2002 before reaching US$60 trillion in 2007. Although growth of the sector slowed immediately after the crisis, it regained momentum in mid-2008 before reaching US$75 trillion in total assets by the end of 2013 (ibid.).

The G20 began addressing the shadow banking system in November 2010 at the G20 leaders' summit in Seoul, South Korea. The G20 requested that the FSB develop recommendations to strengthen the regulation and oversight of the shadow banking system by mid-2011 (G20 2010). In response, the FSB and other SSBs proposed a set of reforms that include the five following measures: "1) mitigating risks in banks' interactions with shadow banking entities; 2) reducing the susceptibility of MMFs [money market funds] to 'runs'; 3) improving transparency and aligning incentives in securitisations; 4) dampening pro-cyclicality and other financial stability risks in securities financing such as repos and securities lending; and 5) assessing and mitigating financial stability risks posed by other shadow banking entities and activities" (FSB 2014b, 1).

The FSB's shadow banking standards were particularly relevant to China's financial system amidst the rapid growth of the sector over the past five years, which coincided with the dramatic expansion of lending in China. Since the Chinese government injected RMB 4 trillion (US$568 trillion) into the economy as part of a stimulus package in November 2008 (Barboza 2008), credit in China has grown from 150 percent to 250 percent of GDP between 2008 and 2014 (Anderlini 2014). Continuing restrictions on deposit and lending rates and insufficient access to credit for small to medium-sized enterprises and households has led to the migration of credit outside the traditional banking system toward the shadow banking sector. Although estimates of China's shadow banking system vary widely, JP Morgan's assessment concludes that it is worth RMB 36 trillion (approximately US$5.7 trillion) and 69 percent of GDP (Zhu, Ng and Jiang 2013). Shadow banking grew by 28 percent in 2011 and by 42 percent in 2012 (Wen and Arias 2014). Despite the growth of the shadow banking sector, in absolute terms, it remains a small proportion of global shadow banking assets and a smaller proportion of China's total financial assets relative to other jurisdictions.[3]

However, outside commentators expressed their concern that China's shadow banking system presents a clear and present danger to financial stability. Moody's lowered China's credit outlook from positive to stable in 2013 as a

---

3   China's shadow banking system represented only four percent of the world's US$75 trillion in global shadow banking assets at the end of 2013 (FSB 2013, 2). In contrast, shadow banking in the Netherlands, the United Kingdom, Switzerland and the United States stands at 760 percent, 348 percent, 261 percent and 170 percent of GDP respectively (FSB 2014a, 11).

consequence of concerns about the rapid growth of credit in China and the systemic risks posed by shadow banking (Bloomberg 2013). The IMF's 2014 report on shadow banking also drew attention to the rapid growth of shadow banking in China and, in particular, the growth of off-balance-sheet activities through China's WMPs as a potential source of systemic risk in China's financial system (IMF 2014, 77). In contrast, the FSB has remained relatively quiet on the growth of China's shadow banking system. The FSB suggested that China improve its collection of data in relation to shadow banking in 2012 (FSB 2012, 5) and emphasized the lack of reporting data on the relationship between non-bank and banking intermediaries in 2013 (FSB 2013, 5).

China has taken a balanced approach to shadow banking since the crisis. Chinese regulators have both supported the development of the sector and addressed its risks as the shadow banking system grew in size and systemic importance. Since 2008, China, like other states,[4] has provided conditional support for the growing shadow banking system, viewing the system as a vehicle for the liberalization of China's financial markets. Both the PBoC and the government have been keen to draw attention to the positive benefits of shadow banking for China's financial system. China's State Council viewed the sector as "a complement to the traditional banking system, shadow banks play a positive role in serving the real economy and enriching investment channels for ordinary citizens" (quoted in Parker 2014). The PBoC also provided support for the shadow banking system in 2013 when it argued that "[shadow banking] meets the financing demand of real economy. Investment channels are branched out for residents and enterprises. The whole financial market gets a shot in the arm by shadow banking in liquidity and dynamics" (PBoC 2013, 204).

The Chinese government has also sought to downplay the risks of the sector. Using a very narrow definition of shadow banking, China claimed that its shadow banking sector held only US$0.4 trillion in assets in 2012 (FSB 2012, 8). It has emphasized that the shadow banking sector remains small compared to its international counterparts. The PBoC's 2013 Financial Stability Report downplayed the risks of the sector: "With regard to size and risk, China's shadow banking is dwarfed by its international counterparts. The financing channels are similar to those in the traditional banking, and the access to capital and credit from regular banking system is limited" (PBoC 2013, 203).

---

4   Although jurisdictions have been concerned about its growth, many have also promoted a revival of securitized lending, an important component of the shadow banking system. The Bank of England and the European Central Bank released a document in March 2014 discussing how to promote the revival of securitization in the euro zone (European Central Bank and Bank of England 2014).

Chinese regulators have conditionally supported the growth of the shadow banking system but have responded to its rapid growth by instituting a set of reforms aimed at strengthening the transparency and resiliency of the shadow banking system and the exposure of corporate banks beginning in 2013. The CBRC issued a directive requiring corporate banks to disclose the extent of their off-balance-sheet vehicles, mostly in the form of WMPs, and register them with local regulators (Rabinovitch 2013). That same year, the State Council issued Circular 107, requiring banks' capital adequacy requirements to reflect their material exposures to shadow banking assets, trusts and WMPs (Clifford Chance 2015). In 2014, the CBRC issued Document 99, which overhauled the trust sector by introducing a strict approval process for firms entering the market, requiring shareholders to provide additional capital when trusts suffer losses and requiring trusts to be restructured so that they do not bear the burden of risk but act as the distributor risks (Asian Banking and Finance 2014; Bloomberg 2014a).

The PBoC has also tried to manage emerging risks and bring greater transparency to the sector. The PBoC tried to temper the growth of the shadow banking sector and its reliance on short-term funding by inducing a liquidity crunch in money markets twice over the course of 2013 (Davis and Wei 2013; Parker 2013). The PBoC placed further pressure on the sector when it announced that it would incorporate lending to non-bank-deposit-taking institutions in its loan calculations for corporate banks to identify the extent to which lending institutions are a source of liquidity for non-bank intermediated debt. The PBoC justified the measure by saying, "the changes in calculating deposit and loan items are aimed at making [Chinese standards] gradually be in line with usual international practices" (Reuters 2015b), further demonstrating the use of financial standards in informing domestic reforms.

The reform process has also regressed at times. In 2014, Industrial and Commercial Bank of China (ICBC) announced that it would not compensate investors from losses incurred on a credit line for a Chinese coal mine project. The WMP was marketed by ICBC but issued by China Credit Trust Co. Ltd. (Reuters 2014a). Eight days later, ICBC announced that it would restructure the deal to allow the debtor to meet its obligations at a later date, indicating that the Chinese government would not accept a full default (Bloomberg 2014b; Reuters 2014b). The measure raises concerns about whether China is willing to instill market discipline and the extent and clarity of the exposure of Chinese corporate banks. China has also failed to introduce MMF reforms, instead continuing to retain a stable net asset value approach, making it more susceptible to runs, while the United States and Europe have introduced measures that require MMFs to adopt a variable net asset value approach (Clifford Chance 2015).

China's considerable efforts to improve the regulation and oversight of the shadow banking system started to take effect by the end of 2014, as growth of the sector had slowed according to Moody's (2015). Moody's Chief Credit Officer for the Asia-Pacific Michael Taylor said, "Although shadow banking has continued to grow, it has done so more slowly in recent quarters as regulatory measures to rein in the sector's growth appear to be having an effect....These tighter regulations have also prompted a shift in credit activity back to the formal banking system, and overall credit growth has been sustained well above nominal GDP growth." Reforms have not only slowed the growth of shadow banking, but have also channelled funds back into the traditional banking system.

China has not played a passive role in the standard-setting process at the FSB, according to Zheng Liangshen. Zheng says China utilized its position on the FSB's Standing Committee for Supervisory and Regulatory Cooperation (SCSRC) and made important contributions to the FSB's work on shadow bank reforms. At the SCSRC's meeting in London on January 31, 2012, China proposed a set of principles that should guide the standard-setting process. Importantly, China emphasized that reforms "should respect the judgements and standards of national regulatory authorities based on the economic functions defined by the FSB and reality of different countries" and that reforms take into account the relationship between the shadow banking and traditional banking systems (Zheng 2015, 9). Although China actively participated in the standard setting process, it is not apparent that its preferences substantively diverged from those of industrialized economies. Rather than opposing the FSB's standards, Chinese regulators viewed the standard-setting process as a way "to better understand the dynamic development of regulation of this sector, to better absorb other experiences and to achieve more comprehensive, effective and efficient regulation" (ibid.). This suggests that China maintained the regulatory status quo rather than opposing the content of financial standards at the FSB.

Conclusion

The expanded membership of SSBs after the GFC raised important questions about the extent to which China and other emerging market powers could or would choose to influence the content of financial standards. IPE scholars suggested that China's relative power in SSBs remained limited by its lack of financial market power in the global financial system and by its limited regulatory capacity and expertise relative to advanced industrialized economies. However, the most important aspect of China's role in SSBs after the crisis was that Chinese regulators viewed financial standards as an opportunity for reform. Amidst efforts to liberalize China's financial sector and promote a more effective and efficient domestic financial system, financial standards have provided a road map for reform. An analysis of China's patterns of compliance with Basel III capital adequacy standards and the FSB's shadow banking standards demonstrates that financial standards have largely been consistent with China's domestic political preferences. China has also criticized the standard-setting process for failing to take into account meaningful differences between developed and emerging market financial systems and has advocated for a more flexible approach to financial regulatory standards. Despite this, China has largely complied, even over-complied, with international financial standards and has been an enthusiastic adopter of reform.

China's patterns of compliance suggest that it is likely to remain a status quo political actor in SSBs. The power of China to influence financial standards will depend on a number of factors, including its structural power in the global financial system, the sophistication, experience and expertise of its financial regulators, and the extent to which the financial sector becomes an influential actor in the domestic policy process. More importantly, the extent to which China exerts influence over financial standard setting will be contingent on whether it develops an alternative set of preferences for financial regulation. It remains to be seen whether China will develop its own unique regulatory preferences that would inform a set of rival standards for global finance in the future.

Works Cited

Alexander, Kern, Rahul Dhumale and John Eatwell. 2006. *Global Governance of Financial Systems*. Oxford, UK: Oxford University Press.

Anderlini, Jamal. 2014. "China Debt Tops 250% of National Income." *Financial Times*, July 21. www.ft.com/intl/cms/s/0/895604ac-10d8-11e4-812b-00144feabdc0.html#axzz3Qi2OSW9P.

Asian Banking and Finance. 2014. "Here's the Potential Impact of China's New Trust Regulation on Banks." April 16. http://asianbankingandfinance. net/wholesale-banking/news/heres-potential-impact-chinas-new-trust-regulation-banks.

Asian Development Bank. 2009. "Beyond the Crisis: Regulatory Reform in East Asia." http://aric.adb.org/pdf/aem/jul09/Jul_AEM_special.pdf.

Bach, David. 2010. "Varieties of Cooperation: The Domestic Institutional Roots of Global Governance." *Review of International Studies* 36 (03): 505–28.

Bach, David and Abraham L. Newman. 2010. "Transgovernmental Networks and Domestic Policy Convergence: Evidence from Insider Trading Regulation." *International Organization* 64 (3): 561–89.

Bair, Sheila. 2012. *Bull By the Horns: Fighting to Save Main Street from Wall Street and Wall Street from Itself.* New York, NY: Free Press.

Baker, Andrew. 2009. "Deliberative Equality and the Transgovernmental Politics of the Global Financial Architecture." *Global Governance* 15 (2): 195–218.

Bandeira, Fernanda Martins. 2015. *Emerging Countries and Implementation: Brazil's Experience with Basel's Regulatory Consistency Assessment Programme*. New Thinking and the New G20 Series Paper No. 3. March.   www.cigionline.org/publications/emerging-countries-and-implementation-brazils-experience-basels-regulatory-consistency.

Barboza, David. 2008. "China Plans $586 Billion Stimulus." *The New York Times*, November 9. www.nytimes.com/2008/11/09/business/worldbusiness/09iht-yuan.4.17664544.html?_r=0.

BCBS. 2012. "Regulatory Consistency Assessment Programme: Assessment of Basel III Regulations — China." September. www.bis.org/bcbs/implementation/l2_cn.pdf.

———. 2014. "Regulatory Consistency Assessment Programme: Assessment of Basel III Regulations — European Union." December. www.bis.org/bcbs/publ/d300.pdf.

Bloomberg. 2013. "China Shadow Banking Poses Systemic Risks to Banks, Moody's Says." May 13. www.bloomberg.com/news/2013-05-13/china-shadow-banking-poses-systemic-risks-to-banks-moody-s-says.html.

———. 2014a. "China Tightens Oversight of Trusts as Default Risk Rises." April 14. www.bloomberg.com/news/articles/2014-04-14/china-tightens-oversight-of-trust-companies-document-shows.

———. 2014b. "China Credit Says It Reached Pact on Troubled Product." January 27. www.bloomberg.com/news/2014-01-27/china-credit-trust-says-it-reached-accord-on-troubled-investment.html.

Blustein, Paul. 2013. *Off Balance: The Travails of Institutions That Govern the Global Financial System*. Waterloo, ON: CIGI.

CBRC. 2010. "CRBC Feedback on the BCBS Documents." April 10. www.bis.org/publ/bcbs165/cbrc.pdf.

———. 2011. "The CBRC Responds to Questions of the Press Relating to the *Guiding Opinions on the Implementation of New Regulatory Standards in China's Banking Industry*." www.cbrc.gov.cn/EngdocView.do?docID=20110613FCE47ABD05FA4204FF5BCBC854991A00.

———. 2012. "Decree of China Banking Regulatory Commission." June 7. www.cbrc.gov.cn/EngdocView.do?docID=86EC2D338BB24111B3AC5D7C5C4F1B28.

Chen, Wenxian. 2010. "Basel III and China's Potential Interests: Interview with Ge Qi, the CEO of Bank of China (Britain)." [In Chinese.] *Ennweekly*, April 26. www.ennweekly.com/2010/0426/1554.html.

Chey, Hyoung-kyu. 2015. *Changing Global Financial Governance: International Financial Standards and Emerging Economies since the Global Financial Crisis*. New Thinking and the New G20 Series Paper No. 1. Waterloo, ON: CIGI. February. www.cigionline.org/publications/changing-global-financial-governance-international-financial-standards-and-emerging-eco?.

Chwieroth, J. M. 2008. "Normative Change from Within: The International Monetary Fund's Approach to Capital Account Liberalisation." *International Studies Quarterly* 52 (1): 129–58.

Clifford Chance. 2015. "Shadow Banking and Recent Regulatory Developments in China." January. www.cliffordchance.com/briefings/2015/01/clifford_chance_clientbriefing-shadowbankin.html as of 3 February 2015.

Cohen, Benjamin J. 2008. "The International Monetary System: Diffusion and Ambiguity." *International Affairs* 84 (3): 435–70.

Davis, Bob and Wei, Lingling. 2013. "China's Central Bank Acts on Cash Crunch." *The Wall Street Journal*, June 26. www.wsj.com/articles/SB1000 14241278873236835045785566842205728724.

De Sousa, Mariana Magaldi. 2015. "Financial Inclusion and Global Regulatory Standards: An Empirical Study Across Developing Economies." New Thinking and the New G20 Series Paper No. 7. Waterloo, ON: CIGI. March.   www.cigionline.org/publications/financial-inclusion-and-global-regulatory-standards-empirical-study-across-developing-e.

Drezner, Daniel. 2007. *All Politics Is Global: Explaining International Regimes.* Princeton, NJ: Princeton University Press.

———. 2010. "Afterword: Is Historical Institutionalism Bunk?" *Review of International Political Economy* 17 (4): 791–804.

———. 2014. *The System Worked: How the World Stopped Another Great Depression.* Oxford, UK: Oxford University Press.

European Central Bank and Bank of England. 2014. "The Impaired EU Securitisation Market: Causes, Roadblocks and How to Deal With Them."   www.ecb.europa.eu/pub/pdf/other/ecb-boe_impaired_eu_securitisation_marketen.pdf.

ECB. 2015. "Statistics Data Warehouse: Financial Data." February 5. http://sdw.ecb.europa.eu/reports.do?node=1000004817 .

Fioretos, Orfeo. 2010. "Capitalist Diversity and the International Regulation of Hedge Funds." *Review of International Political Economy* 17 (4): 696–723.

FSB. 2008. "Financial Stability Forum Chairman Supports the G20 Call to Broaden the FSF's Membership." November 13. www.financialstabilityboard.org/wp-content/uploads/pr_081113.pdf.

———. 2012. "Global Shadow Banking Monitoring Report 2012." November 28. www.financialstabilityboard.org/2012/11/r_121118c/.

———. 2013. "Global Shadow Banking Monitoring Report 2013." November 14. www.financialstabilityboard.org/wp-content/uploads/r_131114.pdf.

———. 2014a. "Global Shadow Banking Monitoring Report 2014." November 4. www.financialstabilityboard.org/wp-content/uploads/r_141030.pdf.

———. 2014b. "Transforming Shadow Banking into Resilient Market-based Financing: An Overview of Progress and a Roadmap for 2015." November 14. www.financialstabilityboard.org/wp-content/uploads/Progress-Report-on-Transforming-Shadow-Banking-into-Resilient-Market-Based-Financing.pdf.

G7. 1995. "Halifax Summit Communiqué." June 16. www.g8.utoronto.ca/summit/1995halifax/communique/index.html#strengthen.

G20. 2010. "The Seoul Summit Document." November 12. www.g20.utoronto.ca/2010/g20seoul-doc.html#finsector.

Global Partnership for Financial Inclusion. 2014. "2014 Financial Inclusion Action Plan." September. 2. www.gpfi.org/sites/default/files/documents/2014_g20_financial_inclusion_action_plan.pdf.

Hanemann, Thilo. 2014. "China's International Investment Position: 2014 Update." Rhodium Group, April 9. http://rhg.com/notes/chinas-international-investment-position-2014-update%29.

Helleiner, Eric. 2010. "A Bretton Woods Moment? The 2007–2008 Crisis and the Future of Gobal Finance." *International Affairs* 86 (3): 619–36.

———. 2014. *The Status Quo Crisis: Global Financial Governance After the 2008 Meltdown.* Oxford, UK: Oxford University Press.

Helleiner, Eric and Stefano Pagliari. 2010. "Crisis and the Reform of International Financial Regulation." In *Global Finance in Crisis: The Politics of International Regulatory Change,* edited by Eric Helleiner, Stefano Pagliari and Hubert Zimmerman, 1–18. London, UK: Routledge.

———. 2011. "The End of an Era in International Financial Regulation? A Postcrisis Research Agenda." *International Organization* 65 (Winter): 169–200.

Ikenberry, John. 2008. "Rise of China and the Future of the West: Can the Liberal System Survive?" *Foreign Affairs* 87: 23.

IMF. 2009. "The Financial Sector Assessment Program After Ten Years: Experience and Reforms for the Next Decade." August 28. www.imf.org/external/np/pp/eng/2009/082809B.pdf.

———. 2011. "People's Republic of China: Financial Stability Assessment." November. www.imf.org/external/pubs/ft/scr/2011/cr11321.pdf.

———. 2012. "People's Republic of China: Detailed Assessment Report: IOSCO Objectives and Principles of Securities Regulation." April. www.imf.org/external/pubs/ft/scr/2012/cr1280.pdf.

———. 2014. "Shadow Banking Around the Globe: How Large, and How Risk?" www.imf.org/external/pubs/ft/gfsr/2014/02/pdf/c2.pdf.

Kapstein, Ethan. 1989. "Resolving the Regulator's Dilemma: International Coordination of Banking Regulations." *International Organization* 43 (2): 323–47.

———. 1992. "Between Power and Purpose: Central Bankers and the Politics of Regulatory Convergence." *International Organization* 46 (1): 265–87.

Kempthorne, David. 2013. "Governing International Securities Markets: IOSCO and the Politics of International Securities Standards." Ph.D. dissertation, University of Waterloo.

Knaack, Peter. 2015. "From Laggard to Primus — Why Is China Exceeding Global Banking Standards?" Paper Prepared for the Annual Meeting of the International Studies Association, February 18–21.

KPMG. 2009. "China Board Room Update: Regulatory Developments." January. www.kpmg.com/CN/en/IssuesAndInsights/ArticlesPublications/ Newsletters/China-boardroom-update/Documents/China-boardroom-update-0901-01.pdf.

Lane, Philip. 2012. "Financial Globlisation and the Crisis." BIS Working Papers: No. 397. December. www.bis.org/publ/work397.pdf.

Luo, Ping. 2008. "Enhancing Risk Management and Governance in the Region's Banking System to Implement Basel II and to Meet Contemporary Risks and Challenges Arising from the Global Banking System." Presentation given at APEC summit, December 8–12. www.apec.org.au/docs/08_ TP_BRM/2.1_Luo.pdf.

Moody's. 2015. "China's Shadow Banking Growth Slows on Regulatory Tightening, But New Areas Emerge." January 22. www.moodys. com/research/Moodys-Chinas-shadow-banking-growth-slows-on-regulatory-tightening-but--PR_316856.

Oatley, Thomas and Robert Nabors. 1998. "Redistributive Cooperation: Market Failure, Wealth Transfers, and the Basle Accord." *International Organization* 52 (1): 35–54.

Parker, James. 2013. "China Faces Cash Crunch Again." *The Diplomat*, December 23. http://thediplomat.com/2013/12/china-faces-cash-crunch-again/.

———. 2014. "China's Shadow Banking Challenge." *The Diplomat*, January 20. http://thediplomat.com/2014/01/chinas-shadow-banking-challenge/?allpages=yes.

PBoC. 2013. "Financial Stability Report 2013: Financial Stability Analysis Group of the People's Bank of China." www.pbc.gov.cn/image_public/UserFiles/english/upload/File/%E4%B8%AD%E5%9B%BD%E9%87%91%E8%9E%8D%E7%A8%B3%E5%AE%9A%E6%8A%A5%E5%91%8A2013%EF%BC%88%20E8%8B%B1%E6%96%87%E7%89%88%20EF%BC%89.pdf.

Porter, Tony. 2001. "The Democratic Deficit in the Institutional Arrangements for Regulating Global Finance." *Global Governance* 7 (4): 427–39.

———. 2005a. *Globalization and Finance*. Cambridge, UK: Polity Press.

———. 2005b. "Private Authority, Technical Authority, and the Globalization of Accounting Standards." *Business and Politics* 7 (3): 1–30.

Posner, Elliot. 2009. "Making Rules for Global Finance: Transatlantic Regulatory Cooperation at the Turn of the Millennium." *International Organization* 63 (4): 665–99.

Rabinovitch, Simon. 2013. "China to Tighten Shadow Banking Rules." *Financial Times*, February 26. www.ft.com/intl/cms/s/0/223777b6-7fec-11e2-adbd-00144feabdc0.html#axzz3Q2MzaHlq.

Reuters. 2014a. "China's ICBC Says Won't Compensate Investors in Troubled Shadow Banking Product." January 14. www.reuters.com/article/2014/01/16/china-icbc-idUSL3N0KQ1MT20140116.

———. 2014b. "China's ICBC Says Will Help Repay Investors in Troubled Shadow Banking Scheme." January 23. www.reuters.com/article/2014/01/24/us-china-trust-idUSBREA0N07Q20140124.

———. 2015a. "Update 1: Global Bank Watchdog to Review Rule on Zero-Risk Weighting for Sovereign Debt." January 23. http://uk.reuters.com/article/2015/01/23/basel-sovereign-regulations-idUKL6N0V22ZO20150123.

———. 2015b. "Update — China Central Bank Tightens Loan, Deposit Measurement as Shadow Banking Surges." January 15. www.reuters.com/article/2015/01/15/china-economy-pboc-lending-idUSL3N0UU27020150115.

Rodrik, Dani. 2009. "A Plan B for Global Finance." *The Economist*, March 12.

Simmons, Beth. 2001. "The International Politics of Harmonization: The Case of Capital Market Regulation." *International Organization* 55 (3): 589–620.

Singer, David Andrew. 2007. *Regulating Capital: Setting Standards for the International Financial System*. Ithaca, NY: Cornell University Press.

Sommer, A. A., Jr. 1996. "IOSCO: Its Mission and Achievement." *Northwest Journal of International Law and Business* 17 (1): 15–29.

Tsingou, Eleni. 2014. "Club Governance and the Making of Global Financial Rules." *Review of International Political Economy* 19 (3): 1–32.

US Department of Commerce. 2014. "International Data: International Transactions, International Services, and International Investment Position Tables." December 30. www.bea.gov/ iTable/iTable.cfm?ReqID=62&step=1#reqid=62&step=6&isuri= 1&6210=5&6200=144.

Wade, Robert. 2008. "A New Global Financial Architecture?" *New Left Review* 46: 113–29.

Walter, Andrew. 2008. *Governing Finance: East Asia's Adoption of International Standards*. Ithaca, NY: Cornell University Press.

———. 2010. "Chinese Attitudes Towards Global Financial Regulatory Co-operation: Revisionist or Status Quo?" In *Global Finance in Crisis: The Politics of International Regulatory Change*, edited by Eric Helleiner, Stefano Pagliari and Hubert Zimmerman, 153–169. London, UK: Routledge.

———. 2015. *Emerging Countries and Basel III: Why Is Engagement Still Low?* New Thinking and the New G20 Series Paper No. 4. Waterloo, ON: CIGI. March. www.cigionline.org/publications/emerging-countries-and-basel-iii-why-engagement-still-low.

Walter, Carl E. and Fraser J. T. Howie. 2014. "China's Disappearing Bad Loans." *Wall Street Journal*, September 4. www.wsj.com/articles/chinas-disappearing-bad-loans-1409845549.

Wen, Yi and Maria Arias. 2014. "How Risky Is China's Shadow Banking System?" The Federal Reserve Bank of St. Louis, March 17. www.stlouisfed.org/on-the-economy/2014/march/how-risky-is-chinas-shadow-banking-system.

Wood, Duncan. 2005. *Governing Global Banking: The Basel Committee and the Politics of Financial Globalisation*. Aldershot, UK: Ashgate.

Xinhuanet. 2012. "China Unveils Financial Reform Plan for 12th Five-Year Plan Period." September 24. http://news.xinhuanet.com/english/indepth/2012-09/24/c_131900170.htm.

Zheng, Liangsheng. 2015. *The Shadow Banking System of China and International Regulatory Cooperation*. New Thinking and the New G20 Series Paper No. 6. Waterloo, ON: CIGI. March. www.cigionline.org/publications/shadow-banking-system-of-china-and-international-regulatory-cooperation.

Zhu, Haibin, Grace Ng and Lu Jiang. 2013. "Economic Research Note: Shadow Banking in China." May 3. https://markets.jpmorgan.com/research/EmailPubServlet?action=open&hashcode=bu8r06sj&doc=GPS-1114535-0.pdf.

13

China's Engagement in Minilateral Financial Cooperation: Motivations and Implications

Hongying Wang

n the spring of 2015, the world had its eyes fixed on a new development bank initiated by China — the Asian Infrastructure Investment Bank (AIIB). China signed a memorandum of understanding with 20 other Asian countries in October 2014 to establish the bank to finance infrastructure in the region. At first, it seemed to be an innocuous attempt to meet the region's huge infrastructure needs. However, as the deadline of March 31, 2015 approached for countries to apply for founding membership, the AIIB quickly gained momentum. Despite US warnings against it, the United Kingdom declared it would join the China-led bank. In the days and weeks that followed, major economies in Europe and elsewhere stampeded to join the AIIB, leaving the United States in a state of shock and embarrassment. Pundits and reporters across the globe quickly portrayed the establishment of the AIIB as a symbol of the emergence of a new international financial/economic order (see, for example, Chhibber 2015; Zhang Zhongkai 2015) and of a power shift from a declining United States to a rising China (see, for example, Merry 2015; Shen 2015).

Whether the establishment of the AIIB constituted a Bretton Woods moment or a power shift from the United States to China is questionable. It did, however, highlight a more activist foreign financial policy on the part of China. The AIIB came at the heels of the New Development Bank (NDB) and the Contingent Reserve Arrangement (CRA), both of which were created by China and the other BRICS countries — Brazil, Russia, India and South Africa — in July 2014. Together they demonstrate China's growing enthusiasm toward and capacity for minilateral financial cooperation. This chapter analyzes this new phenomenon in Chinese foreign policy. After a brief review of the background of this development, the bulk of the chapter examines China's motivations in engaging in minilateral financial cooperation and explores the implications of this development for the existing framework of global financial governance as well as for China's own economic development.

Background

In the early 1990s, after the Tiananmen Square incident and in the midst of the fall of Communist governments in Eastern Europe, the Chinese government faced serious challenges at home and abroad. Chinese leader Deng Xiaoping prescribed the foreign policy strategy of *taoguang yanghui, yousuo zuowei* (keeping a low profile while trying to accomplish something). What he meant was that China should work hard to develop its economy rather than seek international leadership, and that it should make a difference in international affairs as permitted by its capabilities (Wang 2011a). For years, Chinese foreign policy followed the first half of Deng's formulation closely, avoiding getting deeply involved in or taking a strong position on international issues outside the immediate national interests of China. China's participation in various aspects of global governance lagged behind its growing economic capabilities (Wang and French 2013).

But in the last few years, Chinese policy makers and analysts have begun to rethink the virtue and value of keeping a low profile (Chen and Wang 2011). Chinese foreign policy has shown greater assertiveness on some issues, particularly in its approach to territorial disputes with neighbouring countries (Johnston 2013). China has also become more active in participating in global economic governance (Wang and French 2014). There is a notable shift in China's conduct of foreign policy from "keeping a low profile" to "trying to accomplish something." Its growing engagement in financial minilateralism is part of this overall trend.

Minilateralism refers to the gathering of a subgroup of countries within or outside a multilateral institution to solve a problem when the multilateral institution is unable to reach agreements among its members. It has been a salient trend in economic diplomacy in recent years (Naim 2009; Brummer 2014). For instance, as the Doha Round of negotiation under the World Trade Organization remains too stagnant to reach a new multilateral trade agreement, different groups of countries have come together to push for liberalization among themselves. The Trans-Pacific Partnership (TPP) and the Transatlantic Trade and Investment Partnership (TTIP) are prominent examples.[1]

Financial minilateralism is not new. It includes various sub-global financial cooperation schemes such as the Group of Seven and the Group of Twenty (G20). Nor is it unprecedented in Chinese foreign economic policy. In 2000, China joined neighbouring countries in launching the Chiang Mai Initiative (CMI), a series of bilateral currency swaps to provide support for countries faced with liquidity crises. China was also a major force behind the Asia Bond Market Initiative (ABMI) in 2002, which aimed to promote regional bond market development. Later, China played an important role in expanding the CMI, turning the bilateral swaps into multilateral arrangements known as Chiang Mai Initiative Multilateralized (CMIM). Today, CMIM is a regional pool of foreign reserves of US$240 billion.

However, within the last year, China's engagement in minilateral financial cooperation has accelerated, as shown by the establishment of the NDB, the CRA and the AIIB. The NDB, with an initial subscribed capital of US$50 billion and authorized capital of US$100 billion, aims to mobilize resources to invest in infrastructure and sustainable development projects in member countries and other developing countries. The CRA, with a reserve pool of US$100 billion, is designed to help members deal with short-term balance-of-payment pressures and reduce financial instability caused by liquidity problems. The AIIB, according to China's proposal, will have an initial subscribed capital of US$50 billion and authorized capital of US$100 billion and will focus on supporting the development of infrastructure in Asia first.

Compared with the earlier regional financial arrangements — the CMI, ABMI and CMIM, the more recent schemes of minilateral financial cooperation are far more China-centred and China-dominated. What are China's motivations for joining and, more recently, taking a lead in minilateral financial cooperation? What are the implications of the recent minilateral initiatives? The remainder of this chapter attempts to shed light on these questions.

---

1   Some scholars use the term "plurilateralism" to refer to subgroup cooperation (see, for example, Baker 2000; Cerny 1993; Reich 1997). Chinese scholars have used the terms *xiao duobian*, *shaobian* or *zhubian* to refer to "minilateral."

China's Motivations

Reforming Multilateral Financial Institutions

China and other developing countries have often criticized the existing international financial system as being Western-dominated and unfair to developing countries. In particular, they have demanded that multilateral financial institutions give greater voice to the Global South. Western countries have taken some steps in accommodating this demand. The G20, which consists of the largest industrialized countries and a number of dynamic emerging economies, was established in 1999 after the Asian financial crisis. Following the global financial crisis of 2008, these meetings, which had consisted only of finance ministers and central bank governors, were elevated to include state leaders. Although the agenda of these summits has expanded to include more issues, economic cooperation and financial reform remain the major focus. Meanwhile, the World Bank and the International Monetary Fund (IMF) introduced "voice reform" to increase the representation of developing countries in accordance to their growing weight in the world economy. In 2010, agreements were reached at both institutions to shift votes from the developed to the developing countries, in particular to the emerging economies.

However, these reforms did not go very far and have fallen short of the expectations of the international community. The first few G20 summits achieved substantive achievements, including coordinated stimulus packages in response to the global economic crisis and agreements on strengthening financial regulations. However, the more recent meetings have been characterized by disagreements and gridlock. Some worry about the G20's loss of momentum as a forum of global economic governance. At the World Bank and the IMF, the "voice reform" has not changed the imbalance of influence between the developed and the developing countries. The announced shift in voting power at the World Bank has been quite small and the actual shift has been even smaller, leaving developing countries, including China, seriously under-represented (Vestergaard and Wade 2013). At the IMF, the reallocation of votes has been held up by the United States.

China and other emerging economies have been disappointed at the slow pace of reform at multilateral financial institutions. On the one hand, Chinese officials have continued to call for these institutions to carry out their promise of greater inclusiveness and better representation of developing countries (see, for example, Zhou 2014). On the other hand, they see the creation of alternative institutions as a way to apply "reverse pressure" (*daobi*) on these institutions to act (Lu 2013; Zhu 2014). A central theme in the official and popular Chinese discourse is to use minilateral initiatives as leverage to increase China's "right to speak" (*huayu quan*) in global institutions.

For instance, at a press conference in July 2014, the spokesperson of the People's Bank of China (PBoC) stated that the creation of the CRA is a milestone — it provides a platform for BRICS countries to participate in global economic governance and increase their influence and voice (Xinhua 2014a). At the ASEAN [Association of Southeast Asian Nations] Plus Three (APT) foreign ministers' meeting in August 2014, the Chinese foreign minister, Wang Yi, pointed out that by implementing plans for an Asian financing system, monetary stability system and credit system, Asian countries will enhance their voice in global financial governance (Xinhua 2014b). Similar comments by policy analysts about the NDB, the CRA and the AIIB permeate Chinese media (see, for example, Xu 2014; Ding 2014; Li 2015).

Besides its active role in regional and BRICS financial cooperation, China is also a member of a number of other international financial groups, such as the G20, the Financial Stability Board and the Bank for International Settlements. The PBoC's deputy governor, Yi Gang (2011), argues that China's participation in these financial institutions has "clearly improved China's influence and voice on international financial affairs." At this stage, China has not offered a detailed blueprint of what a new framework of global financial governance might look like, except that it will give greater weight to the developing countries, especially the emerging economies, and will help rebalance the political influence between the Global North and Global South. The power redistribution, presumably, will lead multilateral financial institutions to adopt more favourable policies toward the developing countries.

Providing "Public Goods"

Another goal of China's participation in financial minilateralism is to provide a variety of "public goods," which are important to the region and developing countries, but are thus far undersupplied.[2] At the regional level, the CMI/CMIM, ABMI and AIIB are designed to provide common financial security and encourage common economic development. The CMI and CMIM came about after the Asian financial crisis in the late 1990s. China and its neighbours

---

2   The term "public goods" is used loosely here to refer to goods that tend to benefit more than one country. Some of the goods provided by the financial cooperation initiatives are non-excludable and non-rivalrous (for example, prevention of financial crisis), while others do not meet these criteria (for example, infrastructure loans). The latter may be more accurately described as "club goods" (Buchanan 1965).

were not only shocked by the devastating economic and political consequences of the financial crisis across the region, but were also dismayed by the slow and inadequate assistance provided by the IMF to Asian economies struggling with balance-of-payment problems (Higgot 1998; Wade and Veneroso 1998). Although China initially rejected the Japanese proposal of an Asian Monetary Fund in 1997, it welcomed the establishment of the CMI in 2000, which had a much more limited scope of cooperation. Chinese leaders had by then recognized that regional cooperation was necessary for regional as well as national financial security and economic growth in the long run (Jiang 2010). Over the next few years, China actively promoted the expansion of the CMI, which facilitated its multilateralization in 2010.

In addition to the CMI and CMIM, another important step of regional financial cooperation was the launch of the ABMI by the APT in 2002. For years previously, due to the poor development of bond markets locally, East Asian countries channelled their savings into Western bond markets while borrowing heavily from international banks. Many analysts inside and outside the region pointed out that such an approach led to a waste of resources for East Asia. It also created the problem of "double mismatch," i.e., borrowing in dollars in the short term for long-term projects that generate revenues in local currencies. This was, in fact, a main cause of the Asian financial crisis. The ABMI seeks to develop regional bond markets in order to better utilize the region's own financial resources and reduce its dependence on Western markets and associated exchange rate risks.

The AIIB is an attempt to fill a glaring gap in infrastructure financing in the region. According to a study by the Asian Development Bank (ADB), between 2010 and 2020, Asia needs US$8 trillion to finance its infrastructure development (ADB and ADBI 2009). A more recent study by HSBC estimates infrastructure development in the region will require US$11 trillion between 2015 and 2030 (French 2014). While infrastructure development is essential for long-term economic growth, the massive size of the projects and the slow returns make such investment unattractive to most private investors. Some of the countries — including China — have accumulated sufficient public funds to support infrastructure development, but many others are not so fortunate. Moreover, in the last few decades, developed country donors and multilateral development banks have steadily reduced their financing of infrastructure projects in the developing world (Chin 2012). There is a dire need for alternative sources of financing in this area. Chinese officials point out that the World Bank and the ADB have focused their attention on poverty reduction and provided very limited investment in infrastructure. They claim that the new bank will help developing countries in the region, in particular low-income countries, to meet their infrastructure financing needs (Xinhua 2014c). A Chinese scholar noted, "as China's economic power grows, it's a natural process for China to play a bigger role in the region and to give more support to other countries. Now China has the ability to show the real money" (Bloomberg 2014). Like the AIIB, the NDB offers an alternative source of infrastructure financing for the emerging economies and other developing countries.

Similar to the CMI/CMIM, the CRA provides an additional financial safety net for BRICS countries in times of liquidity crises. According to Chinese government officials, the CRA draws from the successful experience of the CMIM (Xinhua 2014a). If the CMIM came out of lessons of the Asian financial crisis, the CRA may, in some ways, be a reaction to the global financial crisis and the more recent European debt crisis. In the aftermath of the Asian crisis, the IMF was slow and arrogant in its response to Asian countries, prompting Asia to develop self-help mechanisms. In contrast, following the European debt crisis, the IMF provided generous support for Greece by bending its own lending rules.[3] Although BRICS leaders have not explicitly related the creation of the CRA with the apparent Western bias of the IMF, such a connection seems quite plausible. Chinese officials state that the CRA is a helpful new mechanism to protect the financial stability of other emerging economies and indirectly serve the economic interests of China (ibid.).

Promoting China's Interests and Influence

Besides the "reverse pressure" on reform of the global financial institutions and the provision of undersupplied public goods for developing countries, another goal of Chinese initiatives in minilateral financial cooperation is to more directly promote Chinese economic interests and political influence.

On the development-financing front, the NDB and AIIB both aim to invest in infrastructure projects such as energy and transportation, in particular in developing countries. This is consistent with China's economic priorities. In the last decade or so, China's own development bank and export-import (Ex-Im) bank have poured large sums of money into building power plants, railways, highways, ports and airports in Africa and Latin America, as well as Asia (Bräutigam and Gallagher 2014). In 2013, the Chinese government unveiled

---

3   In 2010, in response to the euro-zone debt crisis, the IMF introduced "systemic exemption" to its existing lending framework. The exemption allowed some countries to receive financing even if the IMF could not confirm that their debt was sustainable with high probability, as was the case with Greece. The rationale used for the exemption was to prevent contagion from Greece that would cause systemic instability in Europe and beyond. Observers in China and elsewhere view the exemption as inequitable because countries outside major currency unions are unlikely to qualify for it (House, Wang and Xafa 2014; Wang 2014a).

its vision of "One Belt and One Road," a transnational economic development network centred around China. The Silk Road Economic Belt extends from China westward through Central Asia to Europe. The Maritime Silk Road will reach southward across the Indian Ocean to Africa before turning north to meet the land-based Silk Road. The Chinese government is seeking to build networks of highways and high-speed rail to link the Chinese economy with the economies along these paths and expand Chinese trade and investment in these regions (Sun 2014; Ye 2014). With China playing a leading role in both the NDB and the AIIB, it is likely to direct financial resources to such projects in the future, promoting China's growing economic interests overseas.

Infrastructure building is an area where China has both strong competitive advantages and excess capacities. The NDB and the AIIB will serve China's commercial interests in these areas. Chinese leaders have often spoken of China's desire to share its success in infrastructure development with other developing countries to help them grow; policy analysts and commentators have stressed the benefits for China in this "sharing." Because of their experience and competitiveness, Chinese companies are likely to gain a large portion of the contracted work from these infrastructure projects. In fact, shortly after Chinese President Xi Jinping announced the proposal for the AIIB, Chinese companies expressed great expectations for "a feast" of opportunities (*China Daily* 2013). Overseas projects will provide much-needed outlets for the built-up capacity in China. Officials and analysts alike have pointed to China's overcapacity in infrastructure development. As an influential Chinese commentator put it, "This structural problem cannot be solved merely by increasing domestic demand; rather, China must look to the overseas markets to channel this overcapacity" (Hu 2013).

The NDB and the AIIB can also be instruments of China's currency policy in the short and longer term. In the short run, they could help reduce China's large, unprofitable holdings of reserves. In the last decade, the management of the rapidly increasing foreign reserves has been a growing challenge for the Chinese government. Thus far, most of the reserves are invested in US Treasury securities (valued at US$1.24 trillion in January 2015) with low returns (see chapter 7 of this volume). Chinese analysts believe that investment in infrastructure projects abroad could offer a partial solution to this problem (see, for example, Tang 2014). In the long run, the NDB and the AIIB could contribute to the internationalization of the renminbi (RMB). Although the initial contribution from all member countries to these banks is to be made in US dollars, the hope is that, over time, the banks will use more and more local currencies in their lending and thus promote the internationalization of local currencies, including the RMB. This will, in turn, reduce the exchange rate risks for trade and investment among the emerging economies (Xinhua 2014d).

On the monetary side, the CMIM and the CRA can serve China's economic interests and political influence in several ways. First, China recognizes that regional and global financial stability is vital for China's own economic growth. The Asian financial crisis and the global financial crisis have driven home the sensitivity of Chinese foreign trade and investment to financial upheavals abroad. Although China has built up vast foreign reserves for self-assurance, the Chinese government sees regional (and bilateral) swaps as an extra safety net for other countries that are less capable of self-protection (Wang and Lu 2012).

Second, in ways parallel to the NDB and the AIIB, the CMIM and the CRA can help facilitate the adoption of the Chinese currency in the region and globally. Under the CMIM framework and elsewhere, China has signed a large number of currency swap agreements with other countries and administrative regions in Asia and elsewhere. Some of these are based on US dollars, but more and more of them are based on local currencies. Since 2008, China has signed or renewed 35 local currency swaps, totalling RMB 2.8 trillion (about US$440 billion).[4] Chinese officials and analysts view these arrangements as conducive to the cross-border use of RMB for trade and investment. The internationalization of the RMB, in turn, will facilitate China's trade relations with other countries and support Chinese companies' "going out" strategy (ibid.).

In addition to these economic benefits, China's involvement in minilateral financial cooperation is driven by potential political gains. In reviewing China's financial cooperation with regional financial institutions in Asia, Africa, Latin America and the Caribbean, PBoC Deputy Governor Yi Gang (2011) stated explicitly that these financial initiatives are "coordinated with the country's overall foreign policy strategy."

In fact, the economic calculations are likely to be secondary to political considerations. After all, China has its own development bank and Ex-Im bank, which function in ways not dissimilar to the NDB and the AIIB when it comes to promoting Chinese economic interests abroad. About five years ago, these two Chinese banks overtook the World Bank in their magnitude of lending to developing countries. And China's own foreign reserves, at nearly US$4 trillion, dwarf both the CMIM and the CRA. When it comes to fending off the direct impact of financial crises on the Chinese economy, it is unlikely that China will need to resort to borrowing from minilateral or multilateral institutions.

---

4   Calculated from data provided by the PBoC (www.pbc.gov.cn:8080/publish/ huobizhengceersi/3135/index_2.html).

China's initiatives with regard to these and other financial institutions should be understood as part of the overall diplomatic strategy to improve China's global image and political influence. For instance, China's initial reaction to Asian regional financial cooperation was quite negative. But when it became clear that Southeast Asian countries supported some form of financial cooperation after the Asian financial crisis, Chinese policy makers changed their minds. They calculated that some kind of cooperative arrangement was going to happen with or without China's participation. China should thus support the CMI and in doing so improve its image as a responsible and reliable partner (Jiang 2010). More recently, China's continued financial cooperation with its neighbours and active engagement with other BRICS countries on financial matters are also, in part, motivated by its desire to be seen as a "responsible great power" (Huang, Tan and Lei 2013).

Minilateral financial cooperation can also potentially take some of the edge off another aspect of China's more activist foreign policy, i.e., its "going out" strategy. Although the strategy was declared in the late 1990s, it was not until the last several years that China dramatically increased its investment in energy and natural resource-rich countries around the world, in particular in developing countries in Africa and Latin America. Not surprisingly, this has generated concern and alarm from various corners, ranging from governments concerned about China's geopolitical gains to civil society groups disturbed by China's disregard for human rights and the environment. By using minilateral institutions and initiatives, China may be able to ameliorate such negative reactions. Japanese commentators seem to be particularly cynical about the AIIB, arguing it is essentially a Chinese bank dressed up as a multilateral bank, serving China's interests (*Asahi Shimbun* 2014a; 2014b). Chinese officials have made subtle references to the pacifying effect of the bank. China's minister of finance suggested that it could ease the geopolitical tension in East Asia and facilitate joint development of the resources of the East and South China Sea (Lou 2014). Some commentators see the AIIB as a conscious effort by China to step back from its aggressive bilateral economic initiatives, reducing its leverage in exchange for legitimacy (Hung 2015).

Last, but not least, these minilateral financial arrangements provide grounds for China to test its leadership skills. As a rapidly rising power, China faces a steep learning curve on how to turn its new economic weight into legitimate and effective leadership. The development banks and the reserve pools China has helped create promise to provide resources and protection for poorer and more vulnerable countries. In contributing to these institutions, China hopes not only to serve its own broader economic interests, but also to cultivate its political standing (Li 2012).

Compared with the earlier regional financial arrangements (such as the CMI/ CMIM and ABMI), the more recent minilateral schemes (such as the NDB, the CRA and the AIIB), are clearly more China-centred and China-dominated. In earlier regional financial cooperation, China faced a strong competitor in Japan. For instance, the ABMI's initial commitment amounts to a reserve of US\$120 billion, with China and Japan each contributing US\$38.4 billion. In the case of the Credit Guarantee and Investment Facility, an important component of the ABMI, out of the total of US\$700 million, China pledged to contribute US\$200 million, the same as Japan.

In contrast, in the BRICS, China's economy is head and shoulders above the other members (see Table 1): its GDP is much larger than the combined GDP of Brazil, Russia, India and South Africa; its economic growth has been much faster than the other four countries; and its foreign reserves dwarf the combined amount of the other four countries. Within the CRA, China is by far the largest contributor, making up US\$41 billion of the total pool of US\$100 billion and enjoying close to 40 percent of the voting power. As for the NDB, its headquarters will be in Shanghai, which gives China both tangible and intangible advantages in the new bank. In the case of the AIIB, China is the original proponent, has by far the largest shares in the bank, and Beijing will be home to its headquarters.

Table 1: BRICS Economic Indicators (2013)

Country	Brazil	Russia	India	China	South Africa
GDP (US\$ billion)	2,246	2,097	1,877	9,240	351
Economic growth rate (%)	2.5	1.3	5.0	7.7	1.9
Foreign reserves (US\$ billion)	358.8	509.7	289.1	3880.4	49.7

Source: World Bank data.

It is interesting to note that even as China takes on a prominent role in minilateral financial cooperation, Chinese officials and scholars are careful to point out it is not just another great power like the others preceeding it. In their discussions of BRICS cooperation, there is apparent tension between the claim that China is an equal partner and the suggestion that China should take on the responsibility to guide and lead the group (see, for example, Lu 2013). While China's position in the CRA is overwhelming, its approach to the NDB is more egalitarian. Given China's massive financial resources, it could easily have contributed much more capital than the US\$10 billion allocated to each member country and thus have gained greater influence. It has refrained from doing so as a concession to the other member countries (Chen 2014). With regard to the AIIB, in the early days China was said to take 50 percent of the shares. But in response to concerns of other countries over China's dominance, Chinese officials indicated that China could reduce its shares (Xinhua 2014e). In the end, when the bank's Articles of Agreement were signed in June 2015 China only took about 30 percent of the stakes (Zheng 2015). The official rhetoric in China emphasizes that even as China makes the transition from a ruler-taker to a rule-maker, its leadership is fundamentally different from that of the traditional great powers. China's leadership is consultative rather than hegemonic; it is open and inclusive rather than dictatorial (Xia 2015). Time will tell if China's proclamation is indeed mirrored in its action.

Implications of China's Engagement in Financial Minilateralism

Implications for Global Financial Governance

Do China's minilateral financial initiatives threaten the exiting framework of global financial governance? This is a question on the minds of many. Formally, the World Bank and the IMF have politely applauded the NDB, the CRA and the AIIB. At the same time, anxiety about the newer initiatives is easy to discern just below the surface of Western media. Although not often spoken about openly, there are serious concerns that these new institutions undermine the liberal international economic order by providing alternatives to the existing multilateral financial institutions, such as the World Bank and the IMF, and thus weakening the latter's leverage on borrowing countries (see, for example, Von Sant 2014). In the case of the AIIB, the US government actively sought to discourage other countries from joining the China-led bank. The official justification is that the new infrastructure investment bank may not follow good governance practices or international labour or environmental standards (Perlez 2014). But the unstated concern is really about China's challenge to the US-led international order. In early April 2015, following the avalanche of countries applying to join the AIIB despite US opposition, former US Treasury Secretary Larry Summers (2015) commented: "This past month may be remembered as the moment the United States lost its role as the underwriter of the global economic system."

Chinese policy makers and analysts are well aware that many see China's minilateral financial initiatives as a threat to the existing multilateral financial system. They have gone out of their way to calm such fears, emphasizing that these new institutions complement the existing institutions and fill a gap in their operations (see, for example, Lu 2013; Zhu 2014; Ministry of Finance of the PRC 2014). In April 2015 Chinese Premier Li Keqiang held an interview with the *Financial Times*, in which he strongly emphasized China's continued commitment to the existing global financial order, with special reference to the AIIB as a supplement to the current international financial system (Barber, Pilling and Anderlini 2015).

Will China's financial minilateralism threaten the existing framework of global financial governance? To begin with, it is important to put the minilateral arrangements in perspective. Table 2 indicates that in terms of subscribed capital, the CMIM and the CRA are no match for the IMF, and the AIIB and the NDB are considerably smaller than the World Bank and even the ADB. Moreover, the traditional multilateral financial institutions enjoy higher credit ratings and are thus able to raise funds in the international capital market more easily and cheaply than the new minilateral institutions. Some argue the new minilateral institutions are simply not strong enough to undercut the Bretton Woods institutions and system (see, for example, Steil 2014).

Table 2: Minilateral Institutions in Comparative Perspective

Institution	CMIM	CRA	IMF	
Total capital (US$ billion)	240	100	327 (quota) 515 (new arrangement to borrow)	
Institution	AIIB	NDB	World Bank	ADB
Subscribed capital (US$ billion)	50	50	223.2	162.2

Source: World Bank data.

Beyond that, the foundation of some of these new arrangements may be precarious. For instance, the NDB and the CRA are based on cooperation among the BRICS. But BRICS countries are very different from one another. Besides the issue of size mentioned above, they have very different political systems and economic interests. Brazil, India and South Africa are democratic countries, whereas China and Russia are authoritarian states. Brazil, Russia and South Africa are major exporters of commodities, whereas China and India are large importers. Their GDP per capita also varies from about US$4,000 in India to about US$24,000 (using purchasing power parity) in Russia. There may simply not be enough cohesion among these countries to sustain strong cooperation (O'Neill 2013; Runde 2014).

It is too early to draw any definitive conclusion about the impact of the new minilateral financial institutions on the current global financial order. The governance structure and rules of operation of the NDB, CRA and AIIB have not had a chance to be fully implemented. We have had more time to observe the regional institutions China has participated in. From what we can see so far, the new institutions seem to be quite closely tied to the Bretton Woods system. For instance, under the CMIM, 70 percent of the lending to countries facing liquidity problems is linked to the IMF programs for those countries, i.e., they must have an on-track arrangement with the IMF that involves a commitment by the IMF to provide financing to them and a promise by the borrowing countries to comply with the terms and conditions of the arrangement. It is questionable how useful the non-IMF-linked portions (30 percent) of the fund can be. A telling case was that during the global financial crisis, Asian countries faced with liquidity problems did not resort to the CMI/CMIM, but rather sought assistance through bilateral swaps with the United States and other countries. The more recently created CRA has adopted the same IMF link.

In the case of the AIIB, which has been more controversial than the NDB and CRA, the Chinese officials in charge of its creation have bent over backwards to emphasize that the new bank will "play by the rules." China's Foreign Ministry spokesman stated: "the AIIB will follow the principles of openness, inclusiveness, transparency, responsibility and fairness in its governance structure and operational policies" (Ministry of Foreign Affairs 2015). Indeed, according to the official statement of the AIIB (2015a), "its modus operandi will be lean, clean and green: lean, with a small efficient management team and highly skilled staff; clean, an ethical organization with zero tolerance for corruption; and green, an institution built on respect for the environment." Recent news about staff recruitment for the AIIB indicates China aims to bring on board individuals with strong experience in multilateral financial organizations, prompting some observers to conclude that China really wants to build the new bank after the prevailing international model (Zhang Han 2015). The Articles of Agreement specifically state that the new bank will "promote regional cooperation and partnership in addressing development challenges by working in close collaboration with other multilateral and bilateral development institutions" (AIIB 2015b).

Aside from these minilateral financial initiatives, there are other signs that China is not ready to break away from the Bretton Woods system. This should not be surprising given the benefits China has derived from the existing economic order and the gradual convergence of its interest toward that of the dominant Western powers. For instance, in recent years, China has become a major international creditor, making loans to other countries in the world. Contrary to widely shared criticism of the IMF, China's central bank governor has spoken favourably about the Fund's conditionality as a way to discipline countries borrowing internationally (Zhou 2012). On various financial regulatory issues,

China has also been eager to meet the standards set by international agencies dominated by Western countries (see chapter 12 of this volume).

Implications for China

On the surface, China's engagement in minilateral financial arrangements is indicative of a more confident and influential financial power. The establishment of the AIIB in particular has been touted as a triumph for China, just as it has been a diplomatic fiasco for the United States, demonstrating a decline in American influence over other countries. However, these initiatives reflect deep-rooted problems in China and may well delay their timely solution.

China's increasingly activist foreign economic policy since the early 2000s has been driven by a variety of economic and political considerations. Chief among the economic motives are the desire to ensure access to energy and raw materials, to export China's overcapacity and to improve the financial performance of China's external assets. All of these economic necessities are closely related to China's investment- and export-dependent economic growth model.

A large portion of China's energy consumption is investment-driven, in particular investment in manufacturing (Fu et al. 2014). China's demand for resource commodities in recent decades has been in large part the result of its massive exports of manufactured goods (Roberts and Rush 2012). The buildup of overcapacity in China is closely linked to the gap between high investment in production, especially in sectors favoured by the developmental state, and the relatively low level of consumption in China (Cai 2015). The accumulation of massive foreign reserves, most of which have been held in low-yielding US government debt, comes from the persistent current account surplus in recent years, which is ultimately attributable to the high saving rate and low consumption in China (Pettis 2014; Wang 2014a). All of these problems challenge China's sustainable economic development. The last of them — the accumulation of dollar assets — has also led to huge financial losses for China, whose positive net investment position has, ironically, resulted in negative net international income in recent years (see chapter 7 of this volume).

For over a decade, China's leaders have called for a change of development model — a transition to domestic consumption-based economic growth. This would involve reform of the financial sector, liberalizing exchange rates and interest rates, and reform of the public finance system, giving greater weight to social welfare. Despite steps taken in the right direction from time to time, the overall pace of reform has been painfully slow because of the strong political resistance by vested interests (Wang 2014b).

Instead of making fundamental structural changes in the Chinese economy, the Chinese government has chosen to deal with the current model's problems, including overcapacity and the burden of managing large foreign reserves, by encouraging the diversification of its overseas assets. New policies have eased the procedures for Chinese companies to invest abroad. By 2014, China had become the third-largest source country of foreign direct investment. The Chinese government has also set up a number of national wealth funds to look for overseas investment opportunities. The establishment of minilateral financial institutions, such as the AIIB and the NDB, is part of this overall strategy. Alongside these, China has recently launched a US$40 billion Silk Road Infrastructure Fund that serves similar purposes. It has also been in active discussion with other members of the Shanghai Cooperation Organization (SCO) to set up an SCO development bank.

Seen in this light, the NDB and the AIIB, along with various unilateral and bilateral schemes of overseas investments, potentially offer a short-term and partial solution to a much broader problem. To the extent they succeed in helping to export China's overcapacity and improve the income performance of China's foreign assets, they may well further delay the structural reform necessary for China's transition to a new and more sustainable development model. This may be beneficial for the Chinese government and some Chinese corporations involved in the investment projects, but is hardly in the interest of the long-term health of the Chinese economy or the well-being of the general public in China.

Looking Ahead

For many years, the Chinese government sought to "join the world" by learning and selectively following the international rules established by the West (Economy and Oksenberg 1999). Now China's relations with the world have entered a new stage, where China is actively trying to participate in the making of international rules. Its foreign policy strategy is gradually moving away from "keeping a low profile" toward "trying to accomplish something." China's enthusiasm toward financial minilateralism is part of this larger trend. This chapter has analyzed the motivations behind China's new activism in promoting minilateral financial cooperation and its implications so far. Looking ahead, two questions are important to consider: will the minilateral arrangements led by China be effective in accomplishing their stated missions, and will these initiatives continue to be compatible with the exiting international financial system? An affirmative answer cannot be taken for granted for either question.

With regard to the first question, there are reasons to be skeptical as to how successful the minilateral financial arrangements can be. As noted above, during the global financial crisis, Asian countries sought assistance from the Federal Reserve of the United States rather than CMIM to deal with liquidity problems. It was a clear illustration of the persistent structural power of the United States that scholars have been discussing for a long time (Strange 1997; Helleiner 2006). It is questionable how useful the CRA will be in the next crisis, given its much smaller size than the CMIM.

Likewise, the NDB and the AIIB face serious challenges. It is well known that investment under China's statist capitalism has long been inefficient (Chen et al. 2011). Recently, the *Financial Times* reported that Chinese researchers from the government's National Development and Reform Commission reported US$6.8 trillion in wasted investment since 2009. The Chinese government carried out a massive stimulus package after the global financial crisis in 2008. However, much of the funds went into projects that turned out to be abandoned highways, mothballed steel mills and entire ghost cities (Anderlini 2014). Will the NDB and the AIIB be able to move beyond this pattern? Some commentators in China have already expressed doubts (see, for example, *Dongfang Ribao* 2015). Indeed, other financial institutions have also had a checkered record in financing infrastructure in the developing world. Bilateral and multilateral lending to developing countries to develop infrastructure has often led to poor results and defaults. It is not at all clear what will make China-led development banks more effective (Pettis 2015).

With regard to the second question, as noted above, so far the new minilateral institutions do not directly threaten the existing international financial order. However, this situation could change over time, as the result of domestic economic and political development in China. For a number of years, there has been a debate in China between those who believe China should not challenge a US-led international system and those who argue China should do exactly that (Shambaugh 2011). Economic downturns and/or political instability could undermine the moderate forces and give rise to more militant foreign policies.

Change could also come from how Western countries react to the aspirations of China. As a leading scholar of international relations in China puts it, "if the international community appears not to understand China's aspirations…the Chinese people may ask themselves why China should be bound by rules that were essentially established by the Western powers" (Wang 2011b). In the area of financial governance, if reform in multilateral institutions continues to be delayed and if Western countries — especially the United States — continue to adopt a skeptical and even hostile attitude toward China-led initiatives, it will generate resentment and hostility from China. On the other hand, if Western countries and the multilateral financial institutions they dominate acknowledge the legitimacy of China's (and other emerging economies') demand for greater representation, if they work together with the minilateral institutions China has cultivated, and if they can persuade Chinese policy makers that they do not seek to thwart China's pursuit of more economic and political influence, China is likely to continue to support these multilateral institutions rather than to try to supplant them.

Moreover, just as the United States and some of its allies are concerned about Chinese minilateralism, China is suspicious of US-led minilateral projects, such as the TPP and TTIP (Institute of International Relations 2014). If such mutual suspicion continues to deepen, it will undermine multilateral cooperation globally. In order to ensure that China's minilateral initiatives supplement and improve multilateral cooperation at the global level rather than undermine it, the international community should try to accommodate China's reformist agenda, while at the same time encourage China to maintain an open form of minilateralism. The best way to do so is to keep Western minilateral arrangements open to China. Both China and the United States have claimed that their minilateral projects — such as the TPP and the AIIB — are open to all and will seek cooperation with each other. It is important to match their action with that rhetoric.

Works Cited

ADB and ADBI. 2009. *Infrastructure for a Seamless Asia.* Tokyo: ADBI. www.adbi.org/files/2009.08.31.book.infrastructure.seamless.asia.pdf.

AIIB. 2015a. "The Asian Infrastructure Investment Bank." www.aiibank.org/html/aboutus/AIIB/.

———. 2015b. "Asian Infrastructure Investment Bank Articles of Agreement." www.aiibank.org/uploadfile/2015/0629/20150629094900288.pdf.

Anderlini, Jamil. 2014. "China Has 'Wasted' $6.8tn in Investment, Warn Beijing Researchers." *Financial Times,* November 27. www.ft.com/intl/cms/s/0/002a1978-7629-11e4-9761-00144feabdc0.html#axzz3WYRLTtyz.

Asahi Shimbun. 2014a. "Yazhou jichu sheshi touzi yinhang: zhongguo de boyi (亚洲基础设施投资银行 中国的政治博弈)." *Asahi Shimbun,* May 19. http://asahichinese.com/article/opinion/AJ201405190008.

———. 2014b. "Zhongguo zhudao guoji zuzhi, tiaozhan buleidun senlin tixi(中国主导国际组织 挑战布雷顿森林体系)." *Asahi Shimbun,* September 27. http://asahichinese.com/article/opinion/AJ201409270001.

Baker, Andrew. 2000. "The G-7 as a Global 'Ginger Group': Plurilateralism and Four-Dimensional Diplomacy." *Global Governance* 6 (2): 165–89.

Barber, Lionel, David Pilling and Jamil Anderlini. 2015. "Interview: Li Keqiang on China's Challenges." *Financial Times,* April 15. www.ft.com/intl/cms/s/2/38307b3e-e28d-11e4-aa1d-00144feab7de.html#axzz3Yd8hLOZ8.

Bloomberg. 2014. "China's $50 Billion Asia Bank Snubs Japan, India." Bloomberg, May 12. www.bloomberg.com/news/2014-05-11/china-s-50-billion-asia-bank-snubs-japan-india-in-power-push.html.

Bräutigam, Deborah and Kevin P. Gallagher. 2014. "Bartering Globalization: China's Commodity-backed Finance in Africa and Latin America." *Global Policy* 5: 346–52.

Brummer, Chris. 2014. *Minilateralism: How Trade Alliances, Soft Law and Financial Engineering Are Redefining Economic Statecraft.* Cambridge: Cambridge University Press.

Buchanan, James M. 1965. "An Economic Theory of Clubs." *Economica* 32 (125): 1–14.

Cai, Fang. 2015. "Haste Makes Waste: Policy Options Facing China after Reaching the Lewis Turning Point." *China & World Economy* 23 (1): 1–20.

Cerny, Philip G. 1993. "Plurilateralism: Structural Differentiation and Functional Conflict in the Post-Cold War World Order." *Millennium-Journal of International Studies* 22 (1): 27–51.

Chen, Dingding and Jianwei Wang. 2011. "Lying Low No More? China's New Thinking on the Tao Guang Yang Hui Strategy." *China: An International Journal* 9 (2): 195–216.

Chen, Jibing. 2014. "Jinzhuan yinhang yao gan shenme (金砖银行要干什么)？" Tencent, August 10. http://dajia.qq.com/blog/427371068364007.

Chen, S., Z. Sun, S. Tang and D. Wu. 2011. "Government Intervention and Investment Efficiency: Evidence from China." *Journal of Corporate Finance* 17 (2): 259–71.

Chhibber, Ajay. 2015. "New World Bank Order." *The Indian Express*, April 3. http://indianexpress.com/article/opinion/columns/new-world-bank-order/.

Chin, Gregory. 2012. "China as a 'Net Donor': Tracking Dollars and Sense." *Cambridge Review of International Affairs* 25 4: 579–604.

China Daily. 2013. "Yazhou jijian touzi yinhang yure gongcheng chengbaoshang de shengyan (亚洲基建投资银行预热　工程承包商的盛宴)." *China Daily*, October 23. www.chinadaily.com.cn/hqcj/2013-10/23/content_17053992.htm.

Ding, Xin. 2014. "Jinzhuan wuguo ban yinhang guoji huayuquan jiang gengjia wengu(金砖五国办银行　国际话语权将更加稳固)." People.cn, July 17. http://finance.people.com.cn/bank/n/2014/0717/c202331-25292219.html.

Dongfang Ribao. 2015. "习大大杰作　"一带一路"要成最大烂尾楼?" www.backchina.com/news/2015/03/30/354324.html#ixzz3WZQzMtpb.

Economy, Elizabeth and Michel Oksenberg, eds. 1999. *China Joins the World: Progress and Prospects*. New York: Council on Foreign Relations.

French, Gordon. 2014. "How Asia Should Pay for $11tn in Infrastructure Needs." Beyondbrics (*Financial Times* blog). http://blogs.ft.com/beyond-brics/2014/11/26/guest-post-how-asia-should-pay-for-11tn-in-infrastructure-needs/.

Fu, Feng, Linwei Ma, Zheng Li and Karen R. Polenske. 2014. "The Implications of China's Investment-driven Economy on Its Energy Consumption and Carbon Emissions." *Energy Conversion and Management* 85: 573–80.

Helleiner, Eric. 2006. "Below the State: Micro-Level Power." In *International Monetary Power*, edited by David M. Andrews. Ithaca, NY: Cornell University Press.

Higgott, Richard. 1998. "The Asian Economic Crisis: A Study in the Politics of Resentment." *New Political Economy* 3 (3): 333–56.

House, Brett, Hongying Wang and Miranda Xafa. 2014. "Chinese Perspectives on Sovereign Debt Restructuring." CIGI Commentary, July. www.cigionline.org/publications/chinese-perspectives-sovereign-debt-restructuring.

Hu, Shuli. 2013. "China Will Benefit from Investing in Others' Infrastructure Development." *South China Morning Post*, December 4. www.scmp.com/comment/insight-opinion/article/1372991/china-will-benefit-investing-others-infrastructure.

Huang, Zhiyong, Tan Chunzhi and Lei Xiaohua. 2013. "Choujian yazhou jichu sheshi touzi yinhang de jiben silu ku duice jianyi (筹建亚洲基础设施投资银行的基本思路及对策建议)." *Dongnanya Zongheng* (东南亚纵横), no. 10. http://mall.cnki.net/magazine/Article/DLYZ201310001.htm.

Hung, Ho-fung. 2015. "China Steps Back." *The New York Times*, April 5. www.nytimes.com/2015/04/06/opinion/china-steps-back.html.

Institute of International Relations (China). 2014. *Zhongguo guojia anquan yanjiu baogao* (中国国家安全研究报告).

Jiang, Yang. 2010. "Response and Responsibility: China in East Asian Financial Cooperation." *The Pacific Review* 23 (5): 603–23.

Johnston, A. I. 2013. "How New and Assertive Is China's New Assertiveness?" *International Security* 37 (4): 7–48.

Li, Wei. 2012. "Dongya houbi zhixu de zhengzhi jichu – cong danyi zhudao dao gongtong lingdao (东亚货币秩序的政治基础—从单一主导到共同领导)." *Dangdai Yatai* 当代亚太 no. 6.

———. 2015. "Yatouhang zhanshi daguo jirong jueqi de baofu (亚投行展示大国金融崛起的抱负)." http://opinion.china.com.cn/opinion_51_124751.html.

Lou, Jiwei. 2014. "Jiakuai choujian yazhou jichu touzi yinhang (加快筹建亚洲基础设施投资银行)." *Xin Shangwu Zhoukan* (新商务周刊) no. 3.

Lu, Jing. 2013. "Hou weiji shiqi jinzhuan guojia hezuo zhanglue tanxi (后危机时期金砖国家合作战略探悉)." www.cctb.net/llyj/lldt/qqzl/201405/t20140530_307988.htm.

Merry, Brian. 2015. "Will China's New Bank Shift the Global Balance of Power?" Atlantic Council of Canada. March 25. http://natocouncil.ca/will-chinas-new-bank-shift-the-global-balance-of-power/.

Ministry of Finance of the PRC. 2014. "Lou Jiwei tan yazhou jichu sheshi touzi yihang choujian qingkuang (楼继伟谈亚洲基础设施投资银行筹建情况)." www.mof.gov.cn/zhengwuxinxi/caizhengxinwen/201404/t20140411_1066633.html.

Ministry of Foreign Affairs. 2015. "2015年3月17日外交部发言人洪磊主持例行记者会." www.fmprc.gov.cn/mfa_chn/fyrbt_602243/t1246296.shtml.

Naim, Moises. 2009. "Minilateralism: The Magic Number to Get Real International Action." *Foreign Policy* 173 (July-August): 135-36.

O'Neill, Jim. 2013. "So What Do the BRICS Countries Want from Their New Development Bank?" *The Independent*, August 8. www.independent.co.uk/news/business/comment/jim-oneill-so-what-do-the-brics-countries-want-from-their-new-development-bank-8751204.html.

Perlez, Jane. 2014. "U.S. Opposing China's Answer to World Bank." *The New York Times*, October 9. www.nytimes.com/2014/10/10/world/asia/chinas-plan-for-regional-development-bank-runs-into-us-opposition.html?_r=0.

Pettis, Michael. 2014. *The Great Rebalancing: Trade, Conflict, and the Perilous Road ahead for the World Economy.* Princeton, NJ: Princeton University Press.

———. 2015. "Will the AIIB One Day Matter?" http://blog.mpettis.com/2015/04/will-the-aiib-one-day-matter/.

Reich, Arie. 1997. "The New GATT Agreement on Government Procurement — The Pitfalls of Plurilateralism and Strict Reciprocity." *Journal of World Trade* 31 (2): 125–51.

Roberts, Ivan and Anthony Rush. 2012. "Understanding China's Demand for Resource Imports." *China Economic Review* 23 (3): 566–79.

Runde, Daniel. 2014. "The BRICS Bank, Bretton Woods and U.S. Disengagement." *Foreign Policy*, July 20. http://shadow.foreignpolicy.com/posts/2014/07/20/the_brics_bank_bretton_woods_and_us_disengagement.

Shambaugh, David. 2011. "Coping with a Conflicted China." *The Washington Quarterly* 34 (1): 7–27.

Shen, Qing. 2015. "AIIB, A Paradigm Power Shift." Xinhuanet, March 31. http://news.xinhuanet.com/english/2015-03/31/c_134114065.htm.

Steil, Ben. 2014. "The BRICS Bank Is a Feeble Strike against Dollar Hegemony." *Financial Times*, October 1. www.ft.com/intl/cms/s/0/3c84425c-48a9-11e4-9d04-00144feab7de.html#axzz3GzQBjTXf.

Strange, Susan. 1987. "The Persistent Myth of Lost Hegemony." *International Organization* 41: 551–74.

Summers, Larry. 2015. "Time US Leadership Woke Up to New Economic Era." http://larrysummers.com/2015/04/05/time-us-leadership-woke-up-to-new-economic-era/.

Sun, Xingjie. 2014. "Yatouhang de qianjing yu tiaozhan(亚投行的前景与挑战)." *Zhongguo Jingji he Xinxihua* (中国经济和信息化) no. 10.

Tang, Lingxiao. 2014. "Jinzhuan guojia kaifa yinhang chengli de xianshi dongyin (金砖国家开发银行成立的现实动因)." www.qstheory.cn/freely/2014-08/20/c_1112156491.htm.

Vestergaard, Jakob and Robert H. Wade. 2013. "Protecting Power: How Western States Retain the Dominant Voice in the World Bank's Governance." *World Development* 46: 153–64.

Von Sant, Shannon. 2014. "BRICS Bank Viewed as IMF Competitor." Voice of America, August 12. www.voanews.com/content/brics-launches-new-development-bank/2410633.html.

Wade, Robert and Frank Veneroso. 1998. "The Asian Crisis: The High Debt Model v. the Wall Street-Treasury-IMF Complex." *New Left Review* 228: 3–23.

Wang, Dan and Fengling Lu. 2012. "Renmin yinhang huobi huhuan shijian (人民银行货币互换实践)." *Zhongguo Jinrong* (中国金融), 4.

Wang, Hongying. 2014a. *China and Sovereign Debt Restructuring*. CIGI Papers no. 45, September 29. www.cigionline.org/publications/china-and-sovereign-debt-restructuring.

———. 2014b. "The Limits of the Exchange Rate Weapon in Addressing China's Role in Global Imbalance." In *The Great Wall of Money: Power and Politics in China's International Monetary Relations*, edited by Eric Helleiner and Jonathan Kirshner, 99–126. Ithaca, NY: Cornell University Press.

Wang, Hongying and Erik French. 2013. "China's Participation in Global Governance from a Comparative Perspective." *Asia Policy* 15 (1): 89–114.

———. 2014. "China in Global Economic Governance." *Asian Economic Policy Review* 9 (2): 254–71.

Wang, Jisi. 2011a. "Zhongguo de guoji dingwei wenti yu 'taoguang yanghui, yousuo zuowei' de zhanlue sixiang (中国的国际定位问题与'韬光养晦、 有所作为'的战略思想)." *Guoji wenti yanjiu (*国际问题研究）no. 2. www.ciis.org.cn/gyzz/download/201102/20110202.pdf.

———. 2011b. "China's Search for a Grand Strategy-A Rising Great Power Finds its Way." *Foreign Affairs* 90: 68–79.

Xia, Nan. 2015. "Cong genpaozhe dao lingpaozhe: jianzheng zhongguo de daguo lingdaoli (从跟跑者到领跑者：见证中国的大国领导力)." http://www.qstheory.cn/wp/2015-03/29/m_1114799271.htm.

Xinhua. 2014a. "Yanghang: yingji chubei anpai tigao jinzhuan jinzhuan guojia guoji huayuquan (央行：应急储备安排提高金砖国家国际话语权)." Xinhua, July 17. http://rmb.xinhua08.com/a/20140717/1357690.shtml.

———. 2014b. "Wang Yi: jiaqiang 10+3 hezuo, tuijin dongya gongtongti jianshe (王毅：加强１０＋３合作，推进东亚共同体建设)." Xinhua, August 10. http://news.xinhuanet.com/world/2014-08/10/c_1112007246.htm.

———. 2014c. "Yatouhang choubeizu zuzhang: yazhou jichu sheshi touzi gongqiu bu pibei (亚投行筹备组组长：亚洲基础设施投资供求不匹配)." Xinhua, June 29. http://news.xinhuanet.com/fortune/2014-06/29/c_1111368289.htm.

———. 2014d. "Jinzhuan yinhang li women de shenghuo bing bu yuan(金砖银行 离我们的生活并不远)." Xinhua, July 18. http://news.xinhuanet.com/finance/2014-07/18/c_1111687837.htm.

———. 2014e. "Lou Jiwei: sheli yatouhang shi duoying zhi ju zhongfang chuzi bu yiding feida 50% (楼继伟：设立亚投行是多赢之举 中方出资不一定非达50%)." Xinhua, July 3. http://news.xinhuanet.com/fortune/2014-07/03/c_1111448768.htm.

Xu, Bei. 2014. "Lianghao de kaiduan: 'jinzhuan siguo' yaoqiu gengduo huayuquan （良好的开端 '金砖四国'要求更多话语权)." http://e-magazine.bjreview.com/VOL_003/03_N_c.html.

Ye, Hailin. 2014. "Zhongguo shishi 'xiao duobian' duiwai zhanlue dazao quanshi zhongxin （中国实施"小多边"对外战略打造权势中心)." www.ccwe.org.cn/ccwenew/upfile/file/zhongguoshishi.pdf.

Yi, Gang. 2011. "Quanmian canyu guoji jinrong tixi gaige, tigao zhongguo huayuquan （全面参与国际金融体系改革提高中国话语权)." www.pbc.gov.cn/publish/hanglingdao/63/2011/20110113182233985864603/2011011 3182233985864603_.html.

Zhang, Han. 2015. "亚投行今年秋天向全球公开招聘顾问团." http://news.china.com/domesticgd/10000159/20150406/19482412_all.html#page_2.

Zhang, Zhongkai. 2015. "The World Votes for AIIB, New Economic Order." Xinhuanet, April 1. http://news.xinhuanet.com/english/2015-04/01/c_134116630.htm.

Zheng, Yangpeng. 2015. "China Gets 30% Stake in AIIB as Bank Takes Shape." *China Daily*, June 29. http://usa.chinadaily.com.cn/china/2015-06/29/content_21132838.htm.

Zhou, Xiaochuan. 2012. 走出危机僵局需要设计新的激励机制：在中国金融四十人论坛上的讲话. www.pbc.gov.cn/publish/goutongjiaoliu/524/2012/2012091918 1848888417176/20120919181848888417176_.html.

———. 2014. "Statement by the Honorable Zhou Xiaochuan, Governor of the IMF for China to the Thirtieth Meeting of the International Monetary and Financial Committee." Washington, DC, October 11. www.imf.org/External/AM/2014/imfc/statement/eng/chn.pdf.

Zhu, Jiejin. 2014. "Jinzhuan guojia hezuo jizhi de zhuanxing (金砖国家合作机制的转型)." *Guoji Guancha* (国际观察) no. 3. www.chinareform.org.cn/open/governance/201408/t20140826_205298.htm.

Conclusion

Domenico Lombardi and Hongying Wang

he rise of China in the international financial and monetary system has been a momentous development in the twenty-first century. This book examines the issues underlying the process, in particular those concerning the internationalization of the renminbi (RMB), development of the financial sector and, more broadly, China's evolving role in the governance of international finance. The book's contributors have focused on different questions and adopted a variety of approaches in their research. While they do not always agree with one another, their chapters speak to a number of common issues that are crucial to understanding China's role in the international financial and monetary system. Four of these issues are especially worth highlighting: the complex nature and source of international financial power; China's attitude toward the existing financial and monetary order; the linkage between China's foreign financial policy and its domestic political economy; and, finally, the distinctiveness of China's rise in the international financial system.

The Nature and Sources of International Financial Power

The concept of power is notoriously slippery. Many equate power with influence. In the classic definition by Robert Dahl (1957, 202-03), "A has power over B to the extent that he can get B to do something that B would not otherwise do." However, others argue that power does not only mean the ability to influence others, as it also means the ability to act unilaterally, that is, free from the influence of others (Carroll 1972). In other words, there is power over others and there is power to act autonomously. Scholars have also sought to differentiate the various types of power, such as direct and indirect power, active and passive power, relational and structural power, and hard power and soft power (Bachrach and Baratz 1962; Lukes 1974; Strange 1988; Nye 2004). The notion of power continues to be an important and controversial subject of study (see, for example, Baldwin 2013; Cohen 2015). As some lament, "the more we look into the question of power, the murkier the concept becomes" (Reich and Lebow 2014).

The meaning of power on financial and monetary matters is even less developed. In his recent book, Benjamin J. Cohen (2015) comments that many scholars take the concept of financial and monetary power for granted, using it without defining it. He refers to studies that try to measure financial and monetary power (see, for example, Armijo, Mühlich and Tirone 2014; Norrlof 2014) and concludes that "such indicators omit consideration of strategic or political context. They tell us little about how capabilities may or may not translate into influence" (Cohen 2015, chapter 3).

In agreement with Cohen, we believe power is more than quantifiable resources — context matters. Making assumptions about China's financial and monetary power on the basis of the size of the Chinese economy, its share of the global trade and its large foreign reserves has been common. Indeed, this book has underscored the growing significance of China in regards to these factors. However, it remains to be seen, as several chapters in this volume suggest, whether or not these factors have contributed to China's financial and monetary power, and whether or not they have brought benefits to China at all. The one-to-one positive mapping between China's growing economic and financial resources, on the one hand, and China's autonomy and influence in the international financial and monetary system, on the other hand, is highly questionable.

Along these lines, Stuart S. Brown and Hongying Wang show that China's net creditor position in recent years has not brought it as many financial gains or as much political leverage as one might expect. They distinguish between China's net international investment position (NIIP) and its net investment income (NII). Although China has become a net creditor with a large, positive NIIP since the early 2000s, its NII has consistently run in deficit. Brown and Wang argue that a contributing factor to this paradox comes from low rates of return earned on China's large official foreign exchange reserves. Hailong Jin,

Domenico Lombardi and Coby Hu examine this point more closely, showing that since 2007, China's official foreign exchanges have been a burden to some extent. Similar to Brown and Wang, they show that the foreign reserves held by the People's Bank of China (PBoC) have been earning negative returns — the losses exceeded US$180 billion in 2011 alone.

Brown and Wang document that the majority of China's foreign assets are denominated in US dollars. One might naively assume that this position gives the People's Republic of China (PRC) some political leverage in the American macroeconomic discourse. However, the authors argue that the PRC has not had any significant impact on these issues in the United States, and instead its net creditor status makes it subordinate to US structural power within the international capital market. China's status as an international creditor has failed to obtain the financial rewards and tangible political influence that one might expect. As both aforementioned chapters argue, China's large foreign holdings, at least with respect to US assets, have become a burden in recent years, yielding economic losses and rendering China more vulnerable to US policies.

Along similar lines, Bessma Momani and David Kempthorne note that the usual indicators of China's economic weight have not led to greater voice or influence in international financial institutions. Momani argues that, although the country's role in the International Monetary Fund has increased, there is still significant progress to be made in the area of governance and decision making. She questions whether this can be explained by China's unwillingness to assume more power or by the denial of increased Chinese influence by Western nations. In a similar vein, Kempthorne explores China's relation with financial standard-setting bodies and concludes that China has yet to exert any major influence. He argues that this comes from China's lack of structural power in global financial markets relative to the United States and the European Union. Furthermore, China lacks sufficient regulatory expertise to promote its own financial regulatory preferences. Like Momani, Kempthorne also argues that it is unclear whether the PRC has been eager to increase its influence in financial regulatory settings.

These studies find that China's financial and monetary power is limited despite its GDP, trade volume and foreign assets. This is in contrast to — and partly a result of — the enduring structural power of the United States, which is rooted in the dominant role of the dollar in the world as well as in the depth and openness of its financial market. The case of China has much to offer regarding the meaning and sources of financial and monetary power, echoing Cohen's call for moving beyond quantifiable measures and taking into consideration the specific context of financial and monetary relations.

China's Attitude toward the Current International Financial Order

A widely discussed question in the discourse about China's rise in the global economy is whether the country is a supporter or a challenger of the existing international order. Some scholars — taking the perspective of realism, in particular structural realism — firmly believe that a rising China is bound to threaten the current order. For instance, John Mearsheimer (2001) assumes that all rising powers, including China, seek hegemony, and in doing so they will act aggressively toward the current hegemon (and, by implication, the international system led by the current hegemon). Aaron Friedberg (2005) argues that a realist must, by default, be pessimistic about the rise of China because as it becomes more powerful, it will, in turn, become more ambitious, challenging the status quo. Others — drawing insights from liberalism and classical realism — are more optimistic that the current order could accommodate China and other rising powers. For example, G. John Ikenberry (2008) sees the existing liberal order as rule-based and open to newcomers. As such, it is easy to join and difficult to overturn. Accordingly, it is capable of absorbing rising powers such as China. For instance, Jonathan Kirshner (2010) believes that even though a rising China could potentially be a threat to the existing international system, that outcome is not predetermined; much depends on how the domestic political debate in China evolves and how the international community reacts to China's rise.

The chapters in this volume provide nuanced insights on China's attitude toward the existing international financial and monetary order. Juan Carlos Martinez Oliva argues that China does not seek to challenge the position of the US dollar globally, but is rather interested in establishing regional leadership. He acknowledges that the issuer of an international currency has historically been associated with power. To this extent, Martinez Oliva argues that China is using RMB internationalization to increase its power in the East Asian region, while expanding its support and friendship to this region's states at the same time. In doing so, China does not dissolve the current international order, but could strengthen it through the mutual economic interests it shares with its neighbours in the region. Similar to Martinez Oliva, Alex He argues that China perceives its role as complementary to the existing international and monetary order, especially in regards to the Group of Twenty (G20). He contends that, on the whole, China has been a major supporter of the G20 even though it has been critical of it from time to time. He adds that China intends to be a rule follower, rather than a challenger, within the G20, working to improve the relationships it has with member countries and gain political reputation within the international arena.

Along similar lines, Kempthorne points out that China's inclusion in various financial standard-setting bodies does not in itself mean Chinese influence in those bodies, and that, in fact, China has been a model rule follower on most of the regulatory issues. He contends this stems from the fact that the country sees value in the current financial regulatory framework as it promotes resilience and stability of its own domestic financial markets. Similarly, Wang's chapter on China's involvement in minilateral financial institutions outside the traditional multilateral financial organizations shows that China has been interested in reforming rather than overthrowing the existing financial order. She argues that China and other developing economies have been frustrated by the slow pace of reform in the Bretton Woods institutions. By creating new financial institutions, they seek to apply "reverse pressure" to stimulate change in those traditional institutions rather than supplanting them. China has shown a clear and consistent interest in collaboration between the new institutions and the Bretton Woods organizations.

Together, these studies present a picture of China as ambivalent about various aspects of the existing international order, trying to push for reform, but far from seeking to replace it with an entirely new order. Some of the contributors to this volume follow the liberal perspective and emphasize the intrinsically open and flexible nature of the current order. Others, however, take a classical realist approach, stressing the contingent nature of China's relations with the international financial and monetary order, dependent on a combination of domestic and international factors. But all reject the structural realist point of view, which sees the rise of China as inevitably threatening the current international system.

Domestic-international Linkage

Traditional scholarship on international political economy typically neglected domestic dynamics. In recent decades, however, this has changed. In the 1980s, scholars of international trade began to pay attention to the domestic sources and effects of foreign trade and trade policy, highlighting the central role played by political institutions and coalition politics (see, for example, Milner 1988; Rogowski 1989). They were soon joined by researchers studying international investment and finance (see, for example, Frieden 1991; Haggard and Maxfield 1996; Kirshner 2003). Over time, scholarship on international political economy, and indeed on international relations more generally, has increasingly recognized that international relations and domestic politics are inseparable, making diplomacy a two-level game (Putnam 1988).

The study of China has also become more sensitive to the interplay between domestic politics and foreign policy. In the last decade or so, more and more research on China's foreign relations has taken into account the role of domestic politics (see, for example, Lampton 2001; Lai 2010; Zhao 2013). This scholarship suggests the importance of leadership power struggles, bureaucratic competition, interest group politics and public opinion in shaping Chinese foreign policy. To a lesser extent, scholars have also explored the domestic effect of China's interactions with the outside world. For instance, a number of studies shed light on the impact of China's international economic relations on its domestic economic reform (Moore 2002; Steinfeld 2010).

Many chapters in this volume speak directly to the domestic-international connection in the context of China's policy and behaviour with regard to the international financial and monetary system. The linkage is twofold. On the one hand, it involves the domestic *sources* of China's foreign financial policy. A number of contributors explain how China's foreign financial policies have been shaped by the struggle among different interest groups and by well-established domestic political and economic institutions. On the other hand, the domestic international linkage refers to the domestic *consequences* of China's foreign financial policy. Several chapters explore the effect — intended as well as unintended — of China's foreign financial policies on the domestic economy and society.

For both Alex He and David A. Steinberg, interest group politics is crucial in shaping China's foreign financial policies, such as those on currency internationalization, exchange rates and capital account liberalization. He contends that the PBoC has promoted RMB internationalization as a way to pursue domestic economic reforms, especially to overcome the resistance by domestic interest groups and bureaucracies. Steinberg discusses the complex power struggles over exchange and reserve policies between advocates of reform and the anti-reform groups — in particular politically connected firms and the manufacturing sector more generally, which continue to benefit from the current economic policies. According to such a view, the trajectory of China's foreign financial policy depends on the interplay between the different domestic interest groups. Exploring the impact of domestic politics from a somewhat different angle, Randall Germain and Herman Mark Schwartz contend that China's foreign financial policies are severely constrained by its non-democratic domestic political system. Historically, only democratic countries have been flexible enough to adjust to the high domestic costs of currency internationalization. The absence of such a political system in China, they argue, is a major obstacle for the further internationalization of the RMB.

The consequences of China's foreign financial policy, in particular with regard to RMB internationalization and its exchange rates, have also been examined. The chapter by Qiyuan Xu identifies the varied impact of RMB internationalization on China's economy and its financial system. The exchange rate policy is explored extensively by Jin, Lombardi and Hu, who show that the PBoC incurred large losses, including a curtailing of its policy-making autonomy, through its exchange rate policy. Going forward, China is bound to lose even more policy space as its economy becomes more dependent on its trading partners.

In sum, this volume highlights the two-way influence between domestic politics and foreign policy, reinforcing the virtue of studying international relations through the "second image" and "second image reversed" lenses (Waltz 1959; Gourevitch 1978). Indeed, China's involvement with the international financial system provides new and interesting opportunities to explore the complex connections between international political economy on the one hand and domestic interests, institutions and policies on the other.

The Distinctiveness of China's Rise in Finance

Chinese officials are fond of emphasizing the "Chinese characteristics" of their policies, including how their country relates with the rest of the global economy. In some ways, China's rise in the international financial and monetary system is indeed a distinctive phenomenon. Unlike previous rising financial powers, China is a developing country, whose population remains quite poor by international standards, and it is a country that has a non-democratic political system with severe limitations of political and economic freedom. Structural realists discount country characteristics in their analysis of state policies. But other scholars of international monetary relations are quite attentive to the implications of particular Chinese characteristics, including China's particular economic and political institutions, and how they may affect China's rise in international finance.

In an earlier study, Barry Eichengreen (2013) notes that the international and reserve currencies of the nineteenth and twentieth centuries — the sterling and the dollar — were currencies of democracies. Because their citizens could constrain arbitrary action, the policy environment was relatively stable and predictable, encouraging private investors to hold their currencies. In his comparative study of post-World War II financial powers and their efforts to internationalize their currencies — the cases of the Deutsche or German mark, the Japanese yen and the euro — Cohen (2014) points out these countries all had democratic political institutions, strong protection of property rights and rule of law. In contrast to these historical precedents, contemporary China does not have such democratic political institutions or a strong system of rule of law. How far China can go in internationalizing its currency thus remains a big question.

Several contributors to this volume have incorporated a historical and comparative approach to studying China's role in the international financial and monetary system. Echoing the studies cited above, both Martinez Oliva and Eichengreen refer to earlier cases of currency internationalization in their study of RMB internationalization, going back to the Roman and the Spanish empires and the more recent experience of the United Kingdom and the United States. Germain and Schwartz's chapter is the most explicit and extensive in its historical comparison. Their detailed discussion of the political context of sterling and dollar internationalization suggests that the democratic political process played a crucial part in compensating the losers in the currency-issuing countries, and that the absence of democratic politics in China today puts serious constraints on further RMB internationalization. Liu Dongmin compares the bond market in China with bond markets elsewhere, especially in the United States. He argues that the peculiar characteristics of the Chinese bond market, such as its small size, maturity structure, and segmented regulatory system, have hindered its internationalization, which in turn limits the internationalization of the Chinese currency.

On a related issue, Steinberg concludes that China's distinctive political and economic structure makes it behave quite differently from other financial powers when it comes to foreign financial policy. He partly attributes this difference to China's distinct one-party rule since 1949 by the Communist Party, and asserts that this has had a profound impact on the distribution of power. The chapters by Momani, Kempthorne and Wang all refer to China's uniquely ambiguous status in the international financial system, both as a developing country and as a major financial power, suggesting that this has resulted in its dubious positions on various international governance issues. How these unconventional characteristics contribute to China's rise in the international financial and monetary system is an interesting question that deserves more research.

Looking ahead, we see a range of possible scenarios for China's role to evolve in the international financial system. Under an ideal scenario, successful domestic reform combined with reasonable international accommodation will likely facilitate China's emergence as a responsible and effective co-leader of the international system. In the worst-case scenario, China could face major financial and economic crises at home due to mismanagement of financial liberalization and/or prolonged delay of structural reforms. Given the size of the Chinese economy, this could potentially destabilize the international financial system. Under such circumstances, both China and the rest of the world are likely to face serious economic and even political challenges. However, the more likely scenario is between these extremes. As most of the contributors point out, through the competition and struggle between the forces for and against reform, China has been moving cautiously and slowly toward liberalizing its financial sector and rebalancing its economy. The international community has grudgingly come to accept the reality of China's rise, even though the dominant powers in international finance remain passive in integrating China's aspirations in newly reformed global governance arrangements.

Works Cited

Armijo, Leslie E., Laurissa Mühlich and Daniel C. Tirone. 2014. "The Systemic Financial Importance of Emerging Powers." *Journal of Policy Modeling* 36 (Supplement 1): S67–S88.

Bachrach, Peter and Morton S. Baratz. 1962. "Two Faces of Power." *American Political Science Review* 56 (4): 947–52.

Baldwin, David A. 2013. "Power and International Relations." In *Handbook of International Relations*, edited by Walter Carlsnaes, Thomas Risse and Beth A. Simmons, 273–97. 2nd edition. Los Angeles, CA: Sage Publications.

Carroll, Berenice A. 1972. "Peace Research: The Cult of Power." *Journal of Conflict Resolution* 16 (4): 585–616.

Cohen, Benjamin J. 2014. "Will History Repeat Itself? Lessons for the Yuan." Asian Development Bank Institute. www.adbi.org/files/2014.01.17. wp453.will.history.repeat.itself.lessons.yuan.pdf.

———. 2015. *Currency Power: Understanding Monetary Rivalry.* Princeton, NJ: Princeton University Press.

Dahl, Robert A. 1957. "The Concept of Power." *Behavioral Science* 2: 201–15.

Eichengreen, Barry. 2013. "ADB Distinguished Lecture Renminbi Internationalization: Tempest in a Teapot?" *Asian Development Review* 30 (1): 148–64.

Friedberg, Aaron. 2005. "The Future of U.S.–China Relations: Is Conflict Inevitable? *International Security* 30 (2): 7–45.

Frieden, Jeffry A. 1991. "Invested Interests: The Politics of National Economic Policies in a World of Global Finance." *International Organization* 45 (04): 425–51.

Gourevitch, Peter. 1978. "The Second Image Reversed: The International Sources of Domestic Politics." *International Organization* 32 (4): 881–912.

Haggard, Stephan and Sylvia Maxfield. 1996. "The Political Economy of Financial Internationalization in the Developing World." *International Organization* 50 (1): 35–68.

Ikenberry, G. John. 2008. "The Rise of China and the Future of the West: Can the Liberal System Survive?" *Foreign Affairs* (January/February): 23–37.

Kirshner, Jonathan, ed. 2003. *Monetary Orders: Ambiguous Economics, Ubiquitous Politics*. Ithaca, NY: Cornell University Press.

Kirshner, Jonathan. 2010. "The Tragedy of Offensive Realism: Classical Realism and the Rise of China." *European Journal of International Relations* 18 (1): 53–75.

Lai, Hongyi. 2010. *The Domestic Sources of China's Foreign Policy: Regimes, Leadership, Priorities and Process*. Oxford: Routledge.

Lampton, David M. 2001. *The Making of Chinese Foreign and Security Policy in the Era of Reform, 1978–2000*. Redwood City, CA: Stanford University Press.

Lukes, Steven. 1974. *Power: A Radical View*. London: Macmillan.

Mearsheimer, John. 2001. *The Tragedy of Great Power Politics*. New York, NY: Norton.

Milner, Helen V. 1988. *Resisting Protectionism: Global Industries and the Politics of International Trade*. Princeton, NJ: Princeton University Press.

Moore, Thomas Geoffrey. 2002. *China in the World Market: Chinese Industry and International Sources of Reform in the Post-Mao Era*. Cambridge: Cambridge University Press.

Norrlof, Carla. 2014. "Dollar Hegemony: A Power Analysis." *Review of International Political Economy* 21 (5): 1042–70.

Nye, Joseph S. 2004. *Soft Power: The Means to Success in World Politics*. New York, NY: PublicAffairs.

Putnam, Robert D. 1988. "Diplomacy and Domestic Politics: The Logic of Two-level Games." *International Organization* 42 (3): 427–60.

Reich, Simon and Richard Ned Lebow. 2014. *Good-Bye Hegemony! Power and Influence in the Global System.* Princeton, NJ: Princeton University Press.

Rogowski, Ronald. 1989. *Commerce and Coalitions: How Trade Affects Domestic Political Alignments.* Princeton, NJ: Princeton University Press.

Steinfeld, Edward S. 2010. *Playing Our Game: Why China's Rise Doesn't Threaten the West.* New York, NY: Oxford University Press.

Strange, Susan. 1988. *States and Markets.* London: Pinter Publishers.

Waltz, Kenneth. 2001. *Man, the State, and War: A Theoretical Analysis.* New York, NY: Columbia University Press.

Zhao, Suisheng. 2013. "Foreign Policy Implications of Chinese Nationalism Revisited: The Strident Turn." *Journal of Contemporary China* 22 (82): 535–53.

Contributors

Stuart S. Brown is professor of practice of public administration and international affairs at the Maxwell School of Citizenship and Public Affairs (Syracuse University). In addition to holding academic positions at Georgetown University and Smith College, he worked as an economist at the IMF and as chief economist for Eastern Europe, Africa and the Middle East for BNP-Paribas and Bank of America. He has written widely on the transitional economies and has recently authored *The Future of US Global Power: Delusions of Decline* published by Palgrave MacMillan.

Liu Dongmin is a senior research fellow and director of the International Finance Division at the Institute of World Economics and Policy at CASS. Liu has a Ph.D. from CASS, and a master's degree and a bachelor's degree from Tsinghua University. He is the author of numerous journal articles, policy reports and books. His research areas are: reform of international monetary system, internationalization of the RMB, the Asian Infrastructure Investment Bank and the BRICS bank, shadow banking system, financial regulation and construction of China's financial centre.

Barry Eichengreen is a CIGI senior fellow. He is the George C. Pardee and Helen N. Pardee Professor of Economics and professor of political science at the University of California, Berkeley, where he has taught since 1987. He is a research associate of the National Bureau of Economic Research (Cambridge, Massachusetts) and a research fellow of the Centre for Economic Policy Research (London, England). From 1997 to 1998, he was senior policy adviser at the IMF. He is a fellow of the American Academy of Arts and Sciences (class of 1997). At CIGI, Barry's research focuses on the internationalization of the renminbi, including a comparative analysis between regionalization and full-fledged internationalization.

Randall Germain is professor of political science at Carleton University, Canada. His teaching and research focus on the political economy of global finance, issues and themes associated with economic and financial governance, and theoretical debates within the field of international political economy. His most recent book is *Global Politics and Financial Governance* (Palgrave, 2010).

Xingqiang ("Alex") He is a CIGI visiting scholar. Alex is a research fellow and associate professor at the Institute of American Studies at the Chinese Academy of Social Sciences (CASS). At CIGI, he is focusing on interest group politics in China and their role in China's foreign economic policy making, China and the G20, and China and global economic governance. Alex has co-authored the book *A History of China-U.S. Relations* and published dozens of academic papers and book chapters both in Chinese and English. He also periodically writes reviews and commentaries for some of China's mainstream magazines and newspapers on international affairs. Alex has a Ph.D. in international politics from the Graduate School of CASS. Before beginning his Ph.D., he taught international relations at Yuxi Normal University in Yunnan Province, China.

Coby Hu is a CIGI research associate in the Global Economy Program and is a Ph.D. student in the Finance Division at the Sauder School of Business, University of British Columbia. He has a B.A. (honours) in economics and mathematics from McGill University and an M.A. in economics from the University of Toronto. Coby's current research at CIGI covers macroeconomics, monetary economics and international finance.

Hailong Jin is a research consultant in CIGI's Global Economy Program. He has expertise in international economics, monetary economics and Chinese economy. He holds a B.A. in economics from Jilin University in China, a M.Sc. in economics from Tsinghua University in China and a Ph.D. in economics from Iowa State University. Hailong is also a lecturer in the Association to Advance Collegiate Schools of Business-accredited School of Business at the Black Hills State University, SD, and monetary economist for the Global 4C Mitigation Project in the Center for Regenerative Community Solutions, NJ. He has published several articles in peer-reviewed journals such as *China Economic Review*, *Pacific Economic Review* and *International Review of Economics & Finance*.

David Kempthorne joined CIGI as a research fellow in the Global Economy program in September 2013. He holds a B.A. (honours) and M.A. in political science from the University of Otago in New Zealand and a Ph.D. in global governance from the Balsillie School of International Affairs. His research focuses on financial regulatory reforms and the international institutions responsible for setting international financial standards, with an emphasis on the Financial Stability Board.

Domenico Lombardi is the director of the Global Economy Program at CIGI. Previously, he served as an executive board member of the IMF and the World Bank Group. His distinguished career includes positions on the executive boards of major international financial institutions such as the IMF and the World Bank. Domenico's academic interests focus on the global economy and currencies, global governance, the G20 and the reform of the international financial and monetary system. His research has been widely published in peer-reviewed journals as well as policy outlets.

Juan Carlos Martinez Oliva is a principal director in the Directorate General for Economics, Statistics and Research Department at the Bank of Italy and a member of the Academic Committee of the International Monetary Institute of Renmin University, Beijing, China. He was a member of a number of standing committees and working groups at the Organisation for Economic Co-operation and Development and the European Economic Community. Juan Carlos was a member of the executive board of the IMF and a special economic adviser to the Italian minister of economics. From 2010 to 2013 he was a visiting fellow at the Peterson Institute for International Economics, Washington, DC. From 2012 he is a member of Istituto Affari Internazionali. A former visiting scholar at University of California, Berkeley, visiting professor at various Italian universities and frequent guest lecturer, he regularly takes part in the activities of the Asia-Pacific Economic Association, where he has contributed to the organization of academic events. He is the author or editor of numerous books, refereed journal articles and blog articles on quantitative international economics, monetary and exchange rate policy, regional monetary integration, economic history and geopolitics. For his distinguished civilian career he was awarded the knighthood of the Order of Merit of the Italian Republic in 2010.

Bessma Momani is a CIGI senior fellow. She has a Ph.D. in political science with a focus on international political economy, and is an associate professor at the Balsillie School of International Affairs and the University of Waterloo. She has been a visiting scholar at Georgetown University's Mortara Center and a non-resident fellow at the Brookings Institution. Bessma is a 2015 Fellow of the Pierre Elliott Trudeau Foundation and a Fulbright Scholar. She has authored and co-edited over eight books and over 60 scholarly, peer-reviewed journal articles and book chapters that have examined the IMF, the Middle East, and economic liberalization throughout the Arab Gulf and Middle East. She is a current recipient of a research grant funded by Canada's Social Sciences and Humanities Research Council (SSHRC) to study IMF and World Bank cooperation. She is also the past recipient of two previous SSHRC grants on the reform of the IMF executive board and on Middle East urbanization.

Herman Mark Schwartz is a professor in the politics department of the University of Virginia. In addition to over 40 articles and chapters, he has written or co-edited books on economic development, globalization, Denmark's welfare state, employment policy, the politics of housing finance and the global financial crisis. His most recent book is *Subprime Nation: American Power, Global Capital and the Housing Bubble* (Cornell 2009). He has been a Fulbright or visiting scholar at the University of Aarhus (Denmark), University of Calgary (Canada), Radboud University (Netherlands) Kyung Hee University (Seoul, Korea), Oslo School of Management (Norway) and City University (London).

David A. Steinberg is an assistant professor of international political economy at Johns Hopkins University's School of Advanced International Studies. He is the author of *Demanding Devaluation: Exchange Rate Politics in the Developing World* (Cornell University Press, 2015), and of articles in journals such as *Comparative Political Studies*, *International Studies Quarterly* and *World Politics*.

Hongying Wang is a CIGI senior fellow. She is also associate professor of political science at the University of Waterloo, specializing in international political economy, Chinese politics and Chinese foreign policy. She is the author of *Weak States, Strong Networks: The Institutional Dynamics of Foreign Direct Investment in China* (Oxford University Press, 2001) and many articles that have appeared in journals such as *Asian Survey, China Quarterly, Global Governance, Journal of Contemporary China, Review of International Political Economy* and *Third World Quarterly*. Her current research explores the domestic and international politics shaping China's role in global economic governance. She previously taught at Syracuse University, and was the founding director of the East Asia Program at its Maxwell School of Citizenship and Public Affairs.

Qiyuan Xu is a CIGI visiting scholar. Qiyuan is associate professor and the director of the Economic Development Division at the Institute of World Economics and Politics, at the Chinese Academy of Social Sciences. At CIGI, he studies renminbi (RMB) internationalization. Since 2006, Qiyuan has co-authored and published four books about the RMB exchange rate and RMB internationalization in Chinese. He has also published more than 30 academic papers and more than 100 articles both in Chinese and English. Qiyuan has a Ph.D. in international economics from North East Normal University in China.